To my family: Nancy, Todd, and Dana

Contents

Preface   xi

1. Introduction to Computers and Programming   1

1.1 Problem Solving   2
1.2 Algorithms, Flowcharts, and Programs   2
1.3 Functional Units of a Computer   6
    1.3.1 The Memory Unit   6
    1.3.2 The Input Unit   8
    1.3.3 The Output Unit   9
    1.3.4 The Central Processing Unit   11
1.4 Program Statements   12
1.5 Structure of a BASIC Program   13
1.6 Two Examples   14

Exercises   18

2. Using the Terminal   19

2.1 An Overview   20
2.2 System Commands   22
    2.2.1 Naming Your Program   22
    2.2.2 Saving Your Program   22
    2.2.3 Deleting Your Program   23
    2.2.4 Creating a New Version of Your Program   23
    2.2.5 Listing Your Program   23
    2.2.6 Running Your Program   24
2.3 Making Corrections   25
    2.3.1 Correcting a Line   26
    2.3.2 Inserting a Line   28
    2.3.3 Deleting a Line   28

Exercises   29

3. Basic BASIC, Part I: Reading, Writing, Arithmetic   31

3.1 Variables and Constants   32
3.2 Arithmetic Operations   34
3.3 Remarks   35

3.4 The END Statement   37
3.5 The PRINT Statement   37
    3.5.1 Printing Messages (Strings)   38
    3.5.2 More Than One Item on a Line   39
    3.5.3 Printing Tables   42
    3.5.4 Legal Items in PRINT Statements   43
3.6 Assigning Values to Variables: The LET Statement   43
3.7 Assigning Values to Variables: READ and DATA Statements   46
3.8 Assigning Values to Variables: The INPUT Statement   51

Exercises   52

4. Basic BASIC, Part II: Control Statements   57

4.1 The STOP Statement   58
4.2 Conditional Jumps: The IF-THEN Statement   58
4.3 Unconditional Jumps: The GO TO Statement   60
4.4 Loops   62
4.5 An Application of Loops   67
4.6 The FOR-NEXT Statements   72
4.7 Another Application of Loop Construction   79
4.8 Debugging and Program Check-out   87

Exercises   89

5. Structured Programming   95

5.1 Control Structures   96
5.2 The IF-THEN-ELSE Construction   98
5.3 Loop Structures   101
5.4 Describing Structure with REM Statements   102
5.5 The Structured Approach to Program Design   107
5.6 An Application   108
5.7 Another Application   114
5.8 Eliminating Exits   117
5.9 Common Structural Errors   119

Exercises   120

6. Numbers, Arrays, and Functions   129

6.1 Numbers Revisited   129
6.2 Arrays   132
    6.2.1 The DIM Statement   135
    6.2.2 Some Applications   136
    6.2.3 Tables: Two-Dimensional Arrays   147

6.3 Functions   153
    6.3.1 The Built-In Functions   155
    6.3.2 An Application of the INT Function   157
    6.3.3 The SQR Function   161
    6.3.4 Applications of the RND Function   162
    6.3.5 An Application in Physics   167
  Exercises   169

7. Additional Features of BASIC   175

  7.1 Case Structures   175
    7.1.1 An Application   179
  7.2 More Input-Output   183
    7.2.1 The Semicolon   183
    7.2.2 The TAB Function   185
    7.2.3 Editing Output: The PRINT IN IMAGE (USING) Statement   187
    7.2.4 The RESTORE Statement   191
    7.2.5 Two Applications   193
  7.3 The Logical Operators   204
  Exercises   205

8. Matrices, Strings, and Files   213

  8.1 The MAT Instructions   214
    8.1.1 The MAT READ, MAT PRINT, and MAT INPUT Statements   214
    8.1.2 The MAT Arithmetic Assignment Statements   219
    8.1.3 Special Matrix Instructions   224
    8.1.4 Changing Dimensions   228
    8.1.5 An Application   229
  8.2 String Processing   232
    8.2.1 The CHANGE Statement   232
    8.2.2 An Application   237
    8.2.3 Comparing Strings   241
    8.2.4 Additional String Functions   243
  8.3 Files   249
    8.3.1 Sequential Files   250
    8.3.2 Random Files   260
  Exercises   264

9. Functions and Subroutines   271

  9.1 User-Defined Functions   271
    9.1.1 Single-Line Functions   272
    9.1.2 Multiline Functions   279

9.2 Subroutines   287
9.3 Further Considerations of Program Design: Efficiency   291
9.4 The CHAIN Statement   295
9.5 Functions and Recursion   297
9.6 A Final Application: Computer Art   299
9.7 Concluding Remarks   308
Exercises   308

Appendix A   Summary of BASIC Statements, Functions, and Commands   313

A.1 Statements   313
A.2 Functions   316
A.3 System Commands   317

Appendix B   Error Messages   319

B.1 Compilation Errors   320
B.2 Execution Errors   322

Appendix C   A DEC BASIC-PLUS-2 Program   323

Index   325

Summary Card

Preface

The statement "people are taught how to *code;* programming is learned only by bitter experience"[†] summarizes how many people feel about the art of programming. All too often introductory textbooks on programming don't do what they were intended to do: teach students how to write programs. Detailed presentations of the particular language elements are made. Many examples of programs and many exercises are provided. Sometimes flowcharts are shown, but with little emphasis on how to design one.

The result is that a sizable percentage of students never really grasp the concepts necessary to write anything other than the most elementary programs. And of those who do, many write "bad" programs. This book is written to remedy that situation. I try to show what programming really is, with the hope that the learning experience need not be as unpleasant as the first sentence of this preface implies. Thus, I attempt to teach not just programming, but *good* programming. Good habits should be learned early.

This book is intended for teaching beginning programming to a general audience; it is not aimed at any specific class of students. Students of applied mathematics, physics, and other "hard" sciences naturally have embraced the computer as a powerful tool for their work. But the spectrum of disciplines turning to the computer has expanded quickly, first to business and economics, then more recently to such fields as sociology, psychology, and even the arts. Thus, there is a need for textbooks that can be studied not only by mathematicians and scientists, but also by those with a minimal technical background.

As such, the book is appropriate for a general one-semester first course in programming in a university, college, junior college, or even high school. Since a solutions manual containing answers for the exercises is available, the text can also be used for self-study.

This book is written with a problem-solving approach in mind. To write a successful program to solve a problem, one must first thoroughly understand the problem. Thus, a significant by-product of learning to solve problems on a computer is a greater understanding of and appreciation for the ideas behind the problems themselves.

My experience in teaching programming over the past six years has led me to the approach used in this book. I have chosen BASIC for several reasons. First, it is one of the easiest programming languages to learn. Second, it is widespread in educational institutions, and with the expanding minicomputer market, its use is increasing rapidly. Furthermore, because of its string handling capability, it is more appealing for a general class of students than, say, FORTRAN. But this book is more than a study of the BASIC language—its main purpose is to teach a beginner how to solve problems using a computer.

I have attempted to apply, where possible, the principles inherent in structured programming. I have especially adhered to the techniques of "top-down" programming and have followed T. E. Hull's and S. Charmonman and J. L. Wagener's suggestions for

[†]J. M. Yohe, "An Overview of Programming Practices," *Computing Surveys* 6, 4 (1974): 221–243.

producing programs with a "structured look" in languages like FORTRAN and BASIC.[†] Structured programming concepts are introduced in Chapter 5 and are emphasized throughout the rest of the book.

At the same time I cannot state too strongly the fact that this is a book for beginners. Thus, the book is slowly paced in the first four chapters in order to provide a solid foundation in fundamental programming concepts before moving on to more advanced topics. For the most part, the examples are purposefully simple.

Finally, I have tried to follow other principles of successful texts, such as the early presentation of complete programs (Chapter 1) and the use of many examples to motivate understanding of new topics. Flowcharting is presented in outline form, since the detailed outline much more closely resembles the coded program than the outmoded flowcharts with their boxes and arrows. Students are encouraged to begin writing their own programs as quickly as possible. Most examples are juxtaposed with their explanations so that no page turning is necessary to study them. Many varied applications are presented in the text in Chapters 6 through 9, after the fundamentals have been covered. The applications selected illustrate topics covered in the same section or chapter. Furthermore, applications appear as early as the exercises in Chapter 3.

There are references to material yet to come in a number of places in the text. My intent is not to make the reader jump ahead in the text to read the information, but only to let the reader know that the material relevant to questions normally raised at these points will eventually be covered.

A summary card is included which can be removed from the book and used as a handy reference at a terminal, for study, and so forth.

Portions of Chapters 5 and 7 in this text—including the boxed diagrams that appear on pages 99 and 178—are adapted from an article written by the author that appeared in the June 1977 issue of *Datamation* magazine, pages 149-156. This material is reprinted with permission of *Datamation*® magazine, © Copyright by Technical Publishing Company, A Division of Dun-Donnelley Publishing Corporation, A Dun & Bradstreet Company, 1978— all rights reserved.

I am indebted to many people who have contributed to this book, including the reviewers whose comments have helped to improve the book—Waldo Wedel, University of Texas at Austin; John Kropf, Seattle Pacific University; Stephen Waite, Dartmouth College; Ralph Szweda, Monroe Community College; and Lester Richey, Oregon State University; and to Julie Schendel, Anita Eggler, and Nancy Nordgren, who typed the manuscript.

P. B. W.

[†]T. E. Hull, "Would You Believe Structured FORTRAN?" *SIGNUM Newsletter* 8, 4 (1973): 13-16; and S. Charmonman and J. L. Wagener, "On Structured Programming in FORTRAN," *SIGNUM Newsletter* 10, 1 (1975): 21-23.

Introduction to BASIC Programming

1. Introduction to Computers and Programming

You need to find the average of a list of numbers. A bank must compute the balance of each customer's savings account and the interest that accumulates, often on a daily basis. To land a manned spacecraft safely on the moon, National Aeronautics and Space Administration (NASA) engineers must solve thousands of complex equations that determine such factors as escape velocity from the earth, fuel requirements, and the flight path at any instant. A chemist, before beginning a lengthy series of complicated and expensive experiments, needs some way of simulating quickly and efficiently the outcomes of the

FIGURE 1.1   NASA computer control center. (Courtesy of NASA)

experiments under various conditions to eliminate the trials that seem unproductive. A research psychologist would like to know whether there is any relation between voting trends and movie preferences among voting adults in New York State.

1.1   Problem Solving

Each of the situations mentioned is an example of a problem. To the average person some may seem commonplace and others exotic. All represent problems individuals and large institutions face. All have one common characteristic—they can be (and in some cases *must* be) solved by a digital computer.

Computers are synonymous with problem solving. In the thirty years that electronic computers have existed, problems submitted to the computer have become increasingly complex. And the variety of such problems has also grown—the assortment is probably much greater than you could imagine. At the same time, some former dreams have become realities. Without the computer, human footprints would not be on the moon.

Besides making some impossible jobs possible, computers have also relieved us of the burden of many boring and tedious tasks, such as averaging numbers and balancing accounts. And they can perform these tasks with a speed and accuracy that far surpasses human skills.

The computer is a tool, then, for helping us solve problems. But that is another problem in itself; how does one tell the computer to solve a given problem? The central purpose of this book is to help you develop the techniques necessary for successfully using the computer in solving problems. Once this skill is learned, it becomes a new source of power—power to solve many problems, to accomplish some otherwise difficult or even unattainable ends, just as reading and writing increase one's capacity for accomplishment. In this sense, the computer becomes an extension of one's brain.

1.2   Algorithms, Flowcharts, and Programs

The computers we consider in this book are more precisely termed **general-purpose automatic digital computers**. A general-purpose computer can perform a wide variety of tasks, from sorting lists of names or numbers to playing games like tic-tac-toe or checkers. Special-purpose "computers," such as telephone switching circuits or automatic pilots for airplanes, are not considered here.

An important aspect of computers is their *automatic* nature; they can carry out long and complex sequences of operations without human intervention. This is not true of a typical hand-held calculator.

Finally, we shall concern ourselves with *digital* (as opposed to analog) computers. A digital computer computes by discrete units; values increase or decrease in "jumps." Analog computers (of interest mainly to engineers) compute by measuring on a continuous, or "smooth," scale. An abacus is a digital device, whereas slide rules and thermostats are analog devices.

FIGURE 1.2 A small computer system. (Courtesy of Digital Equipment Corporation)

In solving a problem, a computer deals with information. This information may take many forms. From the user's point of view, it can be classified as either **instructions** or **data**. *Instructions* are commands to the computer to perform certain tasks. *Data* are the numbers or other symbols that are manipulated according to the instructions. In either case, the information is represented in symbolic form. The capacity of computers for treating symbols in a very general way is another giant step above electronic calculators. In calculators, symbolic representation is also used for information; but these symbols represent numbers and cannot be used in any other way. They can only be multiplied, added, subtracted, and the like. But the internal symbols representing data in a computer can be thought of and manipulated as people's names, trees in a simulated forest, notes in a musical scale, or just about any other object or idea one could conceive. How we can meaningfully manipulate these symbols to solve problems is what concerns us here.

Once a problem is well defined—objectives specified in detail, potential difficulties described, time and other constraints set down, and so on—the next step in the process is formulating an algorithm.

Definition: An *algorithm* is an unambiguous sequence of steps, or instructions, that specify precisely how a given problem is to be solved.

Many examples of algorithms will be given in Chapter 3. It should be emphasized here that formulating effective algorithms is the most important, and generally the most time-consuming, part of solving problems. For all but the most simple problems, constructing an algorithm requires a systematic analysis in which the solution is first stated in very general terms. Then the solution is increasingly refined as one proceeds to the final stage. The number of levels of refinement depends on the complexity of the problem.

The algorithm, once written down, is also called a **flowchart**. A flowchart can be specified in the form of a sequence of very precise sentences (like the steps in a cookbook), or in a much more formal, diagrammatic form. We shall use a combination of both, a form that resembles an outline. From now on, we shall use the terms *outline* and *flowchart* interchangeably.

After the lowest-stage, or most refined, outline is written, usually an experienced person can easily convert that outline into a program.

Definition: A *program* is a sequence of imperative statements (instructions) that prescribe precisely how a problem is to be solved. It differs from the flowchart in that the instructions must be valid statements in a language that the computer can interpret. Also, the program usually specifies the process in much greater detail than a flowchart does.

A program, then, is simply the realization of a flowchart, or algorithm, on the computer. In summary, the problem-solving process means designing a procedure for solving a problem and then "describing" it to the computer. This requires very precise descriptions of even those portions of the solution that would ordinarily involve common sense, because the computer doesn't have any!

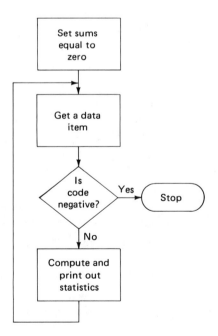

FIGURE 1.3   Example of a flowchart

It may seem strange to you that we must know precisely how to solve a given problem in order to tell the computer to do it. Why then do we need a computer at all? The answer lies essentially in the speed of the computer. Knowing how to solve a problem doesn't mean that the job is done. For example, I may know how to add a million numbers, but I can't do it. And a modern computer could do the job in less than five seconds.

A basic tool for constructing a program is a *computer language.* Over 120 different computer languages have been developed in the United States alone! We shall concentrate on one of the most popular and easy to learn: **BASIC**.

BASIC (Beginner's All-Purpose Symbolic Instruction Code) was developed at Dartmouth College between 1963 and 1964 and became the first widely used language designed for use principally in educational institutions. Unfortunately, there are many versions, or "dialects," of BASIC; every computer manufacturer has its own. It is likely, however, that many BASIC programs written for one computer could, with minor modifications, work correctly on another computer.

Why trouble ourselves with BASIC in the first place? It would be simpler if we could use English to instruct the computer. But computers have their own language, called *machine language,* which consists of operations that are built into the electronic circuitry. Thus any other programming language statements must be translated into machine language before they can be executed.

English (and every other natural language) is hopelessly complex by comparison. Attempts to translate English (or even very restricted subsets of English) unambiguously into machine language have thus far met with only limited success. Programming in machine language, on the other hand, is very tedious and extremely error-prone. Thus we use a language like BASIC—sometimes termed a *high-level language*—instead. This is a compromise. Such languages have much simpler forms than English and are not ambiguous, and at the same time they can be used much more easily than machine language. However, they must be translated (by the computer itself) into the machine language of the computer.

Therefore, to write programs for computers, we learn an intermediate language, and the computer also "learns" that language. In such cases the translation process is called *compiling* and is accomplished by means of another program, called a **compiler**. A different compiler for each language is available on any given computer. It is important to

```
10 REM THIS PROGRAM PRODUCES A TABLE OF INTEGERS FROM
20 REM 1 TO 10, THEIR SQUARES AND CUBES.
30 REM///////////////////////////////////////////////////////
40 REM
50 PRINT, "NUMBER","SQUARE","CUBE"
60 PRINT
70 FOR I = 1 TO 10
80    PRINT  I, I*I, I*I*I
90 NEXT I
100 END
```

FIGURE 1.4 **Example of a BASIC computer program**

remember that an entire program is usually compiled before any of the instructions are executed.

Another type of translating program is called an **interpreter**. The fundamental difference between the two is that a compiler translates all the instructions of the program before the program is executed (that is, before the instructions are carried out), and an interpreter translates, then executes, one instruction at a time. The result is that compiled programs generally proceed faster, and interpreted programs produce better *error messages;* that is, it is easier to find your mistakes. Often one will find translators that have features of both.

1.3 Functional Units of a Computer

The computer, considered as a collection of machinery or hardware, consists of four units, each performing a different logical function. This abstract breakdown is greatly oversimplified, especially in today's rapidly developing field of computer technology, but it is a good place to begin.

1.3.1 The Memory Unit The **memory unit**—also called *storage*—holds items of information (programs and data) as long as they are needed. Thus, in finding the average of a list of numbers, both the numbers and program that computes their average might be stored in the computer memory. After the program has run to completion, the information can be electronically "erased" from the memory since it is no longer needed.

In modern computers, there is usually a hierarchy of different levels of memory. *Main memory* is the memory directly accessible via the computer's control circuitry. When a program is compiled and executed, it must be in main memory. At another level, devices called *auxiliary storage devices* (such as magnetic tape drives, which are like tape recorders—see Figure 1.5) also provide for storage of programs and data. Before stored material can be processed, however, it must be transferred to main memory. Unless we say otherwise, *memory* will mean "main memory" in the following discussion.

The memory is divided into separate units, called **bytes,** each capable of holding one item of information. These locations are numbered consecutively from zero upward; the number is called the **address** of the location to which it refers. The computer uses the address to locate a particular item of information. The size of the memory determines the amount of information that can be stored at one time, and typical memory sizes range from 4,000 to a million bytes.

Within each individual byte, the information appears as a pattern consisting solely of 0's and 1's (called **bits**). Actually, the information is stored electronically as one of the two possible *states,* like current *on* or *off.* We use 0's and 1's on paper for convenience in representing the states. The most common byte lengths are either six or eight bits. Each byte of information, such as a digit 9 or a letter A or an equals symbol, is represented as

FIGURE 1.5   Tape drive. (Courtesy of International Business Machines Corporation)

a unique pattern of bits. The letter A, for example, could be represented as 11000001 on an eight-bit machine or as 010001 on a six-bit computer. Up to 64 different characters can be represented with a six-bit byte and up to 256 characters with an eight-bit byte.[†] Some patterns have particular significance for the computer circuitry and represent instructions to be followed.

Thus, a program written in the BASIC language would be run by placing it in the computer's memory. The BASIC compiler would then translate the program into the machine language of the computer, which would be represented as a sequence of bit patterns. The computer circuitry could then recognize these bit patterns as instructions, starting with the first one, interpreting and executing each instruction in sequence, one at a time.

[†]Most computers also combine a fixed number of bytes into another unit, called the *word.* Typical word lengths are two, four, or six bytes, depending on the computer. Words are used to store numbers for arithmetic operations. Addressing on many computers is also by word rather than by byte.

1.3.2   **The Input Unit**   The **input unit** is used to communicate information to the memory, where it is stored. There are many types of input devices; one of the most common is the *card reader* (Figure 1.6). This device "reads" cards by sensing rectangular holes that are punched into the cards in the form of a code.

      Other common input devices include *teletype terminals* (Figure 1.7), which consist

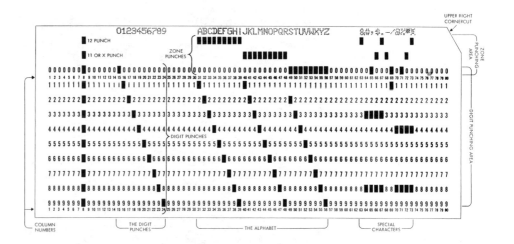

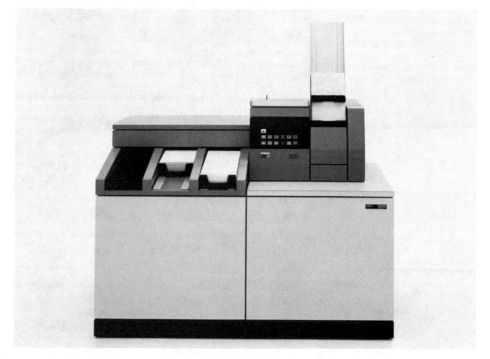

FIGURE 1.6   **Card reader and punched card. (Courtesy of International Business Machines Corporation)**

of a typewriter-like keyboard and a roll of paper to record what is typed, and *CRT* (cathode-ray tube) *display terminals* (Figure 1.8), which also have a keyboard and a screen to display whatever is typed. Often there will be a *paper tape punch* or a *cassette tape drive* attached to such terminals, which enables the user to keep a copy of the program. Then the program does not have to be typed every time it is to be run; the user simply supplies the corresponding tape, which is read by the terminal.

In general, computer systems have more than one input unit, but terminals are by far the most common form of input devices for the BASIC programmer. Consequently, it is probably a good idea for the reader to become familiar now with the terminals to be used (see Exercises, Chapter 2).

1.3.3   The Output Unit   The **output unit** accepts information from the memory and makes it available to the programmer. The teletype unit and the CRT terminals also are output devices; the information from memory is typed on the paper of the teletype or displayed on the CRT screen under the control of the computer. Again, for a BASIC programmer, the most common input/output devices are terminals. Another common

FIGURE 1.7   Teletype terminal. (Courtesy of Teletype Corporation)

FIGURE 1.8   CRT terminal. (Courtesy of International Business Machines Corporation)

output device is the line printer (Figure 1.9), which will print information from the memory at rates that can vary from less than 200 to over 2,000 lines per minute. A CRT terminal may also have a low-speed line printer attached to it.

Such input/output devices can be situated far from the computer itself, perhaps hundreds of miles away. They are linked to the computer by high-quality telephone lines.

1.3.4   **The Central Processing Unit**   The **central processing unit**, or CPU, is the "brain of the computer," as the name implies. It consists of much electronic circuitry and controls essentially all the activities of the computer. Its functions include accepting commands when buttons are pressed and switches set on its console; and it interprets and carries out the instructions in programs, detects errors, and controls the operations of the input/output devices (see Figure 1.10).

FIGURE 1.9   Line printer. (Courtesy of International Business Machines Corporation)

FIGURE 1.10 Central Processing unit (CPU). (Courtesy of International Business Machines Corporation)

1.4 Program Statements

What do the instructions, or statements, in a given programming language look like? What do they do? The definition of a program tells us they are imperative statements; they have a "Do this!" nature. In addition, it is very important for you to understand that essentially all the instructions that appear in any programming language can be grouped into five main categories, although the actual set of instructions available depends on the particular language and even the computer model. The five types are:

1. *Arithmetic assignment instructions* Arithmetic assignment instructions compute a value using one of the arithmetic operations (addition, subtraction, multiplication, and division) or a combination of these operations. Often just a constant value is given and no operation takes place. In either case the value is then stored in memory for later reference.

2. *Data handling instructions* Data handling instructions can be used to transfer information from one part of the memory to another or to compare two sets of information (numbers, names, symbols, and so on) to determine whether they are the same,

whether one is less than the other, or the like. In high-level languages like BASIC, the comparisons are usually combined with other instructions to make them conditional. For example, executing an instruction to add two numbers may depend on whether another number is positive.

3. *Sequence control instructions* Normally, instructions in the memory are executed in the sequence in which they appear, but control instructions are available that can alter the execution sequence. They may be unconditional, or they may be conditional if combined with some comparison as described above.

4. *Input/output instructions* An input instruction provides for data to be read from a particular device, like a terminal, into an area of memory and made available for processing. Output instructions specify to a device that particular data items should be written (they will, for example, specify displaying a number on the CRT).

5. *Data structure instructions* Data structure instructions describe the structure that the various data items are to have. For example, are the data for a given program simply a list of numbers that can be examined one at a time? Or are they a complex collection of records, such as a payroll file, which requires a large area of memory to be reserved for retaining these records while the program is carried out? Generally, these instructions provide information for the compiler; once compiling is finished and execution has begun, no action due to these statements takes place.

Thus, a program consists of a sequence of statements from the above classes. This classification is at best a simplification of reality. Some instructions may represent a combination of several of these types. This is especially true in higher-level languages. The classification was made to emphasize that any BASIC program must be written by such instructions. Thus, the description of an algorithm (the flowchart) must eventually be refined to a point at which it can be written in terms of these instructions. If this cannot be done, the algorithm must be re-examined.

1.5   Structure of a BASIC Program

Each BASIC program consists of a sequence of instructions. The following rules apply to all BASIC instructions:

1. *Each instruction must begin with a line number.* A *line number* is a positive integer less than 100,000 (usually). No two instructions can have the same line number.
2. *Successive instructions must have increasing line numbers.* Line numbers are important in BASIC. For one thing, they will be automatically arranged in ascending sequence, even if they are not transmitted to the computer memory in that sequence. This allows for easy correction of errors (see Chapter 2).
3. *Each line must contain one and only one instruction.*[†]

[†]Some versions of BASIC do not have this restriction.

4. *An instruction cannot be continued onto the next line* (that is, it should not exceed one line in length).[†]

5. *BASIC ignores all blank spaces.*[‡] That is, inserting spaces into an instruction will have no effect on how that instruction is executed. But a programmer's judicious use of spaces is important. First, they can be used to make a program more readable. For example, the statement[§]

$$100IFI-12 > UTHEN111$$

is much easier to read in the form

$$100 \ IF \ I-12 > U \ THEN \ 111$$

Second, and more important, if some instructions are indented as in an outline of an article, the organization, or the *structure,* of the program becomes much clearer. See Example 1.2 in Section 1.6. (Much more will be said on this topic later.)

1.6 Two Examples

Even though individual statements in the BASIC language have not yet been introduced, one can still learn much at this stage by studying complete programs like the ones in the accompanying examples. You should study these examples very carefully. Even though you cannot now be expected to comprehend fully all the points made, hard work at this point will pay off later on.

The first program is very simple. It is so elementary that ordinarily no one would bother to write the program to solve the problem, since it can be done more easily by hand. But learning to program takes time and lots of practice. The first program or two you write will necessarily be simple like this one—"learn to walk before you can run" is the principle used here, rather than "sink or swim."

The first program computes the area of a right triangle; given are two numbers B and H, which represent the length of the base and the height. It then prints out the two dimensions B and H, followed by the computed area.

The program is listed in Example 1.1, with an accompanying explanation. Study it carefully.

[†]Some versions of BASIC do not have this restriction.

[‡]Some versions of BASIC require blanks around *keywords* (for example, IF or PRINT) and following the line number.

[§]Note that the letter O is distinguished from the digit 0 by "slashing" the zero (0). Some computers slash the letter O instead of the zero.

EXAMPLE 1.1

Program:

```
 10 REM//////////////////////////////////////////////////
 20 REM/ EXAMPLE 1.1:  FIND THE AREA OF A RIGHT TRIANGLE AS   /
 30 REM/ 1/2 THE BASE TIMES THE HEIGHT.                       /
 40 REM/ PROGRAMMER:  C. MILQUETOAST.  1/2/80.                /
 50 REM//////////////////////////////////////////////////
 60 REM
 70 INPUT B,H
 80 LET A = .5*B*H
 90 PRINT B,H,A
100 END
```

Input:

Suppose the numbers transmitted to the computer in response to the INPUT statement are

3,4

Output:

The printed output that would be produced by *inputting* the numbers (that is, making them available to the program) 3 and 4 is

3   4   6

Lines 10-60 are comments on the program (indicated by the letters REM for "remark"). Comments provide valuable documentation about what the program does and its limitations and assumptions. Here the programmer's name is included for identification. For ease of reading, ignore the REM part of the comment.

Line 70 is clearly an input instruction. It enables the user to interact with the program during execution. During execution of the program, the computer will pause, displaying a question mark (?) on the terminal. That means it is waiting for the user to input two numbers (in this case). After the numbers are transmitted to the computer, B will take on the value of the first number, and H the second. The symbols B and H are examples of *variables*. A variable is simply a symbolic address in the memory that can be used to represent a value.

Line 80 is an assignment statement; the value computed as 1/2 multiplied by the base by the height is assigned to the variable A. Note that the symbol * is used to represent multiplication.

Line 90 is an output instruction. It will print the current values of B, H, and A, the area, all on the same line.

Line 100 tells BASIC that this is the last statement in the program. It also stops the execution of the program. An END statement is required in every BASIC program.

The second program is more complex. It determines the largest number in a list of *positive numbers*. The procedure simply examines the numbers one at a time in order, comparing them with the largest found up to that point. When the end of the list is reached, the largest number up to that point is the largest in the entire list.

It is assumed that a negative number is the last number (called a *trailer*) in the list, which can have an arbitrary length. A common technique in programming, which you should remember, is to place a special value at the end of a list of data that will enable the program to tell when the list is exhausted. If this is not done, an input instruction will cause an attempt to read another data item in the series when none exists. This usually results in an *error condition,* which causes the CPU to take over—the program "loses control" and is usually terminated with an appropriate error message displayed on the output unit, such as "ERROR—TRIED TO READ BEYOND THE DATA." Thus, we would not get the result we were looking for.

In this example, the choice of a trailer was easy—a negative number is easily distinguishable from the numbers in our list. If we wanted our program to be more general, that is, to apply to lists of negative numbers also, then we should have to devise a different trailer or a different technique altogether.

Because the program is complex, we first present a flowchart, **the algorithm.**

Let L be the name of the largest number found up to the one currently tested.

Let N be the name of the value in the list currently being tested.

1. Temporarily let L have the value zero.
2. Read one number from the list—call it N.
3. If N is not negative (the end of the list), go on to step 4.
   Otherwise go to step 6.
4. Compare N with L. If N is greater than L, replace the current value of L with the current value of N.
5. Repeat—return to step 2.
6. Print out L and then stop.

The BASIC program corresponding to this flowchart is listed in Example 1.2, with an accompanying discussion. You may not understand all the details now, but most of the process should be clear. Again, study it thoroughly, keeping the flowchart above in mind. (References will be made to this program in later chapters.)

EXAMPLE 1.2

Program:
```
 10 REM//////////////////////////////////////////////////////////
 15 REM/ EXAMPLE 1.2:                                             /
 20 REM/ FIND THE MAXIMUM IN A LIST OF NONNEGATIVE NUMBERS.       /
 25 REM/ THE LENGTH OF THE LIST IS ARBITRARY, BUT THE NUMBERS     /
 30 REM/ SHOULD APPEAR ON "DATA" STATEMENTS NUMBERED SEQUENTIALLY/
 35 REM/ FROM 300.  ALSO, THE LAST NUMBER IN THE LIST MUST BE     /
 40 REM/ LESS THAN ZERO.                                          /
 45 REM/ PROGRAMMER: JANE DOAKS, MARCH, 1976.                     /
 50 REM/              THE VARIABLES                               /
 55 REM/ L:  THE LARGEST VALUE                                    /
 60 REM/ N:  THE NUMBER FROM THE LIST CURRENTLY BEING TESTED      /
 65 REM//////////////////////////////////////////////////////////
 70 REM
 75 REM*BEGIN PROGRAM
100 REM INITIAL VALUE OF L LESS THAN ANY POSSIBLE LIST VALUE.
110    LET L = 0
120 REM*BEGIN LOOP
```

```
130          READ N
140 REM*****EXIT FROM LOOP IF AT END OF LIST
150          IF N<0 THEN 230
170          IF L>= N THEN 120
180 REM*        ELSE
190                 LET L = N
200                 GO TO 120
210 REM*END LOOP
220 REM
230    PRINT "THE LARGEST NUMBER IN THE LIST IS";L
300 DATA 12,17,139.6,1,72,311,4,-5
999 END
```

Output:

The printed output, which is produced by executing this program with the data in line 300, is

THE LARGEST NUMBER IN THE LIST IS 311

Lines 10–100 are comments on the program. Note that all the symbolic names used in the program (just L and N here) are defined in this section.

Line 110 is an assignment statement; the value zero is assigned to the variable L, which is used to keep, or store, the largest number in the list.

Line 120 is a remark that indicates the start of a *loop*. A loop is a sequence of instructions that may be repeated. This saves the programmer from having to write the same or similar instructions over and over again.

Line 130 is another form of input instruction. It "reads" one of the numbers from the DATA list and stores it at the symbolic address N. The first time it is executed, it will get the first number; the next time, the second number; and so on.

Line 150 tests whether the trailer was encountered, that is, whether the value is negative. If N is negative, the instruction alters the execution sequence: line 230 will be executed next. If N is not negative, execution will continue in the given sequence. This is an example of a conditional sequence control instruction.

Line 170 tests whether the current value stored at the address L (the current largest value) is greater than or equal to the current value of N (the last number read). If so, the next number is examined; the program will "jump" back to line 120, and a new number will be read and stored at N. The above sequence of instructions (lines 120–170) is repeated, thus forming a loop. If the number at L is less than the current value of N, the next instruction executed is line 190.

Line 190 simply replaces the value of L with the current value of N. After this step is executed, the values of L and N are the same.

Line 200 is an unconditional jump back to line 120, where the cycle is repeated. This completes the loop started at line 120.

Line 230 is an output instruction to print the message in quotes followed by the current value of L on the same line. At this point, L should contain the largest value in the list since the only way to get to this instruction is to jump from line 150.

Line 300 presents the data to be used by the program. This list, we shall see later, can be easily replaced, shortened, or lengthened. It may be anywhere in the program before the END statement.

Exercises

1. Write down five real problems not mentioned in Chapter 1 that you think might be candidates for computer solution. Also, write down two or three problems with which you believe the computer would be of absolutely no help in obtaining a solution. You may be surprised after discussing these with your instructor.

2. Go to the library and browse through the books on computer science and programming. Write down the names of four computer languages besides BASIC. Also, if you can, write down a sample instruction from each language.

3. Write down the names of five different computer manufacturers. Sources for such information are the library and newspaper want ads for programmers and systems analysts. What is the name of the company that manufactured your computer?

4. Tour your school's computer center or a nearby computer center if your school doesn't have one. Your instructor may be able to arrange such a tour.

5. Briefly explain the difference between a hand or desk calculator and a computer.

6. Ambiguity is one of the central problems for a computer in dealing with the translation of English sentences to machine language. How many different meanings can you find in the following sentences:
   a. "The man who saw the boy from the bakery without his glasses fell down the stairs."
   b. "Time flies like an arrow." (This sentence is famous for having many possible interpretations.)

7. Explain the difference between a flowchart and a program.

8. What is a compiler? An interpreter?

9. What is the purpose of computer memory? What are the other three functional units of a computer?

10. Name the five classes of program statements.

11. What is a byte? What is the purpose of an address in the memory unit?

12. Summarize the five rules that apply to all instructions in BASIC.

13. Example 1.1 illustrates the importance of variables. The same output could have been produced by the following program:

$$10 \text{ PRINT } 3, 4, .5 * 3 * 4$$
$$20 \text{ END}$$

In what circumstances is this a better program than Example 1.1? In what circumstances is Example 1.1 better? What must be done to the above example if the base of my triangle is 14 and the height 3? In Example 1.1, does it matter if we input the numbers in the order 4, 3? What will the output look like in that case?

Note: Further questions on the programming examples will be postponed to the end of Chapter 2, where you will have the opportunity to experiment with them on a terminal.

2. Using the Terminal

Terminals provide some tremendous advantages over traditional forms of "batch input," such as decks of cards. Without terminals, one is forced to punch the program onto cards, take the cards to a central processing area, where they are eventually run through a card reader, and finally receive a printout of the results from the line printer. This process could take hours, or even days, depending on the organization and policies of the particular computer center. And if there is a mistake in the program, such as a spelling error, the entire procedure must be repeated after the mistake is corrected. This process

FIGURE 2.1 Using a terminal. (Courtesy of Digital Equipment Corporation)

is extremely frustrating, especially for someone anxiously awaiting the results of such a run.

In all fairness, some much more efficient student-batch systems have been developed —for example, the WATFOR-WATFIV system, originated at Waterloo University in Canada—but in most installations there can still be a significant waiting time with the batch system.

2.1   An Overview

Terminals and time-sharing systems remedy these particular problems, although the cost per job tends to be higher. A **time-sharing system** allows a number of people to have essentially simultaneous remote access to a single computer by means of terminals. In such a system, the computer processes a small part of one user's problem, then switches to another, then to another, and so on. Thus the computer goes through a cycle in which it processes the programs of each of the persons that are using the system at that time. Since the computer is extremely fast and most terminal users' programs quite short, each user may have the impression of being the sole user of the computer. In large time-sharing systems, it is not unusual to have hundreds of people using the terminals at a given moment.

With a terminal at hand, the user types in the program and receives results, either typed out or displayed on the screen. Direct interaction of the computer and the user is of prime importance. Many errors can be corrected immediately at the terminal, and a process that might have taken days with a batch system can be done at a terminal in a few minutes or hours.

The emphasis here is on terminals, since BASIC was designed as a time-sharing language. The overwhelming use of BASIC is on terminals, although it is possible to keypunch BASIC programs on cards and run them in batch mode.

Here is an appropriate place to become acquainted with the terminal you will be using as your input/output device. The discussion will necessarily be brief. There are many kinds of terminals available, and it would be pointless to discuss procedures for operating a particular type. This task will more appropriately be up to your instructor.

The usual first step is to link the terminal to the computer. In some cases this may require little more than turning on a power switch; in others, the link is completed by "calling" the computer (it will have its own telephone number) via a conventional telephone system. However the connection is made, the terminal is said to be **on line**.

At this point you are ready to use the terminal. Terminals accept information *one line at a time*—after each line is keyed in, it must be transmitted to the computer memory by means of a RETURN (or TRANSMIT, SEND, or the like) key.

Before you can begin typing in a program, however, you must **log on**. This involves identifying yourself to the computer, usually by providing an account number to which this job will be charged; computer time costs money. Part of this procedure may include informing the computer which language you intend to use (in this case, BASIC), and whether or not you intend to key in a new program (by typing NEW on some systems) or to use one that is already stored in the computer's auxiliary memory (by

FIGURE 2.2   A typical terminal keyboard. (Courtesy of Teletype Corporation)

typing OLD on some systems). After you have logged on, the computer will usually respond with a message such as READY, to indicate that it is ready to run a program or to accept statements for a new one.

When you work with BASIC, your manipulation of the program and interaction with it are under control of the **BASIC processor**. This is a collection of programs that include the BASIC compiler and that enable you to handle your programs as described below.

After you have run your program, or whenever you must leave the terminal, you should **log off**. This procedure disconnects the terminal from the computer. It varies from one system to another, but usually consists of typing a set of characters that signal the computer to deactivate the terminal. In some systems, you must turn the power off; in others, it is done automatically.

The above details will vary according to the computer system and the kind of terminals you will use. Also, there are other features of various terminals that you should know about, including such options as paper tape or cassette tape readers, attached line printers, and editing capability. We shall not treat these here, as you can get such information locally.

2.2   System Commands

It is important for you to note that the system commands and examples of making corrections discussed here should be treated only as illustrations of the type of considerations that you should take into account when using a terminal. Different systems may use different commands altogether, and specific details must be obtained locally.

2.2.1   Naming Your Program

Once you are logged on to the terminal and have called on the BASIC processor, you are required to enter the word NEW or OLD (on some systems), as explained in Section 2.1. OLD and NEW are examples of *system commands,* which are directives to the BASIC processor to do something with the current program. *Since they are not* BASIC *instructions, they are not preceded by line numbers.* Several examples of system commands follow. Others will be covered in later chapters.

After you transmit OLD or NEW, the computer may respond with a statement like

PROGRAM NAME?

You are then to supply a name for the program for identification. This will allow you to retrieve it at a later date (using the system command OLD) if you should decide to save it.

2.2.2   Saving Your Program

Imagine that you have typed in your program. Depending on the terminal you have, you may be able to keep a copy of your program on paper tape or cassette tape. In addition, you may want to have the computer store the program elsewhere. Just transmit **SAVE** and your program will be filed in a permanent storage area (in auxiliary memory) under its program name. You can then reuse it some other time without retyping the whole program. (See Example 2.1.) This is especially useful if you don't have time to type in the entire program. You simply save what you have and then type in the rest later. You should not save your program this way, however, unless you are definitely going to use it again, since the amount of storage space available for such programs will be limited.

EXAMPLE 2.1 ═══

Suppose you save a program you had named TEST. The next day you want to work with it again. After logging on:

You transmit: OLD

Computer response: PROGRAM NAME?

You respond: TEST

At this point the BASIC processor makes a copy of the program stored in auxiliary memory under the name TEST and makes that copy available to you for further work. If you misspell the name, say as TIST, the BASIC processor will respond with

PROGRAM NOT FOUND.

In that case you simply retransmit the correct name.

2.2.3   **Deleting Your Program** Suppose you saved a program some time ago and now no longer need it. You have a printed listing of the instructions or a copy on paper tape or a cassette. You should then delete your program from the storage area of the computer (Example 2.2). This can be done with the command **UNSAVE**.

EXAMPLE 2.2

   Suppose the program name is TEST.
   You transmit: OLD
   Computer response: PROGRAM NAME?
   You transmit: TEST
   Computer response: READY, or carriage return, or other (varies with terminal)
   You transmit: UNSAVE
At this point the program TEST is deleted from the storage area of the machine.

2.2.4   **Creating a New Version of Your Program** Very often, a program you save will contain errors. You may later access the program and correct it (to do this, see Section 2.3). Or you may want to modify it for other reasons, perhaps to make it more efficient. To save the updated version of your program transmit **REPLACE**. The old version is then replaced in storage by the updated version (Example 2.3).

EXAMPLE 2.3

   Assume that the program name is TEST.
   You: OLD
   Computer: PROGRAM NAME?
   You: TEST
   Computer: READY (for example)
   You: Make corrections or modifications, then transmit REPLACE.

2.2.5   **Listing Your Program** Frequently you may want to examine some portion of a given program or even the entire program. For one thing, this will enable you to make corrections more easily. Also, if the listing of the program is printed on paper, you will always have a permanent copy of the program that you can read (unlike a cassette tape or paper tape).

   This is done with the system command **LIST.** There are three ways to use this command, as shown by Examples 2.4-2.6. In these examples, the program name is EX1.2 (from Section 1.6).

EXAMPLE 2.4 ══

    You: OLD
    Computer: PROGRAM NAME?
    You: EX1.2
    Computer: READY (for example)
    You: LIST
    Computer: Produces an output listing of all instructions in the current program.

EXAMPLE 2.5 ══

    You: OLD
    (Repeat next three steps; see Example 2.4.)
    You: LIST 220
    Computer: Produces an output listing; in this case, all instructions with line numbers
greater than or equal to 220. (On many systems, only line 220 will be listed.)

        220 REM
        230 PRINT "THE LARGEST NUMBER IN THE LIST IS"; L
        300 DATA 12,17,139.6,1,72,311,4,-5
        999 END

EXAMPLE 2.6 ══

    You: OLD
    (Repeat next three steps; see Example 2.4.)
    You: LIST 110,135
    Computer: Produces an output listing; in this case, all instructions between 110
and 135, inclusive.

        110   LET L = 0
        120 REM * BEGIN LOOP
        130   READ N

2.2.6   **Running Your Program** To execute, or run, your current program, whether it is a new or an old program, transmit **RUN**. Example 2.7 illustrates this command and also shows how new data can easily be supplied to a program that was saved previously.

EXAMPLE 2.7

You want to run the stored program TEST, but you first must supply the three numbers Ø, 1, 2 as data for the program. Suppose line number 5ØØ can be used for data.

You: OLD
Computer: PROGRAM NAME?
You: TEST
Computer: READY (for example)
You: 5ØØ DATA Ø,1,2
Computer: Line feed (paper advance, or equivalent)
You: RUN
Computer: Executes the program.

2.3   Making Corrections

You won't be able to use a terminal effectively unless you know how to correct errors. As you learn to program, you will make many mistakes. Some will be so-called logic errors, which occur because the algorithm you designed to solve a given problem was inadequate. Perhaps you failed to take all possible situations into account, or perhaps you expect your procedure to do some job and it does something completely different. In short, there is an error in your logic (as applied to a given problem). Logic errors are common to senior programmers with years of experience as well as to beginners.

Less serious, but perhaps more frustrating, are typing errors. You misspell a word, accidentally omit a line, leave out a single period, and your program fails to run. Instead the computer responds coldly with an error message (or perhaps a whole collection of them) such as

ILLEGAL CHARACTER IN 15Ø
RUN STOPPED

(See Appendix B.) These errors are frustrating, because slight mistakes, like typing 1oo instead of 1ØØ could safely be ignored by a person. But they might be the cause of a catastrophic failure of the computer program. Imagine how frustrating it would be to have a secretary tell you, "I'm sorry, but I can't type your letter since you didn't dot the third 'i' on line 12." After many similar experiences in typing programs at a terminal, one learns to be very careful!

There are reasons that the computer demands such accuracy. Essentially, the precision is required by the compiler. More flexibility could be provided, but with it would come the possibility of ambiguity and misinterpretation. At best, the compiler would have to be much more complex. Programs would take more time to compile and would therefore cost more to run.

Fortunately, these errors are easy to correct, particularly in BASIC. At this point, all that is necessary is to consider three procedures:

1. How to correct a line that is in error
2. How to insert a line
3. How to delete a line

These three procedures are all that are necessary to make any changes. Most terminals and BASIC processors have other features, such as powerful editing abilities, which allow changes to be made more quickly and easily than with the above three procedures. Again, since these features vary greatly with the particular system, Examples 2.8–2.12 should be considered only as illustrations.

2.3.1   Correcting a Line To correct a line after it has already been transmitted to the computer, simply retype it; the BASIC processor will automatically replace duplicate line numbers with the last such line that you transmit. But remember that this correction applies only to the working copy of the program in main memory. If you want the change to apply to the saved version in auxiliary memory, before you log off you must replace the old version. If you don't, the next time you access the old program, the changes would not have been made. This applies to procedures for inserting and deleting lines as well, and to all changes to a given program.

EXAMPLE 2.8 ═══

Suppose that in reproducing program Example 1.2, you type

130 REED N

After you transmit this line, the computer will respond with

ILLEGAL INSTRUCTION IN 130

To correct it, type

130 READ N

and this line will take the place of the former.

EXAMPLE 2.9

Suppose you make an error in the line number itself, for example,

1300 READ N

To correct this, two things must be done. First, type

130 READ N

The BASIC system will insert this line in the proper sequence in the memory. Second, you must *delete* the line 1300 READ N. See Section 2.3.3.

EXAMPLE 2.10

Suppose you type

13O READ N

that is, the letter O in place of the number 0. BASIC will respond with

ILLEGAL INSTRUCTION IN 13

or something similar.

Why? Because BASIC interprets this as line 13 with the letter O as part of the instruction (recall that blank spaces are ignored). Since there is no command of the form OREAD, this line is not accepted. Just retype

130 READ N

Procedures for correcting a line not yet transmitted to the computer vary greatly from system to system. On some CRT's, you can simply backspace to the error and retype the line. On devices like a Teletype (that is, devices with a typewriter keyboard and roll of paper), backspace keys (— or RUBOUT or @ or #) exist that can be used to delete the last character typed on the current line. Thus, two characters are erased if a backspace key is struck twice, three characters if it is struck three times, and so on. The correct characters can then be typed after the appropriate number of deletions have been made. For example, 10 PRIMT A — — — — NT A would be transmitted to the computer as 10 PRINT A.

Furthermore, some terminals have special keys, such as ALTMODE or ESC, that cancel the current line before it has been transmitted to the computer. This is useful if you want to retype the entire line.

2.3.2 Inserting a Line To insert a line, just type it anywhere in the sequence. BASIC always automatically readjusts the internal sequence of the statements in the order of their line numbers.

EXAMPLE 2.11

Typing

```
100 PRINT A + B
 50 LET B = 5
110 END
 10 LET A = 10
```

becomes

```
 10 LET A = 10
 50 LET B = 5
100 PRINT A + B
110 END
```

Try it!

2.3.3 Deleting a Line To delete a line, type the line number alone and transmit it. The corresponding instruction is automatically erased from the program.

EXAMPLE 2.12

Typing

```
10 LET X = 5
20 PRINT X
30 PRINT X*X, X-1
40 END
30
```

becomes

10 LET X = 5
20 PRINT X
40 END

___

Exercises

It is especially true in programming that you learn by doing. At this point you should be ready to practice using the terminal.

1. Enter the program Example 1.2 using a terminal. In doing so, make some intentional mistakes—misspell words, change some of the numbers, or leave out some lines; then observe what happens. Some particular changes are given in the exercises below, but you are also encouraged to experiment on your own.

2. Enter the program Example 1.2 exactly as given (that is, correct the spelling errors and the like made in problem 1). Run it and observe the results.

   In the remaining exercises you are asked to make certain changes to Example 1.2. Before making a change, be sure to start first with the corrected version; don't leave any changes from a previous exercise. In each case try to predict what will happen as a result of a given change, and then run the program to see the actual results.

3. Delete line 150 from the program. What was the function of the deleted instruction? Look at the data (line 300) for a clue.

4. Delete line 200. What was the function of the deleted instruction?

5. Insert a line: 290 DATA 12,500. What do you expect to happen? This shows how easily data can be added.

6. Insert a line: 400 DATA 6666,42. Why are the results the same as in the second problem, even though 6666 is now the largest number in the list?

7. Delete lines 120, 140, 180, and 210. Why are the results unchanged?

8. Delete line 110 and run the program. Note that the results are identical to those in the unaltered version. This is because BASIC automatically sets variables equal to zero if they are not assigned some other value.[†] Thus, line 110 is redundant in the sense that BASIC would have done it automatically anyway. Initializing variables to some value is a good practice for a programmer to follow, however. Otherwise it is easy to neglect doing it when this step is necessary, as when a variable should be set to a nonzero value.

___

[†]This is not true on some BASIC systems, which detect such undefined variables and give a corresponding error message.

9. Interchange the following: lines 11Ø and 13Ø; lines 19Ø and 2ØØ.

10. Replace the number –5 in line 3ØØ with 5. Observe what happens. Why? This is another way to terminate a program—simply let the program run out of data. However, the technique is generally considered a poor way to end a program, and we do not recommend it. There are many situations in which it will not work properly, and you may not obtain the results you were looking for. Second, the printed output will include the unwanted error message.

11. What changes would have to be made to find the minimum of a list of positive numbers? the minimum and the maximum?

3. Basic BASIC, Part One: Reading, Writing, Arithmetic

BASIC is a simple language as programming languages go; there are less than 100 words in its "vocabulary." And it is necessary to know relatively few of them to write reasonably complex programs. The minimal set of instructions forms what is often called basic BASIC.

FIGURE 3.1 Starting out

3.1   Variables and Constants

Before we examine such instructions, it is necessary first to consider *variables.* A program consists of a sequence of commands to manipulate a set of numbers, names, or other symbols. However, most programs do not deal specifically with each of these elements—variables are used instead.

For example, rather than have an instruction compute the value 17 - 8, it would generally be preferable to have one that computed A - B instead, where A and B can then assume the values 17 and 8 respectively. The expression A - B could then be used for subtracting any pair of numbers, not just 17 and 8. In this way, a program becomes generalized; the procedure can be applied to many different sets of data without being changed.

The symbols A and B in this example are called **variables,** (or variable names), since they can assume different values during the execution of a program. The numbers 17 and 8 are **constants**, since they do not change value. Look again at the following segment from Example 1.1:

$$70 \text{ INPUT B, H}$$
$$80 \text{ LET A} = .5 * B * H$$
$$90 \text{ PRINT B, H, A}$$

In that program A, B, and H are variables, and .5 is a constant.

Actually, variables represent locations in memory. They are *symbolic addresses* into which values can be placed. In the above example we have

$$A = 17 \qquad B = 8$$

The variable A has 17 stored electronically in its location and B has the value 8. Here, A is said to be equal to 17, even though in reality A represents the location at which 17 is currently stored. But in BASIC we use variables like A as if the variable were the value itself; it is enough to refer to the variable in a program to get the value at that location.

Variables such as A are created during the compiling process. They are like boxes that can hold only one object at a time; that is, a variable can store a single value—the *current value*—at a given instant. When a new value is placed in A, the previous value that was stored there is destroyed. Later we shall discuss several kinds of instructions that can change the value of a variable.

Look again at this segment of Example 1.2:

```
110        LET L = 0
120 REM*BEGIN LOOP
130            READ N
140 REM*****EXIT FROM LOOP IF AT END OF LIST
150            IF N < 0 THEN 230
170            IF L > = N THEN 120
180 REM*          ELSE
190                  LET L = N
200                  GO TO 120
```

L and N are the only variables in that program. The value of N is changed in line 13Ø:

13Ø READ N

and L is changed in line 19Ø:

19Ø LET L = N

In BASIC, constants are classified as either *numeric* or *string*. Examples of valid constants are

NUMERIC CONSTANTS	STRING CONSTANTS
52	"JOHN DOE"
Ø	"X + Y + Z"
–7.36259	"THIS SENTENCE IS A STRING CONSTANT"
129357	"*!//??*!"
+12	"52"

Numeric constants, or numbers, can have signs and decimal points, but not commas. Thus, 7,276.3 should be written as 7276.3. The number of digits that a numeric constant can have depends on the system but is usually limited to either 6, 8, or 9. Numeric constants can also be expressed in another form called *exponential notation,* which allows for much larger numbers to be represented. We will discuss this form in a later chapter.

A string constant is any sequence of letters, numbers, or other symbols. On most systems, this sequence must be enclosed in quotation marks. There is a limit to the length, and again, this depends on the particular system. Some common limits are 60, 256, and 4,095 characters. Usually a string cannot contain any quotation marks, since quotation marks are used to delimit them. Note that "52" is a string constant, not a numeric, since it is enclosed in quotes.

Similarly, variables are either numeric variables or string variables. A numeric variable can store only numbers and is specified by a *single letter* optionally followed by a *single digit.* As examples,

X
P1
AØ

are valid numeric variables, whereas

1A
BB
C12

are invalid. A string variable is capable of storing numbers as well as nonnumeric data such as names, sentences, and algebraic symbols. (However, arithmetic operations cannot be done on strings; the strings are used mainly as text, instructions, messages, and the like.) A string variable is specified as a variable name (as above) followed by a dollar sign ($). For example, the symbols A$ and Q5$, are valid string variable names.

3.2   Arithmetic Operations

There are five arithmetic operations in BASIC:

OPERATION	SYMBOL	EXAMPLE
Exponentiation	$\wedge$ (or ↑ or **)[†]	$A \wedge 2$ (means A^2)
Multiplication	*	$5 * 2.3$ (= 11.5)
Division	/	$C1 / D \left(\text{means } \dfrac{C1}{D}\right)$
Addition	+	$7.1 + 2.1$ (= 9.2)
Subtraction	–	$3.0 - 3$ (= 0)

More than one operation may appear in a given expression. For example,

$$A * 5.5 / B + C1 - 2.3$$
$$3.7 \wedge .5 \wedge B$$

The above operations are performed in BASIC in the following order:

1. All exponentiations first, in the order in which they occur from left to right[‡]
2. All multiplications and divisions second, from left to right
3. All sums and differences third, from left to right

Each example below is evaluated as the steps indicate, according to the above rules:

$$
\begin{aligned}
3 + 2 * 5 - 2 \wedge 3 - 1 &= 3 + 2 * 5 - 8 - 1 \\
&= 3 + 10 - 8 - 1 \\
&= 13 - 8 - 1 \\
&= 5 - 1 \\
&= 4
\end{aligned}
$$

$$
\begin{aligned}
3 \wedge 2 \wedge 3 / 9 &= 9 \wedge 3 / 9 \\
&= 729 / 9 \\
&= 81
\end{aligned}
$$

$$
\begin{aligned}
12 / 4 / 2 * 2 &= 3 / 2 * 2 \\
&= 1.5 * 2 \\
&= 3
\end{aligned}
$$

Parentheses override these rules; that is, parentheses can be used to change the order of operations. In BASIC, expressions in parentheses are evaluated *first,* according to the above rules. Also, a parenthetical expression may be part of another expression that is enclosed in parentheses. The computer evaluates the innermost expression first and then works outward.

[†]We shall use the symbol $\wedge$.
[‡]Some versions associate right to left.

Compare the following examples with those above:

$$(3 + 2) * 5 - 2 \wedge (3 - 1) = 5 * 5 - 2 \wedge (3 - 1)$$
$$= 5 * 5 - 2 \wedge 2$$
$$= 5 * 5 - 4$$
$$= 25 - 4$$
$$= 21$$

$$12 / (4 / (2 * 2)) = 12 / (4 / 4)$$
$$= 12 / 1$$
$$= 12$$

$$-(5 - (4 - (3 - (2 - 1)))) = -(5 - (4 - (3 - 1)))$$
$$= -(5 - (4 - 2))$$
$$= -(5 - 2)$$
$$= -3$$

Thus, the expression $\dfrac{4 + 3}{9 + 2 \times 6}$ is represented in BASIC as

$$(4 + 3) / (9 + 2 * 6) = .33333333$$

rather than

$$4 + 3 / 9 + 2 * 6 = 16.33333333$$

Note also that we can represent roots of numbers by fractional exponents. For example, $\sqrt{27} = (27)^{1/2}$ is represented by

$$27 \wedge (1/2) \quad \text{or} \quad 27 \wedge .5$$

Another example, $\sqrt[3]{1/4} = (1/4)^{1/3}$, is shown by

$$(1/4) \wedge (1/3) \quad \text{or} \quad (.25) \wedge (1/3)$$

Negative exponents are valid; for example,

$$2 \wedge (-2) = .25$$

and

$$(1/3) \wedge (-3) = 27$$

However, negative values cannot have a fractional exponent. For example, using

$$(-2) \wedge (1/2)$$

in a program would cause an error message to be displayed.

3.3   Remarks

It is very important for a programmer to list the variables used in a program and to describe their function briefly. This is helpful in keeping one's ideas clear both during the writing of the program and afterward. The following scenario is not uncommon.

A student, Roger Rapidwriter, writes and uses a somewhat complicated program without comments or documentation of any sort. He gets the results and stores the program away, with the idea that he will probably never use it again. Then, perhaps a year later, he finds that he needs the program; perhaps it has to be modified, although only slightly, for this new application. On looking at the program, Roger finds that he has completely forgotten how it works, what each of the variables is used for, and even how to use the program for the original application. He finally gets it to work after several frustrating weeks of hard work.

The student's difficulties could have been avoided by sufficient documentation—that is, writing down exactly what each group of instructions accomplishes, what each of the variables does, and so forth. Experienced professional programmers ideally spend as much time documenting programs as they do in coding the program itself. Many large computer installations include workers whose sole task is to document programs.

One way to easily provide such documentation for BASIC programs is by using the REM (remark) statement. Each line of a program starts a new statement. Statements beginning with REM are not instructions to be executed but simply comments for the programmer's benefit. They are important for anyone reading the program to modify it, to correct errors, or to understand what is going on. The more complex the program, the more necessary their use. They can be used to describe what the program does as well as how it does it and how the program itself is constructed. An important advantage of REM statements is that the documentation always stays with the program.

Recall Example 1.2 and the REM statements used there. The number of REM statements is probably somewhat excessive for that problem, but the remarks used depend largely on the audience for whom they are intended. If this program were to be used by experienced programmers, some remarks could be omitted.

Judicious comments are used and should be written *during the coding* of the program and not after the program has been written. We are strongly emphasizing documentation, since you will be tempted to neglect it. When you think you understand how to solve (or write the program for) a given problem, you will want to code it as quickly as possible. **Don't do it!**

Resist such temptations and put in the remarks. Any experienced programmer will tell you that it is worth the effort, even if you think you will never use the program again. The time spent on remarks will more than likely be gained in finding and correcting errors alone. (You will learn that it is nearly impossible to write a program that is error-free in its first trial.) You will have to force yourself at first, but after a while it will become a valuable habit.

Remarks can be used in a second way, helping describe the *structure* of a program. This will be explained more fully in Chapter 5, but for now, we want to indicate how a program is composed—how its "pieces" fit together, again for purposes of documentation. This approach will make programs more readable. For example, look at the following segment of Example 1.2:

```
110      LET L = 0
120 REM*BEGIN LOOP
130             READ N
140 REM*****EXIT FROM LOOP IF AT END OF LIST
150         IF N < 0 THEN 230
170         IF L > = N THEN 120
180 REM*            ELSE
190                    LET L = N
200                    GO TO 120
210 REM*END LOOP
```

Lines 120 and 210 indicate the beginning and end of a loop (a sequence of instructions that are repeated); line 180 indicates alternatives (ELSE).

3.4 The END Statement

On most BASIC systems, the END statement is required, and it must have the largest line number in the program. The END statement consists simply of the word END, preceded by a line number (Example 3.1). There can be only one END statement in a program.

EXAMPLE 3.1 ═══

Program:

```
10 REM THIS IS A SHORT, COMPLETE, BUT MEANINGLESS PROGRAM.
20 END
```

In this and all examples to follow, only the program and output are shown. Other information that would appear on the terminal, such as the amount of computer time used, is omitted. Also, comments that might ordinarily be included with programs in REM statements appear instead in the accompanying text if the volume of remarks is large.

3.5 The PRINT Statement

The PRINT statement is used to display the output—the "answers"—from a program. The statement consists of a line number, followed by the word PRINT, followed by whatever information you want the computer to print. There is a rich variety of formats that the PRINT statement uses. A few examples follow; the remaining features will be treated in Chapter 7.

EXAMPLE 3.2

```
Program:
 1Ø REM  THIS PROGRAM ILLUSTRATES THE USE OF THE PRINT
 2Ø REM  STATEMENT TO PRINT NUMBERS AND THE RESULTS OF
 3Ø REM  SIMPLE ARITHMETIC EXPRESSIONS.
 4Ø REM
 5Ø PRINT 137
 6Ø PRINT 1+27
 7Ø PRINT 5-4-3-2-1
 8Ø PR I NT  5    4     3
 9Ø PRINT2/3
1ØØ END

Output:

 137
 28
-5
 543
 .66666666
```

In Example 3.2, we see that each PRINT statement produces a separate line of output. Also, we see from line 7Ø that subtractions are carried out from left to right. Line 8Ø shows that BASIC ignores blank spaces. Note that the output from line 9Ø includes eight digits. This varies with the system used. Many systems will *round off* such a result to .666666667.

Note that line numbers go up by increments of 10 in this example. This is optional. Usually some gap is left between successive line numbers in case the programmer wants later to insert some extra lines into the program. It is easy to forget something; and without such a gap, many line numbers might have to be changed to make room for such an addition. Many systems have editors that automatically change line numbers to remedy such oversights.

3.5.1   **Printing Messages (Strings)**   Remarks are used to describe a program. It is often useful to print words, sentences, or special symbols to describe the output from a program. This is accomplished with quotation marks.[†] During execution of the program, every-

---

[†]Double quotes (") are used here. Single quotes (') are used in some systems.

thing that is enclosed in quotation marks is printed exactly the way it was typed (see Example 3.3). Note that blank spaces are not ignored if they appear inside quotes.

EXAMPLE 3.3 ═══

Program:

```
1Ø PRINT "THIS IS THE FIRST LINE OF OUTPUT."
2Ø PRINT "THIS LINE WILL NOT BE PRINTED."
3Ø PRINT "31 + 12"
4Ø PRINT 31 + 12
5Ø END
2Ø PRINT "THIS LINE REPLACES LINE 2Ø, ABOVE."
```

Output:

```
THIS IS THE FIRST LINE OF OUTPUT.
THIS LINE REPLACES LINE 2Ø,ABOVE.
31 + 12
 43
```

Note that the second line in the program has been replaced. Another PRINT statement with line number 2Ø has been entered later (after END). Notice also the difference in the output from the expression in quotation marks (line 3Ø) and the one without such marks (line 4Ø). The quotation marks in line 3Ø mean that the expression is a *string* constant, and thus no operation is carried out. In line 4Ø there are no quotation marks, and thus the expression is treated as an arithmetic expression; the addition does take place.

3.5.2 **More Than One Item on a Line** To print more than one string and/or number per line, separate the items in the PRINT list by commas.

EXAMPLE 3.4

Program:
```
1ØØ REM THIS PROGRAM ILLUSTRATES THE USE OF THE PRINT
11Ø REM STATEMENT TO PRINT MORE THAN ONE ITEM PER LINE.
12Ø REM
13Ø PRINT -1,+2,3
14Ø PRINT "A =", 2 ^ (1/2), "SUM IS", 12.7+14.2
15Ø PRINT
16Ø PRINT 1,2,3,4,5,6,7,8,9,10,11,12
17Ø END
```

Output:
```
-1              2               3
A =             1.4142136       SUM IS        26.9

1               2               3             4             5
6               7               8             9             10
11              12
```

From Example 3.4, we see that if a number is negative, a minus sign is printed, and if a number is positive, no sign is printed.

Note also how the items are spaced on output. There are five columns across the page in BASIC, each 15 spaces wide.[†] If there are more than five items in the PRINT list (as in line 16Ø), the sixth item is automatically printed in the first column under the first item, the seventh under the second item, and so on.

Strings can be mixed with numeric items, as in line 14Ø.

In line 15Ø there is no list at all—the result is a blank line in the output. This allows for variation in spacing in the output; for example, if you require two blank lines simply put two statements (like line 15Ø) in succession; for example,

15Ø PRINT

151 PRINT

Study carefully the output from Example 3.5 to review the evaluation of arithmetic expressions. First evaluate each expression in the PRINT statements by hand, and compare your results with the output. The expressions have been spread out in the PRINT lists to improve legibility.

[†]Some systems have only four columns.

EXAMPLE 3.5

Program:

```
 10 REM THIS EXAMPLE ILLUSTRATES THE PRINT STATEMENT AND THE
 20 REM EVALUATION OF ARITHMETIC EXPRESSIONS.
 30 REM
 40 PRINT 5-4*6/2^3-1        ,        (5-4)*6/2^3-1
 50 REM
 60 PRINT 5-4*(6/2)^3-1      ,        ((5-4)*(6/2))^3-1
 70 REM
 80 PRINT 2^3^2  ,  2^(3^2)  ,  -2^4  ,  (-2)^4
 90 REM
100 PRINT 4+3/9+2*6          ,        (4+3)/(9+2*6)
110 END
```

Output:

```
 1              -.25
-104            26
 64             512           -16           16
 16.333333      .33333333
```

Suppose you have more items to print than what will fit in a single PRINT list. (There are 72 columns in a line, including blank spaces.)[†] Then you must provide a sufficient number of PRINT statements to accommodate all the items. To print the words ONE, TWO, . . . , TWELVE, for example, you could write a program like Example 3.6.

EXAMPLE 3.6

Program:

```
 10 REM THIS PROGRAM PRINTS THE WORDS: ONE, TWO, ..., TWELVE
 12 REM IN TWO DIFFERENT WAYS.  NOTE THAT THE STATEMENTS
 14 REM ARE EXECUTED IN THE ORDER OF THE LINE NUMBERS.
 16 REM LINE 24 PRODUCES THE FIRST LINE OF OUTPUT, LINE
 18 REM 27 PRODUCES THE NEXT TWO LINES, AND LINE 29 THE
 20 REM LAST LINE.
 22 REM ///////////////////////////////////////////////////////////
 27 PRINT "ONE","TWO","THREE","FOUR","FIVE","SIX","SEVEN","EIGHT","NINE"
 29 PRINT "TEN","ELEVEN","TWELVE"
 24 PRINT "ONE TWO THREE FOUR FIVE SIX SEVEN EIGHT NINE TEN ELEVEN TWELVE"
100 END
```

Output:

```
ONE TWO THREE FOUR FIVE SIX SEVEN EIGHT NINE TEN ELEVEN TWELVE
ONE             TWO             THREE           FOUR            FIVE
SIX             SEVEN           EIGHT           NINE
TEN             ELEVEN          TWELVE
```

[†] There are 80 columns in the system used in this book.

3.5.3   Printing Tables   Example 3.7 shows us how to print tables.

EXAMPLE 3.7 ═══

Program:

```
10 REM THE "COLUMNS" FEATURE OF BASIC IS USEFUL IN SETTING
20 REM UP TABLES.  NOTE FROM LINE 100 THAT IF MORE THAN
30 REM 15 COLUMNS ARE REQUIRED BY AN EXPRESSION, THE NEXT
40 REM COLUMNS ARE USED TO COMPLETE IT.
50 REM /////////////////////////////////////////////////////
100 PRINT "PRINCIPAL AND INTEREST TABLE FOR: ","EXAMPLE 3.7"
110 PRINT
120 PRINT "PRINCIPAL","INTEREST"
130 PRINT 5226.00,.12*5226.00
140 PRINT 29000.00,.08*29000.00
150 PRINT 795.30,.18*795.30
200 END
```

Output:

```
PRINCIPAL AND INTEREST TABLE FOR:        EXAMPLE 3.7

PRINCIPAL       INTEREST
5226            627.12
29000           2320
795.3           143.154
```

It is sometimes useful to "shift" the columns in a table, as in Example 3.8. Blank spaces enclosed in quotes are used for this purpose.

EXAMPLE 3.8 ═══

Program:

```
10 REM THIS PROGRAM IS ESSENTIALLY THE SAME AS EXAMPLE 3.7,
15 REM EXCEPT THAT SUMS ARE ALSO GIVEN.  NOTE HOW "BLANK STRINGS"
20 REM USE UP A COLUMN, THEREBY SHIFTING THE NEXT ITEM IN THE
25 REM LIST TO THE NEXT COLUMN.  THIS ALLOWS FOR THE "TOTAL ="
30 REM AND "SUM IS" EXPRESSIONS IN THE BOTTOM LINE.
35 REM//////////////////////////////////////////////////////
40 PRINT " ","PRINCIPAL"," ","INTEREST"
45 PRINT " ",5226.00," ",.12*5226.00
50 PRINT " ",29000.00," ",.08*29000.00
55 PRINT " ",795.30," ",.18*795.30
60 PRINT " ","--------"," ","---------"
65 PRINT "TOTAL =",5226+29000+795.30,"SUM IS",.12*5226+.08*29000+.18*795.30
100 END
```

Output:

```
          PRINCIPAL                  INTEREST

          5226                       627.12
          29000                      2320
          795.3                      143.154
          --------                   ----------
TOTAL =   35021.3      SUM IS        3090.274
```

3.5.4   Legal Items in PRINT Statements   Each item in the PRINT list must be one of the following (as shown in Example 3.9):

1. A number
2. A string of letters, digits, symbols, and so forth enclosed in quotes
3. Numeric variables
4. Arithmetic expressions containing constants and/or variables
5. String variables
6. Function values (see Section 6.3)

EXAMPLE 3.9   ══

Program:

```
 1Ø REM PRINTING VARIABLES.
 2Ø REM IN THIS EXAMPLE THE WARNING MESSAGE IS PRODUCED
 3Ø REM BECAUSE THE STRING VARIABLE D$ IS NOT ASSIGNED
 4Ø REM A VALUE PRIOR TO PRINTING: THUS, NOTHING IS
 5Ø REM PRINTED BY LINE 12Ø.  SINCE NO VALUE IS ASSIGNED
 6Ø REM TO A AND B, THEY ARE AUTOMATICALLY ASSIGNED
 7Ø REM THE VALUE ZERO BY THE BASIC PROCESSOR.
 8Ø REM/////////////////////////////////////////////////////////
1ØØ PRINT A,B,A+B
11Ø PRINT "A+B"
12Ø PRINT D$
13Ø END
```

Output:

```
STRING VARIABLE  D$  UNASSIGNED.
Ø                Ø                  Ø
A+B
```

Note: On many systems D$ would be initialized to the *null* string, that is, no characters.

3.6   Assigning Values to Variables: The LET Statement

In BASIC there are three statements that assign values to variables:

1. The LET statement
2. The READ statement
3. The INPUT statement

Use of these statements has been shown in Examples 1.1 and 1.2.
An example of the LET statement is

$$1Ø \; LET \; X = A + 2 * B$$

The variable X is assigned the value that is computed in the expression on the right-hand side of the equals sign. The current value of B is multiplied by 2, and that result is added to the current value of A. The resulting number is stored in X. Thus, the old value of X is replaced by this newly computed value, but the values of A and B remain unchanged.

We can assign values to string variables in a similar manner; for example,

1Ø LET A$ = "THE QUICK BROWN FOX"

There is no computation in this statement; A$ simply takes on the value THE QUICK BROWN FOX. Note that the expression must be enclosed in quotation marks.

In general, the two forms of the LET statement are

n LET v = arithmetic expression

and

n LET v$ = "any string of letters, numbers, symbols
(except quotation marks)"

where n is a line number, v a numeric variable, and v$ a string variable. The arithmetic expression may be a single constant or another numeric variable. The use of the LET statement in programs is shown in Examples 3.10–3.12.

EXAMPLE 3.10

```
Program:

10 LET X = 4
20 LET Y = 7
30 LET Z1 = X + Y
40 PRINT X,Y,Z1,Z2
50 LET X = -1
60 LET Z2 = X + Y
70 PRINT X,Y,Z1,Z2
80 END

Output:

4          7          11          Ø
-1         7          11          6
```

Example 3.10 shows how variables take on different values. Note that in line 4Ø, Z2 has the value zero, since it had not previously been assigned a value. In line 5Ø, the original value of X (4) is replaced by the value -1. In line 7Ø, we see that the value of Z1 is still 11 but Z2 is 6. This is because the statements are executed in the numerical order of the line numbers, and even though X was changed, the value of Z1 was not reassigned to a new value after line 4Ø.

EXAMPLE 3.11 ══

Program:

```
 1Ø LET A$ = " A "
 2Ø LET B$ = " B "
 3Ø LET C$ = " C "
 4Ø PRINT A$,B$,C$
 5Ø LET A = 1
 6Ø LET B = A
 7Ø LET C = B
 8Ø PRINT A,B,C
 9Ø LET A = A + 1
1ØØ LET B = B + 2
11Ø LET C = C * 2
12Ø PRINT A,B,C
13Ø LET A = A + 1
14Ø LET B = B + 2
15Ø LET C = C * 2
16Ø PRINT A,B,C
17Ø END
```

Output:

A	B	C
1	1	1
2	3	2
3	5	4

Example 3.11 shows that the same variable may appear on both sides of the equals sign. This is an extremely important feature of BASIC and other programming languages. It allows a programmer to compute a number by using the old value of a variable and then replacing it with the newly computed value. Such statements are sometimes called *iterative statements.*

In this example, the value of A increases by 1 and the value of B by 2, and C is doubled at each stage. The current value of A (1) is added to 1 in line 9Ø; the resulting sum is then stored back in A, replacing the current value. In this way A increases by 1. This step is repeated in line 13Ø. Similarly, B increases by 2 in lines 1ØØ and 14Ø, and C is doubled in lines 11Ø and 15Ø.

Increasing A and B this way illustrates how counting is done in computer programs. Every time something happens—perhaps we print a line of numbers or perform a particular calculation—we can count the number of such occurrences by including with the occurrence a statement similar to line 9Ø. We can also count by twos, as in line 1ØØ. Counting in a program is an important technique to know, and we will discuss it further in Chapter 4.

EXAMPLE 3.12

```
Program:
 1REM THIS PROGRAM ILLUSTRATES SOME COMMON ERRORS.
 2REM
1Ø LET C = 1
2Ø LET C+1=C
C+1    IS AN IMPROPER VARIABLE IN A "LET" STATEMENT IN 2Ø.
3Ø LET SUM = 5 + 1Ø
SUM    IS AN IMPROPER VARIABLE IN A "LET" STATEMENT IN 3Ø.
4Ø LET 1ØA = 1
1ØA    IS AN IMPROPER VARIABLE IN A "LET" STATEMENT IN 4Ø.
5Ø LET A$ = "6"
6Ø LET B$ = "7"
7Ø LET C$ = A$*B$
A$*B$   IS AN IMPROPER VARIABLE IN A "LET" STATEMENT IN 7Ø.
8Ø A = 6
9Ø PRINT A,A$
1ØØ END

Output:
6                 6
```

Line 2Ø of Example 3.12 is in error because only a single variable can appear to the left of the equals sign. Given what a LET statement does—assigning a value to a variable —we find that any other form, like line 2Ø, does not make sense. Lines 3Ø and 4Ø are in error because SUM and 1ØA are not proper variable names in BASIC. Line 7Ø is in error since it is illegal (and meaningless) to do arithmetic on string variables.

Note that in each of these cases, the BASIC processor immediately detected the error. That is because the errors were in the *form* of the statement; in other words, the rules that specify how a given type of statement is written were violated. Thus, the errors could be determined without considering the context of the rest of the statements. On some systems, these statements in error are consequently not compiled, and line numbers 2Ø, 3Ø, 4Ø, and 7Ø would be missing from the version that was executed. On other systems, the lines would not be discarded and the program would stop execution at the first error with a message such as

ILLEGAL STATEMENT AT LINE 2Ø

Line 8Ø did not produce an error on our system, but omitting the word LET in an assignment statement would be an error on some systems. Check to see whether this omission is acceptable to yours.

3.7   Assigning Values to Variables: READ and DATA Statements

The second method for assigning values to variables is the READ statement. The READ statement must be used together with the DATA statement or statements. DATA presents the list of numbers and/or string constants, and READ assigns these values to its list of variables in the corresponding order.

The READ statement is similar in format to the PRINT statement, except that only variable names (numeric and/or string) may appear in the READ list; arithmetic operations are not allowed.

DATA statements can be placed anywhere in the program (before the END statement). They are ignored by the BASIC processor during execution except where data items are required by a READ statement. Usually, however, a BASIC programmer will place all data together at the end of the program for ease of access, readability, and modification.

EXAMPLE 3.13

Program:

```
10 READ X,Y
20 LET Z = X + Y
30 PRINT X,Y,Z
40 DATA 4,7
50 END
```

Output:

```
4                7                11
```

Example 3.13 reads two numbers, computes their sum, and prints out the result. It essentially duplicates lines 10–40 of Example 3.10. Here, however, the values X and Y are assigned by a READ statement. Like the PRINT list, the READ statement and the DATA statement have their individual components separated by commas. Note that the variables are assigned in the order they appear. Thus the first variable X takes on the first number, 4, in the DATA list, and Y takes on the value 7.

EXAMPLE 3.14

Program:

```
1Ø DATA 1,2
2Ø READ A,B,C
3Ø PRINT A,B,C,D,E
4Ø READ D,E
5Ø PRINT A,B,C,D,E
6Ø DATA 3,4,5,6,7
7Ø END
```

Output:

1	2	3	Ø	Ø
1	2	3	4	5

Note the placement of the DATA statements in Example 3.14. In the first READ, the three variables A, B, and C are to be assigned. Since there are only two numbers in the first DATA statement, the computer must scan the program until it finds the next DATA statement (line 6Ø) so that C can be assigned a value (3).

In line 3Ø, D and E have not yet been assigned values; thus they print as zeros. In line 4Ø, D and E are assigned values beginning with the numbers at which the previous READ left off. Consequently D = 4 and E = 5 in line 5Ø. Note that there is no error in having *extra* data—the numbers 6 and 7 are simply ignored by the program.

EXAMPLE 3.15

Program:

```
1Ø READ A$
2Ø READ B$,B,B1
3Ø PRINT A$
4Ø PRINT B$,B,B1
5Ø READ A$,B$,C$
6Ø PRINT A$,B$,C$

7Ø DATA "July, 4, 1776",July,4,1776
8Ø DATA GEORGE WASHINGTON,THOMAS PAINE, JOHN ADAMS
9Ø END
```

Output:

```
JULY, 4, 1776
JULY            4           1776
GEORGE WASHINGTON           THOMAS PAINE    JOHN ADAMS
```

Example 3.15 illustrates the reading of string data. Note that string data in a DATA list, unlike the PRINT list, can be with or without quotation marks.[†] If the string of characters includes a comma, however, or does not begin with a letter, then it must be enclosed within quotations marks. Thus, JULY, 4, 1776 is assigned to A$, B$ = JULY, B = 4, and B1 = 1776. These rules allow the BASIC compiler-interpreter to distinguish easily between strings and numeric variables. We recommend using quotation marks for all strings in DATA lists to avoid confusion.

Also note that numeric and string data can be mixed in the list. (See also Example 3.16.) Finally, A$ is reset equal to GEORGE WASHINGTON, B$ = THOMAS PAINE, and so on in line 60. Note that blank spaces are preserved in the output.

You should remember that numbers (for instance, 1776) could be assigned to either string variables or numeric variables. If arithmetic operations are to be performed on a number, then of course the number must be assigned to a numeric variable. If it is assigned to a string variable, it must be in quotation marks.

EXAMPLE 3.16

Program:

```
10 READ A
20 PRINT A
30 READ B,C
40 PRINT A ^.5,A/B ^ 2,C
50 DATA 150, 300
60 END
```

Output:

```
150
OUT OF ARITHMETIC DATA IN 30.

RUN STOPPED.
```

Example 3.16 shows a very common error in BASIC, not providing enough data. A program sometimes can be conveniently terminated this way, but there are dangers. First, note that the value of A was printed, but since the program ran out of data, line 40 was not executed. Thus the values of the expressions $A^{.5}$ and A / B^2 were not determined. Second, an unsightly error message appears with the output.

You may be thinking about two questions at this point:

1. Why are variables necessary?
2. How does one decide whether to use READ-DATA statements or LET statements to assign values to variables?

[†]Not in all systems, however.

The answers to these questions become clear with experience. Unfortunately, the simple programming examples in this chapter give no clues to the answers. Consider Example 3.13, shown here again for reference.

EXAMPLE 3.13

```
1Ø READ X,Y
2Ø LET Z = X + Y
3Ø PRINT X,Y,Z
4Ø DATA 4,7
5Ø END
```

This program reads two numbers (4 and 7), computes their sum, and prints the result. This same computation could have been done, for example, by

```
1Ø LET X = 4
2Ø LET Y = 7
3Ø LET Z = X + Y
4Ø PRINT X,Y,Z
5Ø END
```

or

```
1Ø PRINT 4,7,4 + 7
2Ø END
```

To add two *different* numbers in Example 3.13, we should change the DATA statement (line 4Ø). To add two different numbers in the first variation above, we must change the numbers in the LET statements in lines 1Ø and 2Ø. In the second example, we only need to change the numbers in the PRINT statement. The second form may seem preferable to the first and to Example 3.13, since it is shorter and no variables are needed.

However, programs like Example 3.13, which do make use of variables, are generally to be preferred. This will be evident when we examine programs that are more complex. "Useful" programs generally have many statements that refer to given variables many times. (The programs in this chapter are useful—but only as examples and teaching aids. The jobs that these programs do can more easily be done by hand, and there is no need to write programs to do them for us.)

For example, consider a program that calculates the entire payroll for a large company. It computes such things as federal and state income taxes, social security payments, overtime pay, and deductions for health insurance. With variables, only the data, and none of the instructions, have to be changed. If variables were not used, we should need a new set of instructions for every employee!

This idea holds true in general; programs should be written to work independently of specific data. Then none of the instructions needs to be changed to accommodate a change in the data. This may be confusing to a beginning BASIC programmer, since DATA statements appear as part of the instructions in a program, even though the computer ignores them during execution. In other programming languages, the data are usually kept separate from the instructions. It is best, then, not to think of the DATA statement as an instruction.

The above paragraphs have partially answered the second question as well as the first. If there are many data, or if the program will be run many times with different sets of data, the READ-DATA approach is definitely preferable.

If, however, the program is a "one-shot" program—you are going to run it once, with one set of data—and there are only a few data items—using LET statements to assign values to all the variables (or using no variables at all) may be easier. However, any exercises for this course should be written as if they were going to be used many times.

Also, if the program uses quantities that will not differ under any conditions, then one may prefer to use LET statements. It would be pointless, for example, to provide the number 12 in a DATA statement to represent the number of months in a year for a calendar-producing program.

3.8   Assigning Values to Variables: The INPUT Statement

The third method of assigning values to variables is the INPUT statement. Its form is given by

n INPUT list

where n is a line number, and the list may contain only string and/or numeric *variables.* Some examples include

10 INPUT K
20 INPUT A$,B$
30 INPUT A,B,C,D$

The important difference between READ-DATA statements and INPUT statements is that INPUT statements make BASIC *interactive;* that is, the behavior of the program can be modified *during execution* by someone using the program at a terminal. This is an extremely important and powerful feature of BASIC.

When BASIC encounters an INPUT statement, it halts execution temporarily, waiting for data to be transmitted from the terminal. A question mark (?) is displayed to indicate it is waiting for data. The user responds with a list of the corresponding number and type of constants, which are then assigned to the variables in the input list, and execution continues.

INPUT is not useful for assigning large amounts of data—the interaction process is too slow. It is useful, however, for initializing small numbers of variables and especially for interactive processes such as computer-assisted instruction (CAI) or computer games. As you read on, you will see many examples of its use.

EXAMPLE 3.17

Program:

```
 10 REM THIS EXAMPLE ILLUSTRATES THE USE OF THE INPUT
 20 REM STATEMENT, AS IT MIGHT BE USED IN A COMPUTERIZED
 30 REM COURSE IN ARITHMETIC.  THE PROGRAM PAUSES AT
 40 REM LINES 110 AND 140, WAITING FOR INPUT.
 50 REM
100 PRINT "TYPE IN THE THREE NUMBERS YOU WANT TO ADD"
110 INPUT A,B,C
120 LET S = A + B + C
130 PRINT "TYPE YOUR ANSWER FOR THIS SUM"
140 INPUT Z
150 PRINT "YOUR ANSWER:",Z
160 PRINT "TRUE ANSWER:",S
170 END
```

Output:

```
TYPE IN THE THREE NUMBERS YOU WANT TO ADD
?  16,-3,8
TYPE YOUR ANSWER FOR THIS SUM
?  22
YOUR ANSWER:      22
TRUE ANSWER:      21
```

In the output of Example 3.17, the lines containing 16, –3, 8, and 22 were supplied by the user at the terminal. Note the instructional use of the PRINT statements in lines 100 and 130 to inform the user on what kind of data to provide. What would happen, do you think, if the user entered only two numbers in response to line 110? (See problem 20 in the exercises that follow.)

Exercises

1. Write the BASIC instruction or instructions that assign the string STATUS REPORT to the variable A$. Do it in two different ways.

2. What will the following program do?

$$10 \; LET \; A = B$$
$$20 \; PRINT \; A$$
$$30 \; END$$

3. What value is computed by each of the following?

$$10 \; LET \; A2 = (2 * 3 + 1)^{\wedge}3$$
$$20 \; LET \; B \;\; = 2 + 3/6 * (2 + 4)$$
$$30 \; LET \; C \;\; = 4 - 5 * .3 + 6.5$$
$$40 \; LET \; T \;\; = (1 - (2*(3-4)))$$
$$50 \; LET \; T \;\; = T + 2/4 * 2$$

4. For each of the following statements, state what, if anything, is wrong?

$$10 \text{ LET T} = .75 * 3$$
$$20 \text{ READ X,Y} + Z$$
$$30 \text{ PRINT ''A'' * ''B''}$$
$$40 \text{ LET X} + Y = Z$$
$$50 \text{ LET XY} = X + Y$$
$$60 \text{ LET A} = A * B$$
$$70 \text{ LET Q} = \$10,000.00$$
$$80 \text{ LET P1} = A\$$$
$$90 \text{ LET C\$} = A + B$$
$$100 \text{ LET B} = A * (P + C - (D/A + S * Q))$$

5. Write LET statements equivalent to the following equations:

$$x = \frac{12(3 + 2^3)}{4(-8)} \qquad a = \frac{z(2x + y)^3}{b - 12}$$

$$y = \sqrt{1/2} \qquad b = \frac{(3.4 - 2.15)\,(4.7 - 13.3)}{(1.3 - 0.6)\,(2.1 - 5.7)}$$

$$z = \sqrt[3]{(-27)} \qquad c = \frac{7.6(3.5 - 1.7)}{-0.6}$$

$$t = 2^{2^3} \qquad d = \frac{1/3}{x/y}$$

$$u = -3 + \frac{2}{75 - 19 \times 36} \qquad f = \frac{-8 + \sqrt{8^2 - 4 \times 2 \times 4}}{2 \times 2}$$

6. Why, for example, when we want the cube root of 2, should we write the LET statement as

$$10 \text{ LET X} = 2^{\wedge}(1/3)$$

instead of

$$10 \text{ LET X} = 2^{\wedge}.33$$

The latter case is more efficient since it doesn't require a division operation.

7. How can you get the computer to print a plus sign (+) for positive numbers?

8. Write a program to print the author and title for three different books. Do it in two different ways.

9. Write a program to read any three numbers and print out a table consisting of three columns: the number, its square, and its cube. The columns should have headings. For example, the output might look like

NUMBER	SQUARE	CUBE
9	81	729
4.7	22.09	103.823
-3	9	-27

10. Repeat Exercise 9 for five numbers, and input the numbers instead of reading them. What changes are required to make it work for 10 numbers? (There *must* be a better way!)

11. Modify the program written for Exercise 10 to work for the number, its square root and cube root.

12. Write a program to compute the circumference and the area of a circle, and the volume of a sphere whose radius is given as input. The formulas needed are

$$\text{circumference} = 2 \pi r$$
$$\text{area} = \pi r^2$$
$$\text{volume} = \frac{4}{3} \pi r^3$$

where r is the radius and $\pi = 3.1416$.

13. Write a program to print the following pictures (centered on the screen or page):

a.
```
* * * * * * * * *
*               *
*    THE END    *
*               *
* * * * * * * * *
```

b.

c. Make up your own picture.

14. Write a program to compute and print out the simple interest on a bank account and the new balance. The following quantities should be provided by INPUT statements:

P = the original principal
R = the annual rate of interest
D = the number of days of deposit

Compute:

$$S = \frac{PRD}{360} \quad \text{(the simple interest)}$$
$$P2 = P + S \text{ (the new principal)}$$

Print out:

INTEREST = _____
NO. OF DAYS = _____
PRINCIPAL = _____
NEW PRINCIPAL = _____

15. A person has P pennies, N nickels, D dimes, Q quarters, O dollar bills, F five-dollar bills, and T ten-dollar bills. Write a program to compute the total amount of cash for any input values of P, N, D, Q, O, F, and T. Print the answer (1) in pennies and (2) in dollars.

16. A recipe for baked meatballs includes the following ingredients:

> 1 egg
> 1/4 cup milk
> 1-1/2 tablespoons of minced onion
> 1-1/2 slices of bread, cubed
> 1 lb of hamburger
> (Serves two.)

Write a program to compute and print out the amounts of these ingredients needed when this recipe is prepared for X number of people, where X is provided by an INPUT statement.

17. We want to carpet the floors of two bedrooms and the living room. The cost for the bedroom carpet is $11.75/yd^2, and for the living-room carpet, $15.50/yd^2. The bedrooms are 9 ft $\times$ 12 ft and 10 ft $\times$ 15 ft, and the living room is 15 ft $\times$ 19 ft. Write a program to compute and print the cost for each room and the total cost. Make the program flexible enough to be run easily with different carpet prices.

18. The United States is going metric. Write a program that accepts a Fahrenheit temperature as input and prints out the corresponding centrigrade (Celsius) temperature. The conversion formula is C = 5/9 (F – 32).

19. Suppose you have the following data for each of four cars: the miles traveled for one month and the amount of gas used. Write a program that will read that data and print a table showing each car's average miles per gallon and the total mileage driven, the total gas consumed, and the average miles per gallon of all four cars combined.

20. What would happen in Example 3.17 if the user entered only one number in response to the statement in line 11Ø? two numbers? four numbers? Try these modifications.

4. Basic BASIC, Part Two: Control Statements

The programs so far considered have been simple. Indeed, in practice there is no need to write them except to learn how to use the various instructions. Now we examine *control statements*. Without them, only trivial programs could be written, and computers would be of little use except as a toy. A program capable of adding 10,000 numbers would require thousands of instructions! Obviously, programming under such conditions would be very impractical. On the other hand, together with the instructions in Chapter 3, the control instructions described in this chapter form a minimal set that will enable you to write complete, useful, and powerful programs.

FIGURE 4.1 In control

Instructions in a BASIC program normally are executed in the sequence given by their line numbers. But control statements allow the program to change the sequence of execution. Also, this change may depend on some condition in the program, such as the value of a variable. Thus, the behavior of a program may change according to some of the data.

4.1   The STOP Statement

The STOP statement belongs in this chapter because it definitely alters the execution sequence; it stops execution altogether. Although it is not necessary to use the STOP statement, we include it here because it often allows much neater programs. Its form is just like the END statement; for example,

125 STOP

When BASIC encounters a STOP statement, execution is terminated and none of the instructions following the STOP are carried out. Unlike END, however, there may be many STOP statements in a given program, at any location. (Examples are given in later sections.)

4.2   Conditional Jumps: The IF-THEN Statement

The IF-THEN statement permits a conditional transfer of control. The actual change in the execution sequence depends on the result of a computation, the value of a variable, or the comparison of strings and string variables. The general format of the IF-THEN statement is[†]

k IF (expression) (relation) (expression) THEN n

where k and n are different (why?) line numbers. The expressions may be single variables, constants, or arithmetic expressions. They are compared according to the relation in the statement. If the result of the comparison is true, BASIC executes line number n next. If it is false, BASIC continues to the next statement immediately following line k.

There are six relations that can be used in an IF-THEN statement:

SYMBOL	RELATION	EXAMPLE OF USE
=	equal to	50 IF X = Y THEN 10
<	less than	50 IF A1 < X + Y THEN 100
>	greater than	50 IF B$ > Q$ THEN 200
< =	less than or equal to	50 IF A + Y1 < = 27.3 THEN 20
> =	greater than or equal to	50 IF 14/12 > = A − .7 THEN 300
< >	not equal to	50 IF A$ < > "YES" THEN 100

[†]Some systems may substitute the phrase GO TO for THEN.

Note that string constants and variables can be compared as well as numeric expressions. You may ask, "What is meant by B$ < A$?" This can be useful, for example, in sorting lists of names; in the sense of alphabetic order, Smith is greater than Jones. The number following the word THEN can be any line number in the program, except the line number of the IF-THEN statement itself.[†] This restriction is not one of the BASIC compiler; it is that having the same line number is obviously a poor practice.

Example 4.1 illustrates the IF-THEN statement.

EXAMPLE 4.1

Program:

```
 5 PRINT "TYPE A NUMBER."
1Ø INPUT N
2Ø IF N > Ø THEN 6Ø
3Ø IF N = Ø THEN 8Ø
4Ø PRINT "N IS NEGATIVE."
5Ø STOP
6Ø PRINT "N IS POSITIVE."
7Ø STOP
8Ø PRINT "N EQUALS ZERO."
9Ø END
```

Output (1):

```
TYPE A NUMBER.
?   14
N IS POSITIVE.
```

Output (2):

```
TYPE A NUMBER.
?   -8.45
N IS NEGATIVE.
```

This example illustrates the use of the IF-THEN statement to alter the sequence of execution, depending on the value of the INPUT variable N. In the first case, since N is positive, control is transferred from line 2Ø to line 6Ø, which prints the appropriate message. Execution is halted in line 7Ø.

In the second case, the number is negative and the jump to line 6Ø does not take place. Instead, control is passed to the next statement, line 3Ø. Since N is not zero, again execution continues in sequence and line 4Ø is executed.

[†]On most systems. Some do not allow transfer to DATA, REM, DEF (Section 8.2) or DIM (Section 6.2.1) statements.

4.3   Unconditional Jumps: The GO TO Statement

The GO TO statement provides for an unconditional transfer of control to another statement in the program. The general form of the statement is

$$k \text{ GO TO } n$$

where k and n should be different (why?) line numbers in the program. When the GO TO statement is encountered during execution, the next statement executed is the one at line n.

Before we look at some examples, note that GO TO should be used sparingly. As you will see, there will always be BASIC programs that require GO TO statements. But the GO TO is easily abused. It is simple to use, and if you are not careful, you can clutter up your program with GO TO statements that are not really needed. They can make reading a program and following its logic extremely difficult. Thus, finding and correcting errors, or modifying a program later, becomes tedious and time-consuming. Some examples of the use (and misuse) of GO TO statements are given next and in the exercises.

EXAMPLE 4.2

Program:

```
1ØØ REM THIS PROGRAM CALCULATES THE FINAL GRADE AVERAGES FOR STUDENTS
11Ø REM IN A COURSE.
12Ø REM I = STUDENT ID NUMBER       H = HOMEWORK AVERAGE
13Ø REM F = FINAL EXAM SCORE        T1 = TEST 1   SCORE
14Ø REM T2 = TEST 2  SCORE        T3 = TEST 3   SCORE
145 REM
15Ø PRINT "STUDENT", "AVERAGE"
16Ø READ I,H,F,T1,T2,T3
17Ø LET A = .25*H + .3Ø*F + .15*T1 + .15*T2 + .15*T3
18Ø PRINT I,A
19Ø GO TO 16Ø
2ØØ DATA 1725,85,79,75,88,92
2Ø1 DATA 2121,67,65,87,71,65
2Ø2 DATA 3456,89,9Ø,95,92,1ØØ
2Ø3 DATA 5649,75,85,89,67,69
3ØØ END
```

Output:

STUDENT	AVERAGE
1725	83.2
2121	69.7
3456	92.3
5649	78

```
OUT OF ARITHMETIC DATA IN 16Ø.
RUN STOPPED
```

Example 4.2 illustrates how the GO TO statement works. From line 19Ø the program jumps to line 16Ø, by which it reads the next set of data; then it computes the average in line 17Ø and prints the current student ID number and average in line 18Ø. It then jumps back to line 16Ø, repeating this sequence until there are no more data to be read. The program then prints the "OUT OF ARITHMETIC DATA . . ." message and halts.

The repetition of the sequence 16Ø, 17Ø, 18Ø, 19Ø, 16Ø, 17Ø, 18Ø, 19Ø, 16Ø, . . . is a *loop*. This is a valid and useful way to use the GO TO statement.

EXAMPLE 4.3

Program:

```
 1Ø GO TO 4Ø
 2Ø PRINT "LINE 2Ø"
 3Ø GO TO 6Ø
 4Ø PRINT "LINE 4Ø"
 5Ø GO TO 2Ø
 6Ø PRINT "LINE 6Ø"
 7Ø GO TO 8Ø
 8Ø GO TO 1Ø
 9Ø PRINT "LINE 9Ø"
1ØØ END
```

Output:

```
LINE  4Ø
LINE  2Ø
LINE  6Ø
LINE  4Ø
LINE  2Ø
LINE  6Ø
LINE  4Ø
LINE  2Ø
LINE  6Ø
   *
   *
   *
```

Example 4.3 illustrates how not to use the GO TO statement. From line 1Ø, the program jumps to line 4Ø and prints the string; then it jumps back to line 2Ø, prints, and jumps to line 6Ø. After line 6Ø is printed, the GO TO 8Ø in line 7Ø transfers control to line 8Ø. This would have been done anyway since line 8Ø is the next instruction in the sequence. Thus, line 7Ø could be eliminated without any effect on the program's results.

From line 8Ø, the program jumps back to line 1Ø and the cycle is repeated—we jump immediately to line 4Ø, print, and so forth. Thus the successive jumps from line 8Ø to 1Ø to 4Ø were not necessary; we could simply change line 8Ø to read

8Ø GO TO 4Ø

to accomplish the same thing.

The result of this jumping around, which is messy and hard to follow, is a loop. Loops are necessary for most programs, but there must be some way to exit from them. In this example, the program would not terminate by itself. For this reason, this kind of loop is called an *infinite loop*. Eventually, however, the computer would stop executing the program after a preset limit of computer time had been reached (although this is not true for all systems).

Finally, note that the PRINT statement in line 9Ø will never be executed. A poor program indeed!

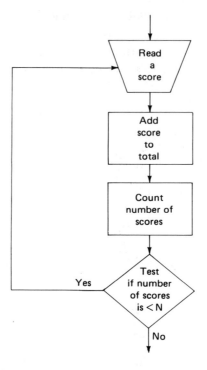

FIGURE 4.2   Flowchart of a simple loop

4.4   Loops

We now have enough instructions in our repertoire to enable us to write "useful" programs. Consider again Example 3.13, which was used to add any two numbers:

```
1Ø READ X,Y
2Ø LET Z = X + Y
3Ø PRINT X,Y,Z
4Ø DATA 4,7
5Ø END
```

Several alternatives were also considered in Section 3.7. But from the standpoint of constructing a generic program to compute sums, all of those examples are poor. Each program is too dependent in some way on the data; any significant changes in the data would call for significant modifications to the program. Example 3.13 has the advantage of being independent of the numbers to be added. *Any* two numbers could be added without changing the program (except, of course, the DATA statement). But it, along with the other examples, suffers because it depends critically on the length of the list of data. To add ten numbers, the programs would require radical changes. To add 5,000 numbers would be impossible for some approaches and impractical for others; the programmer who wants something done 5,000 times must "tell" the computer each of these 5,000 times to do it. To have a program that will function in this general setting means, then, that we must be able to do this without actually writing down 5,000 or so lines of instructions.

This is where loops come in, as illustrated in Example 4.2.

Definition: A *loop* is simply a sequence of instructions that can be repeated again and again.

The net result is as if there were multiple copies of these sequences of instructions, one set after the other. And just as important is that the number of times a given loop is executed can be allowed to vary, depending on the value of a variable or an expression.

To be able to take advantage of these capabilities, then, we must **learn to think in terms of loops in order to construct useful computer algorithms for solving problems.**

Another example for adding numbers (this time, three numbers) is Example 4.4.

EXAMPLE 4.4

```
Program:
    5 LET S = Ø
 ┌10 INPUT N
 └20 LET S = S + N
 ┌30 INPUT N
 └40 LET S = S + N
 ┌50 INPUT N
 └60 LET S = S + N
   70 PRINT S
   80 END

Output:
   ?    17
   ?     5
   ?    32
        54
```

In Example 4.4, the sum is computed as follows. In line 2Ø, the current value of N is added to the current value of S, which was initialized to zero in line 5, and the result is stored back into S, replacing the current value (zero). This is a standard technique for accumulating a sum. Similarly, two more numbers are added to S in lines 4Ø and 6Ø.

Note the repetitions indicated by the brackets. We can easily construct a loop from this sequence. First we write down the two statements in the brackets (the sequence that is repeated):

$$10 \text{ INPUT N}$$
$$20 \text{ LET S = S + N}$$

Then we *transfer control* back to the first statement in the sequence by adding a GO TO statement:

$$10 \text{ INPUT N}$$
$$20 \text{ LET S = S + N}$$
$$30 \text{ GO TO } 10$$

We have now replaced the repetitive sequence in Example 4.4 with a loop. Next we can add the remaining statements in Example 4.4 to get Example 4.5.

EXAMPLE 4.5

Program:

```
 5 LET S = 0
10 INPUT N
20 LET S = S + N
30 GO TO 10
40 PRINT S
50 END
```

Output:

```
?   17
?   5
?   32
?   61
?   74
?   STOP
 PROGRAM STOPPED.
```

This program is shorter than Example 4.4, but it does not work properly. The sequence 10, 20, 30 will be repeated, but we can never exit from this loop (an infinite loop).[†] Line 40 is never executed.

How can we get out of such a loop? The answer is met by another question; When do we want to get out? The answer: When we have added our three numbers; that is, we want to repeat the sequence exactly three times. Thus, we need to be able to count as we go through the loop.

You may recall that in Example 3.11 we counted by using a statement like

$$LET\ C = C + 1$$

This instruction takes the current value of the variable C, adds 1 to it, and stores the result back in C. When such an instruction is placed in a loop, its effect is to count the number of times we pass through the loop. **Counting** is a very important process that is often used in programs. Think of it as a basic tool to keep in your "programmer's file" of useful procedures and techniques. When you want to count, let C be your "counter." Then

$$LET\ C = C + 1 \quad \text{counts by ones}$$
$$LET\ C = C + 2 \quad \text{counts by twos}$$

Accumulating a running total of numbers using a loop is like counting. In fact, counting is nothing more than adding the same number each time through the loop, whereas in a running total the number to be added may change from step to step. Example 4.5 illus-

---

[†]On INPUT we can type STOP (but not on some systems) as shown in the example program, but again, we do not get the answer, since line 40 cannot be executed. On some systems an end-of-file indicator (such as ^Z) can be used.

trates how a sum is computed in this way. This process is called **accumulating**; in it, we let the variable S represent our sum (sometimes called an *accumulator*). Then

> LET S = S + V   adds the current number in V to the current value of S
> LET S = S + V$^\wedge$2 adds the square of V to S

Similar statements could be written for products, quotients, and the like. A statement like this, in which a variable appears on both sides of the equals sign in a LET statement, is called an **iterative** statement. The concept of iteration, of a variable "modifying itself," is important in programming.

Note that a statement like

> LET T = S + N

also computes the sum of S and N (result is T), but S is not changed or updated in the process. Thus, this statement by itself could not be used to compute a running total.

Now back to our example. We can use this counting process to exit from our loop. But before we can use a statement like

> LET C = C + 1

the first time, we must supply an initial value to C. In this case we want

> LET C = 0

initially; in other situations we may want to start our counter at 1 or –1, for example. Although starting C at zero with a LET statement is not necessary (recall that most versions of BASIC would do it automatically), it is strongly recommended that you do so anyway. Otherwise you may forget the initialization step sometime when it is necessary. It's important to form good programming habits early. These comments hold for accumulators as well as counters.

Let's rewrite Example 4.5 with a counter.

EXAMPLE 4.6

```
Program:
10 LET S = 0
20 LET C = 0
25 PRINT "ENTER A NUMBER TO ADD"
30 INPUT N
40 LET S = S + N
50 LET C = C + 1
60 IF C < 3 THEN    25
70 PRINT "THE SUM IS",S
80 END

Output:
ENTER A NUMBER TO ADD
?    17
ENTER A NUMBER TO ADD
?    5
ENTER A NUMBER TO ADD
?    32
THE SUM IS            54
```

Observe that in Example 4.6 the initialization of both S and C occur in lines 10 and 20 respectively *outside the loop.* (What would happen if we had put these statements inside the loop?) The counting operation takes place in line 50, after the summation, although in this case it doesn't matter if it precedes the summation.

The critical difference between this example and Example 4.5 lies in lines 50 and 60; the count combined with the IF-THEN statement provides us with a *test for exit* from the loop. When C is less than three, the IF-THEN statement causes a jump back to line 25 and the sequence is repeated. Since C increases by 1 each time, the third time C will equal 3, and the program will exit from the loop, print S, and stop.

This example is still too dependent on the data (the number of values), but only line 60 has to be changed to accommodate a longer list of data.

Some enhancements have been included here, namely, the PRINT statement in line 25 to accompany the INPUT statement and the string in line 70. Also, further improvements can easily be made, as you will see in Sections 4.5–4.7 and the exercises.

Every useful loop generally has the following properties:

1. Initialization
2. The set of instructions to be executed
3. One or more tests for exit from the loop
4. Modification of one or more variable values for the next repetition

In poorly coded loops, it may be difficult to identify the different properties. Some variables may serve more than one purpose.

Initialization refers to the assignment of the first value to the variable or variables that are modified in iterative statements. In Example 4.6, this occurs in lines 10 and 20.

The set of instructions to be executed are those that would be repeated again and again if we were forced to write the program without a loop. In Example 4.6, these instructions are lines 25, 30, and 40.

The test for exit in Example 4.6 is the IF-THEN statement in line 60. There may be more than one test for exit from a loop, although exactly one is sufficient and desirable (see Chapter 5).

Modification of the loop variable must occur, for otherwise the same computation would be done over and over again. In Example 4.6, the value of N changes—a new value is provided by the INPUT statement each time. Also, the counter C and the sum S change value each time.

4.5   An Application of Loops

Imagine the following scenario: The Third Bank of Omigosh periodically produces a report listing (1) their account numbers, (2) the current balance of the accounts, (3) the interest due (6%), and (4) the new balance. However, the bank has had to fire 37 bookkeepers in the past two years because they made so many errors (the bank pays only $0.89 per hour). So, the bank directors have decided that a program should be written to enable their computer to produce the reports. Let's write it for them.

Input to the program should be (1) account number and (2) the current balance for each person. For concreteness, let us assume we want to process exactly three accounts.

One possible solution is shown in Example 4.7 (the DATA statement and sample output are not included).

EXAMPLE 4.7

```
Program:

10 REM A1, A2, A3 = THE ACCOUNT NUMBERS
20 REM B1, B2, B3 = THE CURRENT BALANCE
30 REM
40 PRINT "ACCOUNT", "CURRENT BAL.", "INTEREST","NEW BAL."
50 READ A1, B1, A2, B2, A3, B3
60 PRINT A1, B1, B1*.06, B1 + B1*.06
70 PRINT A2, B2, B2*.06, B2 + B2*.06
80 PRINT A3, B3, B3*.06, B3 + B3*.06
90 END
```

Suppose now we wanted to do the same thing, but with a list of say 500 accounts. The approach used in Example 4.7 will not work because it cannot be conveniently generalized to form a loop; it is too dependent on the length of the list of data, and we don't want to write 500 lines of instructions.

Again, to construct a proper program we must think in terms of *repetitions*. What is it about this problem that occurs over and over again? One such step is the printing of the numbers, and this repetition does appear in Example 4.7. Is there anything else?

The column headings must be printed only once. The only other part of the program to consider is the reading of the numbers themselves. In Example 4.7, this is done with a single READ statement, but this would not be possible with a long list of numbers. Therefore, it is reasonable to consider reading *one pair of numbers at a time* as well as printing one line at a time.

A repetitive sequence could be formed as follows:

$$
\begin{array}{ll}
\left[\begin{array}{l} \text{read} \\ \text{print} \end{array}\right. & \begin{array}{l} \text{numbers A, B} \\ \text{A,B,B} * .06, \text{ B} + \text{B} * .06 \end{array} \\[1em]
\left[\begin{array}{l} \text{read} \\ \text{print} \end{array}\right. & \begin{array}{l} \text{numbers A, B} \\ \text{A,B,B} * .06, \text{ B} + \text{B} * .06 \end{array} \\[1em]
\left[\begin{array}{l} \text{read} \\ \ \\ \ \\ \ \end{array}\right. & \begin{array}{l} \text{numbers A, B} \\ * \\ * \\ * \end{array}
\end{array}
$$

Note that each pair of statements in this sequence is repeated over and over although required only once in the program as part of a loop.

Let us now construct the loop. If we place a transfer statement after the PRINT statement, we shall have a working program.

EXAMPLE 4.8

Program:

```
10 REM PROGRAM TO COMPUTE INTEREST AND NEW BALANCE
20 REM A = ACCOUNT NUMBER, B = CURRENT BALANCE
30 REM
40 PRINT "ACCOUNT","CURRENT BAL.","INTEREST","NEW BAL."
50 READ A,B
60 PRINT A,B,B*.06,B+B*.06
70 GO TO 50
80 DATA 1126,3400.00,1159,7650.00,1201,290.50,1220,8945.00
90 DATA 1234,5500.00,1400,6225.00,1570,1000.00,1589,2306.00
100 END
```

Output:

ACCOUNT	CURRENT BAL.	INTEREST	NEW BAL.
1126	3400	204	3604
1159	7650	459	8109
1201	290.5	17.43	307.93
1220	8945	536.7	9481.7
1234	5500	330	5830
1400	6225	373.5	6598.5
1570	1000	60	1060
1589	2306	138.36	2444.36

```
OUT OF ARITHMETIC DATA IN 50.
RUN STOPPED
```

At first glance the loop formed by statements 50–70 in Example 4.8 looks like an infinite loop, since there is no test for exit. However, there is an implicit test, carried out by the BASIC processor, which produces an exit from the loop and termination of the program when it runs out of data.

Again, however, it is best to modify the program to include a proper test for exit. This means that we need to include a counter in the loop and to make the unconditional jump (GO TO) conditional (IF-THEN) on the number of values read.

Also, the output isn't quite as polished as we might like, since in some cases there are no decimal points, and in others there is only one digit to the right of the decimal point. Here, for example, 60 means $60.00 and 9481.7 means $9481.70. To print the values in this finished form requires a process called *editing*. (Editing is discussed in a later chapter.)

Consider the revision of Example 4.8 as shown in Example 4.9.

EXAMPLE 4.9

Program:

```
10 REM THIS IS A MODIFICATION OF EXAMPLE 4.8 TO
20 REM INCLUDE A COUNTER (C) AND AN IF-THEN STATEMENT
30 REM EXIT FROM THE LOOP.  THIS EXAMPLE IS DESIGNED
40 REM TO WORK FOR 8 ACCOUNTS; FOR EACH RUN, ONLY LINE
50 REM 130 MUST BE CHANGED TO CORRESPOND TO THE NUMBER
60 REM OF LINES IN THE TABLE.
70 REM
80 LET C = 0
90 PRINT "ACCOUNT","CURRENT BAL.","INTEREST","NEW BAL."
100 READ A,B
110 PRINT A,B,B*.06,B+B*.06
120 LET C = C + 1
130 IF C < 8 THEN 100
140 DATA 1126,3400.00,1159,7650.00,1201,290.50,1220,8945.00
150 DATA 1234,5500.00,1400,6225.00,1570,1000.00,1589,2306.00
160 END
```

Output:

ACCOUNT	CURRENT BAL.	INTEREST	NEW BAL.
1126	3400	204	3604
1159	7650	459	8109
1201	290.5	17.43	307.93
1220	8945	536.7	9481.7
1234	5500	330	5830
1400	6225	373.5	6598.5
1570	1000	60	1060
1589	2306	138.36	2444.36

This version now has a proper test for exit from the loop, and can handle lists of data of varying lengths with only a single change to the program (line 130). This is not too bad, but further improvement can be made.

A test for exit depends on a change in some condition—for example, a condition that was false during the cycling through a loop becomes true, or vice versa. Quite often the condition depends on the value of a single variable. For example, a variable that was positive during previous tests is now negative, or a variable has assumed a value that is now greater than a given number, as in Examples 4.6 and 4.9.

Frequently, the condition we are checking for is *the end of a list of data.* There are two techniques that can be used to check for this condition. One way is to use a **counter** and the second approach is to use a **trailer**. The first method is used in Examples 4.6 and 4.9. But these examples could be improved by reading as the first DATA item a number that equals the total number of DATA items to follow. Then the programs will be completely independent of the data, and none of the instructions has to be changed when the list of numbers changes.

EXAMPLE 4.10

Program:

```
10 REM HERE N REPRESENTS THE TOTAL NUMBER OF ACCOUNTS TO
20 REM BE READ,  C IS THE COUNTER, AND X REPRESENTS THE
30 REM VALUE TO BE PRINTED.
40 REM//////////////////////////////////////////////////////////////////
50 LET C = 0
70 READ N
80 PRINT "ACCOUNT","CURRENT BAL.","INTEREST","NEW BAL."
90 READ A,B
100 PRINT A,B,B*.06,B+B*.06
110 LET C = C + 1
120 IF C < N THEN 90
125 DATA 8
130 DATA 1126,3400.00,1159,7650.00,1201,290.50,1220,8945.00
140 DATA 1234,5500.00,1400,6225.00,1570,1000.00,1589,2306.00
150 END
```

Output:

ACCOUNT	CURRENT BAL.	INTEREST	NEW BAL.
1126	3400	204	3604
1159	7650	459	8109
1201	290.5	17.43	307.93
1220	8945	536.7	9481.7
1234	5500	330	5830
1400	6225	373.5	6598.5
1570	1000	60	1060
1589	2306	138.36	2444.36

In Example 4.10, line 125, which contains a number (8 here) equal to the number of accounts to be read, has been added. This number must be changed when the number of accounts changes.

The main disadvantage with this technique is that the user of the program must know the exact number of items in the DATA list. This can be quite inconvenient if the list is long, if the program is used often and the list varies from day to day, if there are many different lists, and so forth.

The second technique—using a trailer—is often feasible if a counter is not desirable.

This approach depends on having a data item at the end of the list that is in some way different (but not too different) from all the other items. That special item is called a *trailer*.

The trailer must be of the same mode as the rest of the corresponding items in the list; if they are numeric, the trailer must be numeric, and if they are string constants, the trailer must also be a string. (Why?) A counter, then, is not needed. One simply tests whether the current value of the list item equals the trailer or not. If not, the loop continues.

Suppose we agree to use the account number zero (Ø) as a trailer, since this account does not exist. Then we can write the program shown in Example 4.11.

EXAMPLE 4.11

Program:

```
10 REM IN THIS PROGRAM A ZERO ACCOUNT NO. MUST
20 REM BE USED AS A TRAILER.
30 REM
50 PRINT "ACCOUNT","CURRENT BAL.","INTEREST","NEW BAL."
60 READ A,B
70 IF A <> Ø THEN 90
80       STOP
90 PRINT A,B,B*.Ø6,B+B*.Ø6
100 GO TO 60
110 DATA 1126,34ØØ.ØØ,1159,765Ø.ØØ,12Ø1,29Ø.5Ø,122Ø,8945.ØØ
120 DATA 1234,55ØØ.ØØ,14ØØ,6225.ØØ,157Ø,1ØØØ.ØØ,1589,23Ø6.ØØ
130 DATA Ø,Ø
140 END
```

Output:

ACCOUNT	CURRENT BAL.	INTEREST	NEW BAL.
1126	34ØØ	2Ø4	36Ø4
1159	765Ø	459	81Ø9
12Ø1	29Ø.5	17.43	3Ø7.93
122Ø	8945	536.7	9481.7
1234	55ØØ	33Ø	583Ø
14ØØ	6225	373.5	6598.5
157Ø	1ØØØ	6Ø	1Ø6Ø
1589	23Ø6	138.36	2444.36

Example 4.11 is somewhat shorter than Example 4.10 and requires only two variables (A and B). This time the loop includes statements 6Ø–1ØØ, and a STOP statement (line 8Ø) is used to terminate the program. A GO TO statement (line 1ØØ) continues the loop. The GO TO could be replaced by

$$100 \text{ IF } A <> Ø \text{ THEN } 6Ø$$

and lines 7Ø and 8Ø deleted to make the program even more compact, but then the last line of the table would always contain four zeros. (Why?)

One problem with this trailer is that the DATA list is restricted to nonzero numbers; as soon as a zero is encountered the program will terminate. This kind of restriction can be serious for many problems, and for this reason a counter may be preferred.

The trailer approach can be made more flexible by allowing the user to input his or her own trailer. This would require, however, the user to be aware that the item chosen is not in the list of data.

4.6   The FOR-NEXT Statements

The FOR-NEXT statements are used to construct loops. They are not necessary, since any loop that can be written using FOR-NEXT statements can be duplicated using IF-THEN statements and/or GO TO statements. In many cases, however, they make loop construction more simple, and programs become more legible since the beginning and end of a loop are easily recognized.

The generic form of a loop constructed using the FOR-NEXT combination is given by

$$\text{FOR } V = E1 \text{ TO } E2 \text{ STEP } E3$$
$$\cdots$$
$$\text{NEXT } V$$

The symbol V is any numeric variable, sometimes called the *loop index,* and E1, E2, and E3 can be any arithmetic expressions (including constants or single variables). The FOR statement appears at the beginning of a loop and the NEXT statement appears at the end. The value E1 is the *initial value* of the variable V, E2 is the *test value,* and E3 is the *increment.* Collectively, V, E1, E2, and E3 are called *loop parameters,* or sometimes *control variables.*

Some examples of FOR statements are

$$\text{FOR I } = 1 \text{ TO N STEP 1}$$
$$\text{FOR K = X1 TO A + B STEP M}$$

The designations I and K are the loop indices, 1 the initial value of I and X1 of K, N and A + B the test values, and 1 and M the increments.

The operation of the FOR-NEXT loop is as follows. During execution, on entrance into the loop, V is initialized to the value of E1. BASIC then compares the value of V to the value of E2. If either

1. $E3 > \emptyset$ *and* $V < = E2$, or
2. $E3 < \emptyset$ *and* $V > = E2$

then the statements in the loop (that is, between the FOR and the NEXT) are executed. When the NEXT statement is encountered, V is increased by the value of E3, and then a test is made for condition 1 or 2. If either is true, the statements in the loop are repeated. For this reason it is important that for the loop to perform properly, the NEXT statement should be executed during each pass through the loop.

If at any time during these tests (including at the start of the loop) it happens that conditions 1 and 2 are not true, then the statements in the loop are not executed, and control passes to the statement immediately following the NEXT statement.

If N = 5 in the first example above, then the statements in the loop would be repeated, with I taking on the values 1, 2, 3, 4, and finally 5.

None of the values of the variables V nor the values that appear in the expressions E1, E2, *and* E3 *should be altered within the loop (for example, by a* LET *statement).* The results of such modifications are unpredictable, and the outcome depends on the particular version of BASIC used.

Finally, note that STEP E3 can be omitted from the FOR statement, which then has the form

$$FOR \ V = E1 \ TO \ E2$$

If this is done, the increment is set equal to 1. Therefore the first example above is equivalent to

$$FOR \ I = 1 \ TO \ N$$

The FOR-NEXT loop, then, simplifies loop construction by providing an automatic counter and test for exit. It is thus most useful in constructing loops where a counter is used. Consider Examples 4.12–4.16.

EXAMPLE 4.12

Program:
```
10 REM PROGRAM TO COMPUTE INTEREST AND NEW BALANCE USING
20 REM A FOR-NEXT LOOP.
30 REM
60 READ N
70 PRINT "ACCOUNT","CURRENT BAL.","INTEREST","NEW BAL."
80 FOR C = 1 TO N
90     READ A,B
100    LET I = B*.06
110    PRINT A,B,I,B+I
120 NEXT C
125 DATA 8
130 DATA 1126,3400.00,1159,7650.00,1201,290.50,1220,8945.00
140 DATA 1234,5500.00,1400,6225.00,1570,1000.00,1589,2306.00
150 END
```

Output:

ACCOUNT	CURRENT BAL.	INTEREST	NEW BAL.
1126	3400	204	3604
1159	7650	459	8109
1201	290.5	17.43	307.93
1220	8945	536.7	9481.7
1234	5500	330	5830
1400	6225	373.5	6598.5
1570	1000	60	1060
1589	2306	138.36	2444.36

Example 4.12 is a modification of Example 4.10, using a FOR-NEXT loop to replace the counter and the IF-THEN test for exit. Here, then, the statements in the loop will be executed exactly N times, since the STEP portion of the FOR statement is omitted, and the increment therefore equals 1.

Note how the loop stands out in the program—the FOR and the NEXT statements clearly delimit the loop. Also, the program is less cluttered with statements involving counting and tests for exit.

Indenting the statements in the loop is highly recommended to further ease the reading of and, perhaps, the correcting of errors in programs.

EXAMPLE 4.13 ══

Program:

```
1Ø REM THIS PROGRAM COMPUTES THE SUM OF THE FIRST
2Ø REM 2*N EVEN INTEGERS, WHERE N IS AN INPUT VALUE.
25 REM IT ASSUMES THAT N IS AN INTEGER.
3Ø REM
4Ø PRINT "ENTER A POSITIVE INTEGER N"
5Ø INPUT N
6Ø IF N < 1 THEN 11Ø
65 LET S = Ø
7Ø FOR K = 2 TO 2*N  STEP 2
8Ø     LET S = S + K
9Ø NEXT K
1ØØ PRINT "THE SUM IS", S
11Ø END
```

Output:

```
ENTER A POSITIVE INTEGER N
?    5
THE SUM IS                 3Ø
```

Example 4.13 illustrates how the loop index (K here) can be used effectively as part of the computation within a FOR-NEXT loop. In this example, K is the term to be accumulated in successive passes through the loop. It is often the case that a loop index can serve such double duty.

In this example, it is assumed that N is a positive integer. If N is less than one, the program terminates. But suppose that N is positive but not integral; what happens then? Suppose for example that N = 3.4. Then according to rule 1, line 8Ø will be executed for K equal to 2, 4, and 6. (Why?)

EXAMPLE 4.14

Program:
```
10 REM THIS PROGRAM ILLUSTRATES SEVERAL VARIATIONS OF
20 REM THE FOR-NEXT PARAMETERS.
30 REM
50 LET S = 0
60 FOR I = .1 TO 1 STEP .2
70      LET S = S + I
80      PRINT I,S
90 NEXT I
100 FOR I = -1 TO 10 STEP -1
110     PRINT "THIS LOOP WILL NOT BE EXECUTED."
120 NEXT I
130 LET A = 1
140 LET B = 5
150 LET C = 5
160 FOR T = A+B TO C-1 STEP -1
170     PRINT "T = ",T
180 NEXT T
190 END
```

Output:
```
.1                   .1
.3                   .40000009
.5                   .90000009
.7                   1.6
.90000009            2.5
T =                  6
T =                  5
T =                  4
```

The first loop in Example 4.14 (lines 60–90) illustrates the use of parameters that are not integers. The variable I is initialized to .1 and increased to .2. When I is set to 1.1, control passes to line 100. In this example, then, I is never *equal* to the test value.

Take note of the output values such as .90000009. The error, called *round-off error,* happens because a noninteger number like .2 must be converted to *binary*—the number system of the computer—before the computation. Since the number generally cannot be represented exactly in the binary system, an error is introduced. Further errors are introduced when the operations such as addition take place.

Round-off error is usually unavoidable with noninteger arithmetic, although it can be minimized by careful analysis and design of the program. This analysis lies in the domain of *numerical analysis* and is beyond the scope of this book.

The second loop (lines 100–120) is not executed, since the increment is negative and I is initialized to a value (–1) that is less than the test value (10).

The third loop (lines 160–180) illustrates the use of expressions (A + B and C – 1) for the loop parameters.

EXAMPLE 4.15

Program:

```
1Ø LET S = Ø
2Ø FOR I = 1 TO 1ØØØ
3Ø      READ X
4Ø       IF X < Ø THEN 7Ø
5Ø      LET S = S + X
6Ø NEXT I
7Ø PRINT "THE SUM IS",S
8Ø DATA 129,37,4,49,22,6,55,-3
9Ø END
```

Output:

```
THE SUM IS              3Ø2
```

EXAMPLE 4.16

Program:

```
1Ø LET X = Ø
2Ø FOR J = 1 TO 1ØØ
3Ø      LET X = X + 1
4Ø      PRINT X
5Ø END
```

Output:

```
FOR WITHOUT NEXT.
RUN DELETED.
```

   Example 4.15 shows that it is possible to transfer out of a loop independently of the FOR-NEXT control variables. In this example, control is passed to line 7Ø whenever either (1) a negative number is encountered in the DATA list or (2) 1000 numbers have been read. The program is thus limited to adding fewer than 1001 nonnegative numbers. It can, however, be easily generalized.
   Example 4.16 contains a common error; the NEXT statement to complete the loop started in line 2Ø is missing. The error was detected during the compiling of the program, and thus no output was produced.

EXAMPLE 4.17

Program:

```
1Ø REM THIS PROGRAM SHOWS THAT LOOPS CAN BE PLACED
2Ø REM INSIDE OTHER LOOPS.
3Ø REM
5Ø PRINT " X"," Y","X ^ Y","Y ^ X"
6Ø FOR X = 1 TO 5
7Ø     FOR Y = 1 TO 3
8Ø         PRINT X,Y,X ^ Y,Y ^ X
9Ø     NEXT Y
1ØØ NEXT X
11Ø END
```

Output:

X	Y	X^Y	Y^X
1	1	1	1
1	2	1	2
1	3	1	3
2	1	2	1
2	2	4	4
2	3	8	9
3	1	3	1
3	2	9	8
3	3	27	27
4	1	4	1
4	2	16	16
4	3	64	81
5	1	5	1
5	2	25	32
5	3	125	243

Example 4.17 illustrates an important capacity of BASIC, that of placing one loop inside another. This procedure is called the **nesting** of loops and is an extremely important technique for many problems.

Note that *each pass* through the outer loop (lines 6Ø–1ØØ) means a *complete cycle* through the inner loop (lines 7Ø–9Ø). Thus, line 8Ø is executed 15 times (5 × 3), corresponding to the different values of X and Y. Necessarily the inner loop must increase faster than the outer loop. When X is 1, then Y is set to 1, then 2, then 3; then X = 2, and Y becomes 1, 2, then 3; and so on. This can be seen clearly by studying the output.

Observe again the clarity produced by indenting the statements in the loops. Only one level of nesting is shown in this example, but loops can be nested to more than one level. In using nested loops, one must be careful to

1. Use in an inner loop loop parameters that do not change the parameters in an outer loop.
2. Make sure that loops do not cross each other.

Proper and improper nestings of loops are illustrated in Example 4.18.

EXAMPLE 4.18

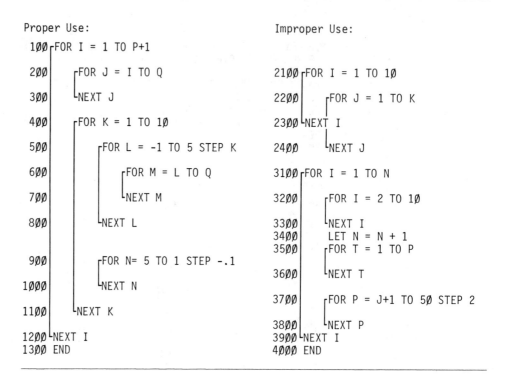

```
Proper Use:                                    Improper Use:
 100 ┌FOR I = 1 TO P+1
 200 │    ┌FOR J = I TO Q                      2100 ┌FOR I = 1 TO 10
 300 │    └NEXT J                              2200 │    ┌FOR J = 1 TO K
 400 │    ┌FOR K = 1 TO 10                     2300 └NEXT I
 500 │    │    ┌FOR L = -1 TO 5 STEP K         2400      └NEXT J
 600 │    │    │    ┌FOR M = L TO Q            3100 ┌FOR I = 1 TO N
 700 │    │    │    └NEXT M                     3200 │    ┌FOR I = 2 TO 10
 800 │    │    └NEXT L                         3300 │    └NEXT I
                                               3400 │    LET N = N + 1
 900 │    │    ┌FOR N= 5 TO 1 STEP -.1         3500 │    ┌FOR T = 1 TO P
                                               3600 │    └NEXT T
1000 │    │    └NEXT N                         3700 │    ┌FOR P = J+1 TO 50 STEP 2
1100 │    └NEXT K                              3800 └NEXT P
1200 └NEXT I                                   3900 └NEXT I
1300 END                                       4000 END
```

Observe that in the first column (proper use) each loop started inside a given loop also finishes inside that same loop. Note that lines 6ØØ–7ØØ form a loop that is contained within three other loops. The nesting is accentuated by the brackets.

Using the variable I as the initial value for J in the loop starting in line 2ØØ is perfectly valid and useful. Also, the increment of an *inner* loop may vary according to a value determined in an *outer* loop (K in line 5ØØ, for example).

Lines 21ØØ–24ØØ (right column) form an improper pair of loops because the loops cross each other (they are not nested properly): the loop 22ØØ–24ØØ begins inside the loop 21ØØ–23ØØ and finishes outside. Note the brackets.

Line 32ØØ is in error because it attempts to change the FOR loop parameter I of the outer loop 31ØØ–39ØØ from inside that loop. Line 34ØØ is in error for the same reason.

Although not strictly in error, line 37ØØ would cause problems. The variable P is used as an index for loop 37ØØ–38ØØ, and P is the limit parameter for the loop 35ØØ–36ØØ. Since both loops are nested within an outer loop, 32ØØ–39ØØ, successive passes through the outer loop have a value of P in loop 35ØØ–36ØØ that is indefinite (that is, it will depend on the version of BASIC that is used). This should be avoided by using a different variable in one of the loops.

FIGURE 4.3 Management by computer. (Courtesy of Tektronix, Inc.)

4.7 Another Application of Loop Construction

Your repertoire of instructions is now large enough for you to write some fairly sophisticated programs. Before we discuss in detail how to go about programming, you need a really solid foundation in constructing loops. Thus, we present another example.

This example illustrates a recurring problem. Perhaps a student is asked to write a program. Since the assignment is straightforward, it is easy to write the program without loops—only a few repetitions are involved. The program is written that way, although some preliminary thoughts on the problem would have produced a program with loops that would greatly reduce the program's size. We shall take our example through the complete procedure for solving it.

Suppose Jane Doaks is working for a college computer center, and the dean asks her to write a program to compute various choices of faculty salary increases so that the dean can quickly determine their effect on the total budget.

An interactive program is desired, one that asks the following questions of the user (the dean):

What is the base salary for full professors?
What is the base salary for associate professors?

The questions go on to cover the four faculty ranks of full, associate, and assistant professors, and instructors. Then the program should ask four more questions, beginning with

What is the annual increment for full professors?

The output from the program should be a response of the form

The cost of the salary schedule will be:

followed by the total cost figure.

Now the cost for all the faculty members *in each rank* is to be determined by the formula

$$COST = E + N * B + A * U$$

where E is the "educational bonus" for faculty members in this rank who have earned the Ph.D. degree, N is the number of faculty members in this rank, B is the base salary figure (as requested above), A is the annual increment (requested above), and U is the *number of units* of annual increments in this rank (for instance, a person who has been an assistant professor for 4 years would have received 3 annual increments and would thus account for 3 units in that rank).

The values E, N, and U for each of the ranks will be supplied by the dean at the beginning of the academic year and can be treated as constants in the program. The other values are to be supplied by INPUT statements, since the dean wants to experiment with different amounts.

Now Jane can begin. She writes down a flowchart, or an outline, of the steps she intends to follow in solving the problem:

1. Initialize the values E, N, and U for the four ranks.
2. Input the base salaries for the four ranks.
3. Compute the cost for each rank.
4. Add the costs and print the total.

With experience, Jane might write the BASIC program directly from this flowchart. But Jane is a novice, and so she decides to refine the flowchart.

First, since she is already close to the final flowchart, she lists all the variables she thinks she will need:

E1, E2, E3, E4 = educational bonus for faculty in each rank (full professor, associate, and so on)
N1, N2, N3, N4 = number of faculty in each rank
U1, U2, U3, U4 = number of units of increments for each rank
B1, B2, B3, B4 = base salaries for each rank
A1, A2, A3, A4 = annual increments for each rank
C1, C2, C3, C4 = cost for each rank

She now refines the outline:

1. Assign the constant values.
    a. Assign values to E1, E2, E3, E4.
    b. Assign values to N1, N2, N3, N4.
    c. Assign values to U1, U2, U3, U4.
2. Input the base salaries.
    a. For full professors (B1)
    b. For associate professors (B2)
    c. For assistant professors (B3)
    d. For instructors (B4)
3. Input the annual increment.
    a. For full professors (A1)
    b. For associate professors (A2)
    c. For assistant professors (A3)
    d. For instructors (A4)
4. Compute cost per rank.
    a. C1 = E1 + N1 * B1 + A1 * U1
    b. C2 = E2 + N2 * B2 + A2 * U2
    c. C3 = E3 + N3 * B3 + A3 * U3
    d. C4 = E4 + N4 * B4 + A4 * U4
5. Total cost T = C1 + C2 + C3 + C4
6. Print out the total cost T.

Note that Jane overlooked T in her list of variables, and she would include it now.

With this much detail, it is relatively easy to convert the above outline into a BASIC program; what Jane gets looks like Example 4.19.

EXAMPLE 4.19 ===

Program:

```
1ØØ LET E1 = 6ØØØØ
11Ø LET E2 = 3ØØØØ
12Ø LET E3 = 45ØØØ
13Ø LET E4 = Ø
14Ø LET N1 = 35
15Ø LET N2 = 4Ø
16Ø LET N3 = 32
17Ø LET N4 = 15
18Ø LET U1 = 15Ø
19Ø LET U2 = 12Ø
2ØØ LET U3 = 2ØØ
21Ø LET U4 = 22
22Ø PRINT "WHAT IS THE BASE SALARY FOR FULL PROFESSORS?"
23Ø INPUT B1
24Ø PRINT "WHAT IS THE BASE SALARY FOR ASSOCIATE PROFESSORS?"
25Ø INPUT B2
26Ø PRINT "WHAT IS THE BASE SALARY FOR ASSISTANT PROFESSORS?"
27Ø INPUT B3
28Ø PRINT "WHAT IS THE BASE SALARY FOR INSTRUCTORS?"
29Ø INPUT B4
3ØØ PRINT "WHAT IS THE ANNUAL INCREMENT FOR FULL PROFESSORS?"
31Ø INPUT A1
32Ø PRINT "WHAT IS THE ANNUAL INCREMENT FOR ASSOCIATE PROFESSORS?"
33Ø INPUT A2
34Ø PRINT "WHAT IS THE ANNUAL INCREMENT FOR ASSISTANT PROFESSORS?"
35Ø INPUT A3
36Ø PRINT "WHAT IS THE ANNUAL INCREMENT FOR INSTRUCTORS?"
37Ø INPUT A4
38Ø LET C1 = E1 + N1 * B1 + A1 * U1
39Ø LET C2 = E2 + N2 * B2 + A2 * U2
4ØØ LET C3 = E3 + N3 * B3 + A3 * U3
41Ø LET C4 = E4 + N4 * B4 + A4 * U4
42Ø LET T = C1 + C2 + C3 + C4
43Ø PRINT "THE TOTAL COST OF THIS SCHEDULE IS",T
999 END
```

Output:

```
WHAT IS THE BASE SALARY FOR FULL PROFESSORS?
?    185ØØ
WHAT IS THE BASE SALARY FOR ASSOCIATE PROFESSORS?
?    155ØØ
WHAT IS THE BASE SALARY FOR ASSISTANT PROFESSORS?
?    125ØØ
WHAT IS THE BASE SALARY FOR INSTRUCTORS?
?    1Ø5ØØ
WHAT IS THE ANNUAL INCREMENT FOR FULL PROFESSORS?
?    6ØØ
WHAT IS THE ANNUAL INCREMENT FOR ASSOCIATE PROFESSORS?
?    5ØØ
WHAT IS THE ANNUAL INCREMENT FOR ASSISTANT PROFESSORS?
?    4ØØ
WHAT IS THE ANNUAL INCREMENT FOR INSTRUCTORS?
?    2ØØ
THE TOTAL COST OF THIS SCHEDULE IS              21944ØØ
```

The program is straightforward, but extremely long for such a simple application. Has Jane missed something? If we examine the program, we see that there is much repetition. And we know that repetition to a programmer is spelled "L-O-O-P."

The repetition occurs as we move from one rank to the next; the computation for each rank is the same, only the numbers change. Thus, we should be able to write statements that assign variables and carry out the computation only once. These statements can then be placed inside a loop to complete the job.

Before we can do this, however, we must examine the outline again. Reorganization is in order. A little thought will show that to use a loop here, we must have a sequence of steps that can be repeated for each rank. Thus, we must do the entire computation for a given rank before we go on to the next rank. (Why?)

It was somewhat logical to organize the procedure as Jane did; the process was written in the same order of the requests that the dean supplied. The main point is that one must put a lot of thought into the overall design of the program. *Design* (which includes organization) is an extremely important aspect of programming, just as it is in writing a report or in constructing a building. Chapter 5 examines this topic in more detail.

Let us now outline a second approach.

1. For *each* rank:
   a. Initialize the values of E, N, and U.
   b. Input the base salary B.
   c. Input the annual increment A.
   d. Compute the cost and add it to the running total.
2. Print out the total cost.

Again we refine this outline to approach the form of the final program (first we list the variables we will need):

E = educational bonus
N = number of persons in the current rank
U = number of units of increments for the current rank
B = base salary for this rank
A = annual increment for this rank
C = cost for this rank
T = total cost

Before we refine the outline, we must clarify a few items. First, how can we initialize the values E, N, and U? We can't use LET statements, for then we would need four copies of these statements for each rank. We could use INPUT or READ statements; since the data for these values are the same each time and since the dean doesn't want to supply these values each time (they remain constant for a whole year), reading seems the most reasonable approach.

Second, we want to print an appropriate rank-dependent comment when asking for input (for example, "What is the base salary for full professors?"). Thus, it seems that we need four different print statements just for the base salary question. We could use a sequence of IF-THEN statements to select the appropriate PRINT statement, for instance,

```
5Ø FOR I = 1 TO 4
        . . .
1ØØ       IF I = 1 THEN 14Ø
11Ø       IF I = 2 THEN 16Ø
12Ø       IF I = 3 THEN 18Ø
13Ø       IF I = 4 THEN 2ØØ
14Ø       PRINT "WHAT IS THE BASE SALARY FOR FULL PROFESSORS?"
15Ø       GO TO 3ØØ
16Ø       PRINT "WHAT IS THE BASE SALARY FOR ASSOCIATE PROFESSORS?"
          . . .
3ØØ       INPUT B
          . . .
4ØØ END
```

But this is messy, and some thought will show that it is unnecessary. Again we see repetition. The only difference between each of these statements is the rank itself; we are printing the same sentence with only the rank changing. Now a changing value suggests using a *variable.* In this case, the changing values are words; therefore a *string* variable should be used.

Thus we can initialize R$, say, to "full professor" the first time through the loop, and so on, using a READ statement. We can now refine the outline as follows:

I.   Print an introductory comment.
II.   Initialize the cost T to zero.
III. For each of the four ranks
    A. Read the corresponding values of E, N, U and R$.
    B. Provide the value of B.
       1. Print "What is the base salary for", R$
       2. Input B.
    C. Provide the value of A.
       1. Print "What is the annual increment for", R$
       2. Input A
    D. Compute the cost for this rank.
       1. C = E + N * B + A * U
       2. Accumulate the total cost: T = T + C
IV. Print T with an appropriate comment.

It is very easy to forget an instruction like step II above and consequently forget to include it in the program. We recommend that to minimize this possibility, you should include in the description of the variables used a word to indicate the "iterative" variables that need initialization.

Observe that step III, "For each of the four ranks," implies that a loop is involved, and an arrow is included for emphasis.

Working from this outline then, we can write the program shown in Example 4.20.

You will agree that this example is a big improvement over Example 4.19. With some thought and experience, a careful programmer would be able to arrive at a similar result without producing coded programs for the previous versions. Careful consideration of solutions to a problem in the beginning can produce good first results and eliminate much reworking later.

With the extras like the remarks and extra PRINT statements disregarded, this program required essentially 16 lines, including the DATA statements, as opposed to 34 lines in Example 4.19. Note the use of the remarks to explain the calculation (lines 332-339).

EXAMPLE 4.20

Program:

```
 10 REM *****************************************************************
 15 REM PROGRAM NAME: FACSAL                                            *
 20 REM PROGRAM TO COMPUTE THE COST OF VARIOUS ALTERNATIVES IN FACULTY  *
 30 REM SALARIES.  WRITTEN BY J. DOAKS, 9/11/75.                        *
 40 REM                                                                 *
 50 REM E=EDUCATIONAL BONUS                                             *
 60 REM N=NUMBER OF PERSONS IN CURRENT RANK                             *
 70 REM U=NUMBER OF UNITS OF INCREMENTS FOR THE CURRENT RANK            *
 80 REM R$=RANK                                                         *
 90 REM B=BASE SALARIES FOR EACH RANK                                   *
100 REM A=ANNUAL INCREMENT FOR EACH RANK                                *
110 REM C=COST FOR THIS RANK                                            *
120 REM T=TOTAL COST; INITIALIZED TO ZERO                               *
130 REM *****************************************************************
140 REM
200 PRINT "GOOD MORNING, DEAN SMITH."
210 PRINT "THE PURPOSE OF THIS PROGRAM IS TO HELP YOU DETERMINE THE"
220 PRINT "IMPACT OF CHANGES IN THE FACULTY SALARY SCHEDULE FOR 1975-76."
230 PRINT
240 PRINT
250 LET T=0
260 FOR I=1 TO 4
270      READ E,N,U,R$
275      PRINT
280      PRINT "WHAT IS THE BASE SALARY FOR",R$
290      INPUT B
300      PRINT
310      PRINT "WHAT IS THE ANNUAL INCREMENT FOR"
320      PRINT R$
330      INPUT A
332 REM
335 REM THE COST PER RANK EQUALS THE SUM OF THE EDUCATIONAL
336 REM BONUS, THE PRODUCT OF THE BASE TIMES THE NUMBER
337 REM IN THIS RANK, AND THE PRODUCT OF THE ANNUAL INCREMENT
338 REM TIMES THE NO. OF UNITS OF INCREMENTS.
339 REM
340      LET C=E+N*B+A*U
350      LET T=T+C
360 NEXT I
370 PRINT
380 PRINT "THE TOTAL COST OF THIS SALARY SCHEDULE IS",T
400 DATA 60000,35,150,"FULL PROFESSORS"
410 DATA 30000,40,120,"ASSOCIATE PROFESSORS"
420 DATA 45000,32,200,"ASSISTANT PROFESSORS"
430 DATA 0,15,22,"INSTRUCTORS"
999 END
```

```
Output:
GOOD MORNING, DEAN SMITH.

THE PURPOSE OF THIS PROGRAM IS TO HELP YOU DETERMINE THE

IMPACT OF CHANGES IN THE FACULTY SALARY SCHEDULE FOR 1975-76.

WHAT IS THE BASE SALARY FOR FULL PROFESSORS

?   16000

WHAT IS THE ANNUAL INCREMENT FOR

FULL PROFESSORS

?   1200

WHAT IS THE BASE SALARY FOR ASSOCIATE PROFESSORS

?   14000

WHAT IS THE ANNUAL INCREMENT FOR

ASSOCIATE PROFESSORS

?   1000

WHAT IS THE BASE SALARY FOR ASSISTANT PROFESSORS

?   12500

WHAT IS THE ANNUAL INCREMENT FOR

ASSISTANT PROFESSORS

?   800

WHAT IS THE BASE SALARY FOR INSTRUCTORS

?   11000

WHAT IS THE ANNUAL INCREMENT FOR

INSTRUCTORS

?   500

THE TOTAL COST OF THIS SALARY SCHEDULE IS    2291000
```

Brevity, by itself, is not important, however. Example 4.20 is easy to read and understand; in this case clarity has been enhanced by the brevity, although this is not always so. More important, the program was written only after several approaches were considered and after a careful outline of the procedure was made and then refined.

Note also how including remarks makes it easier to read and understand the program.

An important feature is the description of the meaning of each of the variables used in the program. Including PRINT statements to skip lines in appropriate points makes it easier to read the output.

Finally, if the dean wanted to use this program, as written, next year, only lines 220 and 400–430 (the DATA) would have to be changed. If the dean wanted further changes to the program, such as having a table of values printed, they could be easily made because of the clarity of the program and the documentation the REM statements provide. The exercises at the end of this chapter contain other possible improvements.

4.8 Debugging and Program Check-out

Two classes of errors can appear in programs. First, there are **syntax errors,** or errors in the format of a given statement. Violations of the rules for constructing statements are syntax errors. For example, the statement

$$10 \ X + Y = Z * Z$$

has a syntax error—only a variable name may appear to the left of an equals sign in an assignment statement. Syntax errors are easily found and corrected. The BASIC compiler will find them and flag them with an appropriate error message (see Example 3.12).

The second class of errors, **logic errors,** are much more troublesome. Sometimes a great deal of time and effort is required to correct them, for they cannot be detected by the compiler. What we have told the computer to do via a program is syntactically correct; it just wasn't what we meant to happen. Then we have a logic error.

Suppose that a physics student has written the program in Example 4.21 to produce a table of Celsius temperatures from 0 to 100 degrees and their equivalent Fahrenheit temperatures.

EXAMPLE 4.21

Program:

```
1Ø PRINT "CELSIUS","FAHRENHEIT"
2Ø PRINT "-------","----------"
3Ø LET T1 = Ø
4Ø LET T2 = 1.8*T + 32
5Ø PRINT T1,T2
6Ø LET T1 = T1 + 1
7Ø IF T1 < = 1ØØ THEN 3Ø
8Ø END
```

Output:

CELSIUS	FAHRENHEIT
-------	----------
Ø	32
Ø	32
Ø	32
Ø	32
Ø	32
Ø	32
Ø	32
Ø	32
Ø	32

Note that after the heading, the same line is printed over and over again, and it appears to be in an infinite loop. Before coding the program into BASIC and running it on a terminal, we could have detected the error sooner by "walking through" the algorithm with pencil and paper.

A convenient way of doing this is to set up a table of all the variables used in the algorithm. In Example 4.21, T1 represents the Celsius temperature and T2 the Fahrenheit temperature. We then go through each step of the program by hand, changing the values in the table as we go. For this example we have

T1	T2
Ø	32
1	33.8
Ø	

and we discover at this point that the problem is that we are resetting T1 to zero each time through the loop. The IF-THEN statement in line 7Ø should jump to line 4Ø, not line 3Ø.

Running the program again with this correction, we get

CELSIUS	FAHRENHEIT
Ø	32
1	32
2	32
...	...
1ØØ	32

This time the program gives the correct result for T1 but not for T2. We study the code and discover that the variable named T is used where T1 should be. We make this change and the result is

CELSIUS	FAHRENHEIT
0	32
1	33.8
2	35.6
. . .	. . .
100	212

No matter how careful you are, your program is likely to have some errors. But you can minimize their number by thinking very carefully about the development of your program. (This is discussed in detail in Chapter 5.) Some other suggestions include:

1. Spend time desk-checking your program, studying the program line by line. Be sure that each line will do what you mean it to. You can detect many errors in this way and consequently shorten the time for getting your program working.

2. Setting up a table of the variables and "executing" the statements by hand is a valuable exercise. If the program is reading data, supply a small but representative sample for your test. Otherwise this process will become too time-consuming. But try to choose data so that all parts of the program will be tested. And by all means keep your wits about you in this process—it's too easy to assume that a statement will work the way you had intended. Note that we erred in calculating T2 in the second row of our first table because we assumed that T1 was on the right-hand side of the assignment statement. A careful reading would have revealed the error at that point.

3. Try to correct as much as you can with each run. Just because you found one or two errors doesn't mean that there are no more. Check it again. For most of the programs in the first five chapters of this book you should require no more than three runs on the computer. If you are averaging more than five, you are not doing a very good job of developing and checking your program.

4. The fact that no error messages appear in your program doesn't mean there are no errors. Carefully check the output to be sure that the program is doing what you expect it to do.

Finally, before you leave this chapter, spend some time looking over the list of error messages in Appendix B. There are some helpful hints for pinpointing some of the most elusive errors.

Exercises

1. Why is a statement like

$$20 \text{ IF } A > 10 \text{ THEN } 20$$

not allowed?

2. What will the following program do? (Try it.)

```
10 LET X = 0
20 LET S = 0
30 LET X = X + 1
40 LET S = S + X ^ 3
50 IF X < 10 THEN 25
60 PRINT S
70 END
```

3. Write a program that will read a list of numbers and compute their product. The first number in the list should equal the number of the values that follow. Thus the program should be general enough to handle lists of varying lengths.

4. Modify Example 4.6 to use a trailer, so that consequently it will be suitable for lists of varying lengths. What is a good choice for a trailer in this case?

5. Modify Example 4.10 to read three accounts at a time. Assume that the length of the list is a multiple of three.

6. Several IF-THEN statements are given below. Write correct versions of the invalid statements.[†]
a. 20 IF S <> T THEN 10
b. 50 IF A > B * C THEN X = Y + 1
c. 30 IF N = "YES" THEN 10
d. 100 IF A/B * C >= (A − X) * Y THEN 5
e. 40 IF A$ = 13.5 THEN 60
f. 75 IF X > 0.3 THEN GO TO 40
g. 42 IF A = B THEN C

7. Determine which of the following FOR statements are invalid. If a statement is invalid, write the correct form.
a. 10 FOR X + Y = 0 TO 50 STEP 2
b. 20 FOR I = 10 TO −10 STEP −.5
c. 50 FOR A$ = B$ TO C$
d. 12 FOR Q = Q + 1 TO 100

8. Identify what is wrong, if anything, with the following FOR-NEXT loops:
a. 5 FOR X = A TO B STEP −C

   . . .
   100 NEXT A
b. 10 FOR I = 1 TO N + 1

   . . .
   50 I = I + 1

   . . .
   75 NEXT I

[†]Many versions of BASIC accept the form of the IF-THEN statement in b.

c. 10 FOR K = I TO J

  . . .

  50 FOR L = K TO J + 1

  . . .

  80 NEXT K

  . . .

  110 NEXT L

d. 110 FOR X1 = 0 TO -10 STEP -1

  . . .

  150 FOR X1 = A TO 100

  . . .

  190 NEXT X1

9. Write a pair of FOR-NEXT statements for each of the following situations:

a. A loop is to be repeated 150 times.

b. A loop is to be repeated with the index running from 3 to 100 in steps of 2.

c. A loop is to be repeated with the index increasing from the value of N to a value given by X/Y - 5. Each time through the loop the index increases by a value given by L + M.

10. Write a program that will compute the yearly depreciation for a depreciable item (say a car or a machine). Use (a) the *straight-line* method and (b) the *double-declining-balance* method.

In the straight-line method, the value of the new item is divided by its expected lifetime in years. The quotient is the amount of depreciation each year. For example, if the expected life of a $5000 item is 10 years, the value of the item will decrease by the same amount, $500 = $5000/10, each year.

In the double-declining-balance method, 2 is divided by the life of the item and the result is multiplied by the value of the item at the beginning of each year (not the original value of the item) to get the depreciation for that year. Thus, the value of the item decreases by a constant percentage, but the actual amount will vary from year to year. To depreciate a $5000 item over 10 years, for example, the depreciation factor is 2/10 = 0.2. Therefore the item depreciates 0.2 $\times$ $5,000 = $1,000 the first year; 0.2 $\times$ ($5,000 -$1,000) = $800 the second year; and so on.

The original value and the life of the item should be input values for both a and b.

11. Write a program to tabulate the function

$$y = x^4 - 3x^2 + x - 2$$

for x = -2, -1.5, -1.0, . . . , 4.5, 5.0.

12. Write a program that will compute the total amount of money T accumulated after an original investment of P dollars for N years at an annual rate of interest I that is compounded annually. The value of T is given by

$$T = P (1 + I)^N \qquad (\textit{law of compound interest})$$

In general, if the interest is compounded K times per year, the formula is

$$T = P \left(1 + \frac{I}{K}\right)^{KN}$$

Run the program for several different values of P, I, K, and N and compare the results. These values should be input values, and the user should have the option of continuing with new sets of values.

13. Write a program to tabulate the function

$$y = \frac{x^2 + x + 1}{x - 3}$$

for $x = 0, 1, \ldots, 10$.

14. One technique for finding the square root of a value x (which is *faster* than computing $x^{.5}$) is to use the iterative formula

$$s_{i+1} = 1/2\left(\frac{x}{s_i} + s_i\right)$$

where s_i is the estimate of $\sqrt{x}$ on the ith iteration. Write a program for computing the square root of an input value x and printing out each successive approximation s_i along with the value computed using $x^{.5}$ for comparison. Use 1 for the value of s_0 (the initial value). Stop the iteration when the difference between two successive iterates s_i and s_{i+1} is less than $.5 \times 10^{-5}$, that is, when

$$|s_{i+1} - s_i| < 0.000005$$

Note: The absolute value of x can be computed using the *function* ABS, as in

LET Y = ABS(X).

15. a. Write a program for reading a list of records, each record containing a name, age, and sex (M or F). The program should select and print out only those records of persons who are (1) over the age U, (2) under the age L, and (3) all females between ages U and L, where U and L are input values. Each printed item should have an appropriate heading.
    b. How would you modify the program to allow the user to make the combination for selection that he or she wants?
    Use the following data:

```
900 DATA "SMITH, J.", 32, "M"
901 DATA "LITTLE, C.", 14, "F"
902 DATA "MORRISS, P.", 83, "M"
903 DATA "DUMB, I. M.", 26, "M"
904 DATA "MOUSE, M.", 43, "F"
905 DATA "PIGGY, P.", 38, "M"
906 DATA "DOAKS, J.", 21, "F"
907 DATA "WHITE, S.", 45, "F"
908 DATA "FOX, B.", 45, "M"
909 DATA "WASHINGTON, G.", 66, "M"
910 DATA "LINCOLN, A.", 63, "F"
920 DATA "BETA, A.", 7, "M"
930 DATA "OMEGA, A.", 51, "F"
```

940 DATA "BLKSFST, J.", 30, "F"
950 DATA "YOKUM, A.", 45, "M"
960 DATA "ABNER, L.", 60, "M"
970 DATA "LAST, N.", 35, "F"

16. A list of data has m values of test scores t. Write a program that computes the *mean,* or average score, and the *standard deviation,* a measure of how the scores are spread out. The standard deviation can be computed by the formula

$$s = \sqrt{\frac{1}{m-1}\left(\Sigma t^2 - \frac{(\Sigma t)^2}{m}\right)}$$

where Σt = sum of the values of t
   Σt^2 = sum of the squares of the values of t.

17. Write a program that reads a list of integer numbers and determines the following:
a. The sum of all positive integers
b. The sum of all negative integers
c. The total number of positive integers
d. The total numbers of negative integers
e. The sum of positive integers greater than 10 but less than 90

18. Write a program that will determine the cost of a book based on the following information. The cost of a book is $0.75 plus $0.02 per page if the book is a paperback. If the number of pages is greater than 400, a cloth binding will be used, increasing the base price by $1.50. Also, if the number of pages is greater than 700, stronger binding is used, raising the cost by another $1.00. The maximum that can be bound is 1000 pages, which means that books over 1000 pages will be published in volumes of equal length, each subject to the above restrictions. Finally, if the number of pages is greater than 1500, the charge is reduced to $0.0175 per page. The number of pages should be the only input value required.

19. Write a program to tabulate the function (of two variables)

$$Z = X^3 - X^2 Y + 3 X Y^2 - 4 Y^3$$

for X = 0, .5, 1, 1.5, . . . , 5
   Y = -3, -2, -1, 0, for each value of X
Use nested FOR-NEXT loops.

20. Write a program to tabulate the function (of three variables)

$$T = (X^2 - Y^2)/(X^2 + Y^2 + Z^2)$$

for X = 1, 2, 3
   Y = 2, 4, 6, for each value of X
   Z = 2, 2.5, 3, 3.5 for each value of X and Y
Use nested FOR-NEXT loops.

5. Structured Programming

Having covered basic BASIC, we are now ready to consider solving problems completely from beginning to end. Some of the concepts of *structured programming* will be useful. Structured programming has been mostly an advanced topic, but to promote good habits early, we introduce it now. This approach to programming will be used throughout the rest of the book.

FIGURE 5.1 Unstructured design

Definition: *Structured programming* is a way of designing and writing programs so that they can be easily understood and modified.

Clarity and ease of modification are becoming increasingly important in programming. In the early days of computers (that is, about 25 years ago), computer memories were severely limited. Experienced programmers taxed their skills to write programs that would solve their problems with a minimal amount of memory. Similar efforts were made for the sake of efficiency.

As a result, the programs worked but at the same time were tricky (that is, they used unusual, nonstandard techniques) and consequently difficult to follow. Often, if programmers quit their jobs, the programs they had written were thrown out and rewritten because no one else could interpret them. Sometimes programmers would have difficulty understanding their own programs written perhaps a year before. It was extremely hard to find errors, and all but the most trivial modifications were nearly impossible.

Over the years, programmers' salaries went up and computer costs decreased markedly. Memory sizes increased along with computation speed. The earlier constraints on programs were no longer so severe, and it was soon discovered that an inordinate amount of time and money was spent not on writing the program but on *debugging* (finding and correcting "bugs," or errors, during program development) and *maintenance* (producing modifications, for instance when new capacities are required or when the computer is replaced by another model).

The emphasis is now on good design and clarity. And this is a sound philosophy for anyone who writes programs, not just the professional. Your time is valuable too, and the less time you spend debugging your program the better. A good approach to take is always to write your programs as though others were going to study them, use them, and modify them.

No single definition now exists to describe what is meant by structured programming. It is a collection of ideas—a methodology—whose objective is creating improved programs and better programmers. Structured programming tries to reduce program complexity, promoting a corresponding increase in clarity.

5.1 Control Structures

A program consists of groups of sequences of statements called **control structures**, which are linked in some way. A group might consist of a loop or a sequence of LET and READ statements. The program's *structure* refers to how these groups are linked to complete the program. It is important to realize that *any program function can be performed with one of three elementary control structures, or a combination of them.* These are shown in the accompanying chart.

ELEMENTARY CONTROL STRUCTURE	EXAMPLE
Simple sequence	10 READ X, Y
	20 LET Z = X + Y
	30 LET T = Z/25
	40 PRINT Z, T
Selection	100 IF X < Y THEN 250
	110 ⌈ LET A = X - Y
Alternative 1	*
(false)	*
	*
	240 GO TO 300
	250 ⌈ LET A = Y - X
Alternative 2	*
(true)	*
	*
	300 PRINT X, Y, A
Loop	100 FOR I = 1 TO N
	*
	*
	*
	200 NEXT I

A simple sequence, then, contains no transfer of control statements. A selection structure consists of an IF-THEN statement and its two possible alternative sequences. One of the alternatives is selected, depending on whether the relation tested is true or false. Loops have already been defined. Note that both the loop and the alternatives in the selection structure can contain more control structures (consider nested loops, for instance) or combinations of them.

The goal of structured programming, then, is to build programs based on these three structures and to make the structure of programs as simple as possible by simplifying the control *paths,* the links from one structure to the next.

Much of a program's complexity comes from the jumps from one part of the program to another, jumps both forward and backward in the code. These jumps can make it hard to follow the logic of the program. Also, it becomes difficult to be certain at any given point about what the current conditions of the program are—the current values of variables, which instruction sequences have been executed, and which ones are yet to be executed.

Moreover, a program may undergo many changes as it is developed; debugging may bring about the inclusion of more code. Perhaps the programmer later decides to modify a program to make it applicable to a wider range of problems. New jumps are inserted, increasing the complexity. The programmer inserts more and more code to account for new or forgotten functions, afraid to alter the existing structure for fear of undoing another function that already works. The result is a program that is nearly unintelligible.

The programs you have written are too simple for you to have experienced such problems. But as you learn and begin to write more complex problems, you will face these difficulties. Consequently, it's a good idea to be prepared for them, armed with a good programming style.

Consider again the three control structures described above. *Ideally, each should be written with a single point for entering the structure and a single exit point.* The following structures would be undesirable from this standpoint.

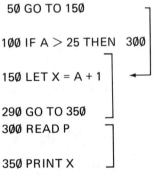

50 GO TO 150

100 IF A > 25 THEN 300

150 LET X = A + 1

290 GO TO 350
300 READ P

350 PRINT X

(This selection structure has two entry points, lines 100 and 150; the line 50 GO TO 150 should be avoided.)

50 FOR I = 1 TO N

90 IF X < 0 THEN 250

150 NEXT I

250 PRINT X

(This loop has two exits, one through line 90, and the other by "falling through" the end of the loop at line 150 where I > N.)

The second example illustrates what is sometimes called an *abnormal termination* of a loop (line 9Ø). This is sometimes acceptable for efficiency if the exit is properly marked (by REM statements; see Example 5.4).

These structures can be combined to form a program that has a single overall structure in that control flows from beginning to end, that is, from top to bottom on the page. **There is no jumping back** (except, of course, to effect a loop structure). This is extremely important. Although the structures may be nested, they usually retain the single entry–exit property.

Furthermore, these structures can be effected in any programming language, although it is more troublesome in some languages. Languages like PL/1 have features that correspond directly to these structures, whereas BASIC is unfortunately more "primitive," requiring more work by the programmer to implement these structures (see Sections 5.2 and 5.3).

This "jumping around" that characterizes a poorly formed program is most often caused by an overzealous use of GO TO statements. Edward Dijkstra, who first introduced the term *structured programming* and who has had much to do with developing its concepts, has observed that "the quality of programmers is a decreasing function of the density of GO TO statements in the programs they produce." He also remarked that "the GO TO statement . . . is too much an invitation to make a mess of one's program."[†]

The GO TO statement will be required much more frequently in BASIC than in equivalent programs written in some other languages because of the lack of some more powerful features. A BASIC programmer should then follow the practice of avoiding the use of a GO TO except to implement one of the elementary control structures.

Fortunately, you will see that if you design the program carefully from the beginning, extraneous GO TO statements will rarely be needed.

5.2   The IF-THEN-ELSE Construction

As we have used it, the IF-THEN statement, and consequently the resulting selection structure, is awkward. We are forced to look past a section of code to continue with the program if the relation is true. It would be logical to have a selection structure that works the other way:[‡]

```
              IF (relation is true)
                 THEN

                    [do this sequence]


                 ELSE (if not true)

                    [do this sequence]


              END IF
```

[†]E. W. Dijkstra, "Go To Statement Considered Harmful," *Communications of the ACM* 11, 3 (March 1968): 147–148.
    [‡]As in DEC's BASIC-PLUS-2 implementation.

This form is more natural to our way of thinking.[†] Furthermore, the END IF statement at the bottom clearly marks the end of the selection structure. We can implement this preferred form in BASIC in the following way:

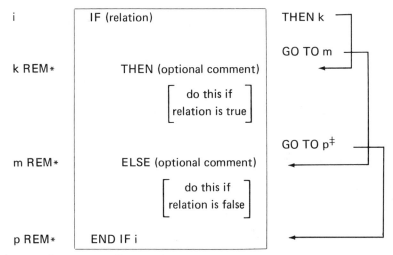

Here i, k, m, and p represent line numbers.

This looks artificial, but it more clearly corresponds to the kind of thinking we should be using in solving a problem. It is much more natural to go from the design of the solution in the outline to this form. Note that we have indented statements to mark more clearly the sections of the selection structure. Also, we have placed the GO TO statements and the THEN portion of the IF-THEN statement far to the right; they are necessary for the structure, but they clutter our view of the logic of the problem. This way you can concentrate on the instructions inside the box. During the actual coding of the program, GO TO statements can be put in last. The box and arrows, which indicate the flows of control, are simply for emphasis. If your version of BASIC does not allow jumps to REM statements, the jumps must then be made to the lines immediately following them.

There is a second form for the case in which no action takes place when the relation is false, which you can see in the following diagram:

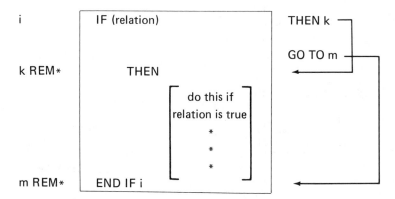

[†]The IF-THEN-ELSE variation is available in most versions of BASIC, but usually in a more restricted form.

[‡]Not always p. The direction STOP can be used if the program is not to continue beyond this structure; also, for efficiency, a jump to another line may be preferred if this structure is nested inside a loop (that is, it is silly to have a GO TO jump to a GO TO statement).

You may be fortunate to have available a version of BASIC that is powerful enough to include control structures like the IF-THEN-ELSE or the IF-THEN forms described herewith. Then your task is easier; using these and other control structures will not require the REM and GO TO statements. The control structures should look like the segments shown in the boxes. You should carefully check the syntax of the control structures on your system, however, since many variations are possible. In this book the assumption is that such structures are not commonly available; REM statements and GO TO's will be used where necessary to implement control structures.

Two programs are given in Example 5.1. The first is a reproduction of Example 4.1; and the second is an equivalent program rewritten in the IF-THEN-ELSE format.

EXAMPLE 5.1

Program (1):

```
 5 REM THIS PROGRAM DETERMINES WHETHER A NUMBER IS
1Ø REM POSITIVE,NEGATIVE, OR ZERO.
15 REM N = THE NUMBER BEING TESTED.
2Ø REM
25 PRINT "TYPE A NUMBER."
3Ø INPUT N
35 IF N > Ø THEN 55
4Ø IF N = Ø THEN 65
45 PRINT "N IS NEGATIVE."
5Ø STOP
55 PRINT "N IS POSITIVE."
6Ø STOP
65 PRINT "N = Ø"
7Ø END
```

Program (2):

```
 5 REM THIS PROGRAM DETERMINES WHETHER A NUMBER
1Ø REM IS POSITIVE,NEGATIVE, OR ZERO.
15 REM N = THE NUMBER BEING TESTED.
2Ø REM
25     PRINT "TYPE A NUMBER."
3Ø     INPUT N
35     IF N > Ø                                    THEN 45
4Ø                                                 GO TO 6Ø
45 REM*    THEN
5Ø             PRINT "N IS POSITIVE."
55             STOP
6Ø REM*    ELSE
65             IF N = Ø                            THEN 75
7Ø                                                 GO TO 85
75 REM*            THEN
8Ø                     PRINT "N = Ø"
82                     STOP
85 REM*            ELSE
9Ø                     PRINT "N IS NEGATIVE."
95 REM*        END IF 65
1ØØ REM*END IF 35
11Ø END
```

The second form is longer than the first, mainly because of all the extra remarks, and at this point you may be saying, "Why must I mess up my program with all those extra statements?"

All we can reply now is, "Have patience!" The techniques we consider here can greatly improve your programming in the long run, especially when you begin to write more complex programs.

Remember that the length of a program is not important unless it seriously affects clarity or efficiency. The second form is to be preferred over the first because it is easier to follow what is going on. To see this, read through both programs from beginning to end.

In reading the first version, you might respond like this (starting at line 35): ". . . Now if N is positive, I go to line 55. Then at line 55 I print out the message and stop. What if N were not positive? Going back to line 35, I go next to line 4Ø. If N equals zero, I go to line 65, where I print the message and stop. And if N is not zero? Going back to line 4Ø, I should then go to line 45, print the message, and stop." Thus in reading this program, you are forced to jump back in the code twice to see what is happening.

Now read the second version (again begin at line 35), concentrating on the main body of the code between the line number on the left and the GO TO statements on the far right. (It contains two selection structures, one nested inside the other.) "If N is positive, then print the appropriate message and stop; otherwise, if N equals zero, then print the message and stop; otherwise print 'N is negative.'"

This time we were able to read through the entire program from top to bottom without backtracking at all. This is an important characteristic of a well-constructed program. See Appendix C for a similar example, written in Digital Equipment Corporation's (DEC) BASIC-PLUS-2, a version of BASIC that has built in the control structures discussed in this chapter.

5.3 Loop Structures

Unless it is awkward to do so, you should write loops with counters using the FOR-NEXT statements, rather than write the counter and test for exit yourself. Counters and tests for exit tend to clutter a program and obscure the main intent of the loop. Example 5.2 makes this clear.

EXAMPLE 5.2

```
Program (segment) 1:
5Ø LET C = Ø
6Ø LET C = C + 1
7Ø LET V = (R*C - 1)^.5
8Ø PRINT C,V
9Ø IF C < 2Ø THEN 6Ø

Program (segment) 2:
5Ø FOR C = 1 TO 2Ø
6Ø     LET V = (R*C - 1)^.5
7Ø     PRINT C,V
8Ø NEXT C
```

Both code segments in Example 5.2 perform precisely the same function. In the first case, the reader has to think about the initialization of C, reads the next two lines, sees the IF, jumps back to line 6Ø, and then begins to see what is going on. In the second segment, the reader can scan the entire sequence without stopping—the loop is clearly delineated and the reader is aware of the loop immediately upon entry (line 5Ø). In a more complex program with several levels of nested loops, the improvement in clarity is magnified many times.

You should not assume, however, that all loops must be constructed using the FOR-NEXT statements. Loops requiring something besides a counter (for example, a trailer) to test for exit must use an IF-THEN statement. In this case, the loop should be clearly indicated by REM statements. (This is discussed further in the next section.)

5.4 Describing Structure with REM Statements

We have already seen how REM statements can be used to emphasize the structure of a program in the IF-THEN-ELSE structures. In this section we propose a formal use for the REM statement to describe structure.

In this procedure, we first use **REM**∗ to indicate structure, keeping the usual REM for ordinary comments about the purpose of the program or for definitions of the variables used. (See Examples 5.1 and 1.2.) This is the book's convention, since an asterisk or anything else can follow REM.

Using the REM∗ statement to effect the selection structure was described in Section 5.2. Also, FOR-NEXT loops require no REM∗ statements. REM∗ statements are, however, extremely useful in delineating loops constructed without FOR-NEXT statements. In that case, we use

k REM∗ BEGIN LOOP k

to indicate the entry point to such a loop, and

l REM∗ END LOOP k

to mark the bottom of the loop, where k and l are line numbers. Loops in which termination does not depend on counters are sometimes called *indefinite loops* (as opposed to *definite* loops).

The sequence in Example 5.3 shows how indefinite loops might be used (note the use of indentations to delineate the loops).

EXAMPLE 5.3

```
Program (segment):
100 REM*BEGIN LOOP 100
110          LET X = X + 1

170          IF S < .1 THEN 100
180 REM*END LOOP 100

250 REM*BEGIN LOOP 250
260          READ A
270 REM*     BEGIN LOOP 270
280              LET B = A^2 - 1.

410              IF X <> 0 THEN 270
420 REM*     END LOOP 270
430          PRINT A,B,C

480          IF A > = B THEN 250
490 REM*END LOOP 250
```

Examine these segments closely. Note how IF-THEN statements are used to implement these loops (lines 170, 410, and 480). If the relations become false, the loops are automatically terminated. Of course, it will not always be possible to place the IF-THEN at the end of the loop like this. Therefore, the REM* statement will be used to indicate an exit from BEGIN-END loops and also to mark an abnormal termination of a loop (see Section 5.1). Its general form is

REM* * * . . . * * EXIT comment

The word EXIT is properly indented in the loop from which the exit is made, with the asterisks running out to the left to indicate the depth of the exit (see below). The comment is optional but can be used to point out the reason for the exit. Consider Example 5.4 (also line 140 of Example 1.2).

EXAMPLE 5.4

```
Program (segment)
11Ø     FOR I = 1 TO 1ØØØ

22Ø         ┌FOR J = 1 TO N

28Ø REM*    │ *****EXIT IF AT END OF LIST
29Ø         │     IF X$ = Z THEN 36Ø┐

35Ø         └ NEXT J
36Ø           LET T = T - 1        ◄──

5ØØ     NEXT I

6ØØ REM*┌BEGIN LOOP 6ØØ
61Ø     │    READ Z
62Ø REM*│*****EXIT FROM LOOP IF VALUE NOT ALLOWED
63Ø     │     IF Z < = -99 THEN 75Ø┐

73Ø     │                                              GO TO 6ØØ
74Ø REM*└END LOOP 6ØØ
75Ø          PRINT Z                    ◄──
```

In Example 5.4, an abnormal termination of the inner loop (lines 22Ø–35Ø) is marked in line 28Ø. The EXIT remark refers to the statement that follows (line 29Ø). The asterisks mark the level of exit. Here we leave the inner loop but not the outer loop (lines 11Ø–5ØØ). Note also that line 29Ø is an example of the standard usage of the IF-THEN statement. The exit from the BEGIN-END loop (lines 6ØØ–74Ø) occurs in line 63Ø and is marked in line 62Ø.

Remember that proper spacing and indentations are important. First, introductory remarks should be set off from the rest of the program. These include a statement of the purpose of the program, special rules or restrictions on the use of the program, the name of the programmer, the date the program was coded, and the definition of the variables used. Setting off can be accomplished by enclosing these remarks in a "box"; for example,

```
REM / / / / / / / /
REM / comments /
REM / / / / / / / /
```

(See Example 1.2 again.)

Because REM* occurs in the program, the actual program statements most conveniently should begin in the fifth column after the line numbers. The GO TO and other statements used to implement the selection structure (IF-THEN-ELSE) should appear as far to the right as possible. Indentations should be standard; indent three to five spaces each time you enter a deeper level of nesting.

Some terminals have tabs you can set to help you with this. Alternatively, you can write a program to do it for you, which you will be able to do after you cover the material on strings (Chapter 8).

There is some danger in trying to provide a structured appearance for a BASIC program. Because the control structures described above are carried out using remarks, it is easy to be casual about their use and consequently to use them incorrectly. Some points to remember are the following.

1. Don't use an IF statement in a BASIC program except to exit from a loop or implement an IF-THEN structure or an IF-THEN-ELSE structure.

2. Use GO TO statements as sparingly as possible, ideally only to implement one of the control structures.

3. Exits from loops should be clearly marked.

4. A well-constructed program can be read from beginning to end with little or no backtracking. A program should be written as a sequence of control structures, ideally each with a single entry and single exit. The structures can be nested (such as an IF-THEN structure within a loop or a loop as part of the ELSE clause of a selection structure), but like the nested loops, they must not cross each other. For example, the following sequence is improper because the selection structure begins inside the loop and finishes outside.

```
100 REM*    BEGIN LOOP 100
110             READ X
120             IF X > = 0                    THEN 140
130                                           GO TO 190
140 REM*        THEN
150                     LET N = N + 1
160                     LET S = S + X * X
170                                           GO TO 100
180 REM*    END LOOP 100
190 REM*        ELSE
200                     LET A = S/N
210                     PRINT A
220 REM*    END IF 120
```

5. By no means should you first code the program, without considering the structured approach, and then try to rewrite the proper structure into it. A good structure should develop naturally as part of the process of designing the program. (This aspect is considered in the next section.)

6. If the structure is good, you should be able to understand the program by reading only the code between the line numbers and the GO TO's. You should not have to look at the GO TO's and line numbers at all.

Next we present Example 5.5, which incorporates several of the above recommendations.

EXAMPLE 5.5 ══

Program:
```
10 REM/////////////////////////////////////////////////////////////////
15 REM/ PROGRAM NAME:  CREDIT                                          /
20 REM/ THIS PROGRAM READS A LIST OF NAMES AND A NUMBER CORRESPONDING /
30 REM/ TO EACH NAME.  IF THE NUMBER IS NEGATIVE IT IS TREATED AS A   /
40 REM/ DEBIT; IF POSITIVE A CREDIT.  A REPORT IS PRINTED WITH THE    /
50 REM/ NUMBER IN THE APPROPRIATE COLUMN.  TOTALS ARE PRINTED.        /
60 REM/ THE DUMMY NAME "ZZZZ" MUST APPEAR AS A TRAILER.               /
70 REM/ PROGRAMMER JOHN DOE, 8/11/76                                  /
80 REM/ X = CURRENT VALUE                                             /
90 REM/ N$ = CURRENT NAME                                             /
100 REM/ S1 = RUNNING SUM OF CREDITS (INITIALIZE TO ZERO)             /
110 REM/ S2 = RUNNING SUM OF DEBITS  (INITIALIZE TO ZERO)             /
120 REM/////////////////////////////////////////////////////////////////
130 REM
200     LET S1 = 0
210     LET S2 = 0
220     PRINT "NAME","CREDIT","DEBIT"
230 REM* BEGIN LOOP 230
240         READ N$,X
250 REM* *****EXIT IF AT END OF LIST
260         IF N$ = "ZZZZ" THEN 390
270         IF X >= 0                                    THEN 290
280                                                      GO TO 330
290 REM*           THEN (CREDIT)
300                 PRINT N$,X
310                 LET S1 = S1 + X
320                                                      GO TO 230
330 REM*           ELSE (DEBIT)
340                 PRINT N$," ",-X
350                 LET S2 = S2 - X
360 REM*     END IF 270
370                                                      GO TO 230
380 REM* END LOOP 230
390     PRINT
400     PRINT "TOTALS ARE",X1,S2
500 DATA "ALBERTS,F.",23.75,"BROWN,J.",72.55,"MORRIS,P.",-9.37
510 DATA "TESTA,K.",-71.32,"YOUNG,A.",14.25,"ZZZZ",0
999 END
```

Output:
```
NAME           CREDIT          DEBIT
ALBERTS,F.     23.75
BROWN, J.      72.55
MORRIS, P.                     9.37
TESTA, I.                      71.32
YOUNG, A.      14.25

TOTALS ARE     110.55          80.69
```

Note the abnormal exit from the loop in line 260 as marked in line 250. Note also the placement of the GO TO's far to the right, away from the mainstream of the program text. The GO TO in line 320 jumps back to the beginning of the loop and not to the end, for efficiency. Otherwise a "double jump" would occur. (Why?)

In any case, Example 5.5 is not constructed as well as it could be; in reading the program we would normally follow the exit from the loop, but then we must jump back into the loop at line 27∅ to follow the rest of the program. Can you improve it (see problem 2 in the Exercises)? This example was given to show how to use REM statements and indentation to emphasize structure.

5.5   The Structured Approach to Program Design

Structured programming has two aspects—program design and program coding. Coding was considered in Sections 5.1–5.4, and you have already been introduced to the structured approach to program design (Section 4.7). We will consider the design aspect in more detail here and then combine two features in some examples.

Sometimes structured program design is referred to as top-down programming. A program should not be coded immediately from the statement of the problem to be solved, and then patched by inserting and deleting statements until it finally works. Rather, it should represent a systematic development of the entities natural to the problem itself. Briefly, *top-down design* means this: Start with the definition of the purpose of the program and then decompose it into a set of descriptions of procedures for solving the problem. Then progressively decompose each description into subdescriptions, thus providing more and more detail as you proceed to lower levels of refinement. This step-by-step refinement continues until you reach a level that can be coded directly (that is, one statement in the description yields exactly one statement in the program) into a high-level programming language—BASIC, for example.

In general, the more complex the problem, the more numerous the levels of refinement necessary. As the procedure is refined, all vagueness and imprecision are gradually filtered out when the lowest level, the program itself, is reached. There can't be any vagueness or imprecision in a computer program. With this approach, the original problem is generally analyzed quite naturally and classified into a sequence of smaller, and usually simpler, subproblems. In turn, each of these subproblems may require further analysis.

Each description of how the problem is to be solved—the algorithm—from the first to the most refined, should be presented in outline (see Sections 4.7 and 1.5). The indentations and subheadings in the outline reflect the eventual structure of the program. Arrows can be used to emphasize loops (recall the development of Example 4.20).

After a preliminary outline is constructed, before you refine it, you should consider your approach very carefully. Are you quite certain it will work? One way to check is to run through the solution by hand. If the program will be handling large sets of data, you can still check your approach with a small but representative set. For example, if you must write a program that will sort lists of names alphabetically, there is no need to hand-test your method with a list of a thousand names; four or five will do, so long as the order is sufficiently jumbled to take all possibilities into account. (For instance, one question to ask would be, "Will the method work if only the last name is out of order?")

You should realize that it is still quite possible that your procedure is not feasible, however so it appears at this stage. But the top-down approach still has the advantage that most potential failures will become apparent as early as possible. If there is an error, it is important for you to restart the program design at the top rather than patch up the outline that is in error.

If you are reasonably certain of success with this method, you should now ask your-self, "Is there a better way?" Often, some hard thinking at this point will pay off later with a much better program. It is quite possible, however, that you may have several methods for solving a problem but cannot be sure which approach is best. In that case, go with one of the schemes, and don't worry about the others. A sophisticated study could be made, if the program were important enough, using a branch of mathematics called analysis of algorithms, but that is beyond the scope of this book.

Once you have determined a procedure and have a rough outline, you can start re-fining; each step may require a more detailed description of how it is to be carried out. Resist the temptation to begin writing BASIC immediately. Much time should be de-voted to designing (as much as 80 percent of the total), compared with program coding, which will become more or less automatic as you gain experience.

One other programming technique that you should know about now (more will be said in Chapter 9) is how to use **modularity**.

If a problem is complex, it is reasonable to classify it into a set of smaller problems; then an independent design and program can be developed for each subproblem. Each resulting *subprogram,* or *module,* can be compiled and tested individually. The modules should be combined to form the complete program only when they have been shown to work independently. At this point, the relation between the modules must be clearly defined. This technique along with structured programming can significantly reduce the complexity of the problem and the time required to debug the program. This ap-proach is often taken when teams of programmers work on a large project; each pro-grammer works on a separate module.

In a sense, modular programming is the inverse of top-down programming. In modular programming, we start with the components and combine them to form the complete program. In structured programming, we first view the whole problem and refine it to produce eventually the fine detail. For large problems, then, both schemes are used; this approach will be used on selected examples.

5.6   An Application

Here is what seems to be a very simple problem. Write a program that accepts three numbers on INPUT and then determines and prints out the one that is the middle value in magnitude. (For example, if 3, 7, and 2 are the numbers, the program will select 3; if 2, -7, -7 are the numbers, -7 is printed.)

Consider now the thoughts of our mythical novice programmer, Jane Doaks, as she attempts to solve the problem (a good exercise at this point is to try it yourself before reading further).

First, I'll write down the statement of the problem:

Find the middle value of three numbers.

Let's see, how would I do this by hand? I'll take an example, the sequence 3, 7, 2.

I recognize immediately that 3 is the value—but I can't ask the computer to do that. In BASIC, it can make only one comparison at a time.

For reference I'll use A, B, and C as my values. Now suppose I compare A with B (3 with 7) and pick out the smaller (A), which I then compare with C. The largest number in the last comparison must be my middle value (A here).

That's it! It seems to work, and I can outline my procedure:

I. If A $\geqslant$ B,

   then

   ⌈ A. If B $\geqslant$ C, then B is the middle value.
   ⌊ B. If C $>$ B, then C is the middle value.

   else

   ⌈ A. If A $\geqslant$ C, then A is the middle value.
   ⌊ B. If C $>$ A, then C is the middle value.

Before proceeding further, I'd better try another example or two: 7, –3, 5, say. If A is greater than B, that means compare B with C. The value C is greater than B, which means that C is in the middle. Right. Well, one more. Try 0, 1, 3. Here, since A is less than B, compare A with C; C is larger, which implies that C is the middle value. Oops! I guess if C is the largest of the three numbers, this won't work.

This is tougher than I thought. What are the different possibilities? I can write them all down:

$$A \geqslant B \geqslant C$$
$$A \geqslant C \geqslant B$$
$$B \geqslant A \geqslant C$$
$$B \geqslant C \geqslant A$$
$$C \geqslant A \geqslant B$$
$$C \geqslant B \geqslant A$$

Six cases—I could test separately for each case; but there must be a better way. Can I combine any of those cases and in so doing reduce the number of possibilities?

Aha! What if I know the largest number? Then finding the middle number means simply finding the larger value between the other two. I can see this will work as I examine the above six cases, and my basic outline is:

I.   Find the largest number of the three.
II. Find the larger of the remaining two; that is, the middle value.

Have I forgotten anything? What about equality—is that a problem? No, I can compare *less than or equal* or *less than,* and in either case I shall select one of the two values (and if they are equal, it doesn't matter which one).

Now I can simply design a procedure to find the largest of three numbers. Then I just compare the remaining two—hold it. There's a problem here—comparing the remaining two implies knowing the location in the list (first, second, or third), not the value, of the largest number. I'd better revise my outline:

I.   Find the location of the largest number.
II. Find the larger of the remaining two numbers; that is, the middle value.

That's better, and I can refine the whole. The original problem has become two simpler subproblems (modules). I can now consider each independently.

Finding the location of the largest number can be done by a series of comparisons, as follows:

I. If $A \geqslant B$,

    then

    A. If $A \geqslant C$,

        ⌈ 1. *then* A is the largest.
        ⌊ 2. *else* C is the largest.

    else

    B. If $B \geqslant C$,

        ⌈ 1. *then* B is the largest.
        ⌊ 2. *else* C is the largest.

In the second problem, finding the larger of the two remaining numbers, we have three cases: one if A is largest, one if B is largest, and one if C is largest. Each can be solved with a single comparison.

I. If A is the largest,

    then

    A. If $B \geqslant C$,

        1. *then* B is the middle value.
        2. *else* C is the middle value.

Similar outlines can be written for the other two cases.

I can now put the two outlines together to produce the complete solution:

I. If $A \geqslant B$,

    then

    A. If $A \geqslant C$, A is the largest;

        then

        ⌈ 1. If $B \geqslant C$,
        | a. *then* B is the middle value.
        ⌊   b. *else* C is the middle value.

        else, C is the largest.

        ⌈ 2. If $A \geqslant B$,
        | a. *then* A is the middle value.
        ⌊   b.

Hold it! Step I. A. 2 isn't necessary. At that point I already know that $A \geqslant B$ and consequently that A is the middle value in that case. Thus, my next refinement is as follows:

I. If A ⩾ B,
    then
  A. If A ⩾ C, A is the largest;
      then
      1. If B ⩾ C,
        a. *then* B is the middle value.
        b. *else* C is the middle value.
      else, C is the largest.
      2. A is the middle value.
    else
  B. If B ⩾ C, B is the largest;
      then
      1. If A ⩾ C,
        a. *then* A is the middle value.
        b. *else* C is the middle value.
      else, C is the largest.
      2. B is the middle value.

This looks good, and it works on every example I've tried. But before coding it, I'll refine it once more to make it complete.

I. Input A, B, and C.
II. If A ⩾ B,
    then
  A. If A ⩾ C, A is the largest;
      then
      1. If B ⩾ C,
        then
        a. Print B.
        b. Stop.
        else
        c. Print C.
        d. Stop.
      else, C is the largest;
      2. Print A.
      3. Stop.
    else
  B. If B ⩾ C, B is the largest;
      then
      1. If A ⩾ C,
        then
        a. Print A.
        b. Stop.
        else
        c. Print C.
        d. Stop.
      else, C is the largest;
      2. Print B.
      3. Stop.

Note how the selection structures are marked clearly with brackets. A similar approach can be used with loops. This outline is sufficiently refined to be converted easily into the program shown in Example 5.6.

EXAMPLE 5.6

Program:

```
 10 REM/////////////////////////////////////////////////////////////
 15 REM/ PROGRAM NAME: MIDDLE
 20 REM/  THIS PROGRAM DETERMINES THE MIDDLE VALUE OF THREE NUMBERS.
 30 REM/  PROGRAMMER: DOAKS, J.  2/28/76
 40 REM/  A,B,C ARE THE NUMBERS GIVEN IN THAT ORDER.
 50 REM/////////////////////////////////////////////////////////////
 60 REM
100      PRINT "TYPE IN THE THREE NUMBERS."
110      INPUT A,B,C
120      IF A > = B                                        THEN 130
125                                                        GO TO 260
130 REM*      THEN
140               IF A > = C                               THEN 155
150                                                        GO TO 230
155 REM*               THEN  (A IS THE LARGEST)
160                         IF B > = C                     THEN 170
165                                                        GO TO 200
170 REM*                         THEN
180                                  PRINT B
190                                  STOP
200 REM*                         ELSE
210                                  PRINT C
220                                  STOP
225 REM*                    END IF 160
230 REM*               ELSE  (C IS THE LARGEST)
240                         PRINT A
250                         STOP
255 REM*          END IF 140
260 REM*      ELSE
270               IF B > = C                               THEN 285
280                                                        GO TO 360
285 REM*               THEN  (B IS THE LARGEST)
290                         IF A > = C                     THEN 305
300                                                        GO TO 330
305 REM*                         THEN
310                                  PRINT A
320                                  STOP
330 REM*                         ELSE
340                                  PRINT C
350                                  STOP
355 REM*                    END IF 290
360 REM*               ELSE  (C IS THE LARGEST)
370                         PRINT B
380                         STOP
385 REM*          END IF 270
390 REM*END IF 120
500      END
```

Output 1:

```
TYPE IN THE THREE NUMBERS.
?  1,2,3
2
```

```
Output 2:
TYPE IN THE THREE NUMBERS.
?  3,1,2
2

Output 3:
TYPE IN THE THREE NUMBERS.
?  2,1,3
2
```

Note how closely Example 5.6 resembles the last refinement of the outline. Because of the careful design, the program has a nice structure; you can read from top to bottom without backtracking once.

Clearly, some awkwardness remains because of the multinested IF's. At this point we really have no other options; alternatives are given in Chapter 7.

Finally, observe the important use of REM statements in the text of the program itself. This technique is useful, especially in complex programs, for describing in English the purpose of a segment of code. (See also Example 1.2.)

For another example of this use, imagine a program containing a loop with the statement

250 LET C = C + X

It would be silly to label this loop or statement with a remark like

REM ADD X TO C

since that's obvious. It would be much more informative to include a comment like

REM COMPUTE THE TOTAL COST OF THE PRODUCTION.

Comments like this one can be extremely helpful in reading and trying to understand the procedures in a program.

Let us compare the previous example with the program in Example 5.7, written by a beginner, without any attempt to "structure" the program.

EXAMPLE 5.7

Program:

```
 1Ø INPUT A,B,C
 2Ø IF A > = B THEN 7Ø
 3Ø IF B > = C THEN 14Ø
 4Ø IF B > = A THEN 16Ø
 5Ø PRINT A
 6Ø STOP
 7Ø IF A > = C THEN 9Ø
 8Ø GO TO 5Ø
 9Ø IF B > = C THEN 12Ø
1ØØ PRINT C
11Ø STOP
12Ø PRINT B
13Ø STOP
14Ø IF A > = C THEN 5Ø
15Ø GO TO 1ØØ
16Ø IF B > = C THEN 18Ø
17Ø GO TO 12Ø
18Ø IF C > = A THEN 1ØØ
19Ø GO TO 5Ø
2ØØ END
```

Try following both Example 5.6 and Example 5.7 using the data 2,1,2; 1,2,3; and 2,1,3. Which program do you prefer? Which one can be more easily generalized?

$$A \div B = C, \text{REMAINDER} = ?$$

FIGURE 5.2 Elementary arithmetic

5.7 Another Application

In this example, we begin with the design of the procedure, having already chosen the algorithm. The problem is to write a program that will do the following: Given two positive integers N and D, find the integer quotient and remainder on division of N by D. Furthermore, the program should be written to allow the user to continue to input values of N and D so long as he or she wishes to do so.

This problem can be done with essentially one statement, using the INT function (see Chapter 6), but it is interesting to solve the problem without it.

If we let Q be the *exact* quotient (not necessarily an integer), I the *integer* quotient, and R the remainder, then these values satisfy the following equations:[†]

$$N = Q * D \text{ and } N = I * D + R$$

For example, let N = 18 and D = 4. Then Q = 4.5, I = 4, and R = 2. That is, I will be the integer portion of Q. The problem, then, restated in these terms is: Given N and D, find I and R. Our algorithm is

1. Let Q = N/D.
2. Find I, the integer part of Q.
3. Compute the remainder R.

How shall we find I? We can simply count by ones until $I \leqslant Q \leqslant I + 1$. We can now refine the above version:

1. Let Q = N/D.
2. Count (using I as the counter) until $I \leqslant Q \leqslant I + 1$.
3. Compute the remainder, R = N – I * D.
4. Print I and R.

Before we code this in BASIC, another refinement is needed. We have forgotten several elements.

1. We must input N and D.
2. To be safe, we should make sure that N and D are both positive or both negative; otherwise the procedure may not work. A simple way to do this is to examine the sign of the product N * D; if it is negative, N and D have different signs.
3. The entire procedure should be embedded in a loop to allow the user to try more than one example.

Also, we should consider at this stage how to accomplish step 2 in the procedure. A little thought will show that a FOR-NEXT loop is ideal for this purpose. The refinement then becomes

I.   Input N and D.
II. If N * D < Ø,
        then
        A. Print error message.
        else
        B. Let Q = N/D
        C. For K = Ø TO Q, set I = K
        D. Compute R = N – I * D
        E. Print I, R
III. If the user wants to continue, repeat steps I and II.
IV. Stop.

This version is sufficiently detailed to be coded directly into BASIC, resulting in the program and output shown in Example 5.8.

[†] If there is no round-off error; see Chapter 6.

EXAMPLE 5.8

Program:

```
10 REM/////////////////////////////////////////////////////////////////////
15 REM/ PROGRAM NAME:  QUOREM                                              /
20 REM/ THIS PROGRAM FINDS THE QUOTIENT AND REMAINDER ON DIVISION OF ONE  /
30 REM/ INTEGER BY ANOTHER.  THE INTEGERS MUST HAVE THE SAME SIGN.        /
35 REM/ INPUT OF NONINTEGERS IS UNPREDICTABLE                            /
40 REM/ PROGRAMMER: DOAKS, J.  5/4/76                                     /
50 REM/ N IS THE DIVIDEND                                                /
60 REM/ D IS THE DIVISOR                                                 /
70 REM/ Q IS THE "EXACT" QUOTIENT                                        /
80 REM/ I IS THE INTEGER QUOTIENT                                        /
90 REM/ R IS THE INTEGER REMAINDER                                       /
95 REM/////////////////////////////////////////////////////////////////////
100 REM
110 REM* BEGIN LOOP 110
120          PRINT "INPUT THE INTEGER DIVIDEND AND DIVISOR."
130          INPUT N,D
140          IF N*D < = 0                                       THEN 160
150                                                             GO TO 190
160 REM*          THEN
170                    PRINT "ERROR--OPPOSITE SIGNS."
180                                                             GO TO 270
190 REM*          ELSE
200                    LET Q = N/D
205 REM/ THIS LOOP DETERMINES INTEGER QUOTIENT I.
210                    FOR K = 0 TO Q
220                         LET I = K
230                    NEXT K
235 REM/ COMPUTE REMAINDER R.
240                    LET R = N - I * D
250                    PRINT "QUOTIENT","REMAINDER"
260                    PRINT I,R
270 REM*     END IF 140
280          PRINT "DO YOU WISH TO TRY ANOTHER PAIR?  (YES OR NO)"
285          INPUT A$
290 REM* ****EXIT FROM LOOP IF USER DOES NOT WANT TO CONTINUE.
300          IF A$ = "YES" THEN 110
310 REM* END LOOP 110
320      END
```

Output:

```
INPUT THE INTEGER DIVIDEND AND DIVISOR.
?  37,5
QUOTIENT       REMAINDER
 7               2
DO YOU WISH TO TRY ANOTHER PAIR? (YES OR NO)
?  YES
INPUT THE INTEGER DIVIDEND AND DIVISOR.
?  32,4
QUOTIENT       REMAINDER
 8               0
DO YOU WISH TO TRY ANOTHER PAIR? (YES OR NO)
?  NO
```

Clearly, Example 5.8 could be improved to make it fail-safe. The program could, for example, check to be sure that N and D are integers and print an error message if they are not. It could also ensure a yes or no response in line **285** (see Exercise 5.4).

Many of the programs in this (or any other) book could be so improved. We do not do this here in the interest of space and lest the additional detail conceal the points being highlighted in each example.

Such improvements are necessary, however, for any program that will be used by other persons besides the programmer who writes it. What seems clear to the programmer may not be clear to the user, and information entered as input data to a program may be completely unexpected. The result is a program that doesn't do what it is supposed to.

5.8 Eliminating Exits

Section 5.1 pointed out that sometimes multiple exits from a loop structure are necessary, especially in a language like BASIC, which does not have some of the powerful structures required to eliminate this problem. Multiple exits from structures are undesirable, since they can make a program unnecessarily difficult to follow.

If one is clever, however, the problem can be avoided in BASIC too, although at a price. Refer now to Example 5.9.

EXAMPLE 5.9

Program (segment):

```
100      FOR K = 1 TO N
110          READ X,Y
120          LET Z = X + Y
130          IF Z < R                               THEN 150
140                                                 GO TO 190
150 REM*         THEN
160                  LET Z = R
170 REM* ***********EXIT FROM LOOP
180                  GO TO 290
190 REM*         ELSE
200              IF Z > T                           THEN 220
210                                                 GO TO 260
220 REM*                 THEN
230                          LET Z = T
240 REM* *******************EXIT FROM LOOP
250                          GO TO 290
260 REM*             END IF 200
270 REM*     END IF 130
280     NEXT K
290     PRINT X,Y,Z
```

Example 5.9 has three exits from the loop—the normal exit, or "falling through" the end of the loop when K is greater than N, and the two abnormal terminations, lines 180 and 250. To avoid this multiple exit, we can introduce a switch. A **switch** is simply a variable that takes on one of several possible values. Then the value of the switch determines which of several sequences of instructions will be executed next; each sequence corresponds to one of the values of the switch.

Improving the structure this way produces some loss of efficiency. Extra steps must be introduced for initializing the switch and resetting it to another value whenever any of the conditions for exit are met. Consequently, the programmer must decide whether the reduction in the number of exits is too costly. The conditions for setting and testing such a switch may become too complex, and the programmer may then decide to keep the multiple exits. If a switch is used, to promote clarity the reader should not use that variable for any other function. Furthermore, REM statements should be used to explain each value of a switch and its significance.

Example 5.9 can be repaired easily with a switch, as we can see by Example 5.10.

EXAMPLE 5.10

Program (segment):

```
100      LET S = 0
110      LET K = 1
120 REM* BEGIN LOOP 120
130          READ X,Y
140          LET Z = X + Y
150          IF Z < R                                    THEN 170
160                                                      GO TO 210
170 REM*         THEN
180                  LET Z = R
185 REM* SET SWITCH S TO EXIT CONDITION
190                  LET S = 1
200                                                      GO TO 280
210 REM*         ELSE
220                  IF Z > T                            THEN 240
230                                                      GO TO 280
240 REM*                 THEN
250                          LET Z = T
255 REM* SET SWITCH S TO EXIT CONDITION
260                          LET S = 1
270 REM*         END IF 220
280 REM*     END IF 150
290          LET K = K + 1
300          IF K > N                                    THEN 320
310                                                      GO TO 340
320 REM*         THEN
325 REM* SET SWITCH S TO EXIT CONDITION
330                  LET S = 1
340 REM*     END IF 300
350 REM* ****EXIT FROM LOOP IF SWITCH SET TO 1
360          IF S = 1 THEN 390
370                                                      GO TO 120
380 REM* END LOOP 120
390
```

Example 5.10 essentially duplicates the results of Example 5.9. Here, however, there is *only one exit* from the loop, line 360. This is accomplished by means of the switch S. The value S is initialized to zero in line 100 and is set to 1 if any of the conditions for exit are met, that is, if $K > N$, $Z < R$, or $Z > T$. The exit occurs in line 360 by testing for S equal to 1. Thus, the three separate conditions tested in the loop of Example 5.9 are combined into a single test in Example 5.10.

But we have paid a price. Example 5.10 requires ten more statements, most of them being used to test and define values for S. What we have gained is a more readable program (to see this, read both examples from top to bottom).

The variable S is an example of a two-way switch; that is, it takes on two values. Three-way, four-way, and more complicated switches are possible. (A way of exploiting the general case is examined in Chapter 7.)

5.9   Common Structural Errors

Writing well-constructed programs requires a good deal of discipline. Since a poorly constructed program may be correct (having neither syntax errors nor logic errors), it is perhaps easier to commit "errors" in structure; one may not bother to correct the structure of a working program. In this section, three examples of common structural errors demonstrate the kind of code sequences to avoid. Other errors are possible. One should generally avoid program logic that uses GO TO statements, if possible (except to effect the control structures described in this chapter and in Chapter 7).

One error, which is shown in the following segment (and also considered in Section 5.4), concerns *overlapping structures.*

```
100 REM* BEGIN LOOP
        . . .
150          * * * EXIT FROM LOOP
        . . .
180             IF X > Y            THEN 200
190                                 GO TO 320
200 REM*          THEN
210                  . . .
300                                 GO TO 100
310 REM* END LOOP
320 REM*          ELSE
330                  . . .
410 REM*    END IF
```

The fault with this sequence is that the loop overlaps the IF-THEN-ELSE structure; the IF begins inside the loop and finishes outside. In a language like PL/1, for which such control structures are standard, the above logic would generate several error messages. The rule to remember is: *If a control structure begins inside another control structure, it must also terminate inside.* In other words, control structures may be nested, but they must not overlap. A segment such as the one above can be corrected by reexamining the outline of the solution. In the above case, for example, the IF-THEN-ELSE could often be replaced by an IF-THEN statement that remains nested inside the loop. Multiple exits from the loop could be eliminated with a switch, as shown in Section 5.8.

The accompanying segment illustrates *jumping past a structure.*

```
20          IF S < 60       THEN 40
30                          GO TO 110
40 REM*     THEN
50
    . . .                                    . . .
90                          GO TO 200 ─┐
100 REM* END IF
110         IF S < 70       THEN 130
120                         GO TO 190
130 REM*    THEN
140
    . . .                                    . . .
190 REM*  END IF
200 . . .                              ◄─────┘
```

At the conclusion of the first IF-THEN, the GO TO 200 jumps past the second IF-THEN. This is not an error in the strict sense of the word, but it does represent a violation of the principle of using a GO TO statement for other purposes besides implementing a control structure. The above segment could be handled more effectively by an IF-THEN-ELSE structure (How? Try it!) or by a CASE structure (Chapter 7).

The third and final illustration is the omission of END IF remarks (the GO TO statements and line numbers are not shown here).

```
IF X > C1
   THEN
       IF A-1 < 0
           THEN
               . . .
       ELSE
          IF P <> Q
              THEN
                  . . .
       ELSE
```

The resulting sequence of code looks ambiguous, especially with the last ELSE improperly indented. The program may work correctly, but one must examine the GO TO statements in detail to discover what is intended, while the goal is to write a program which one can read without looking at the GO TO's. This is simply a case of carelessness, and one can provide the appropriate END IF statements by studying the GO TO's or by following what is intended in the outline.

Exercises

1. Example 1.2 is not as well constructed as it could be. Rewrite and run it, using the structured approach described in this chapter. Don't try to convert the example di-

rectly to a structured form; instead, begin with the statement of the problem and design a solution using the top-down approach.

2. Do the same for Example 5.5.

3. Following the advice of problem 1, rewrite Example 5.6 using the following approach: Let L = 1, 2, or 3, depending on whether A, B, or C is the largest value. Save the other two values as N1 and N2. Compare this approach with Example 5.6.

4. Modify Example 5.8 to ensure that N and D are integers and to accept only a yes or no response in line 285.

Problems 5–9 present segments of programs that have poor structure. In each case, explain what is wrong.

```
5.      50       IF A$ = "YES"                                   THEN 70
        60                                                       GO TO 190
        70 REM*        THEN
        80                      IF K < N                         THEN 100
        90                                                       GO TO 140
       100 REM*              THEN
       110                           LET S = S + X
       120                           LET K = K + 1
       130                                                       GO TO 190
       140 REM*              ELSE
       150                        PRINT S
       160                        LET K = 0
       170                                                       GO TO 230
       180 REM*          END IF 80
       190 REM*      ELSE
       200                  PRINT K,N
       210                  LET K = 1
       220 REM*END IF 50
       230       LET A = X – 1.5

6.     100       READ X,Y
       110       IF Y > 0                                        THEN 130
       120 REM*  BEGIN LOOP 120
       130 REM*      THEN
       140                  LET C = C + 1
       150                  LET S = S + Y/C
              . . .
       300 REM*  END LOOP 120
       310 REM*      ELSE
       320                  LET A = S/C
       330                  PRINT A
              . . .
       400 REM*  END IF 110
```

```
7.      100 REM*  BEGIN LOOP 100
        110           READ X
        120           IF X > = 0                              THEN 140
        130                                                   GO TO 200
        140 REM*               THEN
        150                         LET S = S + X
        160                         LET S1 = S1 + X * X
        170                         LET N = N + 1
        180                                                   GO TO 100
        190 REM*  END LOOP 100
        200 REM*               ELSE
        210                         LET A = X/N
        220                         LET A1 = S1/N
        230                         PRINT A,A1,N
        240 REM*        END IF 120
        250      STOP
        260      END

8.      80 REM*  BEGIN LOOP 80
        85            IF X + Y > 1000                          THEN 115
        90 REM*        THEN
        95                  LET A = X + Y
        100                 PRINT X,Y,A
        105 REM*  **********EXIT FROM LOOP
        110                 GO TO 150
        115 REM*        ELSE
        120                 READ X
        125                 LET Y = Y + X + N
        130                 LET N = N + 1
        135                                                   GO TO 80
        140 REM*    END IF 85
        150 REM* END LOOP 80

9.      200      FOR K = N TO 1 STEP -1
        210           READ X,Y
        220           LET Y = Y - K
        230 REM* ******EXIT FROM LOOP
        240           IF Y > X THEN 260
        250      NEXT K
        260      PRINT X,Y
```

10. Consider the following unstructured program segment. Rewrite it in a well-constructed form. (You are again cautioned against taking this approach in general. It can be extremely difficult to create an equivalent structured program directly from one that is not structured.)

```
100 IF A < B THEN 130
110 LET I = I + 1
120 GO TO 150
130 LET A = C * D
140 IF C < D THEN 170
150 LET F = F + 1
160 LET B = C - 2 * D
170 LET I1 = I1 + 1
180 LET I2 = I2 - 1
```

11. Write a structured program to read a sequence of integer numbers and determine whether each is even. If a number is even, the computer should print the number followed by the string "IS EVEN." A comparable output should appear if the number is odd. Use 0 as a trailer for the list. The INT function (see Chapter 6) can be used to do this conveniently. Note that LET A = INT (B) assigns the integer portion of B to A; for example, INT (5.7) equals 5, INT (0.95) equals 0, INT (-1.4) equals -1, and so on. Thus to see whether B is even, we compute INT (B/2) * 2. If that expression equals B, then B is even. (For example, INT (7/2) * 2 = INT (3.5) * 2 $\neq$ 7, which implies that 7 is odd.)

12. A student wrote the following program to compute the *prime factors* of each of the positive integers from 2 to N. (A prime number is an integer greater than 1 that is exactly divisible by only itself and 1. Thus, 11 is prime but 12 is not prime. The prime factors of N are all the primes that exactly divide N. Thus, 6 has 2 and 3 as prime factors, and 12 has 3, 2, and 2 as prime factors.) Write a structured version of this program, using the INT function as it is used in this program to determine whether a number exactly divides another.

```
10 INPUT N
20 LET I = 2
30 LET K = I
40 PRINT K
50 LET T = 2
60 IF INT(K/T) * T <> K THEN 110
70 PRINT T
80 LET K = K/T
90 IF K = 1 THEN 130
100 GO TO 60
110 LET T = T + 1
120 GO TO 60
130 LET I = I + 1
140 IF I <= N THEN 30
150 END
```

13. Consider the following outline of a segment of a program. Because of multiple exits, it is not constructed as well as it could be. Rewrite the outline so that the loop has exactly one exit.

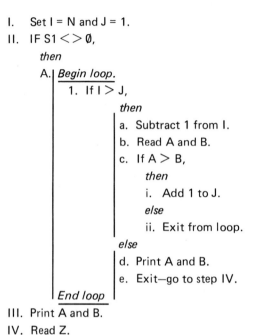

I. Set I = N and J = 1.
II. IF S1 <> Ø,
>   *then*
>   A. | *Begin loop.*
>   >   1. If I > J,
>   >   >   *then*
>   >   >   a. Subtract 1 from I.
>   >   >   b. Read A and B.
>   >   >   c. If A > B,
>   >   >   >   *then*
>   >   >   >   i. Add 1 to J.
>   >   >   >   *else*
>   >   >   >   ii. Exit from loop.
>   >   >   *else*
>   >   >   d. Print A and B.
>   >   >   e. Exit—go to step IV.
>   >   *End loop*
III. Print A and B.
IV. Read Z.

The remaining exercises involve writing programs. In each case, design a solution to the given problem using a top-down approach, and try to construct a well-structured program.

14. The real roots of $ax^2 + bx + c = Ø$ can be computed using the formula

$$x = \frac{-b \pm \sqrt{b^2 - 4ac}}{2a}$$

so long as $a \neq 0$ and $b^2 - 4ac \geqslant 0$. Write a program to compute the roots and print them out along with one of the following strings, whichever is appropriate:

> "NOT AN EQUATION—A = B = Ø, C <> Ø—NO ROOTS"
> "LINEAR—ONLY ONE ROOT"   ($a = 0$)
> "TWO DISTINCT ROOTS"   ($b^2 - 4ac > 0$)
> "TWO EQUAL ROOTS"   ($b^2 - 4ac = 0$)
> "COMPLEX ROOTS"   ($b^2 - 4ac < 0$)

No roots should be printed in the first and last cases. The program should accept A, B, and C as input values and should be capable of handling an indefinite number of equations until the user decides to stop.

15. Write a program to accept a positive integer N on input and compute N factorial (N!). N! = 1 · 2 · 3 · · · N; for instance, 4! = 1 · 2 · 3 · 4 = 24. Run the program for N = 4, 6, 11, 50. Note the results for N = 50.

16. A school file has records that contain the following information:

Student ID number (5 digits)
Student name
Student grade point average

Write a program that will search the records, print out the records of Jones, J. D., and Levy, R. A., and all the records of students with a GPA under 2.0. Put the records on DATA statements, separating the items by commas. Make up a set of 10–20 records for your test runs.

17. A company has N (an input value) employees. For each employee there is a record of the form:

ID number
Name
Age
Number of years with the company
Number of days of vacation
Number of days of sick leave

Write a program to do the following:
a. Print the ID number and name of all employees more than 55 years old who have worked for the company less than five years.
b. Determine the employee who joined the company at the earliest age. Print the ID number, name, and age at which this person joined the company.
c. Print the total number of vacation days and sick-leave days.

18. Write a program to balance your checking account. Input the old balance, and then for each check written read the amount and a string showing to whom paid. Also, input any deposits made. Print out the checks (that is, amount and to whom paid), deposits, and the new balance.

19. A number of objects have masses $m_1, m_2, \ldots, m_n$. Each of the objects is located in space given by the coordinates $x_1, y_1, z_1; x_2, y_2, z_2; \ldots$. The center of gravity of these objects is given by

$$\bar{x} = \frac{m_1 x_1 + m_2 x_2 + \cdots + m_n x_n}{m_1 + m_2 + \cdots + m_n}$$

$$\bar{y} = \frac{m_1 y_1 + m_2 y_2 + \cdots + m_n y_n}{m_1 + m_2 + \cdots + m_n}$$

$$\bar{z} = \frac{m_1 z_1 + m_2 z_2 + \cdots + m_n z_n}{m_1 + m_2 + \cdots + m_n}$$

Write a program to read the masses and their coordinates and to determine $\bar{x}$, $\bar{y}$, and $\bar{z}$. Make up your own data.

20. A company uses W widgets per year. A manufacturer charges $10.00 each for the first 900 widgets and $8.50 each for any over 900. The company could make its own at cost of $9,500 + $5.25 per widget. Write a program to accept W as input and to determine the cost of (a) manufacturing and (b) buying the widgets. Print whether the company should make or purchase the widgets to get the lowest cost. Test the program for W = 500, 1,000, 2,000, 5,000.

21. Use the INT function in a program to provide change for a $20 bill that is supposedly provided as payment for a charge which is less than or equal to $20. Input the charge and print out the change; for example, if $12.52 is the charge, the program should print out

                    YOUR CHANGE IS:
                    0 TEN
                    1 FIVE
                    2 SINGLES
                    1 QUARTERS
                    2 DIMES
                    0 NICKELS
                    3 PENNIES

Hint: Represent $20.00 in terms of cents—2,000—and similarly for the change. Compute the difference. Computing the integer quotient on division by 1,000 gives the number of tens; taking the remainder and dividing by 500 yields the number of fives; and so on. Recall that Example 5.8 shows how to compute the remainder and quotient by integer division. The INT function makes this problem easier.

22. Rewrite Example 5.8, using the INT function to compute the remainder and quotient.

23. El Junko Rent-A-Car would like you to write a program to handle its billing procedures. For each bill you should input the following:
a. The total number of hours the car was kept
b. The daily rate (24 hr) for the particular car
c. The miles driven
d. The mileage charge in cents per mile for that car
e. A value 1 if the customer took out insurance at $3 per day, 0 if not.

The bill is computed using the above information plus the following:
a. The minimum charge is one day's rate.
b. The hourly rate is 1/8 the daily rate, but hourly charge should not exceed the daily rate. Thus a period of 30 hr would be charged for 1 day plus 6 hr.
c. If the car is held for 5 days or more, a 10% discount is applied to the daily rental rate and the hourly charge.
d. A 4% sales tax should be added to the total bill.

24. Write a program to help a professor keep statistics on tests. The program should read the student numbers, names, and scores on the test and compute the average scores. Also, determine the maximum mark, the minimum mark, and the number of students (a) 90% and over, (b) 75% to 89%, (c) 60% to 74%, (d) 50% to 59%, (e) under 50%. Finally, for each of these five categories determine the average mark.

25. Write a program that will accept as input the name and appropriate dimensions of any of the following geometrical objects:

                    sphere   right triangle   box
                    circle   cylinder   cone

The program should then ask the user to input what is wanted—volume or surface area, or area or perimeter, whichever is appropriate. The program should then compute the requested value. You can get the formulas for these quantities from geometry books, tables, encyclopedias, and the like.

26. WEGIPM Corporation conducted a survey to determine whether a proposed premium, to be included with each purchase of their "cheap" toaster, was appealing enough to significantly increase sales. Five cities were used as test cities, where the premium was distributed, and five cities as control cities, where the toasters were sold without the premium. The cities were chosen on the basis of certain similarities.

   The results are summarized as follows:

TEST CITIES	% CHANGE IN AVERAGE MARKET SHARE PER MONTH	CONTROL CITIES	% CHANGE IN AVERAGE MARKET SHARE PER MONTH
1	+20	1	+3
2	+16	2	-7
3	+ 6	3	-5
4	+12	4	+1
5	+10	5	0

Write a program to do the following:
a. Find the mean of the change in market share for both the test cities and the control cities.
b. Find the standard deviations for these figures for the test cases and the controls (see problem 16 in chapter 4).
c. Find the difference between the means of part a. This is an estimate of the percent change in sales because of the premium.
d. Compute the average of the two standard deviations in b.
e. Compute the difference in c $\pm$ the average computed in d as a measure of the smallest and largest estimate of the increase in sales.
Print out all of these figures with appropriate headings, for example,

TEST MEAN	CONTROL MEAN
13.2	-2.4

27. Many so-called *combinatorial* problems can be simply solved by counting. Write programs to find the following:
a. How many three-letter words can be formed using the first ten letters of the alphabet if no letter is repeated in the word? (*Note:* Nonsense words count, for example, BDJ.)
b. Same as a if letters can be repeated.
c. If a Scrabble player has seven letters and decides to test all possible five-letter permutations before his or her next play and can test at the rate of one per second, how long will it take the player?
d. What are the number of different poker hands with exactly two aces that can be obtained from a normal 52-card deck?

6. Numbers, Arrays, and Functions

With a good foundation of basic BASIC and the concepts of structured design, you have the background to write useful, nontrivial programs. There are some serious limitations to the kinds of problems you can solve with this background, however. In this chapter we will examine some additional features of BASIC that will significantly increase your computing capacity.

FIGURE 6.1 Into advanced topics

6.1 Numbers Revisited

First we reexamine briefly the representation of numbers (that is, numeric constants) in BASIC. Recall that numbers can be written with or without a sign or decimal point. The number of digits allowed in a number varies from computer to computer and is usually from 7 to 10 digits; the system used in this book generates 8 digits. If you provide more than the limit n, depending on the system two things can happen. One is that the number will be **truncated** to n digits. This means that all digits to the right of the nth digit are dropped; if we transmit, for example,

$$\text{LET X} = 12.3456789\text{1}\emptyset$$

and $n = 8$, then X will have the value 12.345678. The second possibility is that the number will be **rounded** to n digits, which means that the n-digit result is as *close as possible* to the original number. This result can be computed by hand by adding 5 to the $(n + 1)$ digit and then truncating the resulting sum to n digits (the X above becomes 12.345679).

Besides the forms described, there is the so-called **exponential form,** in which numbers are sometimes used. To understand why another form is useful, think of very large numbers, like 27,000,000. Such numbers are often encountered in the sciences and engineering, and it is tedious to work with so many zeros. These numbers are more efficiently represented in *scientific notation,* or exponential form.

We write 27,000,000 as 27×10^6, or equivalently, 2.7×10^7, or 0.27×10^8, and so on. The zeros are not really necessary, since they only serve to place the decimal point in the proper position. To convert a decimal number to scientific notation, count the number of decimal places as you move to the left stopping at the spot at which you wish to put the decimal point. Then use the count as the exponent of 10, and drop the unnecessary zeros to the right of the new position of the decimal point. Thus 1,230 could be written 1.23×10^3.

In BASIC, numbers in scientific notation are represented with the letter E in place of 10 and without a multiplication sign. Thus, 27E6 (or 2.7E7) represents 27×10^6 and $-1.23\text{E}2$ represents -123. (Why do we not use $1.23 * 10^{\wedge}2$? See Exercise 1 at the end of this chapter.) Note that the sign of the number is represented in normal fashion.

Similarly, very small numbers can be represented this way:

$$0.000000653 = 6.53\text{E}{-7}$$
$$0.012345 \quad = 1.2345\text{E}{-2}$$
$$-.0004792 \quad = -47.92\text{E}{-5}$$

Note that the negative exponent corresponds to the number of places the decimal point has been moved to the right. Moving the decimal point a certain number of places to the right is equivalent to multiplying by that power of 10. But we don't want to change the magnitude of the number. To cancel this effect, the negative exponent —the equivalent of *dividing* by that power of 10—results in no change.

BASIC will automatically convert numbers to the appropriate form for printing. But the size range of numbers taking the exponential form depends again on the particular system. Note Example 6.1.

EXAMPLE 6.1

Program:

```
 1Ø LET A = 12ØØØØØØ
 2Ø LET B = 12ØØØØØØØØ
 3Ø LET C = .ØØØ456
 4Ø LET D = .ØØØØØØØ456
 5Ø PRINT A,B,C,D
 6Ø LET E = 1234567891Ø
 7Ø LET F = .1234567891Ø
 8Ø LET G = 12345.678910
 9Ø PRINT E,F,G
1ØØ LET H = 12.36E3
11Ø LET I = 797.2E-2
12Ø PRINT H,I
13Ø END
```

Output:

```
12ØØØØØØ          1.2E+Ø9      .ØØØ456        4.56E-Ø8
1.23456789E+1Ø   .123456789   12345.679
1236Ø            7.972
```

Example 6.1 shows that only numbers with more than the limiting number of digits (8 here) on the left or right of the decimal point are converted to exponential form (compare A to B, C to D, and E to F or G).[†] Note the effect of rounding off on E and F. The printing of H and I (last line of output) shows that a number can be printed in ordinary decimal form if it is less than 10^8 and greater than 10^{-5} (on this system).

Finally, note that the *size range* of numeric constants is also system-dependent. Two of the most common ranges are

$$\pm 1.E-39 \text{ to } \pm 1.E38$$

and

$$\pm 1.E-78 \text{ to } \pm 1.E75$$

An attempt to assign values outside the range of a particular system will produce an error message similar to

CONSTANT 1.E95 IS TOO LARGE.

or

CONSTANT 1.E-45 IS TOO SMALL.

The size range of numeric constants can be important. Most fractions cannot be represented in decimal form without some error. This is true whether one is working by hand or with a desk calculator or computer. Thus, on the system used in this book, the most

[†]Some systems can provide more than 8 digits through the specification *"double precision."*

accurate representation of the number 1/3 is .33333333, which is in error by approximately 0.3×10^{-8}. If we compute $3 * (1/3)$ the result is not 1, but .99999999. This error is known as **round-off error,** and you have undoubtedly encountered such errors when you programmed some of the exercises. The situation is actually worse than this; computers work in powers of 2, not 10, and thus even a number like 0.3 will not be represented exactly.

Now such errors may not seem serious to you because of their relatively small size. Certainly they can be irritating. "Why must that blasted computer print out a stupid number like 469.49999 when we *know* the answer should be 469.50?" you may ask. But the errors can be serious. Programs dealing with monetary figures must have precautions against accumulating round-off errors into the cents column. Many scientific problems require large numbers of calculations in which round-off errors can become serious enough to produce completely useless results.

For example, suppose we want to compute

$$y = \frac{100}{1 - x^2}$$

for $x = 0.99900000$. We find that because of round-off error x is computed as 0.99900060, an error in the seventh digit. The true result for y is 50025.012, but the result the computer gives is 50052.555, an error in the *fourth* digit. The error has been magnified a thousandfold. Further computation with this result can produce larger errors.

It is the accumulation of round-off errors, then, that causes problems. Sometimes algorithms must be completely reformulated to avoid these errors successfully. Some errors can be avoided by working in integers as much as possible. For example, use

FOR I = 0 TO 1000 STEP 1

rather than

FOR I = 0 TO 1 STEP .001

The study of round-off errors falls in the domain of *numerical analysis,* which is beyond the scope of this book. The intent here has been simply to make you aware of possible problems.

6.2 Arrays

Often a program must have systematic and convenient access to an entire collection of items at one time. A collection that can be approached this way is referred to as an array.

Definition: An *array* is a collection of variables with the same name.

The variables we have considered so far can represent exactly one value at a given instant. (Recall that a variable name represents an address in the computer's memory unit where the value is stored.) An array name, on the other hand, represents a whole set of addresses, each one capable of storing an item at a given moment.

But how can the individual items in an array be distinguished from one another? To distinguish them requires another aspect besides the array name: the individual items, or *elements,* are referred to by the **subscript,** which can be any valid arithmetic expression that has a nonnegative integral value. Another term for the subscript is *index.* Each element in an array is referred to by (1) *the name of the array,* followed immediately by (2) *the subscript enclosed in parentheses.*

An array can be thought of as a list; the subscript simply refers to the site of the corresponding element relative to the beginning of an array. Thus in the array A, the representation A(1) is the first element, A(3) the third, A(K) the Kth element in the list, and so forth. We note here that arrays can have two or more subscripts (see Section 6.2.3 for further on this).

Examples of valid array elements, which are also called subscripted variables, include:[†]

A(3)	T(S(I + 1))	M(M)
K(I)	Q$(R - 1)	N(9.2)
X(A + B)	B(T * R + 2)	Y(∅)

Note that array names must consist of a single alphabetic character if they are to contain numeric information, and a single alphabetic character followed by a $ for nonnumeric values. Nonintegral subscripts are valid on most systems, but they are necessarily truncated to integers when evaluated (N(9.2), for instance, is effectively N(9)).[‡] Note also the example M(M). Here the subscript M is an ordinary variable, and M(M) is a *subscripted variable,* that is, an element of the array M. Otherwise the two names are unrelated. Although it is possible, as in this instance, to use an array and a nonsubscripted variable with the same name, such use is confusing and therefore not recommended. Incidentally, if all the rules for subscripts bother you, remembering that the subscript represents a position in the list will help you keep these straight.

Finally, it is important to remember that a subscripted variable can be used anywhere an ordinary variable can be used. Like ordinary arithmetic variables, numeric array elements are set initially to zero (on most systems) until they are assigned a value during execution of the program. On many systems, string array elements are initialized to the *null string* (that is, zero characters).

Some invalid subscripted variables are:[§]

B1(5)	(The array name must be a single letter.)
T(-7)	(The subscript is negative.)
A	(The name must have a subscript.)
P2$(A)	(The array name must be a single letter.)
Q * (N + 1)	(If N + 1 is a subscript of the array Q, then * should be omitted.)

Whenever a program must deal with lists of data, arrays should be considered a way of handling them. Study Example 6.2.

[†]Zero is not a valid subscript on some systems.
[‡]Some systems *round* the number to an integer.
[§]There are exceptions to the requirement for a subscript (see Chapter 7, Section 3).

EXAMPLE 6.2

Program:

```
10 REM//////////////////////////////////////////////////////////////
15 REM/ PROGRAM NAME:  INCOME-TAX                                    /
20 REM/ THIS PROGRAM READS A COLLECTION OF NAMES OF PERSONS AND THEIR /
30 REM/ GROSS EARNINGS, AND COMPUTES A TAX OF 20 PERCENT ON THAT      /
40 REM/ AMOUNT IF THE EARNINGS ARE LESS THAN $12,000, AND 25 PERCENT  /
50 REM/ OTHERWISE.                                                    /
60 REM/                       VARIABLES                               /
70 REM/ N$ = ARRAY OF NAMES     E = ARRAY OF EARNINGS                 /
80 REM/ T = TAX FOR EACH PERSON   N = NO. OF RECORDS                  /
90 REM//////////////////////////////////////////////////////////////
95       LET N = 1
100 REM* BEGIN LOOP 100: READ DATA
110         READ N$(N),E(N)
120 REM* ***EXIT FROM READ LOOP IF END OF DATA
130         IF E(N) < 0  THEN 160
140         LET N = N + 1
145                                                     GO TO 100
150 REM* END LOOP 100
160     LET N = N - 1
163     PRINT "NAME","EARNINGS","TAXES"
166     PRINT
170     FOR I = 1 TO N
180         IF E(I) > = 12000                           THEN 200
190                                                     GO TO 230
200 REM*      THEN
210               LET T = .25*E(I)
220                                                     GO TO 250
230 REM*      ELSE
240               LET T = .2*E(I)
250 REM*    END IF 180
260         PRINT N$(I),E(I),T
270       NEXT I
300 DATA "ACRE,T.",37500,"BRIL,C.",12520
310 DATA "MILSAP,P.",9500
320 REM TRAILER FOLLOWS
330 DATA "DUMMY",-1
340 END
```

Output:

NAME	EARNINGS	TAXES
ACRE, T.	37500	9375
BRIL, C.	12520	3130
MILSAP, P.	9500	1900

There are two loops in Example 6.2. The first, lines 100–150, reads the data into the array N$ and E. The names are stored in N$ and the earnings in E. The variable M is used as a counter and as a subscript for the current location in the arrays where the data are stored. The value –1 is used as a trailer. Note that at the end of the loop, N is reduced by one in line 160. (Why?)

At the end of the first loop, the array N$ has the form

N$(1): | ACRE, T. |
N$(2): | BRIL, C. |
N$(3): | MILSAP, P. |
N$(4): | DUMMY |
N$(5): ⎫
    •   ⎬ undefined
    •   ⎭
    •

and N equals 3. The fourth value is simply a trailer, or "dummy" value to terminate the read loop.

The second loop, lines 17Ø-27Ø, computes the taxes and prints the results. The variable I is used as a loop index and subscript, and N is the limit value. Observe that the tax T is not stored in an array; for each person it is printed immediately after it is computed. There is no need to keep all the taxes available for later processing, although we could have done it that way. We could have stored the Ith tax in T(I) and then set up a third loop to do the printing.

This program could have been written without any arrays at all (see problem 27 in the exercises). There was no need in this case to store all the names and earnings before computing the taxes.

What the last point indicates is that arrays provide a programmer with flexibility. You are no longer always forced to write a given program in only one way. With such available choices, you will sometimes have the difficulty of making one, but with some experience, choosing the best approach to use should become easy for you. However, as you will see later, there are also many problems for which arrays are essential.

Arrays provide other important advantages besides flexibility.

1. Since whole collections of data can be stored in the memory simultaneously, the data need not be processed item by item in sequence; the third item, for instance, can be compared with the eighty-first.
2. An array can be processed systematically in a loop, relating the loop index to the array subscript.
3. An entire array can sometimes be processed with a single statement that refers to the array name (see Chapter 7).
4. The Ith (for example, the tenth or fifty-second) item in an array A can be obtained simply by referring to A(I).
5. The size of an array can be changed easily without changing any statements that process the array.

6.2.1 **The DIM Statement** With regard to the size (that is, the number of elements) of an array, you should now be wondering how BASIC determines how many storage locations to allocate. Unless it is instructed to do otherwise, BASIC automatically reserves ten locations for each array used in the program (or eleven, if the Ø subscript is allowed). For the array A, for example, valid items would be (A(Ø)), A(1), A(2), . . . , A(1Ø). Thus, Example

6.2 is implicitly limited to handling up to nine names. If we provided more than that, the program would terminate with an error message to the effect that the subscript is out of range.

To provide for more elements we must include a **DIM** (dimension) statement. The DIM statement should be the first statement in the program following the documentation remarks. The statement consists of the keyword DIM, followed by a list of array names with constant subscripts. These subscripts specify the range of the subscripts that can be used in the program. For example,

100 DIM A(100), K(5), B$(20)

provides space for 100 elements in array A, 5 in K, and 20 in the string array B$.[†] Again, it is not necessary to include K in this list, since it requires less than 10 elements. We recommend doing so anyway for consistency and documentation. More than one DIM statement can be used so long as a given array name appears only once in the DIM lists. For example,

50 DIM A(50), B(25)
60 DIM C(100)

is valid, but

100 DIM A(1), B(60), C(25)
110 DIM B(20)

is not on most systems. Some systems do accept the latter combination, using the last DIM for B.

The need for specifying the amount of array space before the program runs can cause problems. You may not know beforehand how much space you will need because the quantity of data may vary from run to run. All you can do in this case is to dimension your arrays at what you believe will be the maximum required. Familiarity with the data to be used should give you a good idea about the approximate sizes required. For example, if your program works with student scores in high school classes that are typically less than 50 members, it would be pointless for you to set the array sizes at over 100.

Dimensioning arrays too large can create other problems. The amount of memory space available for your program—for the instructions and for the variables and arrays—is limited. The amount of space varies from system to system, from as little as 1,000 locations to more than 20,000, with a typical range perhaps 3,000–5,000. Thus, if you use too many large arrays you will be unable to run your program.

6.2.2 Some Applications The following example illustrates a case where the use of an array is essential.

Professor Thisselsith has given some exams, and for grading purposes he wants to determine the median score. Since he wants to do this for all his classes, he would like a program that would enable him to do this easily, regardless of the sizes of the classes.

[†]On some systems, all strings must be dimensioned. The dimension size is then the number of characters that can be stored in the string.

FIGURE 6.2 Computing statistics on tests for large classes can be tedious.

The *median score* is the one for which the number of scores above it is the same as the number below it. If there is an even number of scores, the median is computed as the average of the two numbers closest (in sequence) to the middle point. For example, given scores 50, 60, 72, and 76, the median is $(60 + 72)/2 = 66$.

We have already seen a special case of this problem when we wrote a program to pick out the middle value of three numbers (Chapter 5). There too it was essential to have all the numbers available for comparison purposes. But we were able to use different variable names for each number. Here this is not possible.

How does one find the median? It would be a simple task if all the numbers were first sorted into ascending or descending order. Therefore, to find the median, we

1. Read all the scores into an array A.
2. Sort the elements of A into ascending order.
3. Compute and print the median.

Each of these steps requires some refinement before we code the program. Following the *modular approach,* we shall refine each of them independently. This will allow us to concentrate on smaller problems instead of on the single large one.

First, to put the scores into an array, we need a loop. We shall use a trailer (a negative "score" will work well here).

I.   Initialize loop index I to 1.

II.   Repeat the following until the score S(I) < Ø:
   A. READ a score into array location S(I).
   B. Set I = I + 1.

III. Set N = I – 1, the total number of scores.

That wasn't difficult, since we have met similar problems before. But how can we sort the elements of an array? Actually there are many different sorting algorithms, and we shall concentrate on a simple and straightforward method, even though it may not be the most efficient.

Let us begin by looking at a simple example:

$$\text{(first) } 81\ 63\ 54\ 100\ 70\ 62 \text{ (last)}$$

To understand how we can sort this list into ascending order on the computer, we first consider how we should do it by hand if we were restricted to comparing just two numbers at a time. Suppose we compare two successive numbers, starting at the beginning. If they are already in sequence, we shall move on to the second and the third; if not, we shall first interchange them and then move on. In either case our sequence of comparisons will be first with second, second with third, third with fourth, and so on.

Applying this approach to the above list, we get

$$63\ \underline{81}\ 54\ 100\ 70\ 62$$
$$63\ \underline{54}\ \underline{81}\ 100\ 70\ 62$$
$$63\ 54\ \underline{81}\ \underline{100}\ 70\ 62$$
$$63\ 54\ 81\ \underline{70}\ \underline{100}\ 62$$
$$63\ 54\ 81\ 70\ \underline{62}\ \underline{100}$$

(Each line here represents the results of comparing two successive underlined numbers with possible interchanges.) We note that some interchanges have taken place but that the list is not sorted, even after the final comparison. Why not?

We observe that our method will tend to move large elements toward their proper positions at the end of the list (in fact, the largest number will always be in the last position). The element moved back (to the left) by an interchange is not examined again, however.

But suppose we apply the procedure again. A second pass through the list yields

$$54\ 63\ 70\ 62\ 81\ 100$$

Another pass yields

$$54\ 63\ 62\ 70\ 81\ 100$$

Finally, the fourth pass results in

$$54\ 62\ 63\ 70\ 81\ 100$$

and this time the list is sorted. But how could a program determine this in general?

Note that another pass through the list produces the same result, but this time there are no interchanges. An effective general way to tell whether a list is sorted is to test whether any interchanges have taken place. If there were none, the list must be in order. (Why?)

This procedure can also be used to arrange a list into descending order—an interchange would take place only if the first element were less than the second.

The test for interchanges can be handled easily by a *switch*. We can set a variable W equal to zero initially. If there is an interchange, we set W to 1 inside the loop used to make comparisons. We test for zero outside this loop; if W isn't zero, we repeat the process with W reset to zero again. When the list is sorted, W will still be zero when we exit from the loop. Thus, our revised outline for the sorting procedure becomes:

IV. Set L = N - 1, the number of comparisons to be made, that is, one less than the number of items in the list.

V. Begin loop:

    A. Set switch W = 0.

    B. For I = 1 to L

        1. If S(I) > S(I + 1)

           then

             a. Interchange S(I) and S(I + 1)

             b. Set W = 1

    C. If W = 0, exit from loop.

Note that we have used I for the loop index again, since we no longer need it for the loop to read the scores.

Before we go on we must consider how to do the interchange.[†] If we simply write

$$\text{LET } S(I) = S(I + 1)$$
$$\text{LET } S(I + 1) = S(I)$$

the original value of S(I) is *destroyed* by the first instruction and the result is *two* copies of S(I + 1)! We need a temporary location to store S(I) before we copy S(I + 1) into S(I). Thus, we further refine this part of our outline to read:

IV. Set L = N - 1, the number of comparisons.

V. Begin loop:

    A. Set switch W = 0

    B. For I = 1 to L

        1. If S(I) > S(I + 1)

           then

             a. Set T = S(I)

             b. Set S(I) = S(I + 1)

             c. Set S(I + 1) = T

             d. Set W = 1

    C. If W = 0, exit from loop.

This scheme is a variation of the so-called *simple exchange sort*.

Now we can consider the third part of this problem, computing the median. Since the median is computed differently according to whether N is even or odd, we first have

[†]Some versions of BASIC have an exchange function that handles this problem.

to determine this. We can use the INT function for this purpose (see problem 1 of the exercises in Chapter 5, and Section 6.3). The INT function returns the integer part of the value supplied to it; for example, if C = 3.7, then INT(C) equals 3. To see whether N is odd or even, then, we divide it by two and retain the integer portion (call it I). If N = 2 * I, then N must be even. Otherwise it is odd. For example,

$$N = 7 \longrightarrow I = INT(N/2) = INT(3.5) = 3 \longrightarrow N = 7 \neq 2 * I = 6$$
$$N = 12 \longrightarrow I = INT(N/2) = INT(6) = 6 \longrightarrow N = 12 = 2 * I$$

If N is odd, we take as the median

$$M = S(I + 1) \qquad (Why?)$$

If N is even, we compute the median using

$$M = (S(I) + S(I + 1))/2 \qquad (Why?)$$

The resulting refinement for this problem is then

VI.   Set I = INT(N/2)

VII.   If N = 2 * I

     then (N is even)
     a. Set M = (S(I) + S(I + 1))/2
     else (N is odd)
     b. Set M = S(I + 1)

VIII. Print M and stop.

After carefully checking each of the three segments alone and then combined, we are now able to put the segments together into a complete program. This program is a good example of the value of modularity. The program logically divided into three sections, and each section was relatively easy to develop compared to the whole problem. The program is shown in Example 6.3.

EXAMPLE 6.3

Program:

```
10 REM/////////////////////////////////////////////////////////////
15 REM/ PROGRAM NAME: MEDIAN                                        /
20 REM/ THIS PROGRAM COMPUTES THE MEDIAN VALUE OF A LIST OF NON-    /
30 REM/ NEGATIVE NUMBERS.  A NEGATIVE TRAILER MUST BE USED.  DATA  /
40 REM/ SHOULD BE SUPPLIED BEFORE RUNNING THE PROGRAM USING DATA    /
50 REM/ STATEMENTS NUMBERED STARTING AT 600.                        /
60 REM/ PROGRAMMER:  TERRY TINKERTOY                                /
70 REM/                    VARIABLES                                /
80 REM/ S = THE ARRAY OF SCORES    N = THE NUMBER OF SCORES         /
90 REM/ W = SWITCH TO DETERMINE WHEN SORT IS COMPLETE               /
100 REM/ L = NO. OF COMPARISONS FOR EACH PASS THROUGH SORT LOOP     /
110 REM/ I = COUNTER FOR LOOPS:  INTEGER PART OF N/2                /
120 REM/ T = TEMPORARY STORAGE FOR INTERCHANGE                      /
130 REM/////////////////////////////////////////////////////////////
200     DIM S(75)
210     LET I = 1
215 REM  READ IN THE SCORES.
220 REM* BEGIN LOOP 220
230       READ S(I)
240 REM* ***EXIT FROM LOOP IF END OF LIST
```

```
250          IF S(I) < Ø    THEN 29Ø
260          LET I = I + 1
270                                                      GO TO 22Ø
280 REM* END LOOP 22Ø
290      LET N = I - 1
3ØØ      LET L = N - 1
3Ø4 REM
3Ø5 REM  SORT THE NUMBERS INTO ASCENDING ORDER
31Ø REM* BEGIN LOOP 31Ø
32Ø      LET W = Ø
33Ø      FOR I = 1 TO L
34Ø          IF S(I) > S(I+1)                            THEN 35Ø
345                                                      GO TO 4ØØ
35Ø REM*          THEN (EXCHANGE)
36Ø                  LET T = S(I)
37Ø                  LET S(I) = S(I+1)
38Ø                  LET S(I+1) = T
39Ø                  LET W = 1
4ØØ REM*          END IF 34Ø
4Ø5          NEXT I
41Ø REM* ***EXIT FROM LOOP IF SORT COMPLETE
42Ø          IF W <> Ø    THEN 31Ø
43Ø REM* END LOOP 31Ø
434 REM
435 REM COMPUTE THE MEDIAN M.
44Ø      LET I = INT(N/2)
45Ø      IF N = 2*I                                      THEN 47Ø
46Ø                                                      GO TO 5ØØ
47Ø REM*    THEN (N IS EVEN)
48Ø          LET M = (S(I) + S(I+1))/2
49Ø                                                      GO TO 52Ø
5ØØ REM*    ELSE (N IS ODD)
51Ø          LET M = S(I+1)
52Ø REM* END IF 45Ø
53Ø      PRINT "THE NUMBER OF VALUES IS ",N
535      PRINT
54Ø      PRINT "AND THE MEDIAN IS        ",M
6ØØ DATA 75,63,69,89,82,57,94,99,76,8Ø,84,53,73,85,7Ø,66,71
6Ø1 DATA 97,47,79,78,79,65,83,8Ø,78,9Ø,72,83,75,82,92,65,86
6Ø3 DATA 56,79,88,84,76,73,85,-1
999 END
```

Output:

```
THE NUMBER OF VALUES IS      41

AND THE MEDIAN IS            78
```

In Example 6.3 it is assumed that the user provided the lines of data before the program was run. Note that the array of scores has been dimensioned at 75 (line 2ØØ). If a user required more than that, only the DIM statement would have to be changed, since variable limits are used elsewhere in the program.

It would have been advisable during the checkout of the program to print out the contents of the array after line 43Ø to be sure that the sorting procedure was working properly. Also, the program should have been tested using both odd- and even-numbered lists, which can easily be checked by hand.

Finally, observe again that an array is absolutely necessary here. Can you think of any other way to find the median?

Our second application for which arrays are essential deals partly with arrays of string variables.

Grungy Department Store would like to automate part of the bookkeeping process so that their 103-year-old clerk, Miss Ivy Piffle, can retire.

Every month the sales employees turn in cards that list the salesperson's name and the amount of a particular sale. Miss Piffle's job is to compute the bonus due each salesperson. The bonus is simply 2 percent of the gross sales per month for all amounts less than $3,000, plus 3 percent on anything between $3,000 and $6,000, plus 4 percent on anything between $6,000 and $9,000, and so on. The bonus goes up by 1 percent for each $3,000 increment in sales. The job is tedious because the cards can be stacked in any order; Miss Piffle must keep running totals for each salesperson.

Once again we shall use the modular method in attacking a problem. Observe that a program to carry out this function requires an array N$ of salespersons' names and an array T of total sales for each person, T(I) corresponding to N$(I). This is because the sales cards—input data for the program—may be stacked in any order; the program cannot completely process all the sales for one person before going on to the next. (Note however that if the sales cards were grouped by salesperson, no arrays would be needed. Why?) We can store the names as data and read them into the name array at the beginning of the program:

I. Read the names into the name array N$.

Next, suppose we examine the first sales card. What should be done with it? We can search the array N$ until we find the name corresponding to the one on the card. Then we can add the amount on the card to that person's running total of sales. We should also print an error message in the event that the person isn't in the array N$; this could easily happen if, for example, the user of the program mistypes the name on the card. We assume here that all the names are unique, although in reality we would have to be more careful; we could use a unique identifier like a social security number. We would also need checks against errors in the amounts recorded.

From this discussion, we can now construct an outline for the second part of the program:

II. Repeat the following until there are no more sales "cards":
    A. Read a sales card: name = P$, amount = A.
    B. Search array N$ until P$ = N$(I), say; if not found, print an error message.
    C. Add A to T(I).

After the totals are computed, we can compute the bonuses. Also, as a security check we add up and print the total of all the totals:

III. For each salesperson:
    A. Compute the bonus.
    B. Accumulate the sum of total sales.
    C. Print the name and corresponding bonus.

IV. Print totals check and stop.

FIGURE 6.3 Many bookkeeping tasks can be automated. (Courtesy of International Business Machines Corporation)

Part I doesn't require much refinement. We note that Grungy doesn't expect ever to have more than 100 salespersons (why do we need this information?). Also, since there is a high turnover in staff, we shall first read the number of salespersons. Finally, we learn that on similar programs the terminal users at Grungy sometimes forget and run the programs without first providing the data. We should therefore include an input question to guard against this.

Part I becomes

I′: Has the user provided the data?

II′: If *yes* to I′:

    then

      A. Read K, the number of salespersons.

      B. For I = 1 to K

          1. Read N$(I)

    else

      C. Print: "Provide data starting at line ____ before run."

      D. Stop.

The refinement of Part II is straightforward:

III′: Begin loop (on sales cards):
   A. Read a sales card: P\$, A
   B. Exit from loop if A < 0 (trailer).
   C. Set X = 1 (switch to show if record found).
   D. For I = 1 to K
       1. If N\$(I) = P\$
          then
          a. Set T(I) = T(I) + A
          b. Set X = –1 (found).
          c. Exit from loop D.
   E. If X > 0,
      then
      1. Print P\$, "NOT FOUND—ERROR IN CARD"

The switch X is used to enable us to terminate the loop more cleanly and efficiently; at the step E following the loop, we need to know whether or not the P\$ was found—if X is positive the name was not found. Can you rewrite this part of the outline without a switch?

We note for part III that the bonus can be computed by

$$B = 0.2 * T(I) + .01 * (T(I) - 3000) + .01 * (T(I) - 2 * 3000) + .01 * (T(I) - 3 * 3000) + \ldots$$

where the number of terms equals the integer part of T(I)/3000. This sum is easily computed in a loop; each parenthetical expression in each term is 3000 less than the corresponding expression in the previous term.

Part III then becomes

IV′: Initialize S = Ø (sum of all the sales for the month).
V′: For I = 1 to K
   A. Set S = S + T(I) (accumulate sum).
   B. Set V = INT(T(I)/3ØØØ) (number of terms).
   C. Set B = .Ø2 * T(I) (first term of bonus sum).
   D. Set R = T(I) – 3ØØØ
   E. For F = 1 to V
      1. Set B = B + .Ø1 * R (accumulate bonus sum).
      2. Set R = R – 3ØØØ
   F. Print N\$(I), T(I), B
VI′: Print S and stop.

After thorough desk checking, we can produce the program shown in Example 6.4 from the outline parts I′–VI′.

EXAMPLE 6.4 ===

```
 10 REM//////////////////////////////////////////////////////////////
 15 REM/ PROGRAM NAME: MOBONS                                          /
 20 REM/ THIS PROGRAM COMPUTES THE MONTHLY BONUS FOR SALES PERSONNEL   /
 30 REM/ OF THE GRUNGY DEPARTMENT STORE USING THE FORUMULA:            /
 40 REM/ B = .02*T + .01*(T - 3000) + .01*(T - 2*3000) + ...           /
 50 REM/ WHERE T IS THE TOTAL SALES/PERSON.  DATA SHOULD BE GIVEN      /
 60 REM/ STARTING AT LINE 1000 IN PAIRS -- NAME FOLLOWED BY AMOUNT OF  /
 70 REM/ SALE.                                                         /
 80 REM/ PROGRAMMER:  DINGLEKLAPPER,M.    11/12/78                     /
 90 REM/                    VARIABLES                                  /
100 REM/ N$ = ARRAY OF NAMES      T = ARRAY OF ACCUMULATED TOTAL SALES /
110 REM/ P$ = CURRENT NAME        A = AMOUNT OF CURRENT SALE           /
120 REM/ K = NUMBER OF SALESPERSONS      B = BONUS                     /
130 REM/ I = LOOP COUNTER: INDEX      J = LOOP COUNTER                 /
140 REM/ X = SWITCH TO INDICATE FOUND OR NOT FOUND                     /
150 REM/ S = SUM OF ALL SALES                                         /
160 REM/ V,R = TEMPORARY QUANTITIES TO COMPUTE BONUS                   /
170 REM//////////////////////////////////////////////////////////////
200     DIM N$(100),T(100)
210     PRINT "HAVE YOU ALREADY PROVIDED THE DATA (YES OR NO)?"
220     INPUT Q$
230     IF Q$ = "YES"                                        THEN 250
240                                                          GO TO 310
250 REM*    THEN (INITIALIZE ARRAY OF SALES PERSONNEL)
260            READ K
270            FOR I = 1 TO K
280               READ N$(I)
290            NEXT I
300                                                          GO TO 340
310 REM*    ELSE
320            PRINT "PROVIDE DATA BETWEEN LINES 1000-4900 BEFORE"
321            PRINT "RUNNING THE PROGRAM."
330            STOP
340 REM* END IF 230
350 REM* BEGIN LOOP 350 -- ACCUMULATE SALES
360         READ P$,A
370 REM* ***EXIT FROM LOOP IF END OF LIST
380         IF A < 0 THEN 570
385 REM   INITIALIZE SWITCH X.
390         LET X = 1
400         FOR I = 1 TO K
410            IF N$(I) = P$                                  THEN 430
420                                                          GO TO 480
430 REM*          THEN (NAME FOUND)
440                  LET T(I) = T(I) + A
450                  LET X = -1
460 REM*      **********EXIT FROM INNER LOOP
470                                                          GO TO 500
480 REM*       END IF 410
490         NEXT I
500         IF X > 0                                          THEN 520
510                                                          GO TO 360
520 REM*       THEN
530               PRINT P$,"NOT FOUND -- ERROR IN CARD"
540 REM*    END IF 500
```

```
550                                                                    GO TO 360
560 REM* END LOOP 350
570      PRINT
571      PRINT "NAME","TOTAL SALES","BONUS"
572      PRINT
574 REM  S IS TOTALS CHECK.
575      LET S = 0
580 REM COMPUTE BONUSES:
585 REM B = .02*T(I) + .01*(T(I)-3000) + .01*(T(I)-2*3000) ...
590      FOR I = 1 TO K
600         LET S = S + T(I)
610         LET V = INT(T(I)/3000)
620         LET B = .02*T(I)
630         LET R = T(I) - 3000
640         FOR J = 1 TO V
650            LET B = B + .01*R
660            LET R = R - 3000
670         NEXT J
680         PRINT N$(I),T(I),B
690      NEXT I
700      PRINT
710      PRINT "THE TOTAL OF ALL SALES IS:",S
740 DATA 5
750 DATA "ARFA, T.","BAILEY, B.","MUMPHUS, Q."
760 DATA "TREESORE, K.","WITTLEDOWN, R."
1000 DATA "TREESORE, K.",429.00,"MUMPHUS, Q.",95.00
1001 DATA "WITTLEDOWN, R.",1950.00,"WITTLEDOWN, R.",4210.00
1002 DATA "ARFA, T.",700.00,"WITTLEDOWN, R.",2300.00
1003 DATA "TREESORE, K.",1100.00,"MUMPHUS, P.",480.95
1004 DATA "WITTLEDOWN, R.",5700.00
4999 REM TRAILER FOLLOWS
5000 DATA "TRAILER",-1
6000 END
```

Output:

```
HAVE YOU ALREADY PROVIDED THE DATA  (YES OR NO)?
?   YES
MUMPHUS, P.      NOT FOUND -- ERROR IN CARD

NAME            TOTAL SALES        BONUS

ARFA, T.        700                14
BAILEY, B.      0                  0
MUMPHUS, Q.     95                 1.9
TREESORE, K.    1529               30.58
WITTLEDOWN, R. 14160               549.6

THE TOTAL OF ALL SALES IS:         16484
```

Only a few comments are necessary here, since the procedures have been explained as we developed the program.

We used only a few names in Example 6.4 to illustrate its performance. Note that the trailer can be provided by the programmer, not the user, so long as the line number is large enough to prevent its being overwritten by the data. Also note that since the array T was not assigned values before line 44Ø, the elements of T were initialized to zero by the system.

The output shows that an error occurred because Mumphus's first initial was typed P, not the correct Q. Also, Bailey has zero totals and bonus since he evidently sold nothing this month.

Since space is limited, the program is not as complete as it should be to be used in a real environment. Such a program should be fail-safe in that a user should not be able to obtain erroneous results without at least being warned by the program. For example, there should be a check to be sure that the number of salespeople entered in line 74Ø is correct. The program might, for example, print out the value and ask the user whether it is correct. The program could have other sophisticated checks on amounts of sales; say a negative or an unusually large value could produce a warning message. Can you think of other improvements?

Looking at the entire program at the completion stage would impress many persons that it is somewhat long and difficult. The top-down, modular design greatly simplified the development. It makes good sense to break up a large, complex problem into several smaller and more tractable ones. But if the last two examples seem very difficult for you, don't be troubled. Your skills will improve with each new program you study, with each new program you write. Remember, the presentation from this chapter on is not quite like reality, since all the silly mistakes, the errors in judgment that normally occur in even the most experienced programmer's work cannot possibly be shown here. We are simply trying to illustrate good programming habits.

6.2.3 **Tables: Two-Dimensional Arrays** The arrays discussed in the previous sections are sometimes called **one-dimensional arrays.** They are, as we have seen, nicely suited for dealing with lists of data items. Such lists, whether they consist of numeric or nonnumeric information, can always be ordered in some fashion.

But what about tabular data? How can arrays be used to handle such data as

1. Addition and multiplication tables
2. Tables of population versus state
3. Calendars—week by day
4. Tax tables—income range versus number of dependents
5. Tables of monthly rainfall by region

Let us consider a specific application. Suppose that a table of monthly rainfall as measured over one year at weather stations in various regions in Chillywilly County comprises our data.

MONTHLY RAINFALL—CHILLYWILLY COUNTY

	J	F	M	A	M	J	J	A	S	O	N	D
Region 1	.2	.1	.5	1.1	1.5	2.1	1.3	1.1	.9	.5	.1	0
Region 2	0	.1	.3	.9	1.2	1.5	1.5	1.2	.7	.4	.2	0
Region 3	0	0	.1	.4	.8	.9	.9	.5	.3	.1	0	0
Region 4	.1	.1	.2	.3	.5	.6	1.0	1.1	.3	.4	.3	.2
Region 5	0	.2	.4	.9	.9	1.3	2.0	1.5	.8	.7	.3	.1

FIGURE 6.4 Computers are widely used for weather prediction. (Courtesy of NASA)

Suppose that the weather bureau wants a computer program that will compute the average rainfall in each region over the whole year. In this case we could write the program without any arrays at all if we are strict about the order in which the data are provided.

But suppose that the weather bureau wants also the average rainfall for each month over the whole county. In this case the data must be presentable for both computations in a systematic way, and consequently it should be stored in an array.

It would be convenient to store the data in five different one-dimensional arrays, one for each region. In this example, it is possible to process the table as a single one-dimensional array, but the program would be messy and hard to follow. The problem with five different arrays is that each array must have a different name. Thus, for each statement processing one of the arrays there must be four more otherwise identical statements to handle the others; that is, to sum the rows, for each region we might have

$$\text{LET S1} = \text{S1} + \text{A(I)}$$
$$\text{LET S2} = \text{S2} + \text{B(I)}$$

where A, B, . . . represent arrays of the row elements. Furthermore, a similar approach for tables with fifty rows and columns, for example, would require fifty different arrays! Clearly this is an impractical approach for all tables except possibly those with only two or three columns.

What is needed is the ability to conveniently refer to all the elements of the table, to be able to process the rows and columns of the table systematically. **Two-dimensional arrays** provide us with this capacity. Just as one-dimensional arrays are used to represent lists, so two-dimensional arrays are appropriate for tables. There are also problems for which three- or higher-dimensional arrays are most suitable. Since most versions of BASIC are restricted to one and two dimensions, we shall confine our discussion to those.

Elements of two-dimensional arrays are represented by subscripted variables with two subscripts. The subscripts are enclosed in parentheses and separated by commas. For example, the elements of the two-dimensional array B are given by[†]

$$B(1,1), B(1,2), B(1,3), \ldots, B(2, 1), B(2,2), \ldots$$

The rules for naming arrays and for subscripts are the same as for one-dimensional arrays. The DIM statement should be used to specify the upper limits for both subscripts. If, for example, we have the following DIM statement in a program[‡]

$$DIM\ A(5, 20), B(10,10), C\$(7,15)$$

then the following are valid array elements:

$$A(3,7) \quad B(10,1) \quad C\$(1,1)$$
$$A(I,3) \quad B(I + J,I) \quad C\$(I,J)$$

so long as $1 \leqslant I \leqslant 5$ for A, $1 \leqslant I + J \leqslant 10$ for B, and $1 \leqslant J \leqslant 15$ for C\$.[§] The following are invalid:

$$A(-3,7) \quad \text{(negative subscript)}$$
$$B(10) \quad \text{(missing subscript)}$$
$$C\$(8,15) \quad \text{(first subscript out of range)}$$

Two-dimensional arrays conveniently represent tables with the first (left) subscript corresponding to the row number and the second (right) to the column number. (For this reason the first subscript is called the *row index* and the second the *column index.*) Thus an element in the fourth row and the twelfth column of the array A would be referred to as A(4,12).

Referring to an entire row and column is quite simple with this arrangement. To print the entire third row of the array A, one element per line, where A is dimensioned at A(5,20), we could write

$$FOR\ I = 1\ TO\ 20$$
$$PRINT\ A(3,I)$$
$$NEXT\ I$$

Note that the row index is fixed and that the column index corresponds to the loop index.

[†] Again, 0 is a valid subscript on many systems; $B(0,0)$, $B(0,5)$, and $B(3,0)$ are valid subscripted variables, for instance.

[‡] Many systems do not accept two-dimensional string arrays.

[§] On some systems the subscripts must evaluate to integers.

To print the fifth column of B (dimensioned at B(10,10)), with two elements per line, we could write

```
FOR I = 1 TO 1Ø STEP 2
    PRINT B(I,5), B(I + 1,5)
NEXT I
```

This time the column index is held constant.

Processing all the elements of an array generally calls for a pair of nested loops—one to increase the row index and one to increase the column index. For example, to print the entire array A, one value per line, we allow both subscripts to vary:

```
FOR I = 1 TO 5
    FOR J = 1 TO 2Ø
        PRINT A(I,J)
    NEXT J
NEXT I
```

Here we are printing the elements of A in row order, that is,

$$A(1,1)$$
$$A(1,2)$$
$$\cdots$$
$$A(1,2Ø)$$
$$A(2,1)$$
$$A(2,2)$$
$$\cdots$$
$$A(5,2Ø)$$

A point to remember is that the subscript defined by the inner loop will always be the quickest to change.

Again, since memory space is limited, you must be especially careful not to dimension such arrays too large, since the number of memory locations used is the product of the subscripts in the DIM statement. The array A above, for example, takes up $5 \times 20 = 100$ locations (if there is no zero subscript) whether they are all used or not.

Returning to the weather bureau's problem, we can see that a two-dimensional array can be used to represent the rainfall table—the row index as the region number, and the column index as the month of the year. The table thus requires a dimension of 5×12 locations. The yearly averages for each region can be obtained by summing over each of the rows individually, and the monthly averages for the county are given by the sums over each column.

The outline of the solution can now be written:

I.   Read the data into the rainfall table R.
II.   For each row of R
      A. Add the entries and divide by 12.
      B. Print the average.
III. For each column of R
      A. Add the entries and divide by 5.
      B. Print the average.

One possible problem with this approach concerns the loop limits 5 and 12. If the weather bureau should change the number of regions or the time periods (say, to weekly), several lines of the program would have to be changed. It would be no more difficult to treat these values as parameters to be read; the program could handle different-size tables with possibly only a change to the DIM statement.

With this in mind, we can now refine the above outline as follows:

I. Read L, the number of regions, and M, the number of time periods.

Read in the tabular data:

II. For I = 1 to L
    A. For J = 1 to M
       1. Read R(I,J)

Compute the average rainfall per region:

III. Print heading.
IV. For I = 1 to L
    A. Set S = 0
    B. For J = 1 to M
       1. Set S = S + R(I,J)
    C. Print S/M, the average rainfall for region I.

Compute the average rainfall per time period:

V.   Print heading.
VI. For J = 1 to M
    A. Set S = 0
    B. For I = 1 to L
       1. Set S = S + R(I,J)
    C. Print S/L, the average rainfall for time period J.
VII. Stop.

Note that an array is not needed for the different sums since they are printed out immediately after they are computed. Also, for both averages S is reset to zero inside the outer loop and outside the inner loop. Otherwise the sums would not be correct. The loop IV.B sums the individual rows of the table and loop VI.B sums the columns.

The program in Example 6.5 is now easily generated from the above outline.

EXAMPLE 6.5

Program:

```
1Ø REM////////////////////////////////////////////////////////////////
15 REM/ PROGRAM NAME:  RAIN                                            /
2Ø REM/ THIS PROGRAM COMPUTES THE AVERAGE RAINFALL PER REGION OVER     /
3Ø REM/ A GIVEN TIME PERIOD,  AND THE AVERAGE RAINFALL PER TIME PERIOD /
4Ø REM/ AVERAGED OVER ALL THE REGIONS.  THE TABLE OF AVERAGES IN EACH  /
5Ø REM/ PERIOD AND REGION MUST BE PROVIDED AS DATA STARTING AT LINE    /
6Ø REM/ 5Ø1 ORDERED BY TIME PERIOD WITHIN REGION, I.E., REG.1--PER.1,  /
7Ø REM/ REG.1--PER.2,...,REG.2--PER.1,REG.2--PER.2, ETC.               /
75 REM/ THE NO. OF ROWS FOLLOWED BY THE NO. OF COLS SHOULD BE ENTERED  /
76 REM/ AS DATA ON LINE 5ØØ.                                          /
8Ø REM/ PROGRAMMER:  HOLLY HONEYDEW, 5/6/78                            /
9Ø REM/                     VARIABLES                                 /
1ØØ REM/ R = TABLE OF RAINFALL DATA                                    /
11Ø REM/ L,M = NO. OF ROWS, COLUMNS OF TABLE, RESPECTIVELY             /
12Ø REM/ S -- USED TO STORE APPROPRIATE SUMS FOR AVERAGES              /
13Ø REM/ I,J = INDICES FOR LOOPS, SUBSCRIPTS                           /
14Ø REM/////////////////////////////////////////////////////////////////
15Ø REM  CHANGE DIM IF NO. REGIONS/PERIODS CHANGE.
2ØØ      DIM R(5,12)
21Ø      READ L,M
215 REM  READ IN THE TABLE
22Ø      FOR I = 1 TO L
23Ø         FOR J = 1 TO M
24Ø            READ R(I,J)
25Ø         NEXT J
26Ø      NEXT I
265 REM COMPUTE THE AVERAGE RAINFALL/REGION
27Ø      PRINT "THE AVERAGE RAINFALL PER REGION"
28Ø      PRINT "REGION #","AVERAGE"
29Ø      FOR I = 1 TO L
3ØØ         LET S = Ø
31Ø         FOR J = 1 TO M
32Ø            LET S = S + R(I,J)
33Ø         NEXT J
34Ø         PRINT I,S/M
35Ø      NEXT I
355 REM COMPUTE THE AVERAGE RAINFALL/TIME PERIOD
36Ø      PRINT
37Ø      PRINT "THE AVERAGE RAINFALL PER TIME PERIOD"
38Ø      PRINT "TIME PERIOD","AVERAGE"
39Ø      FOR J = 1 TO M
4ØØ         LET S = Ø
41Ø         FOR I = 1 TO L
42Ø            LET S = S + R(I,J)
43Ø         NEXT I
44Ø         PRINT J,S/L
45Ø      NEXT J
5ØØ DATA 5,12
5Ø1 DATA .2,.1,.5,1.1,1.5,2.1,1.3,1.1,.9,.5,.1,Ø
5Ø2 DATA Ø,.1,.3,.9,1.2,1.5,1.5,1.2,.7,.4,.2,Ø
5Ø3 DATA Ø,Ø,.1,.4,.8,.9,.9,.5,.3,.1,Ø,Ø
5Ø4 DATA .1,.1,.2,.3,.5,.9,1.4,1.1,.9,.4,.3,.2
5Ø5 DATA Ø,.2,.4,.9,.9,1.3,2.Ø,1.5,.8,.7,.3,.1
999 END
```

Output:

```
THE AVERAGE RAINFALL PER REGION
REGION #      AVERAGE
   1           .78333331
   2           .66666666
   3           .33333332
   4           .53333332
   5           .7583333

THE AVERAGE RAINFALL PER TIME PERIOD
TIME PERIOD      AVERAGE
   1             .Ø6
   2             .1
   3             .3ØØØØØØ9
   4             .71999998
   5             .97999998
   6            1.34
   7            1.42
   8            1.Ø8
   9             .72ØØØØØ9
  1Ø             .42
  11             .18
  12             .Ø6
```

6.3   Functions

Before we explore how functions are handled in BASIC, we should review briefly the mathematical meaning of the term *function.* For us, the following definition will suffice.

Definition: A *function* is a rule that assigns to each element from a given collection a unique value, called the value of the function.

For example, $f(x) = x^2$ defines a function (whose name is f) that assigns to each value x from a collection of numbers the quantity x^2. The rule says, in mathematical shorthand, "Take the value x from the given collection of numbers and square it." Thus, if $x = 3$, then the value of the function is 9, and so forth. The symbol $f(x)$ represents the value of the function when f is applied to $x;$ the symbol x is called the *argument* of f.

A more complex example is

$$g(t) = \begin{cases} t \text{ if } t < 0 \\ t^3 - t + 1 \text{ if } t \geq 0 \end{cases}$$

We have given the name g to this function, which is defined by a composition of two different rules—one that applies if the argument t is negative, the other if t is nonnegative.

Sketching a graph of a function is often helpful in visualizing the relation between a set of values and the corresponding function value. To do so, you will find it convenient to compute a table of values and function values. This can be done conveniently in BASIC. (See Example 4.17 and problems 12 and 13 in the exercises at the end of this chapter.)

Thus far you have been exposed to a few functions that are easily defined by a single statement. The function f is such an example; but what about g? The function g can be defined in BASIC by a segment of code similar to the following:

$$\begin{array}{l} \text{IF } T < \emptyset \\ \quad \text{THEN} \\ \qquad \text{LET } G = T \\ \quad \text{ELSE} \\ \qquad \text{LET } G = T^{\wedge} 3 - T + 1 \\ \text{END IF} \end{array}$$

There are many extremely useful functions that, like g, require multiple lines of BASIC code. Each field of application (engineering, for instance) requires programs that use such functions very heavily.

An example of a valuable function is the **greatest integer function,** which for a number x computes the largest integer that is less than or equal to x. This function was introduced in problem 1 in the exercises of Chapter 5 and again in the discussion of Example 6.3. We saw this function applied in Example 5.8.

To review, if we give this function the name I, then by the above notation, $I(3.7) = 3$, $I(.999) = 0$, and $I(-5.6) = -6$. It is useful, for example, for computing the quotient and remainder in dividing one integer by another and for rounding off numbers to a desired number of decimal places.

To operate as defined above for negative as well as positive arguments, the function can be represented by the program in Example 6.6.

EXAMPLE 6.6

Program:

```
10 REM//////////////////////////////////////////////////////////
20 REM/ PROGRAM NAME: GRINTF                                    /
30 REM/ THIS PROGRAM COMPUTES THE GREATEST INTEGER LESS THAN OR /
40 REM/ EQUAL TO THE INPUT VALUE X.                             /
50 REM//////////////////////////////////////////////////////////
100     PRINT "TYPE A NUMBER"
110     INPUT X
120     IF X > = 0                                    THEN 140
130                                                   GO TO 190
140 REM*    THEN (COUNT NO. OF INTEGRAL VALUES <=X)
150         FOR K = 0 TO X
160            LET I = K
170         NEXT K
180                                                   GO TO 280
190 REM*    ELSE (COUNT NO. OF INTEGRAL VALUES BETWEEN 0 AND X--PLUS 1)
200         FOR K = 0 TO -X
210            LET I = -(K+1)
220         NEXT K
```

```
230              IF X = I + 1                                    THEN 250
240                                                              GO TO 270
250 REM*            THEN (ADD 1 IF X IS NEGATIVE INTEGER)
260                    LET I = I + 1
270 REM*        END IF 230
280 REM* END IF 120
290      PRINT "CORRESPONDING TO THE INPUT VALUE",X
300      PRINT "THE VALUE OF THE FUNCTION IS     ",I
310 END
```

```
Output 1:

TYPE A NUMBER
?    3.7
CORRESPONDING TO THE INPUT VALUE            3.7
THE VALUE OF THE FUNCTION IS                3

Output 2:

TYPE A NUMBER
?    .999
CORRESPONDING TO THE INPUT VALUE            .999
THE VALUE OF THE FUNCTION IS                0

Output 3:

TYPE A NUMBER
?    -5.6
CORRESPONDING TO THE INPUT VALUE            -5.6
THE VALUE OF THE FUNCTION IS                -6
```

In Example 6.6, the loop given by lines 150–170 is executed I(X) times if X is non-negative. The symbol I represents the function value desired. If X is negative, I is assigned the corresponding negative value in the loop 200–220; if X is negative and integral (say X = –8), we must add one to I (line 260).

Example 6.6 is neither a long nor a difficult program, and it would be easy enough to incorporate the code into any program that required this function. However, many programs require the evaluation of a given function at several points. Then it would be extremely inefficient to write the code sequence to evaluate the function each time it is needed. Fortunately BASIC and other programming languages make such frequently used functions available so that the value can be obtained in a single line. Most of these functions actually need more than one instruction for the value to be computed, but the user does not have to provide them. The instructions are actually supplied by the BASIC processor for each *reference* to (use of) the function (the function name and argument) in the program.

These special functions are called, for obvious reasons, built-in functions.

6.3.1   **The Built-In Functions**   The set of built-in functions varies from system to system. We present the more common and important ones in Table 6.1. Also, these are essentially all numeric functions—the function value is numeric. There are two other classes of built-in functions: (1) string functions and (2) matrix functions, both of which are discussed in Chapter 8. Study Table 6.1 carefully.

TABLE 6.1
BUILT-IN
FUNCTIONS

		Examples	
Function	Definition	Use in Statements	Values for Specific Arguments
INT	Greatest integer $\leqslant$ argument	LET Y = INT (X/2) + 1	INT (3.99) = 3 INT (–5.8) = –6
ABS	Absolute value of argument	LET K = ABS (Y – 5)	ABS (3.65) = 3.65 ABS (–23) = 23
SQR	Square root of argument	LET Z = SQR (INT (X + 1))	SQR (16) = 4 SQR (5) = 2.236068
RND[1]	Random number x where $0 \leqslant x < 1$	IF RND < .5 THEN 200	RND = .17635298 (for example)
SGN	Sign (–1, 0, 1) of argument	IF SGN (INT (T)) = 1 THEN 50	SGN (36.5) = 1 SGN (0.0) = 0 SGN (–3) = –1
CLK[†,‡]	Time of day in hours, minutes, seconds	PRINT CLK	CLK = 151020 (for 3:10:20 P.M.)
SIN[§]	Sine of argument	LET T = SIN (P/2)	SIN (3.1416) = –7.3591073E-6
COS[§]	Cosine of argument	LET C1 = 1 – COS(X) * 2	COS (3.1416) = –1
TAN[§]	Tangent of argument	FOR I = 1 TO TAN(P)	TAN (3.1416) = –7.359080E-6
ATN[11]	Arctangent of argument	PRINT ATN (X–22.7)	ATN (1) = .78539814
COT[§]	Cotangent of argument	IF COT (X) < .1 THEN 5	COT (–1) = –.64209264
EXP	Exponential (e raised to a power equal to argument)	LET Y = EXP (–X)/2	EXP (1) = 2.7182818
LOG	Logarithm of argument, base e	PRINT LOG (T^2) – LOG (T)	LOG (10) = 2.3025851
LGT[‡]	Logarithm of argument, base 10	LET A = LGT(X)/LGT(2.71)	LGT (10) = .99999999
MAX[‡]	Maximum of two arguments	LET M = MAX (A,B)/A	MAX (10,5) = 10
MIN[‡]	Minimum of two arguments	PRINT MIN (MAX (X,Y), MIN (Y,Z))	MIN (–3,1) = –3

[†]As shown here, many systems require no argument for this function.
[‡]This function is not available on some systems.
[§]The argument is assumed to be in radians.
[11]The result is in radians.

First, note that the function value corresponding to an argument generally is given by the name of the function followed by the argument enclosed in parentheses (but functions such as CLK are independent of an argument and thus may have no argument at all on some systems).

The argument itself may be a single constant, a variable name, or any arithmetic expression that can be evaluated as a constant that does not violate the restrictions of the function (you cannot, for instance, take the square root of a negative number). The argument, the entire expression in parentheses, is evaluated before the function is applied to it. Thus, in the example for SQR in Table 6.1, if X has the value 8.4, then Z equals 3. The steps are:

1. X + 1 = 9.4
2. INT (9.4) = 9
3. SQR (9) = 3

From this example and from the examples for SGN and MIN, it is clear that the function values themselves can be used as arguments for other functions. In fact, a function value can be used like an ordinary variable on the right-hand side of an arithmetic assignment, in an IF-THEN statement, in a PRINT statement, and in a FOR statement (except as the index). But a function value cannot appear in a READ statement or on the left-hand side of an assignment statement. Remember that the function value is really a reference to the code that BASIC used to generate that value. Thus, it doesn't make sense to use it on the left, or in a READ statement—that would imply an attempt to assign the function two different values at the same time.

Observe the value of SQR(5), the example for SQR. The function SQR and others can compute only approximations to the exact function values, usually to the accuracy of the particular computer (for example, seven or eight digits). Thus, SQR(5) * SQR(5) = 4.9999998 and not 5.

Observe that the trig functions SIN, COS, and the like assume that the argument is in radians. That is, if you intend to apply the SIN function, say, to an argument X that is not in radians, you should instead apply SIN to P * X/180, where P = 3.1416.

Finally, note that most of the functions have exactly one argument, a few have none at all, and two—MAX and MIN—have two arguments. Many functions, particularly in other programming languages, use arrays as arguments. You will encounter some of these when you study the MAT functions (Chapter 8).

6.3.2   **An Application of the INT Function**   The following example demonstrates the INT function. Mr. Smith doesn't trust his bank. He should be getting 6 percent interest, compounded annually. Each year for the past 10 years he has deposited $450.00 on January 2. This is sometimes called an annuity. Mr. Smith would like to have a program to check the bank's figures against his own. Let us write it for him.

The formula to compute the maturity value S on an original investment of P dollars at the end of n years at an interest rate of $100i$ percent is

$$S = P (1 + i)^n$$

FIGURE 6.5 Banks use computers extensively. (Courtesy of International Business Machines Corporation)

Thus the first $450.00 is worth

$$S = \$450.00(1 + .06)^{10} = \$805.88$$

at the end of the 10-year period. But the second $450.00 is worth only

$$S = \$450.00(1 + 0.06)^{9} = \$760.27$$

since it has been invested for only 9 years, and so forth.

The total maturity value, then, at the end of 10 years is simply the sum of each of these terms. Note that all the terms are the same except that the exponent is reduced by 1 for each successive year. This suggests setting up a loop, with the index starting at 1 and increasing by 1 up to 10. Furthermore, since we are troubling ourselves with writing the program, we should make it as general as we can. To do so, we shall make P, i, and n variables dependent on input values from the user (of course, we could make it even more flexible; see problem 6 in the exercises).

From the above analysis of the problem, we can now begin to outline our solution:

I.   Input P, i, and n.
II.   Sum up the values $S(j) = P(1 + i)^{j}$ for $j = 1, 2, \ldots , n$.
III. Print the sum and stop.

We can easily refine this outline as follows:

I.   Input P, I, and N.

II.   Set S = 0.

III. For J = 1 to N

      ⌐→ A. Compute $S = S + P * (1 + I)^{\wedge} J$

IV.   Print S and stop.

We are now almost ready to code the program, but there is one aspect of the above outline we should consider first. Although we have not emphasized efficiency, this is a good example to study in that regard. Note that each time through the loop we compute the quantity $P * (1 + I)$, even though it hasn't changed. There are nine multiplications and additions that are unnecessary and only add to the execution time. The cost of these extra operations is only in terms of microseconds here, but in general such costs can be substantial; think about statements that are unnecessarily executed millions of times in programs that run daily. Just as in structural design, considerations of efficiency at this point will lead to better programming habits later. (The topic efficiency is discussed in greater detail in Chapter 9.)

We can easily move the above-mentioned operations outside the loop in the current example. Our revised outline then becomes

I.   Input P, I, N.

II.   Set S = 0.

III. Set V = 1 + I

IV.   For J = 1 to N

      ⌐→ A. Compute $S = S + V^{\wedge} J$

V.   Set S = P * S

VI.   Print S and stop.

Line V. is possible since P is common to every term in the sum. The resulting BASIC program is that in Example 6.7.

EXAMPLE 6.7

Program:

```
10  REM/////////////////////////////////////////////////////////////////////
15  REM/ PROGRAM NAME: COMPINT                                               /
20  REM/ THIS PROGRAM COMPUTES THE MATURITY VALUE OF AN ANNUAL INVEST-       /
30  REM/ MENT OF A FIXED AMOUNT AT A FIXED RATE OF INTEREST COMPOUNDED       /
40  REM/ ANNUALLY.  INPUT TO THE PROGRAM IS THE NUMBER OF YEARS, PRIN-       /
50  REM/ CIPAL, AND INTEREST RATE.  NOTE: THE INTEREST MUST BE GIVEN AS      /
60  REM/ PERCENTAGE DIVIDED BY 100 (E.G., 5% = .05).                         /
70  REM/ PROGRAMMER: F. FIFOFUM, 10/12/79                                    /
80  REM/              INPUT VARIABLES                                        /
90  REM/ P = PRINCIPAL   I = INTEREST (%/100)                               /
100 REM/ N = NUMBER OF YEARS INVESTED                                        /
110 REM/              OTHER VARIABLES                                        /
120 REM/ S = SUM -- MATURITY VALUE     V = 1+I    J = INDEX FOR LOOP         /
130 REM//////////////////////////////////////////////////////////////////////
200     PRINT "TYPE THE PRINCIPAL,INTEREST(%/100),AND NO. OF YEARS"
210     PRINT "INVESTED, IN THIS ORDER, SEPARATED BY COMMAS."
220     INPUT P,I,N
230     LET S = 0
240     LET V = 1 + I
250     FOR J = 1 TO N
260        LET S = S + V^J
270     NEXT J
280     LET S = P*S
285     PRINT
290     PRINT "THE MATURITY VALUE ON THIS INVESTMENT IS:",S
300     END
```

Output:

```
TYPE THE PRINCIPAL,INTEREST(%/100),AND NO. OF YEARS
INVESTED, IN THIS ORDER,  SEPARATED BY COMMAS.
?   450.00,.06,10
THE MATURITY VALUE ON THIS INVESTMENT IS:      6287.2383
```

Since Mr. Smith is easily confused, the four digits to the right of the decimal point in the output in Example 6.7 bother him. Because the result represents a dollar amount, we should really round off the result to the nearest two decimal places (for example, .256 would become .26 and .794 would be .79). This is where the INT function comes in.

If we multiply the result by 100, we get 628723.83. Adding .5 to that amount, we have 628724.33. If we now apply the INT function to this amount, the result is a *truncation,* or loss of the digits to the right of the decimal point, that is, 628724.[†] Dividing this by 100 gives us the result we want, 6287.24.

Thus, to modify the program to round the result to two decimal places, we simply include the following line:

$$285 \text{ LET } S = \text{INT}(S * 100 + .5)/100.$$

[†]If the INT function rounds, rather than truncates, in your BASIC, don't add the .5 value.

The figure 6287.24 was obtained by carrying all the digits to machine accuracy (eight digits here) through the entire computation and rounding to two decimal places only at the last step. The bank's figure was $6287.18, which was obtained by truncating the maturity value at the end of each year and for each $450 invested. See problem 7 in the exercises.

Consequently, Mr. Smith was right! What is more important, such very small differences can accumulate to substantial amounts when millions of dollars are being invested. Note also that because of BASIC's accuracy limitations, monetary values with more than eight digits (on this system) cannot be handled in BASIC.

The INT function can usually be used for truncation or rounding to any specified number of digits.[†] *To truncate or round off a number N to D digits to the right of the decimal point, use the statement*

$$\text{LET } N = \text{INT}(N * 10^D + R)/10^D$$

where $R = \begin{cases} 0.5 \text{ if rounding is desired} \\ \\ 0 \text{ if truncation is desired} \end{cases}$

For example, if $N = 3.1415926$, $R = 0.5$ and $D = 4$, we obtain

$$\begin{aligned} N &= \text{INT}(3.1415926 * 10^4 + .5)/10^4 \\ &= \text{INT}(31416.426)/10000 \\ &= 3146/10000 \\ &= 3.1416 \end{aligned}$$

Finally, you should note that the same statement can be used to truncate or round a number D digits to the left of the decimal point by taking D to be negative.

6.3.3   **The SQR Function**   This is a very short discussion of the SQR function, principally to answer the question, "Why do we need it at all?" We remark first that the only restriction on the SQR function is that it may not be applied to negative numbers.

Consider Example 6.8.

[†]Again, the computed values must be within the computer's limits of accuracy, and R must be zero if the INT function rounds.

EXAMPLE 6.8

```
Program:

10 LET X = 16.0
20 LET A = SQR(X)
30 LET B = X^.5
40 LET C = X^ (1/2)
50 LET D = X^ 1/2
60 LET E = SQR(SQR(X))
70 PRINT A,B,C,D,E
80 END

Output:

4               4               4               8               2
```

First note that A, B, and C are the same. That is, we can use the exponent 1/2 or its equivalent to compute the square root. Why use SQR? The answer is *speed*. The SQR method is much faster than the routine using the fractional exponent; SQR is designed specifically for square roots, whereas the machine language program generated by the BASIC compiler to handle $X^{.5}$ is general enough to work for any positive fractional exponent (like 1/3 for cubic roots). Thus, you should always use the SQR function when you want square roots (see exercise 5 in this chapter and also problem 14 in Chapter 4).

Line 50 illustrates a common error, forgetting the parentheses for the exponent. Observe that D = 8, not 4 (why?). Finally, the square root of the square root of X (that is, the *fourth* root) is computed in line 60 using SQR.

6.3.4 Applications of the RND Function The RND function computes a *random number* between 0 and 1, excluding 1. Here the term *random* means that any number in this range (that is, any number that can be represented in the computer—seven to ten digits in BASIC) is equally likely to be generated.

How are the numbers generated? In actual practice, the number must be computed by a formula (see problem 20 in the exercises). The formula generally uses a starting value X_0 (often called a *seed*) to generate a "random" value X_1. The next time the RND function is called on, it uses X_1 to generate the next number, X_2, and so forth. Thus a sequence of numbers is generated by successive uses of the RND function in the program.

A typical sequence is the following:

.38770953
.93416906
.78649784
.01478871
.98985752
.36702404

Suppose you run a program for which RND generated the above sequence. If you run the program again you will get exactly the same sequence of random numbers (the exceptions are noted below). This is because the RND function uses the same seed each time to start the sequence. For this reason the numbers are not really random in the sense of statistics (they are often called *pseudorandom* numbers).

Even so, this is a useful property to have. For one thing, it facilitates debugging of a program that uses the RND function. It could be a nuisance dealing with a different sequence each time it is run. Also simulations of outcomes of experiments that use random processes can be duplicated precisely (this does not always happen under real laboratory conditions).

On the other hand, if one needs a more truly random sequence, this will not do. For example, if one wants to require a computer-assisted instruction (CAI) program to select a subset of a collection of questions at random, RND could not be used in this way, since the same set of questions would be chosen every time.

Fortunately, most BASIC systems have the capacity for generating a different set of numbers each time RND is used. If RND has no argument (say it is used as in LET Y = RND), it is likely that either (1) a different set of numbers is always generated or (2) a different set will be generated if the use of the RND function is preceded by the statement RANDOM or RANDOMIZE. The computer can do this since in this case it uses its internal clock (that is, the time of day) to generate a seed. Thus, the sequence is different each time, unless you happen to run the program at precisely the same millisecond on two different days.

Note the two different sequences in the Example 6.9.

EXAMPLE 6.9

```
Program:
1Ø RANDOMIZE
2Ø PRINT RND,RND,RND
3Ø END

Output 1:
.ØØ171295         .35298Ø32         .Ø635ØØ61

Output 2:
.ØØ18954          .92311981         .74941213
```

Also, on some systems RANDOM or RANDOMIZE is not used; the argument itself determines the function value:

1. If $X < 0$ RND(X) generates different sequences each time it is used
2. If $X = 0$ the sequences are the same
3. If $X > 0$ the value of RND(X) is always the same for that value of X.

The RND function produces numbers in the range $0 \leqslant X < 1$. Frequently one needs random numbers over a different range. If we assume here no argument for RND, since

$$\emptyset \leqslant \text{RND} < 1$$

then

$$\emptyset \leqslant 5 * \text{RND} < 5$$

and

$$1\emptyset \leqslant 5 * \text{RND} + 1\emptyset < 15$$

for example. Consequently

$$\textbf{M} \leqslant \textbf{N} * \textbf{RND} + \textbf{M} < \textbf{M} + \textbf{N}$$

in general, where M, N $\geqslant$ 0.

Thus, to generate *random integers* (useful, for example, in selecting a random sample of questions, people, and the like) we apply the INT function to the above expression. If M and N are integers, $N > 0$, $M \geqslant 0$, then

$$\textbf{INT(N} * \textbf{RND} + \textbf{M)}$$

generates a random integer in the range M to (M + N – 1).

Let us consider the following application of the RND function, the so-called birthday paradox. The problem is this: Given a class containing n students, what is the probability that at least two people have the same birthday? It is called a paradox, since the answer defies intuition. For example, if $n \geqslant 23$, the odds are greater than 50 percent, and if $n \geqslant 50$ the odds are greater than 97 percent!

This problem can be solved precisely with probability theory, but it is interesting to simulate the process in BASIC. We want to write a program that will:

1. Allow us to select a class size
2. Assign birthdays at random to each class member
3. Determine whether more than one member has the same birthday

We can then run the program many times to see how often the third situation is true. We then divide this value by the total number of runs to get an estimate of the probability. It would also be interesting to compare the results for different n with the theoretical values. For a large number of runs, these values should be close.

Running the program many times would be tedious, however. We can instead write the program to allow us to select several classes of size n, and then determine the ratio of successes (meaning at least two persons with the same birthday) to the number of classes. This ratio is our experimental probability. Let us assume 28 days in February.

We can now produce the following outline:

I.   Input C, the number of classes.
II.   Input N, the number of students per class.
III. Repeat the following C times:
      A. Using RND, assign a birthday to each class member.
      B. Count the number of birthdays falling on day 1, day 2, . . . , day 365
      C. If there is a day with more than one birthday,
          then
            1. Add 1 to counter X.
IV.   Print the probability X/C and stop.

On inspecting this outline, we see that it is not necessary to assign all the birthdays; we can stop as soon as the number of birthdays on any day is greater than 1. Also, we need more details, such as the initialization of variables, before we code the program in BASIC. And we note that an array is needed to store the counts for each of the 365 possible birthdays.

Our revised outline is therefore

I.   Input C, the number of classes.
II.   Input N, the number of students per class.
III. Set X = 0 (counter for the number of successes).
IV.   Repeat the following C times:
      A. Initialize the array D to zero (the Ith element of D represents the Ith day of the year).
      B. Repeat the following N times:
          1. Set B = INT(365 * RND + 1) (generate a random birthday).
          2. If D(B) > 0,
             then
               a. Add 1 to X.
               b. Exit from this inner loop (B).
             else
               c. Set D(B) = 1

Note that step IV.B.1. determines the integer B, so that $1 \leqslant B \leqslant 365$. Once $D(B) > 1$, we have a success (step IV.B.2.). This version is complete enough, and after careful desk-checking, we code it into BASIC as in Example 6.10.

EXAMPLE 6.10

Program:

```
 10 REM//////////////////////////////////////////////////////////////////
 15 REM/ PROGRAM NAME:  BIRTHDAY                                         /
 20 REM/ THIS PROGRAM SIMULATES OUTCOMES FOR THE BIRTHDAY PARADOX,       /
 30 REM/ USING RANDOM ASSIGNMENT OF BIRTHDAYS.  THE PROGRAM ASSUMES      /
 40 REM/ CLASS SIZES ALL THE SAME SIZE FOR EACH RUN.                     /
 50 REM/ PROGRAMMER:  I. M. HAMPERDUCK           7/7/77                  /
 60 REM/                  INPUT VARIABLES                                /
 70 REM/ C = NO. OF CLASSES    N = NO. OF STUDENTS PER CLASS             /
 80 REM/                  OTHER VARIABLES                                /
 90 REM/ D = ARRAY OF DAYS OF THE YEAR (SUBSCRIPT REPRESENTS THE DAY)    /
100 REM/ B = RANDOM BIRTHDATE (1 <=  B  <= 365)                         /
110 REM/ X = NO. OF SUCCESSES    I,J = COUNTERS FOR LOOPS                /
120 REM//////////////////////////////////////////////////////////////////
200       DIM D(365)
205       RANDOMIZE
210       PRINT "WHAT IS THE NUMBER OF CLASSES YOU WISH TO TRY?"
220       INPUT C
230       PRINT "HOW MANY STUDENTS ARE IN EACH CLASS?"
240       INPUT N
250       FOR I = 1 TO C
255 REM   INITIALIZE ARRAY OF BIRTHDAY COUNTERS TO ZEROS
260          FOR J = 1 TO 365
270             LET D(J) = 0
280          NEXT J
285 REM   GENERATE RANDOM BIRTHDAYS
290          FOR J = 1 TO N
300             LET B = INT(365*RND + 1)
310             IF D(B) > 0                                    THEN 330
320                                                            GO TO 370
330 REM*            THEN (AT LEAST TWO HAVE SAME BIRTHDAY)
340                    LET X = X + 1
350 REM*     ********EXIT FROM LOOP
360                                                            GO TO 410
370 REM*            ELSE (ONLY 1 BIRTHDAY ON DAY B SO FAR)
380                    LET D(B) = 1
390 REM*         END IF 310
400          NEXT J
410       NEXT I
415       PRINT
420       PRINT "THE NO. OF SUCCESSES/NO. OF CLASSES IN THIS CASE IS",X/C
430       END
```

Output:

```
WHAT IS THE NUMBER OF CLASSES YOU WISH TO TRY?
?   20
HOW MANY STUDENTS ARE IN EACH CLASS?
?   25
THE NO. OF SUCCESSES /NO. OF CLASSES IN THIS CASE IS        .55
```

Further runs of Example 6.10 produced the following results:

C (NUMBER OF CLASSES)	N (NUMBER OF STUDENTS)	SUCCESS RATIO
20	25	0.4
20	25	0.3
20	25	0.75
20	25	0.6
40	25	0.58
20	50	1
20	50	0.95
20	50	0.95
20	10	0.15
20	10	0.2
40	10	0.16
40	10	0.12

These results differ from run to run, even for the same values of C and N, but on the average—particularly for large C—they agree fairly well with the theoretical values. Note that if we delete line 2Ø5 from the program, the results will be the same for each run when C and N are unchanged.

6.3.5   An Application in Physics Most of the functions represented by the built-in functions are important in physics, mathematics, and chemistry.

Fred D. Gauss has a problem to solve for his physics homework. He is supposed to tabulate a complex function and construct a graph. The tabulation part is quite tedious, even with a hand calculator. Therefore Fred decides to write a BASIC program to do the job.

The function he is to tabulate is given by

$$V = \frac{2aq}{4\pi E_0} \cdot \frac{\cos \theta}{r^2}$$

Fred is only interested in the case in which

$$q = 1.28 \times 10^{-17}$$
$$a = 1.50 \times 10^{-6}$$
$$E = 8.85 \times 10^{-12}$$
$$r = 3.00 \times 10^{-5} \quad \text{(units not shown)}$$

Thus $V = V(\theta)$ is a function of the angle θ. The symbol V represents the electric potential (in volts) at a point P in the field of an electric dipole with charge q. The value P is at a fixed distance r from the midpoint of the dipole. Note to nonscientific readers: Concentrate on the problem of tabulation, not the meaning of the function.

Here Fred is to tabulate V, varying θ from $0°$ to $180°$ in steps of $5°$. The program is reasonably easy to write. The only critical point Fred must remember is that the cosine function COS applies to radians, and so he must convert θ to radians by multiplying by $\pi/180$.

FIGURE 6.6 Many physics problems could not be solved without computers. (Courtesy of Tektronix, Inc.)

We omit the outline of the program, which is straightforward. The program is shown in Example 6.11.

EXAMPLE 6.11 ═══

Program:

```
10 REM/////////////////////////////////////////////////////////////////////
15 REM/ PROGRAM NAME:  DIPOLE                                               /
20 REM/ THIS PROGRAM PRINTS A TABLE OF THE ELECTRIC POTENTIAL AT A          /
30 REM/ POINT THAT IS AT A FIXED DISTANCE R FROM THE MIDPOINT OF THE        /
40 REM/ DIPOLE, FOR ANGLES VARYING FROM Ø TO 18Ø DEGREES.                   /
50 REM/ PROGRAMMER:  FRED D. GAUSS                                          /
60 REM/                     VARIABLES                                       /
70 REM/  T = THE ANGLE     V = POTENTIAL       K = 2*A*Q/(4*PI*E)           /
80 REM/  Q = CHARGE    2*A = DISTANCE BETWEEN DIPOLES                       /
90 REM/  E = PERMITTIVITY CONSTANT                                          /
95 REM/////////////////////////////////////////////////////////////////////
```

```
100 PRINT "ANGLE(DEGREES)"," POTENTIAL"
110 READ Q,A,R
115 LET E = 8.85E-12
120 LET P = 3.1416
125 REM USE C TO CONVERT ANGLE TO RADIANS
130 LET C = P/180
140 LET K = 2*A*Q/(4*P*E)
150 LET K = K/R^2
160 FOR T = 0 TO 180 STEP 5
170     LET V = K*COS(C*T)
180     PRINT T,V
190 NEXT T
200 DATA 1.28E-17,1.50E-6,3.00E-5
210 END
```

Output:

ANGLE(DEGREES)	POTENTIAL
0	.00038365
5	.00038229
10	.00037782
15	.00037058
20	.00036051
25	.0003477
30	.00033225
35	.00031427
40	.00029399
45	.00027128
50	.0002466
55	.00022005
...	...
150	-.00033225
155	-.00034771
160	-.00036051
165	-.00037058
170	-.00037782
175	-.00038229
180	-.00038365

It would be reasonably easy to plot the function $V(\theta)$ from the output of Example 6.11. Note that the program reads the constants q, a, and r. Thus, it would be easy to run the program for different values. Also, to treat V as a function of *both* θ and r would not be difficult; in this case a pair of nested loops is required.

Observe how the function is computed. Since A, Q, P, E, and R are constants here, part of the function is computed outside the loop (K in lines 140 and 150). This is more efficient than computing the same value of K over and over again in the loop. The angle is converted to radians by multiplying by C before applying the COS function.

Exercises

1. What is the difference between the following two statements:

$$10 \text{ LET X} = 7.93 * 10^5 \quad \text{and} \quad 10 \text{ LET X} = 7.93E5$$

2. Write the following numbers in exponential form (BASIC):
   - a. 999,999.93   b. $-17{,}000{,}000$
   - c. .0000006329   d. $-.0000036$
   - e. 1   f. 3,100,005

3. Write BASIC statements corresponding to each of the following equations:
   - a. $y = \sin x - 1$
   - b. $z = \sin^2 x + \cos^2 y$
   - c. $y = ae^{-bx} \, |\tan (x + 1)|$
   - d. $x_1 = \dfrac{-b + \sqrt{b^2 - 4ac}}{2a}$
   - e. $a_1 = \dfrac{\sqrt{\log_e (n + b)}}{\tan \sqrt{x}}$
   - f. $b_2 = \tan^{-1} a - \log_e (\sin y) + \log_e \sqrt{|a - y|}$
   - g. $y = \begin{cases} x^2 - 1 & \text{if } x \leqslant 1 \\ |\sin x \cdot \cos x| & \text{if } x > 1 \end{cases}$

4. Write segments of BASIC programs to
   - a. Add the odd-numbered elements of the one-dimensional array A that has N elements altogether.
   - b. Add the elements in the Kth and Jth columns of the two-dimensional array P, where P is dimensioned as P(15, 50).
   - c. Compute the product of the elements on the main diagonal of the two-dimensioned array B (B has 10 rows and columns), that is, B(1,1) * B(2,2) * B(3,3) * . . . .
   - d. Compute the product of elements of the array B in c above on the diagonal that runs from lower left to upper right, that is, B(1Ø,1) * B(9,2) * . . . .
   - e. Add all the elements of the array C, which is dimensioned as C(20, 20).

5. If your BASIC system does not print the execution time for a program, use the CLK function or something equivalent to it to determine the amount of computer time necessary to compute SQR(3) a thousand times. Do the same for $3^{\wedge}.5$. Is there a time difference?

6. Modify Example 6.7 so that it is more flexible. The principal P should be allowed to change from year to year (read the principal for each year into an array). Secondly, the interest rate may be compounded k times a year. In this case, the formula to compute the maturity value S on an original investment of P dollars at the end of n years on an annual interest rate of $100i$ compounded k times per year is

$$S = P \left(1 + \frac{i}{k}\right)^{kn}$$

Make up your own data. The values i and k should be constant for the n-year period.

7. Modify Example 6.7 to truncate to two decimal places the maturity value of Mr. Smith's investment at the end of each year. Compare your output with the output of the bank.

8. A list of data contains n test scores t_i. Write a program that computes the standard deviation of the scores using the formula

$$s = \sqrt{\frac{1}{n} \Sigma (t_i - \bar{t})^2}$$

where $\bar{t}$ is the mean of the scores and

$$\Sigma (t_i - \bar{t})^2 = (t_1 - \bar{t})^2 + (t_2 - \bar{t})^2 + \cdots + (t_n - \bar{t})^2$$

How does this formula differ from the one given in exercise 16 in Chapter 4? Which one is better to use on a computer? Why?

9. Write a program that reads the dimensions of two matrices A and B and computes either the sum A + B or the matrix product A * B, giving the user the option. (A *matrix* is a two-dimensional array.) If A has N rows and L columns and B has L rows and M columns, the product A * B is well defined; and C = A * B, with N rows and M columns, is defined by

$$C(I,J) = \sum_{K=1}^{L} A(I,K)*B(K,J)$$
$$= A(I,1)*B(1,J) + A(I,2)*B(2,J) + \cdots + A(I,L)*B(L,J)$$

10. Write a program to compute the transpose of a matrix. The matrix B is the transpose of A if B(I, J) = A(J, I) for every element of A.

11. Write a program to sort a list of names into inverted alphabetical order; for instance, BASS should appear before ABNER on the list.

12. Write a program that will produce a table of x, $\sin x$, $\sin^2 x$, $\csc x$, $\csc^2 x$ at 51 equally spaced values of x between 0 and 3.141593 radians. Be sure to have column headings for the table.

13. Write a program to tabulate the function

$$y = 5e^{-0.2x} \cos 2\pi x$$

for x between 0 and 2. The spacing between the x values should be entered on INPUT.

14. Write a program that reads a list of test scores and computes and prints out (1) the total number of students with scores in the range 90-100, 80-89, 70-79, . . . , 0-10, and (2) the percentage of scores in each of these ranges.

15. Write a program to read a list of student names and test scores, and then print out the student's name, score, and that score's *deviation* from the mean score.

16. Use the INT function in a program that reads a five-digit integer number and prints that number with the digits in reverse order; for example, 57193 should print as 39175.

17. Write a program that will add two integer numbers, each having up to 50 digits. Read the first number, one digit at a time, into the array A and the second number into the array B. Print the result, five digits per line. For example, if the first number is 527, then it could be represented as

900 DATA 5,2,7

which means that A(1) = 5, A(2) = 2, and A(3) = 7. Each number should be preceded in the data list by its number of digits.

18. An election for alderman was held in Mushville, and the outcome is summarized in the following table:

| | Total Votes | | | |
Candidate	Precinct 1	Precinct 2	Precinct 3	Precinct 4
Abadaba	410	639	540	731
Clunker	15	110	650	75
Plodder	382	457	610	812
Washdup	87	59	17	39

Write a program that will read this data and compute (1) the total number of votes, (2) the total number of votes for each candidate, (3) the percentage of the total for each candidate, and (4) a table giving the percentage vote for each candidate in each precinct.

19. The Tri-State Tollway allows motorists to enter and leave at different points. When you enter, you get a card indicating the entry point; the distance from the entry point to the exit gate determines how much you pay. Suppose the rates to be as given in the following table:

| Exit point | Entry Point | | | | | | | |
	1	2	3	4	5	6	7	8
1	——	.25	.65	1.10	1.45	1.80	2.10	3.00
2	.25	——	.45	.90	1.30	1.65	1.95	2.85
3	.65	.45	——	.50	.85	1.25	1.55	2.45
4	1.10	.90	.50	——	.40	.75	1.10	2.00
5	1.45	1.30	.85	.40	——	.40	.75	1.65
6	1.80	1.65	1.25	.75	.40	——	.35	1.30
7	2.10	1.95	1.55	1.10	.75	.35	——	.95
8	3.00	2.85	2.45	2.00	1.65	1.30	.95	——

The tollway authority would like to have a program to audit the eight toll collectors. Input to the program is, for each toll collector, the total amount of money the collector reports and a number representing the entry point for each motorist passing through that exit gate. The program should print a report showing the amount of money turned in and the amount that should have been turned in. Write the program.

20. The RND function uses a procedure known as a *random number generator* to produce a sequence of pseudorandom numbers. There are many such schemes. One of them computes the sequence $x_0, x_1, x_2, x_3, \ldots$ by the following procedure. Suppose each number x_i to have four digits. Then x_i has eight digits, counting leading and trailing zeros. Obtaining the middle four digits yields the next random number. For example,

$$
\begin{aligned}
x_0 &= .7192 \longrightarrow x_0{}^2 = .51\underline{7248}64 \\
x_1 &= .7248 \longrightarrow x_1{}^2 = .53\underline{5335}04 \\
x_2 &= .5335 \longrightarrow x_1{}^2 = .28\underline{4622}25 \\
x_3 &= .4622 \longrightarrow \text{and so on} \ldots
\end{aligned}
$$

Write a program that accepts a four-digit seed x_0 on INPUT and generates a sequence of random numbers using the above procedure.

21. Write a program to merge two arrays of names, N$ and M$, that are already sorted into alphabetical order. The lengths of the arrays may be different. *Hint:* Create a third array P$, which will contain the merged lists. Do not solve this problem simply by copying N$ and M$ into P$ and then sorting P$. It is easier to write this program, but it is inefficient since N$ and M$ are already sorted.

22. Professor Bea Twinky of the sociology department in Dimwitty University has an idea for a research project, and to conduct a survey, she needs a random sample of the student body. Write a program for her that will allow her easily to generate random samples. Assume that the student records consist of (1) name, (2) sex (M or F), and (3) year in school (1, 2, 3, or 4), which are provided in DATA statements. The program should allow the user to specify on input whether the sample is to be restricted to a given year or sex or both. Make up your own data. The program should print out the names in the sample. Be careful that each name selected appears only once.

23. Write a program that will read two dates in the form month, day, year (for example, 8, 17, 1978 for August 17, 1978) and compute the number of days between them. Ignore leap years. Use an array that contains the number of days in each month.

24. The probabilities in the birthday paradox problem that were computed experimentally in Example 6.9 can be determined precisely with probability theory. The probability that at least two persons from a group of N people have the same birthday is given by

$$
P(N) = 1 - Q(N)
$$

where

$$
Q(N) = \frac{365 \times 364 \times 363 \times \cdots \times (365 - N + 1)}{365^N}
$$

Write a program that will produce a table of probabilities for N = 5 to 90 in steps of 5. You must organize the computation of Q carefully to avoid overflow or underflow.

25. The exchange-sort algorithm introduced in Example 6.3 is compact but inefficient. Another sorting procedure, called the *bubble sort,* is about twice as fast as the exchange

sort on the average. For an array A to be sorted in ascending order, the procedure works this way:

    1. Find the smallest element among the elements A(I), I = 1, 2, . . . , N and put it in A(1).

    2. Find the smallest element among the elements A(I), I = 2, 3, . . . , N and put it in A(2).

    3. Find the smallest element among the elements A(I), I = 3, 4, . . . , N and put it in A(3).

                      ⋮

N – 1. Find the smallest element among the elements A(I), I = N – 1, N and put it in A(N – 1).

Using this description produce an outline of the solution with refinements and write the program.

26. A much more efficient sorting algorithm (see problem 25 of the exercises) is the *binary merge-sort*. For simplicity, we shall assume that our list contains 2^N elements. We show how it works by a simple example. Suppose we want to sort the array A, with eight elements, into ascending order. In the first step, A(1) and A(2) are compared, the smaller value (15) being copied first into the array B, followed by the larger element. Similarly for A(3) and A(4), A(5) and A(6), and so forth. The array B now contains four sublists, each of which is in ascending order. In step 2, the first sublist (B(1) and B(2)) is *merged* with the second sublist (B(3) and B(4)) into A to form a sorted sublist of four elements. The procedure is similar for the last half of B. The final step produces the sorted list in B.

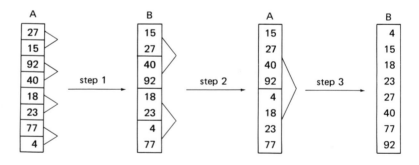

This procedure is easily extended to any list of length 2^N; note that the number of merging steps is N (for example, $2^3 = 8$). The procedure can be made more efficient by using a two-dimensional array with two columns, each column replacing A and B. Write a program to sort by merging.

27. Modify Example 6.2 so that it produces the same results without arrays.

7. Additional Features of BASIC

Several features discussed in this chapter are not included in some versions of BASIC. If your BASIC system does not have these features, omitting the corresponding sections should not create any difficulties with the rest of the text.

FIGURE 7.1   Extras

7.1   Case Structures

Another fundamental structure, the **case structure**, can be included with the simple sequence, loop, and selection structures. Case structures, unlike other structures, are not essential to the construction of a program, but they can provide a more elegant solution to some programming problems.

The case structure is simply a generalization of the IF-THEN-ELSE construction that provides for the selection of one of two procedures based on a test of some criterion. If a problem requires picking one of more than two possibilities, it still can be handled by a combination of IF-THEN-ELSE structures.

But this treatment is awkward (recall Example 5.6, finding the middle value of three numbers). For example, suppose we have a program that requires different computational sequences depending on the range of test scores S: $0 \leqslant S < 60$, $60 \leqslant S < 70$, $70 \leqslant S < 80$, $80 \leqslant S < 90$, and $90 \leqslant S \leqslant 100$. With the IF-THEN-ELSE construction, a program for this would have the form shown in Example 7.1 (brackets emphasize the grouping).

EXAMPLE 7.1

```
Program (form only):
    IF  S  <  6Ø

        THEN
         ┌ *
         │ *  } computation for Ø ≤ S < 6Ø
         │ *
         └

        ELSE
         ┌
         │ IF  S  <  7Ø
         │
         │     THEN
         │      ┌ *
         │      │ *  } computation for 6Ø ≤ S < 7Ø
         │      │ *
         │      └
         │
         │     ELSE
         │      ┌
         │      │ IF  S  <  8Ø
         │      │
         │      │     THEN
         │      │      ┌ *
         │      │      │ *  } computation for 7Ø ≤ S < 8Ø
         │      │      │ *
         │      │      └
         │      │     ELSE
         │      │      ┌ *
         │      │      │ *  } continue as above
         │      │      │ *
         │      │      └
```

A better way is to use a CASE structure which is designed around the **ON–GO TO STATEMENT.** The general format of the ON–GO TO statement is:[†]

$$n \text{ ON } e \text{ GO TO } n_1, n_2, n_3, \ldots$$

where e is any arithmetic expression and n_1, n_2, n_3, ... are line numbers different from line number n. During execution, BASIC evaluates the integer part of e (that is, INT(e))[‡] and then jumps to line n_1 if INT(e) = 1, to line n_2 if INT(e) = 2, to line n_3 if INT(e) = 3, and so on. The number of lines that can be specified is limited by the collection of line numbers that will fit on one line.

For example,

$$5Ø \text{ ON } X + Y \text{ GO TO } 1ØØ, 15Ø, 2ØØ, 15Ø, 3ØØ$$

[†]Some systems use one of the following formats:
n GO TO (n_1, n_2, n_3, ...) e
n GO TO n_1, n_2, n_3, ..., e
n ON e THEN n_1, n_2, n_3, ...
n GO TO e OF n_1, n_2, n_3, ...
[‡]Again, some systems round rather than truncate. The examples in this book assume truncation.

transfers control to line 1ØØ if INT(X + Y) = 1, to line 15Ø if INT(X + Y) = 2 or 4, to line 2ØØ if INT(X + Y) = 3, and to line 3ØØ if INT(X + Y) = 5. Note that the same line number can appear more than once in the list. Although it is also legal to jump back (that is, one of the $n_i < n$), we do not recommend it, since jumping back violates the principles of good structure (except to implement a loop).

Thus, the expression e acts like a generalized switch that can transfer control to one of many alternatives. If the value of INT(e) is less than one or greater than the number of lines in the list, the computer will, depending on the particular BASIC system, either respond with an appropriate error message, such as

ON OUT OF RANGE IN LINE 5Ø

or simply go on to the next line. Thus, INT(X + Y) = 6 in the above example would give rise to such a condition, since there are only five numbers in the list.

The appearance of a line number in the list but nowhere else in the program will definitely cause an error.

Since the ON–GO TO statement restricts the expression e to integer values within the range of the number of lines in the list, you may have to be inventive to use it properly. Consider again Example 7.1. The selection depends on the intervals Ø-59, 6Ø-69, 7Ø-79, 8Ø-89, and 9Ø-1ØØ. The expression to be used in the ON–GO statement might vary from 1 to 5. Dividing S by 10 will result in values from 0 to 10 (that is, for INT(S/1Ø)). Furthermore, we can shift the scores to the range 1 to 11 by adding 1. Since the ranges are not of equal size, we must provide enough values to handle the smallest range; we account for the larger ranges by repeating the line number in the list the appropriate number of times. Then we can implement the above example as shown in Example 7.2.

EXAMPLE 7.2

```
Program (form only):
 80 ON S/10 + 1 GO TO 90, 90, 90, 90, 90, 90, 200, 300, 400, 500, 500

 90    *  ⎫
       *  ⎬   computation for 0 ≤ S < 60
       *  ⎭

200    *  ⎫
       *  ⎬   computation for 60 ≤ S < 70
       *  ⎭

300    *  ⎫
       *  ⎬   computation for 70 ≤ S < 80
       *  ⎭

400    *  ⎫
       *  ⎬   continue as above
       *  ⎭
```

Note that line 500 is given twice to account for the cases $90 \leqslant S < 100$ and $S = 100$. This approach is a much neater solution to the general selection problem. Just as the IF-THEN-ELSE construction is used to provide a well-constructed formulation for a two-case selection, a CASE structure can be easily formulated using the ON–GO TO statement. What is also needed is a clear indication of the beginning of each case. This can be treated as in the accompanying exhibit:[†]

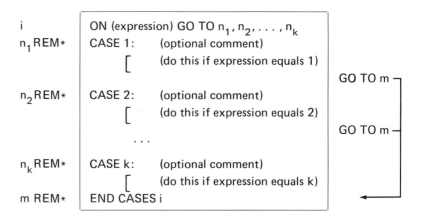

Again, the REM* and GO TO statements are necessary to effect the structure and should be placed as shown so as not to clutter your reading of the program. The arrows and the box are shown simply for emphasis. The CASE remarks may also be indented, if desired. Note that this generalized form assumes that all line numbers n_1, n_2, . . . , n_k are unique; in practice there should be only as many cases as there are unique numbers in the list. Also, each of the GO TO statements after each case jumps to the end of the structure; in this way program control will flow smoothly from top to bottom. Finally, since structures may be nested, each case may consist of another case structure, a sequence of loops, selection structures, and so on.

Using this form, we may now write our example as shown in Example 7.3.

EXAMPLE 7.3 ═══

```
Program (form only):
 5Ø      ON S/1Ø + 1 GO TO 9Ø, 9Ø, 9Ø, 9Ø, 9Ø, 9Ø, 2ØØ, 3ØØ, 4ØØ, 5ØØ, 5ØØ

  9ØREM*    CASE 1:

              [ (computation for Ø ≤ S < 6Ø) ]

 19Ø                                                               GO TO 6ØØ

 2ØØREM*    CASE 2:

              [ (computation for 6Ø ≤ S < 7Ø) ]

 29Ø        ...                                                    GO TO 6ØØ

 5ØØREM*    CASE 5:

              [ (computation for 9Ø ≤ S ≤ 1ØØ) ]

 6ØØREM*    END CASES 8Ø
```

7.1.1   An Application   Let us consider a more concrete example to see how we might use the CASE structure effectively. Mr. Rodney Tufmup, the director of physical education at the Pillpuff Elementary School, has derived a set of formulas to compute what he feels is the minimum time in which boys should be able to run a half-mile. The formulas are used to single out boys who need special training to get them into proper shape.

The formulas vary according to age group and are given by the accompanying table (note that A = age and W = weight).

AGE	FORMULA
5-7	$2AW - A^3 - 100$
8-9	$(18 - A) \sqrt{W} + 150$
10-11	$2W - \sqrt{A^2 + 2A} + 25$
12-14	$3(W^2 - 2W)/(1 + A + A^2) - 75$

The values obtained with each formula are multiplied by a constant whose value is such that the resulting units are in seconds.

Mr. Tufmup would like to have a program that will carry out the computations for him and print a report listing the percentage differences between the minimum times computed by the above formulas and each boy's time. If Mr. Tufmup's theory is correct, negative values will indicate boys who need work, whereas large positive values may pinpoint good track prospects.

We propose the following outline for the problem solution:

I. For each boy in the school:

    A. Read his name N\$, age A, weight W, and time T for his trial run (in seconds).

    B. Compute his minimum time M according to the above formulas.

    C. Compute the percentage difference: $P = 1\emptyset\emptyset(M - T)/M$.

    D. Print name, age, time T, and P, marking * for students with negative P and **for students with $P \geqslant 2\emptyset$.

Parts B and D need some refinement. We note that a case structure will handle part B nicely if we can set up an expression that will enable the program to select the appropriate formula according to the age. Since there are four cases (age groups), we shall need at least four line numbers in one list. We see that the age intervals start at five and range over three years, two years, two years, and three years in that order. Since $5 \leqslant A \leqslant 14$, then $1 \leqslant A - 4 \leqslant 1\emptyset$. The intervals are too irregular to reduce the range further, which means that our list must contain ten line numbers.

To be safe, we should also test for the possibility that $A > 14$, in which case the student will not be evaluated. There are no students less than five years old in the school.

Part D can also be handled using a case structure if we are clever. Depending on P, we must print one of three possible lines:

1. $P < \emptyset$
2. $\emptyset \leqslant P < 2\emptyset$
3. $P \geqslant 2\emptyset$

To use a case structure, we need an expression that will be valued at one, two, or three. Fortunately the SGN function can be used to conveniently compute this value. Recall the $SGN(P) = -1, \emptyset$, or 1 according to whether $P < \emptyset$, $P = \emptyset$, or $P > \emptyset$, and similarly for $SGN(INT(P/2\emptyset))$.

Thus, SGN(INT(P/2Ø)) will be valued at –1, Ø, or 1 for P $<$ Ø, Ø $\leqslant$ P $<$ 2Ø, or P $\geqslant$ 2Ø, respectively. (Try it!) If we add 2 to this expression, its value will fall in the range 1 to 3. This is sufficient for our case structure. Note that the expression (5 + SGN(P) + SGN(P – 2Ø))/2 would give the same result.

Our refinement, based on the above discussion, takes the form:

I. Print heading for report.
II. For each boy in school,
    A. Read N\$, A, W, T (name, age, weight, time).
    B. If A $\leqslant$ 14
        then (valid age)
           1. Select one of the following (using A–4):
              a. If 5 $\leqslant$ A $\leqslant$ 7, set M = 2 * A * W – A$^\wedge$3 – 1ØØ
              b. If 8 $\leqslant$ A $\leqslant$ 9, set M = (18 – A) * SQR(W) + 15Ø
              c. If 1Ø $\leqslant$ A $\leqslant$ 11, set M = 2 * W – SQR(A$^\wedge$2 + 2 * A) + 25
              d. If 12 $\leqslant$ A $\leqslant$ 14, set M = 3 * (W$^\wedge$2 – 2 * W)/(1 + A + A$^\wedge$2) – 75
           2. Let P = 1ØØ * (M – T)/M
           3. Select one of the following (using SGN(INT(P/2Ø)) + 2):
              a. If P $<$ Ø, print N\$, A, T, P, "*"
              b. If Ø $\leqslant$ P $<$ 2Ø, print N\$, A, T, P
              c. If P $\geqslant$ 2Ø, print N\$, A, T, P, "**"
        else
           4. Print N\$, "STUDENT TOO OLD"

We can now code the program directly from this outline. In this example the data were provided before the program was run.

EXAMPLE 7.4

Program:

```
10 REM//////////////////////////////////////////////////////////////////
15 REM/ PROGRAM NAME: PHYED                                             /
20 REM/ THIS PROGRAM PRODUCES A REPORT OF EXCEPTIONAL MALE STUDENTS     /
30 REM/ WITH RESPECT TO PHYSICAL CONDITIONING AT PILLPUFF SCHOOL,       /
40 REM/ ACCORDING TO THE THEORY OF MR. R. TUFMUP.  AGEGROUPS ARE        /
50 REM/ 5-7,8-9,10-11, AND 12-14. STUDENT DATA SHOULD BE PROVIDED       /
60 REM/ IN THE FORM:                                                    /
70 REM/ NAME, AGE, WEIGHT IN POUNDS, TIME FOR TRIAL 1/2 MILE IN SECS.   /
80 REM/ STARTING AT LINE 600.  A TRAILER HAS BEEN PROVIDED.             /
90 REM/ PROGRAMMER:  MR. RING DINGER          12/23/77                  /
100 REM/                         VARIABLES                              /
110 REM/ N$ = STUDENT NAME      M = MARGINAL TIME AS COMPUTED BY FORMULA /
120 REM/ A = AGE IN YEARS       W = WEIGHT IN POUNDS                     /
130 REM/ T = TRIAL TIME IN SECONDS                                      /
140 REM/ P = PERCENTAGE DIFFERENCE BETWEEN T AND M                      /
150 REM//////////////////////////////////////////////////////////////////
190      PRINT "NAME","AGE","TRIAL TIME","% DIFFERENCE"
200 REM* BEGIN LOOP
210         READ N$,A,W,T
220 REM* ***EXIT FROM LOOP IF END OF LIST OF STUDENTS
230         IF N$ = "ZZZZ" THEN 999
240         IF A < = 14                                          THEN 260
250                                                              GO TO 520
260 REM*         THEN (VALID AGE)
270               ON A-4 GO TO 290,290,290,320,320,350,350,380,380,380
280 REM*              CASE 1:  5 < = AGE < = 7
290                     LET M = 2*A*W - A^3 - 100
300                                                              GO TO 390
310 REM*              CASE 2:  8 < = AGE < = 9
320                     LET M = (18-A)*SQR(W) + 150
330                                                              GO TO 390
340 REM*              CASE 3: 10 < = AGE < = 11
350                     LET M = 2*W - SQR(A^2 + 2*A) + 25
360                                                              GO TO 390
370 REM*              CASE 4: 12 < = AGE < = 14
380                     LET M = 3*(W^2-2*W)/(1 + A + A^2) = 75
390 REM*         END CASES 270
395 REM  COMPUTE % DIFFERENCE P
400              LET P = 100*(M - T)/M
410              ON SGN(INT(P/20)) + 2 GO TO 420,450,480
420 REM*              CASE 1:  P < 0
430                     PRINT N$,A,T,P,"*"
440                                                              GO TO 500
450 REM*              CASE 2:  0 < = P < 20
460                     PRINT N$,A,T,P
470                                                              GO TO 500
480 REM*              CASE 3:  P > = 20
490                     PRINT N$,A,T,P,"**"
500 REM*         END CASES 410
510                                                              GO TO 200
520 REM*         ELSE (INVALID AGE)
530                 PRINT N$,"STUDENT TOO OLD"
540 REM*     END IF 240
550                                                              GO TO 200
560 REM* END LOOP 200
600 DATA ANDERSON A.,10,90,201
610 DATA MUDDER D.,5,50,275
620 DATA MOTO K.,16,150,131
```

```
63Ø DATA SMITH A.,14,125,112
64Ø DATA SZENCZYK T.,9,82,26Ø
65Ø DATA WALTON P.,12,11Ø,15Ø
9ØØ DATA ZZZZ,Ø,Ø,Ø
999 END
```

Output:

NAME	AGE	TRIAL TIME	% DIFFERENCE	
ANDERSON A.	1Ø	2Ø1	-3.5839269	*
MUDDER D.	5	275	Ø	
MOTO K.	STUDENT TOO OLD			
SMITH A.	14	112	22.ØØ66	**
SZENCZYK T.	9	26Ø	-12.311761	*
WALTON P.	12	15Ø	1.3199241	

Example 7.4 should require no further explanation. To some readers, determining an appropriate expression for a case structure may seem unreasonably difficult. In problems like those above, however, the alternative is an overly complex set of nested IF-THEN-ELSE selection structures.

7.2 More Input-Output

The PRINT statement, as we have used it thus far, has the advantages of simplicity and convenient features, allowing users to concentrate on the difficult concepts in solving problems without having to think about the intricate details of output production. The automatic five-column format is an example of such features.

On the other hand, our use of the PRINT statement has been extremely limited. Many problems, such as the graphing of functions by computer or the production of complex reports for a business, require expanding it. Many applications programs consist mainly of instructions describing the output of information. Other computer languages such as FORTRAN and COBOL provide extremely flexible (and correspondingly complex) equivalents of the PRINT statement. The same is true for input. Fortunately, BASIC has a few more PRINT features that widen its scope.

7.2.1   The Semicolon   The automatic five-column feature is convenient, but many times it is too restrictive. Often you will need to print more than five values per line. This may be accomplished by using semicolons (;) in place of commas to separate the arguments.

The rules are:

1. If the expressions in the PRINT list are numeric, the output values are separated by two spaces, one of which is used for the sign when the value is negative.
2. If the expressions represent strings, the values are *concatenated*, that is, they are printed as a single string with no spaces between them.
3. If a semicolon separates a string expression from a numeric expression, the output values are separated by a single space.

There may be slight variations in these rules on some systems.

EXAMPLE 7.5

Program:
```
10 REM THIS PROGRAM ILLUSTRATES USING THE SEMICOLON
20 REM IN PRINT STATEMENTS.
30 REM//////////////////////////////////////////////////////////////
50 PRINT 1;-20;300;-4000;50000;-600000
60 PRINT 1;2;3;4;5;6
70 PRINT
80 PRINT 1;2,3,4;5,6
90 PRINT
100 PRINT "ABLE";"WAS";"I";"ERE";"I";"SAW";"ELBA"
110 PRINT "ABLE ";"WAS ";"I ";"ERE ";"I ";"SAW ";"ELBA. "
120 PRINT
130 LET S = 525.12
140 LET S$ = "$"
150 LET T$ = "TOTAL IS   "
160 PRINT T$;S$;S
170 END
```

Output:
```
1 -20   300 -4000   50000 -600000
1  2   3  4   5   6

1  2              3              4  5              6

ABLEWASIEREISAWELBA
ABLE WAS I ERE I SAW ELBA.

TOTAL IS    $ 525.12
```

Lines 50 and 60 of Example 7.5 illustrate how numeric values are printed using semicolons. You may note that one disadvantage of this feature is that values with varying numbers of digits will not be properly aligned in columns (for example, the first two lines of output)—hence, the need for the columns feature or the TAB and PRINT IN IMAGE features (Sections 7.2.2 and 7.2.3).

Line 80 shows that it is possible to mix semicolons and commas in the same list. Each comma has the effect of moving the next variable in the list to the next available column.

Line 100 illustrates the concatenation of strings. Note the effective use of blanks in each of the individual strings to separate the words in line 110.

Lines 130–160 illustrate a more practical example of how this feature can be used to produce more attractive and readable reports. Note the placement of the words TO-TAL IS in the output and the use of blanks in line 150 to separate the words from the amount. Also, observe the placement of the $ sign.

Another useful feature is that a semicolon or comma may appear at the end of the PRINT list. If it does, the next PRINT statement to be executed will continue printing on the same line on which the previous PRINT statement finished rather than on a new line. This can be useful if it is convenient to carry out some computation before the print line is completed (see Section 7.2.2). Example 7.6, which should be self-explanatory, shows how it works.

EXAMPLE 7.6

Program:

```
1Ø REM/ THIS PROGRAM SHOWS HOW THE SEMICOLON AND COMMA
2Ø REM/ FUNCTION AT THE END OF A PRINT LINE.
3Ø REM////////////////////////////////////////////////////////
5Ø PRINT 1,
6Ø PRINT 2
7Ø PRINT
8Ø PRINT "SUPER";
9Ø PRINT "MAN"
1ØØ PRINT
11Ø LET X = 3
12Ø PRINT "FIRST X = ";X;
13Ø LET X = X*X
14Ø PRINT "AND SECOND X = ";X
15Ø END
```

Output:

```
1               2

SUPERMAN

FIRST X = 3 AND SECOND X = 9
```

7.2.2 **The TAB Function** The TAB (tabulate) function operates like the tabular stops on a typewriter. It is used with the PRINT statement to print values in specified positions on the PRINT line. The number of print positions available varies from system to system, but typically the print positions are numbered from 0 through 71, from left to right, giving a total of 72 positions per line.[†]

The general form of the TAB function is

$$TAB(e)$$

where e is any arithmetic expression whose value is nonnegative; the quantity e is evaluated and the integer part of the value determines the print position. Thus, for example,

$$1ØØ \ PRINT \ TAB(32)$$

instructs the computer to skip 32 print positions from the left margin on the current line (Ø to 31); but nothing is printed. To use the function properly, we place the variable or expression whose value we want printed in a given TAB position immediately after the given TAB function and a semicolon. Thus,

$$15Ø \ PRINT \ TAB(15);X$$

will print the value of X starting at print position 15. Generally the TAB function is used with a semicolon; using a comma in the list will automatically space the printer over to the next column.

The TAB function is quite flexible, since its argument may contain variables, and it may appear more than once in a PRINT list. Example 7.7 shows its features.

[†]Depending on the print facilities, some BASIC systems have commands to specify the length of the PRINT line.

EXAMPLE 7.7

Program:

```
10 REM FEATURES OF THE TAB FUNCTION
20 REM/////////////////////////////////////////////////////////
30 PRINT TAB(23);"REPORT"
40 LET N = 20
45 REM (N+1)/2 IS 10.5 HERE
50 PRINT TAB((N+1)/2);"NAME";TAB(35);"WAGE"
55 REM LINES 60-90 PRINT ON 1 LINE
60 PRINT TAB(10);"SMITH, J.";TAB(35);
70 LET H = 40
80 LET R = 3.55
90 PRINT "$";H*R
100 PRINT TAB(82);"ZEE, A. B.";TAB(107);"$";210
110 PRINT
120 PRINT "GRAND TOTAL IS";TAB(5);H*R+210
130 PRINT TAB(21);"END";TAB(10);"REPORT"
140 END
```

Output:

```
                  REPORT

        NAME                WAGE
        SMITH, J.           $ 142
        ZEE, A. B.          $ 210

GRAND TOTAL IS 352

                  ENDREPORT
```

Lines 30 and 50 in Example 7.7 show how the TAB function can be used to set up report headings. "REPORT" is printed starting in column 23. Line 50 prints the string "NAME" starting in position 10. The expression has a value 10.5, but the decimal portion is ignored. Also, note that the TAB function is used twice in line 50. Whenever TAB appears more than once in a PRINT list, it should be in increasing order (left to right) of the values of the arguments; otherwise when the position given by a TAB function has been passed, the TAB function is ignored. Thus, TAB(5) is ignored in line 120 and so is TAB(10) in line 130.

Note carefully lines 60–90. The semicolon at the end of the list in line 60 prevents the PRINT statement from skipping to the next line after printing. The result is that the values computed in the next three statements are printed on the same line by the PRINT statement in line 90.

Although negative values are invalid as arguments for the TAB function (the TAB function is ignored in this case), large positive arguments are valid. If there are 72 print positions, and if $72 \leqslant k < 144$, then TAB(k) = TAB(k – 72) if $144 \leqslant k < 216$, then TAB(k) = TAB(k–2*72), and so forth. In general, the position that is used is equal to the remainder after dividing the argument by 72. We say that TAB(k) is *modulo* 72. Thus, in line 100, TAB(82) is equivalent to TAB(10), and TAB(107) is equivalent to TAB(35), on most systems.

7.2.3 Editing Output: The PRINT IN IMAGE (USING) Statement[†] For many applications, particularly report generation, the TAB function is not sufficient. Much of the information you have seen printed in previous examples has not been under the control of the programmer. For example, numbers (including dollars and cents figures) were printed with varying numbers of digits to the right of the decimal point. Recall that BASIC will not print trailing zeros to the right of the decimal point. Also, the TAB function will align numbers in a column at the left-most digit, for instance,

$$71.263$$
$$-927.1$$
$$61276.51$$

and many reports require the numbers to have their decimal points aligned vertically, others require the numbers in exponential form, and so forth.

Another serious shortcoming occurs in the printing of monetary values, as on a paycheck. With the TAB function, the dollar sign ($) can be printed to the left of the number, but with an embedded blank space, as in

$$\$ \ 500.37.$$

It would be easy in this case for a check forger to insert an extra digit between the $ and the number; consequently, banks prefer that the dollar sign should be placed immediately to the left of the number.

These are only some of the problems that a programmer must deal with in report generation. These tasks are generally referred to as **editing**. Editing is accomplished by means of the PRINT IN IMAGE, or PRINT USING, statement. The format varies from system to system, but perhaps the three most common forms are

1. m PRINT IN IMAGE s: list
2. m PRINT USING s, list
3. m PRINT USING n, list

where m and n are line numbers, s is a string variable, and *list* means the list of variables and expressions to be printed.

The only difference between the first two forms are the phrases IN IMAGE versus USING and the colon versus the comma. We shall use the first form in the examples below. If form 1 or 2 is used, the string s defines the image or format of the line to be printed; s should be defined before execution of the PRINT (line number n in form 3 similarly defines the PRINT image, which must be preceded by a colon). For example, the segment

```
5Ø LET S$ = "PART NO. = %%%%   PRICE = $$$$.$$"

      . . .

28Ø LET P = 398Ø
29Ø LET C = 3.3 * 56.259
3ØØ PRINT IN IMAGE S$: P,C
```

[†]This section is highly system-dependent and can be omitted without loss of continuity. We shall cover some of the details of a specific system; for further details, you should consult the BASIC manual for the system you are using.

would produce the output

PART NO. = 398Ø   PRICE = $185.65

Here the strings of *consecutive* percentage signs or dollar signs represent special editing *fields*. The PRINT IN IMAGE instruction places the values of the variables in the list (P and C here) into the positions temporarily reserved by the percentage signs, one digit for each "%." Once the replacement is made, the image line is printed verbatim. Note that the monetary figure has been rounded to two decimal places.

On most systems, the image string uses six types of editing fields. Study Table 7.1 carefully and apply the rules to Example 7.8, which follows.

**TABLE 7.1
EDITING SYMBOLS**

Type	Editing symbol	Use
Integer numbers	% (# on many systems)	*Example:* %%%% edits 795 as _ 795 (_ represents a blank space). A consecutive string of % symbols represents a single number. There must be at least one % for each digit in the number, plus one more if a sign is present. Extra spaces are filled with blanks, and the number is right-justified in the field. If the field isn't large enough for the number (e.g., 12345 can't fit into %%%%), there is an error. Depending on the system, the number may be truncated, the statement may not be executed, etc.
Decimal numbers	% (# on many systems)	*Example:* %%.%%% edits –5.93 as –5.93Ø. Rules are the same as for integer numbers except that a single decimal point must appear somewhere in the string of % symbols. If the number contains more than the specified number of decimal places, it is rounded (e.g., 6.59 prints as 6.6 if %.% is the editing field). If the number contains less than the number of places, it is zero-filled on the right.

**TABLE 7.1
EDITING SYMBOLS
(continued)**

Type	Editing symbol	Use
Exponential numbers	# (↑ or ! on many systems)	*Example:* #.###### would output –126 as –1.3E+Ø2. The format is the same as for decimal numbers[1] (with % replaced by #) except that there must be at least five # symbols to the right of the decimal point to account for the E, the sign of the exponent, and the two digits of the exponent. With the exceptions of the five rightmost # symbols, the rest of the field is printed according to decimal number rules.
Monetary values	$	*Example:* $$$$%.%% would edit 127.569 as _ $127.57. $ fields consist of a string of $ symbols and/or a single $ followed by integer or decimal fields. The output from the $ (often called the "floating" $) field is similar to the numeric fields (%) except that a character $ will be printed immediately to the left of the numeric data. Although there are exceptions, the $ can usually appear only to the left of the decimal point. The system used in this book is an exception. On some systems there must be at least four consecutive $ symbols, or they will be treated as literal text (see below).
Alphanumeric data	% ('L on many systems)	*Example:* %%% will edit the string ABCD as ABC and the string AB as AB _ . The only restriction is that a decimal point may not appear in the string to be edited. Each character in the string replaces one of the % symbols (on many systems strings are edited by a field of L's preceded

**TABLE 7.1
EDITING SYMBOLS
(continued)**

Type	Editing symbol	Use
		by a single apostrophe ('), rather than %'s). Short strings are always left justified in the field.
Literals	Anything except the above symbols	*Example:* ALPHA123 in the *image string* will print as ALPHA123. All characters in the image string except the editing symbols discussed above are treated as literal text and are printed verbatim.

[1] Many systems use an ordinary decimal number field followed immediately by four ↑ symbols (or four ! symbols).

Some additional points to consider are:

1. Obviously, to use the PRINT IN IMAGE (USING) instruction properly, one must provide enough editing symbols in each field to hold the largest expected value.
2. Different PRINT IN IMAGE (USING) statements can use the same image string.
3. Variation in spacing is accomplished by varying the number of spaces between the image fields.
4. If the PRINT IN IMAGE (USING) statement has *more* variables in the list than fields in the image, the image line is reused, and a second line, third line, and so on, is printed until all the variables in the list are printed.
5. If there are *fewer* variables in the list than fields in the image, the extra fields are ignored.

These features should be kept in mind as you study Example 7.8.

EXAMPLE 7.8

Program:

```
1Ø REM THIS PROGRAM SHOWS THE VARIOUS FEATURES OF THE
15 REM PRINT IN IMAGE STATEMENT.
2Ø REM/////////////////////////////////////////////////////////
5Ø LET A$ = "%%%%%%% $$$$$$.$$ %%%%%%%%%% $$$$.$$"
6Ø LET S = 1526.ØØ
7Ø PRINT IN IMAGE A$: "SAVINGS = ",S,"INTEREST = ",S*.Ø65
8Ø PRINT
9Ø PRINT IN IMAGE A$: -5Ø5,27.6,9273,41.418
1ØØ PRINT
11Ø LET B$ = "%%.% %%%.%%    $$$$.$$    $$$$    #.######   ##.#######"
12Ø LET X = 6
13Ø LET Y = 97.368
14Ø LET Z = 343.6
```

```
15Ø PRINT IN IMAGE B$: X,X,X,X,X,X
16Ø PRINT IN IMAGE B$: Y,Y,Y,Y,Y,Y
165 REM THIS LINE GENERATES AN ERROR MESSAGE SINCE
166 REM Z IS TOO LARGE FOR FIRST EDITING FIELD.
17Ø PRINT IN IMAGE B$: Z,Z,Z,Z,Z,Z
18Ø PRINT
185 REM LINES 19Ø-2ØØ SHOW HOW LITERALS IN THE EDITING STRING ARE PRINTED.
19Ø LET C$ = "LITERAL       %%%%%%%%"
2ØØ PRINT IN IMAGE C$: "ALPHANUMERIC"
21Ø PRINT
215 REM THE NEXT TWO LINES ILLUSTRATE POINTS 4 AND 5 ABOVE.
22Ø PRINT IN IMAGE B$: X,X,X,X,X,X,X,X
23Ø PRINT IN IMAGE B$: Y,Y
24Ø END
```

Output:
```
SAVINGS   $1526.ØØ INTEREST = $99.19

    -5Ø5      $27.6Ø      9273    $41.42

  6.Ø     6.ØØ    $6.ØØ     $6   6.ØE+ØØ   6Ø.ØØE-Ø1
  97.4    97.37   $97.37    $97  9.7E+Ø1   97.37E+ØØ
  OUTPUT VARIABLE EXCEEDED DEFINED LENGTH IN 17Ø -- NOT FATAL
  ****    343.6Ø  $343.6Ø   $344  3.4E+Ø2   34.36E+Ø1

  LITERAL     ALPHANUM

  6.Ø     6.ØØ    $6.ØØ     $6   6.ØE+ØØ   6Ø.ØØE-Ø1
  6.Ø     6.ØØ
  97.4    97.37
```

First, note the correspondence between the four image fields in A$ (line 5Ø) and the expressions in the PRINT list (line 7Ø). Since S is an integer, zeros are filled in to the right of the decimal ($1526.ØØ); this contrasts with an ordinary PRINT. The interest has been rounded to two decimal places because of the image field.

Lines 7Ø and 9Ø both use the same image A$. Note carefully how the same values X, Y, and Z (lines 12Ø-14Ø) are printed using the different image fields of the string B$ (line 11Ø). Since Z=343.6 requires three digits to the left of the decimal point, the first editing field is too small. Thus an error message is produced and the output field is filled with asterisks. Strings that are too long are simply truncated on the right (line 2ØØ).

Line 22Ø contains eight variables in the list, but there are only six fields in the image string B$. Thus the last two values are printed on the next line using the *first two* editing fields. In line 23Ø, the last four editing fields are ignored.

7.2.4   **The RESTORE Statement** We have seen how, by the TAB function and PRINT IN IMAGE (USING) statements, we can customize the output in a BASIC program. Sometimes it is desirable to provide for more flexible input also; COBOL and FORTRAN, for example, can handle richly varied input formats. Because of the limited form in which input data are provided in BASIC, more complex variations of the READ and INPUT statements are not available, except for file processing (see Chapter 8).

There is one feature related to the READ statement that we have not yet considered. Often there is a need to reuse a sequence of data that has been read. Arrays can be provided for this purpose; but if there is a large amount of data, the storage space required for the arrays may exceed the size limitation for a particular system.

Using the RESTORE statement will allow for reusing sequences without the arrays. It allows collection of data to be read and reread any number of times in a program. In BASIC there is a *data pointer*, which keeps track of the next item to be read in a data list during execution of a program. Executing the RESTORE statement simply resets the data pointer to the beginning of the list. The general form is simply

$$n \text{ RESTORE}$$

where n is a line number.[†] Example 7.9 illustrates its use.

EXAMPLE 7.9

Program:

```
10 REM//////////////////////////////////////////////////////////
15 REM/ PROGRAM NAME:  DEVIAT                                    /
20 REM/ THIS PROGRAM DEMONSTRATES HOW THE RESTORE STATEMENT CAN  /
25 REM/ BE USED.  IT COMPUTES THE DEVIATION FROM THE MEAN FOR A  /
30 REM/ LIST OF TEST SCORES.                                     /
35 REM//////////////////////////////////////////////////////////
40 LET S = 0
45 PRINT "WHAT IS THE NUMBER OF SCORES":
46 INPUT K
50 FOR I = 1 TO K
60     READ N
70       LET S = S + N
80 NEXT I
90 LET A = S/K
100 RESTORE
105 PRINT "SCORE","DEVIATION"
110 FOR I = 1 TO K
120     READ N
130       PRINT N,N-A
140 NEXT I
200 DATA 75,90,62,83,97
300 END
```

Output:

```
WHAT IS THE NUMBER OF SCORES?  5
SCORE          DEVIATION
 75            -6.3999996
 90             8.6000004
 62            -19.4
 83             1.6000004
 97            15.6
```

[†]Some versions of BASIC also include the statements

$$n \text{ RESTORE*} \quad \text{and} \quad n \text{ RESTORE\$}$$

The first resets the pointer for numeric data only, and the second for string data only. In this case, RESTORE restores all the data.

Example 7.9 computes the deviation from the mean for a list of test scores. The lines 50-90 compute the mean, line 100 restores the data pointer, and lines 110-140 reread the data and print the difference between the scores and the mean.

7.2.5   **Two Applications**   The mathematics department at Ivy College teaches an introductory course that requires students to plot graphs of functions $y = f(x)$ ($y = x^2 - 1$, for example). Professor Willy Dilly has decided to write a BASIC program that will plot the graphs of functions so that students can check their own results. He also thought that this interesting use of the computer would provide stronger motivation for the students to do their homework.

After some thought Professor Dilly concluded that the program should be easy for students to use; it should tell them how to define the function to be plotted, and it should "ask" (INPUT) for the *range* of the *independent variable x*. He assumed that functions to be plotted can be defined in a single line.

This is not an easy problem, and much thought must go into designing the solution. To begin, Professor Dilly lists some further facts and requirements of the program.

1. He decided it would be easier to print the graph with the independent variable x running from top to bottom rather than from left to right. Then only one point of the graph will be printed per line (why?).

2. Before anything is printed, the program must first determine the maximum and minimum values of y. The difference gives the range of y, which will be divided into equal intervals to cover 55 print positions (instead of 72, since a border is needed—see item 4 below). Thus, each print position will actually represent an interval instead of a single point. This is necessary because of the wide range of possible values here. For example, if minimum $(y) = 0$ and maximum $(y) = 275$, then each print position represents an interval of $(275 - 0)/55 = 5$ values: $0 - 4$, $5 - 9$, $10 - 14$, and so on.

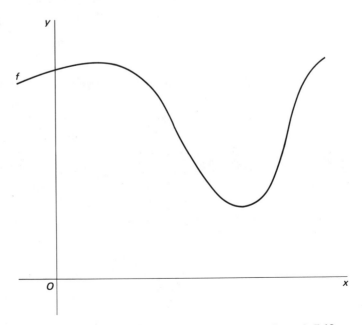

FIGURE 7.2 This graph could easily be reproduced by the program in Example 7.10.

3. The same considerations must be made for x as for y except that the minimum and maximum values of x are given as INPUT and do not have to be determined by the program. We assume here a page size of 50 lines, which determines the interval size.

4. To improve the readability of the graph, a border should be printed at the top and left. The middle value of x for each interval should also label each line; for $15 < x < 20$, for instance, the line should be labeled 17.5. The range of y and the resulting interval size should be printed at the top of the page.

Now Professor Dilly writes down a rough outline of the solution incorporating the above requirements. (In these outlines, Y(X) means the function evaluated at X.)

I. Ask user whether the function to be plotted has been set up.

II. If the answer to I is not "yes,"

    then

    A. Print instructions to the user and stop.

    else

    B. Input min (L) and max (H) values of X.

    C. Compute the min, max values of Y using the function definition.

    D. Compute the interval sizes X1 for X and Y1 for Y(X).

    E. Print the range, interval size for Y.

    F. Print the top border of the graph.

    G. For each interval on the X axis

        1. Compute the midpoint M of each interval.

        2. Print M, a border symbol, and an "*" in the proper print position (representing the function values Y(M)).

The professor, after carefully checking to be sure he had not forgotten something, is ready to refine the outline. He evaluates each step of the outline as a separate module. First, he decides, II.C requires some consideration. How does one find the maximum and minimum of a function with a computer? This problem generally requires extrema techniques of calculus.

Since this can't be done on the computer, he must instead find approximations to the exact values. To do so, he arbitrarily divides the range of X into small steps (he decides that 0.1 is an appropriate stepsize to use); the maximum and minimum are found simply by successively comparing the Y values obtained by evaluating the function at each step in the X range (he could ask the student to input the stepsize since 0.1 may not be a good choice in all circumstances—but for simplicity this is not done).

Part II.C then becomes (since we know how to find the largest value in a list, as given in Example 1.2):

    C.' Set H1 = Y(L) (H1 = the current largest value and L the minimum value of X).

    D.' Set L1 = Y(L) (L1 = the current smallest value).

    E.' For each X from L + 0.1 to H, in steps of 0.1,

        1. If Y(X) < L1

            then

            a. Set L1 = Y(X)

        2. If Y(X) > H1

            then

            a. Set H1 = Y(X)

Note that the max H1 and min L1 values are both initialized to Y(L) before entering the loop.

Part II.D becomes

F'. Set X1 = (H–L)/5Ø, the interval size (or *stepsize*) for X.

G'. Set Y1 = (H1–L1)/55, the interval size for Y.

Steps II.E and F are more or less complete, but II.G needs some work. First, step II.G.1—computing the midpoint of the interval—can be written as

H'. For X = L to H – X1 in steps of X1

    1. Set M = X + X1/2 (the midpoint of the step)

Second, step II.G.2 seems more difficult. How can Professor Dilly write the program to print an asterisk (*) in the "proper position"?

The TAB function is ideally suited for this purpose. Once he has the value Y(X), he only needs to determine the Y interval it belongs to and then to tabulate over that many positions, plus whatever has been reserved for the printing of X values and the axis. Using this idea, Professor Dilly rewrites II.G.2 as:

H'.   2. Set N = INT((Y(M) – L1)/(H1 – L1)*55)

      3. Print M; TAB (14); ":"; TAB (N+15); "*"

Here N determines the print position. It is simply the ratio of the distance of Y(M) from Y's minimum value L1 to the range of Y, multiplied by the total number of print positions. The character ":" is used as the left border, parallel to the X-axis. The value M plus the ":" require 14 characters—hence the addition of 15 to N to properly place the graph. Only 57 positions can be used for the graph; we use 55.

The outline now seems detailed enough, but on restudying it, Professor Dilly has discovered a serious error. There has never been any consideration of how the value Y(X) is obtained. Professor Dilly could require students to enter the expression for the function whenever Y(X) is used in the outline before running the program, but this may be unreasonable, since it would have to be entered at three points: (1) just before C' and D', (2) in the loop E', and (3) in the loop H' before step 2.

Alternatively, the values could be computed in a loop and stored in an array. This would have to be done twice, however, since the X values will most likely differ in loops E' and H'.

The best solution is to allow the programmer to define functions and call up values of such functions as is done with the built-in functions. This would mean that the user would have to supply the function expression at only one line. (This concept is studied in Chapter 9.)

At the moment, we must consider the first solution the best available. Professor Dilly can, however, reduce the number of required function expressions to two by rewriting loop E'. He initializes the min value L1 to +999999 and the max value H_1 –999999, knowing that no function he assigns will have a min or a max outside this range. Thus, these values will be replaced inside the loop. (Why?)

The final version of the outline follows:

I. Print, "Have you entered the function to be plotted?"

II. If the answer is not "yes"

    then

    A. Print instructions and stop.

    else

    B. Input min (L) and max (H) values of X.

    C. Set H1 = -999999, L1 = +999999, the current largest and smallest values of the function, respectively.

    D. For each X from L to H, in steps of .1

        1. Set Y = function value (expression, in terms of X, provided by user).

        2. If Y < L1

            then

            a. Set L1 = Y

        3. If Y > H1

            then

            a. Set H1 = Y

    E. Set X1 = (H-L)/50 (stepsize on X axis).

    F. Set Y1 = (H1-L1)/55 (stepsize on Y axis).

    G. Print range H1-L1, stepsize Y1 for Y.

    H. Print top border of graph.

    I. For M = L to H in steps of X1

        1. Set X = M+X1/2 (midpoints of intervals).

        2. Set Y = function value (expression, in terms of X, provided by user).

        3. Set N=INT((Y(X)-L1)/(H1-L1) * 55)

        4. Print X; TAB(14); " : "; TAB(N+15); "*"

Note that in loop II.I, X and M have changed places and steps 1 and 2 have been switched. Thus, X represents the midpoint of the interval. This is to allow the user to enter the function expression in terms of X in both lines.

The program is given in Example 7.10.

EXAMPLE 7.10

Program:

```
10 REM////////////////////////////////////////////////////////////////
20 REM/THIS PROGRAM IS DESIGNED TO BE USED IN MATH 101 AT IVY COLLEGE. /
30 REM/IT PRODUCES A GRAPH OF A FUNCTION Y=F(X) OVER A RANGE PROVIDED   /
40 REM/BY THE USER.  THE USER MUST ENTER THE FUNCTION IN THE FORM       /
50 REM/          LET Y = (EXPRESSION IN TERMS OF X)                     /
60 REM/AT LINE NUMBERS 330 AND 510 BEFORE RUNNING THE PROGRAM.          /
65 REM/ NOTE: Y VALUES MUST BE IN RANGE: -999999 < Y < 999999.          /
70 REM/    PROGRAMMED BY PROFESSOR WILLY E. DILLY       2/6/78           /
80 REM/    VARIABLES USED:                                              /
90 REM/ X = INDEPENDENT VARIABLE     Y = DEPENDENT VARIABLE             /
100 REM/ L,H = MIN AND MAX VALUES OF X, RESP.                           /
110 REM/ L1,H1 = MIN AND MAX VALUES OF Y, RESP.                         /
120 REM/ X1,Y1 = STEPSIZES ON X,Y AXES, RESP.                           /
```

```
130 REM/ M = STEP NUMBER ON X-AXIS                                                       /
140 REM/ N : USED TO DETERMINE PRINT POSITION FOR POINT ON THE GRAPH.     /
150REM/////////////////////////////////////////////////////////////////////////
200    PRINT "HAVE YOU ENTERED THE FUNCTION TO BE PLOTTED (YES OR NO)?"
210    INPUT A$
220    IF A$ <> "YES"                                          THEN 240
230                                                            GO TO 270
240 REM*    THEN
250            PRINT "ENTER THE FUNCTION DEFINITION IN THE FORM"
252            PRINT "      LET Y = (EXPRESSION AS FUNCTION OF X)"
254            PRINT "IN LINES 330 AND 510; THEN RUN THE PROGRAM AGAIN."
256            PRINT "FOR EXAMPLE:330 LET Y = X ^ 2"
258            PRINT "AND          510 LET Y = X ^ 2"
260            STOP
270 REM*    ELSE
280            PRINT "INPUT MINIMUM AND MAXIMUM VALUES OF X, MIN FIRST,
290            PRINT "SEPARATED BY A COMMA."
295            INPUT L,H
300            LET H1 = -999999
310            LET L1 = 999999
315 REM FIND THE RANGE OF Y.
320            FOR X = L TO H STEP .1
325 REM FUNCTION DEFINED HERE BY USER.
330                LET Y = X ^ 2
340                IF Y < L1                                    THEN 360
350                                                            GO TO 380
360 REM*            THEN
370                    LET L1 = Y
380 REM*        END IF 340
390                IF Y > H1                                    THEN 410
400                                                            GO TO 430
410 REM*            THEN
420                    LET H1 = Y
430 REM*        END IF 390
440            NEXT X
445 REM COMPUTE STEPSIZES ON X,Y AXES.
450            LET X1 = (H - L)/50
460            LET Y1 = (H1 - L1)/55
470            PRINT "Y RANGES FROM";L1;"TO";H1;"IN STEPS OF";Y1
480            PRINT "---------------------------------------------"
485 REM PLOT THE FUNCTION.
490            FOR M = L TO H-X1 STEP X1
500                LET X = M + X1/2
505 REM FUNCTION DEFINED HERE BY USER.
510                LET Y = X^2
520                LET N = INT((Y - L1)/(H1 - L1)*55)
530                PRINT X;TAB(14);":";TAB(N+14);"*"
540            NEXT M
550 REM* END IF 220
560 END
```

Output:

```
(1)
HAVE YOU ENTERED THE FUNCTION TO BE PLOTTED?    NOT YET
ENTER THE FUNCTION DEFINITION IN THE FORM
      LET Y = (EXPRESSION AS FUNCTION OF X)
IN LINES 330 AND 510; THEN RUN THE PROGRAM AGAIN.
FOR EXAMPLE:330 LET Y = X ^ 2
AND          510 LET Y = X ^ 2
```

(User enters:)

330 LET Y = 4*X $^\wedge$ (1/3)-X $^\wedge$ (4/3)
510 LET Y = 4*X $^\wedge$ (1/3)-X $^\wedge$ (4/3)

(2)
HAVE YOU ENTERED THE FUNCTION TO BE PLOTTED?   YES
INPUT MINIMUM AND MAXIMUM VALUES OF X, MIN FIRST,
SEPARATED BY A COMMA.
? 0,4

Y RANGES FROM 0 TO 3.0000001 IN STEPS OF .05454546

```
------------------------------------------------------------
.04           :                                        *
.12           :                                              *
.2            :                                                 *
.28000009     :                                                   *
.36000009     :                                                     *
.44000009     :                                                       *
.52000009     :                                                        *
.60000009     :                                                         *
.67999998     :                                                          *
.75999998     :                                                           *
.83999998     :                                                           *
.91999998     :                                                           *
.99999999     :                                                            *
1.08          :                                                           *
1.16          :                                                           *
1.24          :                                                           *
1.32          :                                                          *
1.4           :                                                          *
1.48          :                                                         *
1.56          :                                                        *
1.64          :                                                        *
1.72          :                                                       *
1.8           :                                                      *
1.88          :                                                    *
1.96          :                                                   *
2.04          :                                                  *
2.12          :                                                 *
2.2           :                                               *
2.28          :                                              *
2.36          :                                             *
2.4399999     :                                           *
2.5199999     :                                          *
2.5999998     :                                        *
2.6799998     :                                       *
2.7599998     :                                      *
2.8399998     :                                     *
2.9199998     :                                   *
2.9999998     :                                  *
3.0799997     :                                *
3.1599997     :                              *
3.2399997     :                             *
3.3199997     :                           *
3.3999997     :                          *
3.4799997     :                        *
3.5599996     :                       *
3.6399996     :                     *
3.7199996     :                   *
3.7999996     :                  *
3.8799996     :                *
3.9599996     : *
```

Note the user's response to the question in the first run. The program was written so that any response except yes will cause the program to print instructions and halt. This program could be further improved to make it fail-safe. It could, for example, check the range of Y to be sure it is valid for this program.

Because of the round-off errors in the calculations, the printed values of X are not quite exact. Also, since the line printer prints in incremented steps rather than in continuous lines, the graph is not ideally smooth.

Lines 33Ø and 51Ø are replaced by the user's function before the program is run.

The second example can be omitted if your system does not have the PRINT IN IMAGE (USING) instruction.

Ittibitty Toy Manufacturing, Inc. (ITM), has three independent divisions, each of which makes purchases and sales. Each division is expected to make a profit. The accounting department produces a monthly report that keeps track of the cash flow for each division. Since the department is computerizing many of their applications, they need a program that will produce this report.

After receiving the assignment, the company's crack programmer-analyst, Henrietta

FIGURE 7.3 Manufacturing companies use computers for a variety of tasks. (Courtesy of International Business Machines Corporation)

Gupp, consulted the accounting department and determined that the necessary input data could be provided in the following form:

1. Vendor-customer name
2. Date paid
3. Amount of check (negative if paid out to vendor)
4. Division code (1, 2, or 3)

The current month and year are also needed. To save time, the amount is typed without the decimal point; for example, 187.25 is typed as 18725.

The department wants the report to look like the following:

```
                    ITTYBITTY TOY MANUFACTURING, INC.
                   CASH FLOW REPORT                NOVEMBER 1977
          VENDOR/CUSTOMER      DATE   DIVISION 1  DIVISION 2  DIVISION 3
          TTW CORP.            11/1   $495.35 DB              $2593.50 DB
          MISS. LIFE INS.      11/4                          $9950.00
          GUMBLES DEPT. STORES 11/25
          J. B. BATES          11/10              $725.95
          FRAMS CORP.          11/11  $150.20 DB
          ABC STORES           11/21  $8550.00
          TTW CORP.            11/15              $1520.00 DB
          TRUCKIT SHOPS        11/28                          $750.27
          PUBLY MANF.          11/19  $27.50
          R. E. WICKER         11/20              $897.50 DB
          TTW CORP.            11/12              $75.50 DB
          SIMPLE SIMON STORES  11/13  $2790.62
          ----------------------------------------------------------------
          TOTALS ARE:                 $10722.57  $-1767.05   $8106.77
          GRAND TOTAL =               $17062.29
```

The abbreviation DB (for debit) is printed if the amount is negative. Henrietta assumes that none of the names is larger than 20 characters and that none of the amounts is greater than $9999.99.

This problem requires very little computation—the initial outline consists mainly of input/output operations:

I.   Read the date (current month and year).
II. Print report headers.
III. Print column headers.
IV. Repeat the following until reaching end of the list:
       A. Read a transaction.
       B. Divide amount by 100 to get true amount.
       C. Print amount in proper column, with "DB" if amount < 0.
       D. Accumulate the three totals.
V.   Print division totals.
VI. Compute and print grand total.

Henrietta decides that steps I to III are detailed enough but that step IV needs refinement. She decides to use a trailer to terminate the loop, testing for a *negative* department number. The READ statement will have the form

READ N$, T$, A, D

where N$ is the name, T$ the date paid, A the amount, and D the division code.

Part IV.B is handled simply by

LET A = A/1ØØ.

Part IV.C, printing the amounts in the proper columns, requires some thought. A case structure will work quite nicely here, one case for each of the three divisions. But how can she take care of printing the "DB"? She could provide six different PRINT IN IMAGE statements to account for the six possible combinations, but that is too messy. An easier way, she decides, is always to print a string Q$, where Q$ = "DB" if the amount is negative, and Q$ = " " (blank) otherwise. She also remembers to drop the sign of A before printing. This is done using the ABS function (actually, this is one detail a programmer might be likely to forget; the error would then be discovered during the testing phase of the program).

Part IV.C expands to:

C'. Set S1$, S2$, S3$ equal to the appropriate image strings for printing the amount for divisions 1, 2, and 3 respectively.

D'. If A < Ø

> *then*
> > 1. Set A1 = ABS (A)
> > 2. Set Q$ = "DB"
>
> *else*
> > 3. Set A1 = A
> > 4. Set Q$ = " "

E'. Select according to D ($1 \leqslant D \leqslant 3$):

> 1. Print in image S1$:N$, T$, A1, Q$
>
> *or*
>
> 2. Print in image S2$:N$, T$, A1, Q$
>
> *or*
>
> 3. Print in image S3$:N$, T$, A1, Q$

Henrietta notes, on examining carefully this segment, that C' should be moved outside the loop IV for better efficiency. Otherwise the strings S1$–S3$, which are not changing, are unnecessarily redefined each time.

For part IV.D of the original outline Henrietta decides that the three division totals can be accumulated using an array V of three elements, one for each total. The division number can be used for the proper subscript:

F'. Set V(D) = V(D) + A

Printing the totals can be handled most effectively with a PRINT IN IMAGE statement:

V'.   Print a line dividing the totals from the rest of the report.

VI'. Set P$ = to an appropriate image string for the three totals.

VII'. Print in image P$:V(1), V(2), V(3)

Computing the grand total is easy. Thus, combining the above refined modules, Henrietta is able to produce the program shown in Example 7.11.

EXAMPLE 7.11

Program:

```
10  REM///////////////////////////////////////////////////////////////////////
15  REM/ PROGRAM NAME: CASHF                                                 /
20  REM/ THIS PROGRAM PRINTS THE CASH FLOW REPORT FOR ITTYBITTY TOY          /
30  REM/ MANUFACTURING, INC.  DATA MUST BE PROVIDED STARTING AT LINE         /
40  REM/ 600 IN THE FOLLOWING ORDER: (1) VENDOR/CUSTOMER.  (2) DATE          /
50  REM/ PAID.  (3) AMOUNT OF CHECK (NEGATIVE IF PAID OUT), WITHOUT THE      /
60  REM/ DECIMAL POINT.  (4) DIVISION CODE.  THE CURRENT MONTH MUST          /
70  REM/ PRECEDE THE REST OF THE DATA.                                       /
80  REM/ PROGRAMMER: HENRIETTA GUPP.   7/7/77                                /
90  REM/                   VARIABLES                                         /
100 REM/ N$ = VENDOR/CUSTOMER NAME       T$ = DATE PAID                      /
110 REM/ D = DIVISION CODE (= 1,2, or 3)                                     /
120 REM/ A = AMOUNT ON INPUT            A1 = TRUE AMOUNT(WITH DECIMAL)       /
130 REM/ V = ARRAY OF TOTALS FOR EACH DIVISION                              /
140 REM/ G = GRAND TOTAL    Q$ INDICATES CREDIT OR DEBIT                     /
150 REM/ S1$,S2$,S3$,P$ = IMAGE STRINGS FOR PRINTING                        /
160 REM///////////////////////////////////////////////////////////////////////
170     DIM V(3)
180     FOR I = 1 TO 3
190        LET V(I) = 0
200     NEXT I
205 REM  DEFINE IMAGE STRINGS
210     LET S1$ = "%%%%%%%%%%%%%%%%%%%% %%%% $$$$$.$$ %%"
220     LET S2$ = "%%%%%%%%%%%%%%%%%%%% %%%%        $$$$.$$ %%"
230 LET S3$ = "%%%%%%%%%%%%%%%%%%%% %%%%                $$$$$.$$ %%"
232     READ T$
233     PRINT TAB(15);"ITTYBITTY TOY MANUFACTURING,INC."
234     PRINT
235     PRINT TAB(19);"CASH FLOW REPORT";TAB(50);T$
236     PRINT
237   PRINT "VENDOR/CUSTOMER      DATE  DIVISION 1   DIVISION 2   DIVISION 3"
240 REM* BEGIN LOOP 240
250        READ N$,T$,A,D
260 REM* ***EXIT FROM LOOP IF END OF DATA
270        IF D < 0 THEN 510
275 REM COMPUTE TRUE AMOUNT
280        LET A = A/100
285 REM SET UP AMOUNT FOR PRINTING
290        IF A < 0                                          THEN 310
300                                                          GO TO 350
310 REM*        THEN
320                LET A1 = ABS(A)
330                LET Q$ = "DB"
340                                                          GO TO 375
```

```
350 REM*        ELSE
360               LET A1 = A
370               LET Q$ = " "
375 REM*      END IF 290
380         ON D GO TO 400,430,460
385 REM SELECT PROPER PRINT COLUMNS.
390 REM*      CASE 1: (DIVISION 1)
400               PRINT IN IMAGE S1$:   N$,T$,A1,Q$
410                                                                     GO TO 470
420 REM*      CASE 2: (DIVISION 2)
430               PRINT IN IMAGE S2$:   N$,T$,A1,Q$
440                                                                     GO TO 470
450 REM*      CASE 3: (DIVISION 3)
460               PRINT IN IMAGE S3$:   N$,T$,A1,Q$
470 REM*      END CASES 380
475 REM COMPUTE DIVISION TOTALS.
480         LET V(D) = V(D) + A
490                                                                     GO TO 240
500 REM* END LOOP 240
510         PRINT "-- -- -- -- -- -- -- -- -- -- -- -- -- -- -- -- -- --"
520   LET P$="%%%%%%%%%%%%%%%%        $$$$$$.$$   $$$$$$.$$   $$$$$$.$$"
530         PRINT IN IMAGE P$: "TOTALS ARE:",V(1),V(2),V(3)
540         PRINT
550         LET G = V(1) + V(2) + V(3)
560         PRINT IN IMAGE P$: "GRAND TOTAL = ",G
600 DATA "NOVEMBER 1977"
610 DATA "TTW CORP.","11/1",-49535,1
620 DATA "MISS. LIFE INS.","11/4",-259350,3
630 DATA "GUMBLES DEPT. STORES","11/25",995000,3
640 DATA "J. B. BATES","11/10",72595,2
650 DATA "FRAMS CORP.","11/11",-15020,1
660 DATA "ABC STORES","11/21",855000,1
670 DATA "TTW CORP.","11/15",-152000,2
680 DATA "TRUCKIT SHOPS","11/28",75027,3
690 DATA "PUBLY MANF.","11/19",2750,1
700 DATA "R. E. WICKER","11/20",-89750,2
710 DATA "TTW CORP.","11/12",-7550.2
720 DATA "SIMPLE SIMON STORES","11/13",279062,1
899 REM TRAILER FOLLOWS
900 DATA "Z","0",0,-1
999 END
```

```
Output:
(See the cash flow report on p. 200.)
```

Note in Example 7.11 first that Henrietta has dimensioned the array V in line 170 and initialized it to zero (lines 180-200). These are not necessary steps here, but they are good programming habits to follow since other programming languages do not perform these tasks automatically.

Also, observe that three different image strings are used in the case structure (lines 380-470). If a string *array* were used, this case structure could be reduced to a *single line.* Also, INPUT IN IMAGE statements could be used to read the data. (See Exercise 7.3.) This is another example of the flexibility you may have in designing a program. It also indicates how one may continue to improve a program even after it has been written.

Finally, note how the negative total was printed in the report.

7.3 The Logical Operators

Many versions of BASIC contain the so-called *logical operators* **AND, OR,** and **NOT,** which enable two or more relational conditions ($<$, $>$, =, and the like) to be combined to form a complex expression in an IF statement. The savings in the number of lines of code and the increased clarity resulting from their use can be significant.

These operators have their normal logical meaning. That is,

A AND B results in a true condition *only if* A and B are both true.
A OR B results in a true condition *only if* A or B (or both) is true.
NOT A results in a true condition *only if* A is false.

BASIC evaluates the expression in an IF statement and transfers control to the line given by the THEN clause only if the expression is true.

Examples of these forms are:

$$100 \text{ IF A} > 0 \text{ AND B} > = 1 \text{ THEN } 500$$
$$200 \text{ IF A} * (I-1) < K \text{ OR Y} > 1000 \text{ THEN } 50$$
$$300 \text{ IF X} > Y \text{ OR } (A < B \text{ AND B} < C) \text{ THEN } 20$$
$$400 \text{ IF NOT A} + B < 12 \text{ THEN } 100$$

In line 100, if *both* A > 0 *and* B ≥ 1, then execution transfers to line 500; otherwise the line immediately following line 100 is executed. The arithmetic operations are always applied first, followed next by the relational operations; the logical operations are applied last. Thus, in line 200, the order of operations would be $-$, $*$, $<$, $>$, OR.

The expression in line 300 has two logical operators. In an expression with more than one logical operator, BASIC applies the NOT operators first, then the AND's, and finally the OR's, left to right, unless they are contained in parentheses. To avoid having to remember this rule, you may enclose the subexpressions you want evaluated first in parentheses, as in this example.

Note that the expression in line 400 is equivalent to

$$A + B > = 12$$

and so the NOT operator is really not necessary.

Look again at Example 5.6, which determined the middle value of three numbers. That program required 40 lines of code, excluding the beginning comments.

Example 7.12 illustrates how using logical operations can reduce the number of nested IF-THEN-ELSE structures. It accomplishes the same result as Example 5.6—finding the middle value of three numbers—with only 17 lines, while improving the clarity and maintaining a structured format.

EXAMPLE 7.12 ==

Program:

```
100       PRINT "TYPE IN THE THREE NUMBERS."
110       INPUT A,B,C
120       IF (B >= A AND A >= C) OR (C >= A AND A >= B)        THEN 140
130                                                            GO TO 170
140 REM*       THEN
150                PRINT "MIDDLE VALUE IS:";A
160                STOP
170 REM* END IF 120
180       IF (A >= B AND B >= C) OR (C >= B AND B >= A)        THEN 200
190                                                            GO TO 230
200 REM*       THEN
210                PRINT "MIDDLE VALUE IS:";B
220                STOP
230 REM*       ELSE
240                PRINT "MIDDLE VALUE IS";C
250 REM* END IF 180
260       END
```

Output:

```
TYPE IN THE THREE NUMBERS.
? 12,1,7
MIDDLE VALUE IS:  7
```

With this approach, there are no nested IF statements at all. Note the use of parentheses to indicate clearly the grouping for the logical operators. Some systems allow only one logical operator in each expression, which means that the above approach would not be possible.

Exercises

1. Use the program in Example 7.10 to plot the *normal distribution function*

$$y(x) = \frac{1}{\sqrt{2\pi}}\, e^{-x^2/2} \qquad \text{for } -3 \leqslant x \leqslant 3$$

2. Use the plotting program of Example 7.10 to plot

$$y(x) = x^3 - x - 1 \qquad \text{for } 0 \leqslant x \leqslant 3$$

and thereby get an estimate of the real root of this function.

3. Rewrite Example 7.11 in such a way that the case structure is omitted. One easy way to do this is to define the image strings using a string array S$ and then to select the appropriate image using the value D, that is, S$(D).

4. Write a program to construct the graph of a function similar to Example 7.10 such that the x-axis runs across the page rather than from top to bottom. (*Hint:* Use a two-dimensional matrix whose elements represent the print positions on the page. Print a digit 1 for each point on the graph and a 0 elsewhere.)

5. Do problem 24 in the exercises of Chapter 5 using a case structure.

6. Do problem 25 in the exercises of Chapter 5 using a case structure.

7. A *scattergram* is a graph of data points based on two variables; the values for one variable run along the horizontal axis and for the other variable along the vertical axis. A scattergram is useful for indicating relations between the two variables, if any. For example, in Figure 7.4 there is a positive linear relation between the variables x and y (the points lie roughly on a straight line), whereas in Figure 7.5 the points seem to be scattered at random, and there is no relation. Write a program that produces a scattergram for a collection of data points. Use an asterisk (*) for each data point.

8. A *histogram* is a graph that displays the relative frequencies of a variable's distribution. The graph is represented in terms of *bars,* the width representing an interval of the variable or a single value (the widths are all the same), and the height representing the frequency. See Figure 7.6. Write a program to produce a histogram, when bars consist of a single line of asterisks. Each bar could represent a single value or an interval of values. (*Hint:* Construct the histogram like the graph in Example 7.10.)

9. Given a data list in which each record consists of (1) an employee name, (2) the employee number, (3) the employee's net pay (as a decimal number), write a program that will read this list and produce a sequence of checks like the one in Figure 7.7. The date, check number, and the name and address of the bank should also be printed. Make up your own data.

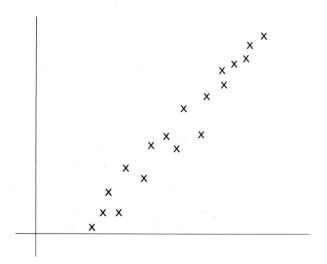

FIGURE 7.4 A linear relation

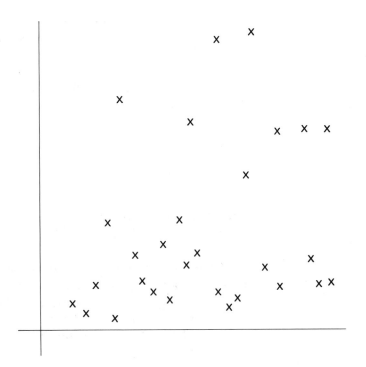

FIGURE 7.5   A random pattern

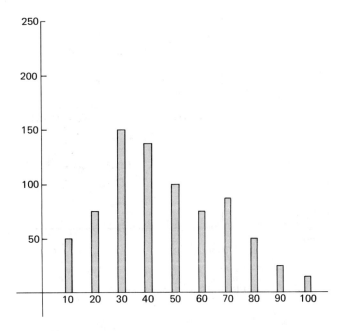

FIGURE 7.6   A histogram

```
┌─────────────────────────────────────────────────────────────┐
│                                                               │
│                      ABC Company                    39546     │
│                   REDLUMP, NEBRASKA                           │
│                                                               │
│      PAY TO THE ORDER OF        DATE      PAYROLL CHECK        │
│                                                               │
│      Willy E. Nilly             7/7/77        $627.52         │
│                                                               │
│                                                               │
│                                                               │
│      THE FIRST BANK                                           │
│      REDLUMP, NEBRASKA                                        │
│                                                               │
└─────────────────────────────────────────────────────────────┘
```

FIGURE 7.7   A sample paycheck

10. Given a data list in which each record consists of (1) a customer name, (2) the customer street address, (3) the customer number, (4) the name of the salesman, (5) a purchased item (a string up to 30 characters), (6) the quantity purchased, (7) the price of the item, write a program that will read the list and produce a sequence of invoices like the one in Figure 7.8. Assume that the city and state are always the same. Be sure to include the delimiting lines.

```
┌─────────────────────────────────────────────────────────────────────┐
│                                                                       │
│                         ABC Company                                   │
│                      REDLUMP, NEBRASKA                                │
│                                                                       │
│   SOLD TO:   DEF Company                  INVOICE NO.   23456         │
│              Skyway, Kansas 00002         INVOICE DATE    7/7/77      │
│                                                                       │
├───────────────────────────────────────────────────────────────────── │
│   SALESMAN:    A. B. Cee                                              │
├──────────┬────────────────────────┬─────────────┬──────────────────┤
│ QUANTITY │       DESCRIPTION       │ UNIT PRICE  │  EXTENDED PR.    │
│    1     │  Red Wizbiz             │   12.95     │    12.95         │
│                                                                       │
│    4     │  Scowl Drapers          │    7.00     │    28.00         │
│                                                                       │
│                                                                       │
├──────────┴────────────────────────┴─────────────┼──────────────────┤
│                                         TOTAL    │    $40.95        │
└──────────────────────────────────────────────────┴──────────────────┘
```

FIGURE 7.8   A sample invoice

11. Generalize problem 10 above to include up to five items on the invoice.

12. Using the outline of an algorithm below, write a program to compute the *greatest common divisor* (GCD) of two positive integers M and N. This algorithm is known as *Euclid's* algorithm.

I.   Repeat the following until R becomes zero:
  A. Divide N by M and compute the remainder R.
  B. If R is not equal to zero
    then
    1. Set N = M
    2. Set M = R
II. Print M, the GCD.
III. Stop.

The GCD of M and N is the largest integer that divides both M and N evenly. The GCD of 12 and 9, for example, is 3.

13. Write a program that will allow the user to play a game of tic-tac-toe with the computer as the second player. The user should have the option of playing first or second. If the computer moves first, generate the first move randomly. The rest of the moves should have a winning strategy. Have the program display the current "board" of X's and O's after each pair of moves.

14. Write a program to simulate a bowling game. Bowling scores are computed by the following rules:

A *strike* (indicated by X) means that all 10 pins are knocked down with *one* ball. This scores 10 *plus* the number of pins knocked down on the next *two* balls.

A *spare* (indicated by /) means that all 10 pins are knocked down with two balls. This scores 10 *plus* the number of pins knocked down on the next ball.

An *open* means that *less* than 10 pins were knocked down with two balls. The score is the number of pins.

There are 10 *frames* per game; a frame represents the throwing of one ball (if a strike) or two. The total score is the sum of the scores for all 10 frames.

The program should use the RND function to represent the number of pins knocked down. If you wish, you may *weight* the random number so that the computer is more likely to get a strike or spare—get a random number between 1 and 13, say, for the first ball. If the number is between 10 and 13, the bowler gets a strike.

The printout should include (1) the name of the bowler, (2) a row containing the frame number, (3) a row containing the number of pins knocked down for both balls (/ for spare, X for strike), and (4) the cumulative score in each frame. Make the printout neat; for example, put lines between each of the rows and between each of the frames.

15. Print a calendar for a year to be determined on INPUT. The starting day (Monday, for example) should also be given as an input parameter.

16. Sinkorswim, Inc., would like to computerize its billing procedures. Over each month the company accumulates sales records containing (1) customer number, (2) customer code (explained below), (3) price of the purchased item (per unit) and (4) the quantity. The company would like the program to read this data and produce a single invoice for each customer. Since there may be more than one sale to a given customer, the invoices cannot be printed until all the records have been read. The customer code is used to indicate the discount for that customer as follows:

CODE	CUSTOMER TYPE	DISCOUNT (%)
1	Sucker	0
2	Friend	10
3	Big shot	15

In addition, there are discounts for large purchases:

TOTAL SALE	DISCOUNT (%)
0 – 99.99	0
100 – 499.99	2
500 – 999.99	4
1000 – 1999.99	8
2000 and over	12

The invoice should include (1) customer number, (2) gross amount, (3) total discount, (4) net amount (= gross – discount), (5) tax (= 6% net).

17. If the expression $(a + b)^n$, where n is a nonnegative integer, is expanded (that is, multiplied out), the coefficients are called the *binomial coefficients*. For example,

$$(a + b)^3 = 1 \cdot a^3 + 3 \cdot a^2 b + 3 \cdot ab^2 + 1 \cdot b^3$$

and the coefficients are 1, 3, 3, 1. These coefficients can be determined from Pascal's triangle, the first portion of which is

$$1$$
$$1 \quad 1$$
$$1 \quad 2 \quad 1$$
$$1 \quad 3 \quad 3 \quad 1$$
$$1 \quad 4 \quad 6 \quad 4 \quad 1$$

Note that the first row corresponds to an exponent of 0, the next to an exponent of 1, and so forth. Each element of the triangle is the sum of the two elements immediately above it (except for the ones on the ends). Write a program to print Pascal's triangle for N = 0 to 15. You can print it in the form

N=0	1
N=1	11
N=2	121
N=3	1331
N=4	14641

18. Use the procedure outlined below to convert decimal numbers to *binary* numbers (that is, numbers with a base of 2). Print the digits separated by a single space. The decimal number should be supplied as input.

Let N = decimal number.

I.   Set I = 1.

II. Repeat the following until Q = 0:
  A. Compute quotient Q = N/2, remainder R.
  B. Save R as the Ith digit of the binary number.
  C. Set N = Q.

III. Print the binary digits in the reverse order from that in which they were computed.

IV. Stop.

For example, if N = 53, we have

	QUOTIENT	REMAINDER
53/2	26	1
26/2	13	0
13/2	6	1
6/2	3	0
3/2	1	1
1/2	0	1

and thus $(53)_{base\ 10} = (110101)_{base\ 2}$.

19. The First Bank of Redlump, Nebraska, to provide better service, wants to be sure that no customer has to wait longer than five minutes in line except on rare occasions. The bank wants to know how many tellers it should hire. Write a *simulation* program to help out the bank. Suppose that *on the average* one customer enters the bank every two minutes during the peak hours and that it takes an average of three minutes per transaction. Use the RND function to produce a sequence of time intervals for incoming customers so that most often the interval is two minutes but that there are shorter and longer intervals also. For example, you could generate a random number between 1 and 6.

If $4 \leqslant N \leqslant 6$, the time interval is set to 2; if $2 \leqslant N \leqslant 3$, the interval is set to 1; and if $N = 1$, the interval is 0 (two people come in together). A similar approach should be used for the transaction times. Compute and print the average times customers must wait in line for two tellers, three tellers, . . . , six tellers. Assume one hour of business at the above rate and do the simulation for a period of several (10, say) days.

20. Humdrum Corporation has a list of employee records that contain (1) employee name, (2) age, (3) sex, (4) number of years with the company, and (5) marital status. Using this list, print the names of all employees who fall into the following categories (also print appropriate headings): (1) over 21 years old but less than 35 years old, and single; (2) 23-year-old women; and (3) men over 45 years of age who have been with the company less than six years. Use the logical operators. Make up your own data.

21. Use the logical operators to write a program to construct a *truth table* for either expression below (your choice). A truth table gives the value of the logical expression (it can be either true or false) for all possible combinations of the logical variables. If two variables are involved, there will be $2^3 = 8$ rows in the table, and so forth. For example, the expression P AND (P OR Q) has the truth table

P	Q	P AND (P OR Q)
T	T	T
T	F	T
F	T	F
F	F	F

The expressions are:
a. (NOT P AND (NOT Q AND NOT R)) OR (P AND (NOT Q))
b. ((P OR Q) AND (NOT P AND Q)) OR (R AND (NOT P))

8. Matrices, Strings, and Files

As we have seen in considering one- and two-dimensional arrays, the ability to process arrays is an extremely important feature of any programming language. Nevertheless, operations on arrays can be tedious. Loops are necessary for such relatively simple problems as adding the numbers in a single row of a two-dimensional array. The much more difficult problem of multiplying two two-dimensional arrays using matrix algebra requires a triply nested loop. (See Exercise 6.9.) The bookkeeping needed for keeping track of the proper subscripts can be formidable.

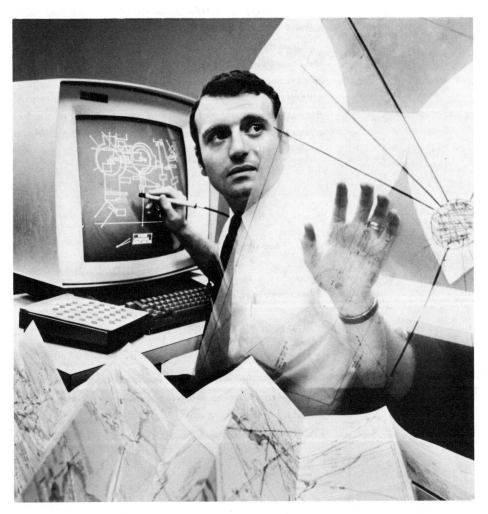

FIGURE 8.1 **More advanced topics. (Courtesy of International Business Machines Corporation)**

8.1   The MAT Instructions

To simplify such problems, most versions of BASIC provide the MAT instructions. With these instructions, we can apply certain operations to entire arrays without referring to each element of the arrays individually. The classification MAT is derived from the word **matrix,** which is the mathematical term for a one- or two-dimensional array. To be more specific, we can use the term **vector** for a one-dimensional array. Unless otherwise noted, we shall use the term *matrix* to mean a two-dimensional array.

The MAT instructions are valid for arrays of both one and two dimensions, and more on some systems. Some systems place more restrictions on the format of the MAT instructions than those given here.

8.1.1   The MAT READ, MAT PRINT, and MAT INPUT Statements

Reading data into a vector with an ordinary READ statement requires a loop, and a matrix requires a nested pair of loops. A single MAT READ statement can do either job simply by referring to the array name.

First, recall that the DIM statement is used by BASIC to reserve space for an array in the computer's memory; it is required for all vectors with more than 10 elements and for all matrices having more than 10 rows or columns. Using MAT instructions also serves another purpose. The MAT instructions use the dimension information to set the *limits* on the number of elements to be read, printed, and the like. Thus, it is important for *all arrays, regardless of size, to be dimensioned with a DIM statement.*

For example, a matrix of the form

$$A = \begin{bmatrix} 4 & -27 & 6.3 & 2 \\ -4 & 15 & 0 & 1 \\ 1 & 6 & 3 & -.5 \end{bmatrix}$$

should have the DIM statement

DIM A(3,4)

Again, the first subscript indicates the row and the second subscript the column in a matrix.

The MAT READ statement has the general form

n MAT READ list of array *names*

where n is a line number. Observe that in its simple form only the array names appear in the list—no subscripts are given. Just like the standard READ statement, it is used in conjunction with one or more DATA statements. The values in the DATA statement or statements are assigned to the matrices in the list row by row; the data are assigned to all the matrix elements in the first row, then the second row, and so forth, until the matrix is completely filled. If there are not enough data to fill all the matrices in the list, an error message similar to

OUT OF DATA

is printed, and the program stops.

For example, the sequence

10 DIM A(2,3), B(4)
20 MAT READ A,B
30 DATA 1,2,3,4,5,6,7,8,9,10

would result in the following assignment:

A(1,1) = 1   A(1,2) = 2   A(1,3) = 3
A(2,1) = 4   A(2,2) = 5   A(2,3) = 6
B(1) = 7   B(2) = 8   B(3) = 9   B(4) = 10

Note that A was completely assigned before any values were assigned to B.

The MAT PRINT statement works in a similar way. Its general form is

n MAT PRINT list of array *names*

but there are two rules to remember regarding the print format, which can be altered by placing a comma or a semicolon after each array name in the MAT PRINT list, including *the last one.* The rules differ depending on the type of array.

First, if a one-dimensional array appears in a list, followed by neither a comma nor a semicolon, it is printed in a single column. For example, if the array B is assigned the values in the previous example, then

100 MAT PRINT B

produces

7
8
9
10

If, on the other hand, a comma or semicolon follows the array name, the array is printed in row form. Thus,

100 MAT PRINT B,

generates

7   8   9   10

using the standard five-column format (if the array contains more than five elements, the extra elements will be printed in the same columns in successive lines).

The statement

$$100 \text{ MAT PRINT B};$$

generates

$$7 \quad 8 \quad 9 \quad 10$$

with minimum spacing (allowing for a sign) between the numbers.

Second, two-dimensional arrays are printed row by row, and each row always begins on a new line. If a comma (or nothing at all) follows the array name, the values are printed in five-column format. If each row contains more than five elements, the additional elements are printed on successive lines. If a semicolon follows the name, the elements are printed with minimum spacing.

If, for example,

$$C = \begin{bmatrix} 1 & 2 & 3 & 4 & 5 & 6 \\ 7 & 8 & 9 & 10 & 11 & 12 \end{bmatrix}$$

then the line

$$200 \text{ MAT PRINT C}$$

generates[†]

```
1              2              3              4              5
6
7              8              9              10             11
12
```

and $200 \text{ MAT PRINT C};$

generates

```
1   2   3   4   5   6
7   8   9   10  11  12
```

Only array names can appear in a MAT PRINT statement; a statement of the form

$$50 \text{ MAT PRINT A} + \text{B}, 10 * \text{C}$$

is illegal.

The MAT INPUT statement enables the user to enter array data during the execution

---

[†]Some BASIC systems print a blank line between each row.

of the program. Like the ordinary INPUT statement, it prints out a question mark and reads in the response. Its general form is[†]

n MAT INPUT name of a vector

Note that most versions of BASIC allow only one array name to appear in the statement.

Most systems allow the number of values entered to be less than or equal to the dimension size of the vector. In this case, you may ask, how does the program determine the number of values that have been entered? The special function **NUM** is used for this purpose. NUM has no arguments. When it is called, it is set equal to the number of values entered by the most recent MAT INPUT statement.

For example, suppose that after the following sequence is executed

10 DIM A(50)
20 MAT INPUT A

the user enters

10,-2,0,14,35,-9.

Then   30 PRINT NUM

would display the value 6.

We complete this subsection with Example 8.1, a short example to illustrate the operation of these MAT input-output statements.

[†]Some versions of BASIC allow matrices also, but the input format is very restricted.

EXAMPLE 8.1 ═══

Program:

```
 10 DIM A(2,3),B(50),C(3,6)
 20 MAT READ A,C
 30 MAT PRINT A,C
 40 PRINT
 50 MAT PRINT A;C;
 60 PRINT
 70 PRINT "ENTER THE ELEMENTS OF B"
 80 MAT INPUT B
 90 MAT PRINT B;
100 PRINT
101 PRINT
110 LET S = 0
120 FOR I = 1 TO NUM
130     LET S = S + B(I)
140     PRINT B(I);
150 NEXT I
160 PRINT
161 PRINT
170 PRINT "TOTAL IS:";S
180 DATA 1,2,3,4,5,6
190 DATA 10,11,12,13,14,15,16,17,18,19,20,21,22,23,24,25,26,27
200 END
```

Output:

```
1               2               3
4               5               6

10              11              12              13              14
15
16              17              18              19              20
21
22              23              24              25              26
27

1   2   3
4   5   6

10  11  12  13  14  15
16  17  18  19  20  21
22  23  24  25  26  27

ENTER THE ELEMENTS OF B
?  -1,-2,-3,-4,-5,-6,-7,-8,-9,-10

-1  -2  -3  -4  -5  -6  -7  -8  -9  -10  0  0  0  0  0  0  0  0  0  0
 0   0   0   0   0   0   0   0   0    0  0  0  0  0  0  0  0  0  0  0
 0   0   0   0   0   0   0   0   0    0

-1  -2  -3  -4  -5  -6  -7  -8  -9  -10

TOTAL IS:-55
```

───

Lines 20–50 of Example 8.1 illustrate the points discussed above. First A and C are printed in the standard five-column format, and then again with minimal spacing because of the semicolons.

Line 9Ø prints all 50 elements of B even though only 10 have been defined by the MAT INPUT statement in line 8Ø; thus the last 40 elements of B are zeros.[†]

Lines 12Ø-15Ø show how the NUM function can be used effectively to process elements defined by MAT INPUT. Note that the use of the semicolon after B(I) in line 14Ø prevents the next element from printing on the next line.

8.1.2   The MAT Arithmetic Assignment Statements   The mathematical operations of addition, subtraction, and multiplication are conveniently done on matrices with MAT statements. These operations, including the assignment of the result to a matrix, involve more than one matrix; thus for the operations to be valid, the matrices must have the proper dimensions. Another common rule is that only one matrix operation is allowed per line. In this section, the term *matrix* includes vectors.

The **simple matrix assignment statement** has the form

$$n \; \text{MAT} \; a_1 = a_2$$

where a_1 and a_2 are array names. Both a_1 and a_2 must have the same dimensions. For example

$$10 \; \text{DIM} \; A(5,10), \; B(5,10)$$
$$20 \; \text{MAT} \; B = A$$

assigns each element of A to the corresponding element of B; that is, A is copied into B.

The general form for the **addition or subtraction of matrices** is given by

$$n \; \text{MAT} \; a_1 = a_2 + a_3$$

where a_1, a_2, and a_3 are the names of arrays with the same dimensions. If the number of rows or columns of a_2 differs from the number for a_3, BASIC generates an error message like

CONFLICTING MATRIX DIMENSIONS

and terminates the run.

Each element of a_1 is set equal to the sum of the corresponding elements of a_2 and a_3. For example, if

$$B = \begin{bmatrix} 1 & 2 & 3 \\ 4 & 5 & 6 \end{bmatrix} \quad \text{and} \quad C = \begin{bmatrix} 1 & -2 & 3 \\ -4 & 5 & -6 \end{bmatrix}$$

then   1Ø MAT A = B + C

results in
$$A = \begin{bmatrix} 2 & 0 & 6 \\ 0 & 10 & 0 \end{bmatrix}$$

and   5Ø MAT A = B - C

yields
$$A = \begin{bmatrix} 0 & 4 & 0 \\ 8 & 0 & 12 \end{bmatrix}$$

[†]On some systems trailing zeros don't print.

Observe that all or any two of a_1, a_2, and a_3 can be the same matrix; for example,

$$100 \text{ MAT A} = \text{A} + \text{B}$$

is valid so long as A and B have the same dimensions. Multiple operations such as

$$50 \text{ MAT A} = \text{B} + \text{C} - \text{D}$$

are illegal, however. Also, it should be emphasized that these instructions are valid for vectors too. If, for example,

$$\text{A} = [1 \quad 2 \quad 3 \quad 4] \quad \text{and} \quad \text{B} = [5 \quad 6 \quad 7 \quad 8]$$

then $$10 \text{ MAT A} = \text{A} + \text{B}$$

yields $$\text{A} = [6 \quad 8 \quad 10 \quad 12]$$

In dealing with operations on matrices, we usually denote ordinary numbers as *scalars* to distinguish them from matrices. **Scalar multiplication** means the multiplication of *all* the elements of a matrix by the *same* single numeric value (the scalar). For example, if

$$A = \begin{bmatrix} -1 & 5 & 2 \\ 7 & 0 & 3 \end{bmatrix}$$

multiplying A by the scalar 3 yields

$$3 * A = \begin{bmatrix} -3 & 15 & 6 \\ 21 & 0 & 9 \end{bmatrix}$$

The general form for scalar multiplication in BASIC is

$$n \text{ MAT } a_1 = (\text{scalar}) * a_2$$

where a_1 and a_2 are matrix names (possibly the same one) and the scalar is *any valid arithmetic expression* that does not include a matrix name. Note that the scalar must be enclosed in parentheses so that the system can distinguish between matrix multiplication (see below) and scalar multiplication. Thus, if A were defined as above, the sequence

$$20 \text{ LET K} = 2$$
$$30 \text{ MAT B} = (3 * K - 1) * A$$

would set

$$B = \begin{bmatrix} -5 & 25 & 10 \\ 35 & 0 & 15 \end{bmatrix}$$

Matrix multiplication is a much more complex operation. The elements of the resulting product matrix are obtained by adding the products of the row elements from the left matrix and the corresponding column elements of the right matrix.

To illustrate, we let a_{ij} represent the element of the matrix A in the ith row and the jth column. Then the product is given by

$$
\begin{array}{cc}
A & B \\
\begin{bmatrix} a_{11} & a_{12} \\ a_{21} & a_{22} \\ a_{31} & a_{32} \end{bmatrix} &
\begin{bmatrix} b_{11} & b_{12} & b_{13} & b_{14} \\ b_{21} & b_{22} & b_{23} & b_{24} \end{bmatrix}
\end{array} =
$$

$$
\begin{array}{c}
C \\
\begin{bmatrix}
a_{11}b_{11}+a_{12}b_{21} & a_{11}b_{12}+a_{12}b_{22} & a_{11}b_{13}+a_{12}b_{23} & a_{11}b_{14}+a_{12}b_{24} \\
a_{21}b_{11}+a_{22}b_{21} & a_{21}b_{12}+a_{22}b_{22} & a_{21}b_{13}+a_{22}b_{23} & a_{21}b_{14}+a_{22}b_{24} \\
a_{31}b_{11}+a_{32}b_{21} & a_{31}b_{12}+a_{32}b_{22} & a_{31}b_{13}+a_{32}b_{23} & a_{31}b_{14}+a_{32}b_{24}
\end{bmatrix}
\end{array}
$$

Note that A and C have three rows and B and C have four columns.

To understand why the mechanics of matrix multiplication are this way requires knowing the mathematics of matrices and matrix algebra, which is outside the scope of this book. The examples below will help you to understand how the product is computed and how to use the MAT instructions to do the job for you.

The general form for matrix multiplication is

$$n \text{ MAT } a_1 = a_2 * a_3$$

where a_1, a_2, and a_3 are matrix names. For this product to be valid, a_2 must have the same number of *columns* that a_3 has *rows*. And a_1 must have the same number of *rows* as a_2 and the same number of *columns* as a_3. Another restriction is that, unlike matrix addition and subtraction, a matrix cannot be updated by multiplication. That is, a_1 cannot be the same as either a_2 or a_3.

Thus, if

$$
X = \begin{bmatrix} 1 & 2 \\ 3 & 4 \end{bmatrix} \quad \text{and} \quad Y = \begin{bmatrix} 5 & 6 \\ 7 & 8 \end{bmatrix}
$$

then

```
5 DIM X(2,2), Y(2,2), Z(2,2)
10 MAT Z = X * Y
```

produces

$$
Z = \begin{bmatrix} 1\cdot5+2\cdot7 & 1\cdot6+2\cdot8 \\ 3\cdot5+4\cdot7 & 3\cdot6+4\cdot8 \end{bmatrix} = \begin{bmatrix} 19 & 22 \\ 43 & 50 \end{bmatrix}
$$

Also, if

$$
A = \begin{bmatrix} 1 & -2 & 3 \\ 4 & -5 & 6 \end{bmatrix} \quad \text{and} \quad B = \begin{bmatrix} 1 \\ 2 \\ 3 \end{bmatrix}
$$

then

```
10 DIM A(2,3), B(3,1)
20 MAT C = A * B
```

generates

$$C = \begin{bmatrix} 1 \cdot 1 + (-2) \cdot 2 + 3 \cdot 3 \\ 4 \cdot 1 + (-5) \cdot 2 + 6 \cdot 3 \end{bmatrix} = \begin{bmatrix} 6 \\ 12 \end{bmatrix}$$

Note that B must be dimensioned as B(3,1) rather than as B(3) so that BASIC will treat B as a matrix with one column (that is, as a column vector) and not as a matrix with one row (a row vector).

To compute B*A in this case where B = [1   2] , we could write

$$10 \text{ DIM } A(2,3), B(1,2)$$
$$20 \text{ MAT } C = B * A$$

which results in

$$C = [1 \quad 2] * \begin{bmatrix} 1 & -2 & 3 \\ 4 & -5 & 6 \end{bmatrix} = [1 \cdot 1 + 2 \cdot 4 \quad 1 \cdot (-2) + 2 \cdot (-5) \quad 1 \cdot 3 + 2 \cdot 6]$$
$$= [9 \quad -12 \quad 15]$$

If a vector is to be multiplied then, it generally must be dimensioned and treated like a two-dimensional array.

Example 8.2 summarizes the MAT arithmetic operations.

EXAMPLE 8.2 ═══

Program:

```
10 REM//////////////////////////////////////////////////////////////////
15 REM/ PROGRAM NAME: MATRIXF                                            /
20 REM/ THIS PROGRAM EVALUATES THE MATRIX FORMULA                        /
30 REM/ F = (A + B)*X - (4)*C                                            /
40 REM/ SINCE ONLY ONE MATRIX OPERATION CAN BE GIVEN PER LINE, MATRICES /
50 REM/ S = A+B AND T = (4)*C ARE USED FOR PARTIAL RESULTS              /
60 REM//////////////////////////////////////////////////////////////////
100 DIM A(3,3),B(3,3),C(3,2),X(3,2),F(3,2)
105 DIM S(3,3),T(3,2)
110 MAT READ A,B,C,X
120 PRINT "MATRICES A, B, AND C ARE:"
130 MAT PRINT A;B;C;
140 PRINT
141 PRINT
150 PRINT "MATRIX X IS:"
160 MAT PRINT X;
161 PRINT
162 PRINT
170 MAT S = A + B
180 MAT T = (4)*C
190 PRINT
200 PRINT "MATRICES A+B AND (4)*C ARE:"
210 MAT PRINT S,T
220 MAT F = S*X
230 PRINT
240 PRINT "MATRIX (A+B)*X IS:"
250 MAT PRINT F;
260 MAT F = F - T
270 PRINT
```

```
28Ø PRINT "THE FINAL RESULT (A + B)*X - (4)*C IS:"
29Ø MAT PRINT F;
3ØØ DATA 1,2,3,4,5,6,7,8,9
3Ø1 DATA 5,6,7,8,9,1Ø,9,8,7
3Ø2 DATA -1,2,-3,4,-5,6
3Ø3 DATA 6,-5,4,-3,2,-1
31Ø END
```

Output:

MATRICES A, B, AND C ARE:

```
1    2    3
4    5    6
7    8    9

5    6    7
8    9    1Ø
9    8    7

-1    2
-3    4
-5    6
```

MATRIX X IS:

```
6    -5
4    -3
2    -1
```

MATRICES A+B AND (4)*C ARE:

```
6            8           1Ø
12           14          16
16           16          16

-4           8
-12          16
-2Ø          24
```

MATRIX (A+B)*X IS:

```
88     -64
160     110
192    -144
```

THE FINAL RESULT (A + B)*X - (4)*C IS:

```
92     -72
172    -134
212    -168
```

Example 8.2 computes the matrix expression

$$F = (A + B) * X - (4) * C$$

where $A = \begin{bmatrix} 1 & 2 & 3 \\ 4 & 5 & 6 \\ 7 & 8 & 9 \end{bmatrix}$ $B = \begin{bmatrix} 5 & 6 & 7 \\ 8 & 9 & 10 \\ 9 & 8 & 7 \end{bmatrix}$ $X = \begin{bmatrix} 6 & -5 \\ 4 & -3 \\ 2 & -1 \end{bmatrix}$ $C = \begin{bmatrix} -1 & 2 \\ -3 & 4 \\ -5 & 6 \end{bmatrix}$

Note how the MAT PRINT statements can be used to print more than one matrix (lines 13Ø and 21Ø), and observe the variations in print form when the semicolon is used instead of the comma.

In line 22Ø the matrix F holds the temporary value (A + B) * X; it is later updated in line 26Ø to store the final result. Another matrix could have been defined, but that would have been an unnecessary waste of memory space. More space could have been saved by using the statements

$$17Ø \text{ MAT A} = \text{A} + \text{B}$$
$$18Ø \text{ MAT C} = (4) * \text{C}$$

in place of those in the program. Then S and T would not be needed. In some problems, however, it is necessary to use temporary results (for instance, if in this program A and C were to be used again in later calculations); Example 8.2 shows that technique.

8.1.3   Special Matrix Instructions   BASIC provides several instructions for generating special matrices that are useful for solving problems in linear algebra, for example, solving simultaneous linear equations. We shall consider such an application later, but first we must examine each of these statements individually.

The **MAT ZER** instruction is used to set all the elements of the given matrix to zero. The general form is

$$n \text{ MAT } a = \text{ZER}$$

where a is a matrix name. For example, the statements

$$1Ø \text{ DIM A (2,3)}$$
$$2Ø \text{ MAT A} = \text{ZER}$$

would set all six elements of A to zero. It is valuable for situations that require a nonzero matrix to be set or reset to zero (that is, all its elements are zero) during execution of the program. It is not necessary on many systems to "zero out" a matrix initially since this is done automatically by BASIC.

Similarly, the **MAT CON** instruction, whose general form is

$$n \text{ MAT } a = \text{CON}$$

sets all of the elements of the matrix a to *ones*. For example,

$$1Ø \text{ DIM B(2,3)}$$
$$2Ø \text{ MAT B} = \text{CON}$$

results in

$$B = \begin{bmatrix} 1 & 1 & 1 \\ 1 & 1 & 1 \end{bmatrix}$$

To fill B with another value besides 1, you simply multiply B by the appropriate scalar, for example,

$$3Ø \text{ MAT B} = (-5) * \text{B}$$

The instruction **MAT IDN** is used to establish an *identity matrix,* that is, a *square* *matrix* (the same number of rows and columns) with ones on the main diagonal and zeros elsewhere. The general form of the instruction is like those above,

$$n \text{ MAT } a = \text{IDN}$$

It establishes the matrix *a* as an identity matrix. But *a* must be dimensioned as a square matrix or an error results. For example,

$$10 \text{ DIM } I(4,4)$$
$$20 \text{ MAT } I = \text{IDN}$$

results in

$$I = \begin{bmatrix} 1 & 0 & 0 & 0 \\ 0 & 1 & 0 & 0 \\ 0 & 0 & 1 & 0 \\ 0 & 0 & 0 & 1 \end{bmatrix}$$

The identity matrix is the matrix analog of the number 1 for scalars; multiplying a matrix A on the left or right by the identity results in a product equal to A. For example,

$$\begin{bmatrix} 7 & -3 & 5 \\ 2 & 1 & 6 \end{bmatrix} \begin{bmatrix} 1 & 0 & 0 \\ 0 & 1 & 0 \\ 0 & 0 & 1 \end{bmatrix} = \begin{bmatrix} 7 & -3 & 5 \\ 2 & 1 & 6 \end{bmatrix}$$

The last two instructions discussed in this section compute matrices as a function of the matrix argument. The first instruction, **MAT TRN**, computes the transpose of a matrix. The transpose of a matrix A, usually written A^T, is simply A with the rows and columns interchanged. The general form of the instruction is

$$n \text{ MAT } a_1 = \text{TRN } (a_2)$$

where a_1 and a_2 are matrices. Both a_1 and a_2 must be compatible in the sense that the row dimension of a_1 must equal the column dimension of a_2, and vice versa. Thus if

$$A = \begin{bmatrix} 1 & 7 & 3 \\ 9 & -6 & -2 \end{bmatrix}$$

the code

$$5 \text{ DIM } A(2,3), B(3,2)$$
$$10 \text{ MAT } B = \text{TRN } (A)$$

produces

$$B = \begin{bmatrix} 1 & 9 \\ 7 & -6 \\ 3 & 2 \end{bmatrix}$$

The second instruction, **MAT INV**, computes the *inverse* of a *square* matrix. The inverse of a matrix A, written A^{-1}, is the unique square matrix such that the products

$$A * A^{-1} = A^{-1} * A = I$$

where I is the identity matrix with the same dimensions.

Finding the inverse of a matrix is an important operation for many mathematical problems. But the computational work, whether one does it by hand or writes a program to do it on a computer, is extremely tedious. Consequently, the availability of an easy-to-use, reasonably accurate matrix inversion algorithm like the MAT INV function can be invaluable for someone working on matrix problems.[†]

Because of the computational problems in finding the inverse— indeed, for some square matrices the inverse doesn't even *exist*—errors, sometimes large, are introduced. In practice then, the product A * INV(A) will only approximate the identity matrix. If DET is near zero or the product A * INV(A) is not close to the identity matrix, or both, the inverse should be considered suspect.

The general form of the statement is

$$n \text{ MAT } a_1 = \text{INV } (a_2)$$

where a_1 and a_2 are different square matrices with the same dimensions. For example, if

$$A = \begin{bmatrix} 1 & 2 & -1 \\ 2 & -1 & 1 \\ 1 & 2 & 2 \end{bmatrix} .$$

then the code

```
10 DIM A(3,3), B(3,3), P(3,3)
20 MAT B = INV (A)
30 MAT P = A * B
```

produces

$$B = \begin{bmatrix} .26666667 & .4 & -.06666667 \\ .2 & -.2 & .2 \\ -.33333333 & 0 & .33333333 \end{bmatrix}$$

and the product

$$P = \begin{bmatrix} .99999999 & 0 & 0 \\ 0 & .99999999 & 0 \\ 0 & 0 & .99999999 \end{bmatrix}$$

which is close to the identity.

A short example will illuminate the above points. Example 8.3 should require no further explanation, but you should study the output carefully.

[†]Once the inverse of a matrix has been computed, the *determinant* of the original matrix can also be found by using the DET function. The DET function requires no argument and returns the value of the determinant of the matrix whose inverse was computed most recently. For example, the code

```
50 MAT B = INV(A)
60 LET D = DET
```

will assign to D the value of the determinant of A. A result DET = 0 indicates that the corresponding inverse is not meaningful. This is an easy way to check for possible errors.

EXAMPLE 8.3

```
Program:
 10 DIM A(3,3),B(3,3)
 20 MAT READ A
 30 PRINT "THE MATRIX A:"
 40 MAT PRINT A;
 50 MAT B = TRN(A)
 60 PRINT
 70 PRINT "THE TRANSPOSE OF A:"
 80 MAT PRINT B;
 90 MAT A = INV(B)
100 PRINT
110 PRINT "THE INVERSE OF THE TRANSPOSE OF A:"
120 MAT PRINT A;
130 PRINT
140 MAT A = ZER
150 MAT B = IDN
160 PRINT "THE ZERO AND IDENTITY MATRICES:"
170 MAT PRINT A;B;
180 DATA 1,-3,2,4,1,-1,-3,2,5
190 END
```

Output:

THE MATRIX A:

```
 1  -3   2
 4   1  -1
-3   2   5
```

THE TRANSPOSE OF A:

```
 1   4  -3
-3   1   2
 2  -1   5
```

THE INVERSE OF THE TRANSPOSE OF A:

```
.0875  -.2125   .1375
.2375   .1375   .0875
.0125   .1125   .1625
```

THE ZERO AND IDENTITY MATRICES:

```
0   0   0
0   0   0
0   0   0

1   0   0
0   1   0
0   0   1
```

Now that we have considered all the most common matrix functions, we note that on many systems several of the MAT instructions (usually MAT READ and MAT INPUT) are valid for arrays of strings, although we have not discussed such use here. These instructions could be useful, for example, in reading entire paragraphs or pages of text into the memory. Thus,

$$10 \text{ DIM A\$(50)}$$
$$20 \text{ MAT READ A\$}$$

would read 50 strings into the array A.

8.1.4 Changing Dimensions The requirements of the MAT instructions for specific dimensions on the matrices can create problems. Sometimes loops might be necessary to copy portions of one matrix into another just so the MAT instructions could be used properly.

Fortunately this is not necessary, since some of the MAT instructions have the option of changing the dimensions of a matrix while the program is being run. For example, each matrix entry in the MAT READ list can take the following form:

$$a \text{ (number of rows, number of columns)}$$

or

$$a \text{ (number of elements)}$$

where a is the name of an array. The number of rows, columns, and elements can be any valid numeric expression for subscripts, with the restriction that the values may not be larger than the number of locations reserved by the DIM statement. Thus

```
10 DIM A(5,5), B(8)
20 READ D
30 MAT READ A(2,3), B(D)
40 DATA 5
50 DATA 1, 2, 3, 4, 5, 6, 7, 8, 9, 10, 11
```

results in

$$A = \begin{bmatrix} 1 & 2 & 3 \\ 4 & 5 & 6 \end{bmatrix} \quad \text{and} \quad B = [7 \quad 8 \quad 9 \quad 10 \quad 11]$$

The point made earlier that subscripts are illegal in MAT instructions therefore is not quite true. Subscripts may be used in some MAT instructions—but only to change dimensions, not to refer to a particular element.

Similarly, the MAT ZER instruction may have either form

$$n \text{ MAT } a_1 = \text{ZER (number of rows, number of columns)}$$

or $\qquad\qquad n \text{ MAT } a_1 = \text{ZER (number of elements)}$

The array a_1 is redimensioned according to the given number of rows and columns, or elements. Thus,

$$50 \text{ MAT P} = \text{ZER (3,4)}$$

defines P as

$$P = \begin{bmatrix} 0 & 0 & 0 & 0 \\ 0 & 0 & 0 & 0 \\ 0 & 0 & 0 & 0 \end{bmatrix}$$

The MAT CON and MAT IDN instructions may be used in the same way, and they have a format like that of the MAT ZER instruction.

Finally, note that after

$$100 \text{ MAT READ A(3)}$$

is used, a reference to A(4) will produce an error on most systems.

8.1.5   **An Application**   Dr. Dexter Doorite has a problem. One of his patients needs a special diet so that he can recover from a rare illness. The diet specifies that he should eat only one meal a day, and further that this meal should have exactly 83 standard units of Vitamin A, 69 of Vitamin B_{12}, and 38 of Vitamin C.

After a long search, the doctor discovered a juice with 4 units of Vitamin A, 3 units of B_{12}, and 1 unit of C per ounce of serving. He also found a vegetable with 5, 3, and 2 units of Vitamins A, B_{12}, and C, respectively, per ounce, and a fruit with 3 units each of vitamins B_{12} and C per ounce, but no A.

Now the doctor needs to know precisely the combination of the three foods that will provide the required amounts of each vitamin. First, he lets f_1, f_2, and f_3 represent the unknown required amounts of juice, vegetable, and fruit. Using the above information, he

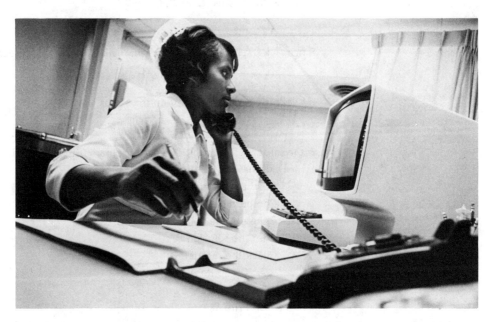

FIGURE 8.2 Computers are used to solve varied medical problems. (Courtesy of International Business Machines Corporation)

is able to write the following set of equations:

$$4f_1 + 5f_2 + 0f_3 = 83 \quad \text{(Vitamin A)}$$
$$3f_1 + 3f_2 + 3f_3 = 69 \quad \text{(Vitamin B}_{12}\text{)}$$
$$1f_1 + 2f_2 + 3f_3 = 38 \quad \text{(Vitamin C)}$$

The equations, an example of a system of linear equations, represent the number of units of vitamins A, B_{12}, and C. The first equation means that f_1 ounces of juice times 4 units per ounce plus f_2 ounces of vegetable times 5 units per ounce should supply 83 units of vitamin A.

Dr. Doorite now faces the problem of solving this set of equations for f_1, f_2, and f_3. Since his mathematics is shaky, he goes to the friendly hospital computer center, where Joe Smarts, a programmer-analyst decides to write a program to solve the problem.

Joe first rewrites the set of equations in matrix form:

$$\begin{array}{ccc} A & F & V \end{array}$$
$$\begin{bmatrix} 4 & 5 & 0 \\ 3 & 3 & 3 \\ 1 & 2 & 3 \end{bmatrix} * \begin{bmatrix} f_1 \\ f_2 \\ f_3 \end{bmatrix} = \begin{bmatrix} 83 \\ 69 \\ 38 \end{bmatrix}$$

or by the matrix names, the equation is

$$A * F = V$$

where F and V are column vectors.

The unknown in this equation is F. Joe notes that if he multiplies both sides of the equation by the *inverse* of A, he gets

$$A^{-1} * A * F = A^{-1} * V$$

Since $A^{-1} * A$ is the identity matrix (call it I here), this becomes

$$(A^{-1} * A) * F \longrightarrow I * F \longrightarrow F$$

by definition of the identity matrix. Thus

$$F = A^{-1} * V$$

is the solution. This will be easy to program using the MAT instructions.

Joe outlines the solution as follows:
  I.   Read the matrix A and vector V.
  II. Compute the inverse of A (call it B).
  III. Compute the matrix product B * V (call it F).
  IV. Print the solution F.
  V.   Check the results:
       A. Compute A * F (call it E).
       B. Compute the *error:* E = E - V.
       C. Print E.

Joe knows enough about matrix problems to check the results carefully. Multiplying the solution F times the original matrix A should produce a product very close to V if the results are accurate.

This outline requires no refinement, and the result is shown in Example 8.4.

EXAMPLE 8.4

Program:

```
10 REM//////////////////////////////////////////////////////////////////////
20 REM/ THIS PROGRAM SOLVES A SET OF THREE SIMULTANEOUS LINEAR EQUATIONS /
30 REM/ IN THREE UNKNOWNS.  THE PARTICULAR APPLICATION HERE IS TO DETER- /
40 REM/ MINE A PATIENT'S DIET.                                           /
50 REM/ PROGRAMMER:  JOE SMARTS            10/12/77                      /
60 REM/                        VARIABLES                                 /
70 REM/ A = 3X3 MATRIX CONTAINING UNITS OF VITAMINS PER OUNCE OF FOOD    /
80 REM/     -- ROWS CORRESPOND TO VITAMINS A, B12, AND C, AND COLUMNS    /
90 REM/        TO THE DIFFERENT FOODS.                                   /
100 REM/ F = UNKNOWN -- AMOUNTS OF FOOD TO BE DETERMINED.                /
110 REM/ V = REQUIRED AMOUNTS OF VITAMINS A, B12, and C.                 /
120 REM/ B = INVERSE OF A.                                               /
130 REM/ E = ERROR VECTOR -- A*F-V.                                      /
140 REM/ G = UTILITY VECTOR USED FOR PRINTING.                           /
150 REM///////////////////////////////////////////////////////////////////////
200 DIM A(3,3),B(3,3),F(3,1),V(3,1),E(3,1),G(3)
210 MAT READ A,V
220 MAT B = INV(A)
230 MAT F = B*V
240 PRINT "AMOUNT, IN OUNCES, REQUIRED FOR DIET."
250 PRINT "JUICE";TAB(16);"VEGETABLE";TAB(34);"FRUIT"
255 MAT G = TRN (F)
260 MAT PRINT G,
270 MAT E = A*F
280 MAT E = E - V
290 PRINT
300 PRINT "THE ERROR VECTOR IS:"
305 MAT G = TRN(E)
310 MAT PRINT G,
320 DATA 4,5,0,3,3,3,1,2,3,83,69,38
330 END
```

Output:

```
AMOUNT, IN OUNCES, REQUIRED FOR DIET.
JUICE           VEGETABLE           FRUIT

 12.             7.0000001       4.0000001

THE ERROR VECTOR IS:

-9.5367432E-07   -9.5367432E-07    0
```

It is interesting that no loops are required in Example 8.4; this can definitely be credited to the MAT instructions. Also, the program would be much longer if these instructions were not available.

In line 200 the vectors F, V, and E are dimensioned as (3,1) instead of simply (3); this is to allow for the matrix multiplication that takes place later in lines 230 and 270. But then, so that the results will be printed in a row rather than in a column, the matrix G is defined as a row vector, the transpose of F in line 255, and the transpose of E in line 305.

The results appear to be accurate according to the error vector.

This program was written to solve a specific problem; but if the headings are changed appropriately, the program could be used to solve any linear system of three equations in three unknowns, so long as the system has a solution that does not tax the accuracy limitations of the computer. It would not be difficult to alter the program to work for larger systems of equations also. See problem 4 in the exercises of this chapter.

8.2   String Processing

We have worked with strings and string data from Chapter 3 on. We have seen how strings can be read, compared, selected from a list of strings, and printed. But sometimes there is a need for examining individual strings in more detail, for breaking up strings into substrings (say a name into last name and first name), or for forming larger strings by combining smaller strings to give them meaning (like arranging words into sentences). There are applications for this kind of processing in the humanities and also in the sciences. These procedures can be accomplished with the help of a single instruction, available on most BASIC systems, the CHANGE statement.

8.2.1   The CHANGE Statement   Recall that string characters are represented in computer memory as coded sequences, and each such sequence can be treated as a number, the numeric equivalent of the character. These numbers can be used conveniently with the CHANGE statement.

The CHANGE statement has two forms. The first is used to translate strings into numeric arrays. The second form permits conversion from numeric arrays to strings. In general, the first form is

$$n \text{ CHANGE string variable TO numeric array name}$$

Each character in the string is translated into its numeric equivalent according to Table 8.1, and the numbers are stored in successive locations in the given array. Thus, the receiving array must be dimensioned at least as large as the number of characters in the string. The element of the numeric array with the subscript zero is convenient to use with the CHANGE instruction, since the total number of characters translated is stored there. This value can be used later to set up limits or loops; strings of variable length are easy to handle, since the length is given by this value. If zero subscripts are not valid, this value must be stored elsewhere.

Once the characters are translated into numeric form, it is easy to deal with them on an individual basis as elements of an array. Again, remember that a numeric 5, say, is different from a string character 5.

TABLE 8.1
ASCII CONVERSION
TABLE: STRING
CHARACTERS AND
THEIR NUMERIC
EQUIVALENTS[†]

Character	Code	Character	Code	Character	Code	Character	Code
Blank	32	/	47	>	62	M	77
!	33	Ø	48	?	63	N	78
"	34	1	49	@	64	O	79
#	35	2	50	A	65	P	80
$	36	3	51	B	66	Q	81
%	37	4	52	C	67	R	82
&	38	5	53	D	68	S	83
'	39	6	54	E	69	T	84
(	40	7	55	F	70	U	85
)	41	8	56	G	71	V	86
*	42	9	57	H	72	W	87
+	43	:	58	I	73	X	88
,	44	;	59	J	74	Y	89
-	45	<	60	K	75	Z	90
.	46	=	61	L	76		

[†]The particular coding scheme varies from system to system, but the ASCII code (American Standards Code for Information Interchange) is perhaps the most common.

For example, consider the segment

```
90 DIM B$(10), A(20), B(30)
100 A$ = "ALPHA"
110 B$(1) = "JOHN DOE"
120 CHANGE A$ TO A
130 CHANGE B$(1) TO B
```

Each of the characters in A$ and B$(1) is translated according to Table 8.1. Therefore,

$$A(\emptyset) = 5 \text{ (the number of characters in A\$)}$$
$$A(1) = 65 \text{ (A)}; A(2) = 76 \text{ (L)}; A(3) = 8\emptyset \text{ (P)};$$
$$A(4) = 72 \text{ (H)}; A(5) = 65 \text{ (A)}$$

Similarly,

$$B(\emptyset) = 8 \text{ (the number of characters in B\$ (1))}$$
$$B(1) = 74 \text{ (J)}; B(2) = 79 \text{ (0)}; B(3) = 72 \text{ (H)};$$
$$B(4) = 78 \text{ (N)}; B(5) = 32 \text{ (blank)}; B(6) = 68 \text{ (D)};$$
$$B(7) = 79 \text{ (0)}; B(8) = 69 \text{ (E)}$$

Note that blank spaces are treated as characters too.

The second form of the statement is

n CHANGE numeric array TO string variable

Each element in the numeric array is translated to its character equivalent according to Table 8.1, and the resulting characters are stored in the given string. For the system to tell how many values to convert, that number must be stored in the zeroth element of the numeric array, or elsewhere if zero subscripts are not allowed.[†]

For example, the code

```
1Ø DIM A(25)
2Ø READ A(Ø)
3Ø MAT READ A(A(Ø))
4Ø CHANGE A TO M$
5Ø PRINT M$
55 REM THIS REMARK SHOWS THE CHARACTER EQUIVALENT
6Ø REM OF THE NUMBERS IN THE DATA STATEMENT
65 REM     T, H, E, ,  B, U, T, L, E, R, ,  D, I, D, ,  I,  T,  !
7Ø DATA 18,84,72,69,32,66,85,84,76,69,82,32,68,73,68,32,73,84,33
8Ø END
```

will print the message

THE BUTLER DID IT!

Consider Example 8.5.

[†] Some versions of BASIC have a more primitive version of the CHANGE statement, which stores several consecutive character equivalents in a single numeric variable. A loop is required for the complete conversion of a string.

EXAMPLE 8.5 ==

Program:

```
5Ø REM////////////////////////////////////////////////////////////////
55 REM/ THIS PROGRAM ILLUSTRATES THE CHANGE STATEMENT.  THE STRING  /
6Ø REM/ A$ IS CONVERTED TO THE ARRAY A OF NUMERIC EQUIVALENTS IN     /
65 REM/ LINE 12Ø WHICH IS PRINTED IN LINE 14Ø.  SIMILARLY B$(1)      /
7Ø REM/ IS CONVERTED TO B; THEN C AND C$ ARE USED TO PULL OFF        /
75 REM/ EACH INDIVIDUAL CHARACTER FROM B$(1) FOR PRINTING IN         /
8Ø REM/ LINE 22Ø. THE LEFT COLUMN LISTS THE NUMERIC EQUIVALENTS,     /
82 REM/ THE RIGHT THE CHARACTERS.                                    /
85 REM////////////////////////////////////////////////////////////////
9Ø REM
1ØØ DIM A(5),B$(1Ø),B(2Ø),C(1)
11Ø LET A$ = "ALPHA"
12Ø CHANGE A$ TO A
13Ø PRINT "NUMERIC EQUIVALENTS OF A$:"
14Ø MAT PRINT A
15Ø PRINT
16Ø LET B$(1) = "JOHN DOE"
17Ø CHANGE B$(1) TO B
18Ø LET C(Ø) = 1
185 PRINT "NUM. EQ. IN B","CHARACTER"
187 REM C AND C$ DEFINE THE INDIVIDUAL CHARACTERS OF B$(1).
19Ø FOR I = 1 TO B(Ø)
2ØØ    LET C(1) = B(I)
21Ø    CHANGE C TO C$
22Ø    PRINT B(I),C$
23Ø NEXT I
24Ø END
```

Output:

```
NUMERIC EQUIVALENTS OF A$:
65              76              80              72              65

NUM. EQ. IN B        CHARACTER IN B$
    74                   J
    79                   0
    72                   H
    78                   N
    32
    68                   D
    79                   0
    69                   E
```

Example 8.5 shows how you can extract words from sentences. It would be easy to search for the numerical equivalent of a blank space (32) and change the preceding array values back into a string. Note that the dimension of the array does not have to be exactly the same size as the string.

In summary, both forms of the CHANGE statement used together provide a powerful tool for manipulating strings. String data can be read one line at a time or as a whole block of strings with one array subsequently translated into a numeric array. If Table 8.1 is stored as data in the program, the resulting array can be studied one character at a time; strings of characters can be compared, inserted, and deleted. When the manipulations are completed, the array can be translated back into strings by the second form of the CHANGE instruction for printing or storage for use later.

FIGURE 8.3 Computers can be used for clandestine purposes.

8.2.2 **An Application** Mrs. Sarah Spade has been receiving cryptographic messages from a secret agent for quite some time. She has deciphered the code, but hand decoding is tedious. She would like to have a program that will enable her to input coded messages on the computer, which will give her the decoded result.

The code is given in Table 8.2.

TABLE 8.2
DEFINITION OF
"SECRET" CODE

Code	Decoded	Code	Decoded	Code	Decoded
A	H	M	Z	Z	D
B	N	N	Y	Ø	J
C	E if C immediately precedes D / T otherwise	O	W	1	C
		P	O the first time P is used / L otherwise	2	V
D	blank			3	6
E	X	Q	Q	4	5
F	2	R	S	5	9
G	·	S	1	6	T
H	R	T	Ø	7	G
I	5 if message starts with B, / M otherwise	U	B	8	E
		V	F	9	M
		W	K	blank	A
J	U	X	E	=	3
K	I	Y	O	>	7
L	P			<	8

Thus, "COME IN" would be coded "1Y9XDKB".

A little thought will show that the above table can be stored in two arrays, D for the numeric equivalents of the decoded characters, and C for the numeric equivalents of the coded ones (from Table 8.1). Thus, the character corresponding to numeric code C(I) can be found using D(I). The program can read a message one line at a time and change it to a numeric array. Then it can scan this array one character at a time, search list C for that value, and replace it in the message with the corresponding value in D. It can then change back to string form for printing. In this example we shall use "3Ø" as the trailer for the input message.

From the above discussion, the following procedure can be given:

I.   Read the numeric equivalents of the characters in Table 8.2 into arrays C and D.

II. Repeat the following until the end of the message is detected:

    A. Read the code message, one line M$ at a time.

    B. CHANGE the string M$ to the array M.

    C. For each element M(I):

        1. Find M(I) in the array C, say at C(J).

        2. Replace M(I) by D(J), the number corresponding to the decoded character.

    D. CHANGE the array M to the string M$.

    E. Print M$.

Because the code is complex, decoding involves more than a simple one-to-one replacement, and Part II.C of this outline must be refined. We must first deal with the special cases. Using Table 8.2, we write in place of C:

C'. If the message starts with "B",

    then

    1. Set numeric equivalent of decode character for code "I" equal to numeric equivalent of character "5."

    else

    2. Set it equal to the numeric equivalent of "M".

D'. Set counter for using code "P": P = $\emptyset$.

E'. For each element M(I) in the message:

    1. If M(I) represents the letter "C" and I is less than M(0),

        then

        a. If M (I + 1) represents the letter "D",

            then

            i.   replace M(I) by the numeric equivalent of "E".

            else

            ii. replace M(I) by the numeric equivalent of "T".

    2. If M(I) represents the letter "P",

        then

        a. Add 1 to counter P.

        b. If P < 2

            then

            i.   Replace M(I) by numeric equivalent of "O".

            else

            ii. Replace M(I) by numeric equivalent of "L".

    3. If M(I) does not represent letters "C" or "P",

        then

        a. Find M(I) in the array C, say at C(J).

        b. Replace M(I) by D(J), the numeric equivalent of the decoded character.

We note after studying this refinement that Part C′ can be improved simply by having the program initialize the decode character corresponding to "I" to the numeric equivalent of "M." Then it requires a change only if the message starts with a "B." The same is true for step E′.1, which handles the letter "C," and E′.2, which handles the letter "P."

Also, we can further refine steps E′.3.a and E′.3.b to be

E′.3 If M(I) does not represent the letters "C" or "P,"

    then

      a. For J = 1 to 4Ø (number of code characters)

          i. If M(I) = C(J)

             then

             a. Set M(I) = D(J)

             b. Exit from loop.

Finally, it will cost little to make the program independent of the computer coding system being used (ASCII here). Using a DATA statement, we can define an array E with E(1) = 66 (the ASCII code for B), E(2) = 53 (ASCII for 5), E(3) = 67 (ASCII for C), E(4) = 84 (ASCII for T), E(5) = 68 (ASCII for D), E(6) = 69 (ASCII for E), E(7) = 8Ø (ASCII for P), E(8) = 76 (ASCII for L), and E(9) = 79 (ASCII for O). These values can be defined by a MAT READ E statement included in Part I above. Then, to run the program on a computer using something else besides the ASCII code, only the DATA statements would have to be changed.

It is reasonable now to construct the program (Example 8.6), but we must be extremely careful to enter the proper numeric values.

EXAMPLE 8.6 ═══

Program:

```
10 REM////////////////////;/////////////////////////////////////////////
15 REM/ PROGRAM NAME: DECODE                                            /
20 REM/ THIS PROGRAM IS DESIGNED TO DECODE MESSAGES WHOSE CODE IS       /
30 REM/ GIVEN BY TABLE 8.2 OF THIS BOOK.  THE MESSAGES MUST BE          /
40 REM/ ENTERED AS DATA STRINGS STARTING IN LINE 800.  A TRAILER,       /
50 REM/ "30", HAS BEEN PROVIDED.                                        /
60 REM/ PROGRAMMER: CHARLIE CHAN                                        /
70 REM/                        VARIABLES                                /
80 REM/ M$ = CODED MESSAGE      M = ARRAY OF NUMERIC EQUIVALENTS TO M$  /
90 REM/ C = ARRAY OF NUMERIC EQUIVALENTS OF CODE CHARACTERS            /
100 REM/ D = ARRAY OF NUMERIC EQUIVALENTS OF DECODED CHARACTERS        /
110 REM/     CORRESPONDING TO C                                        /
120 REM/ P = COUNTER FOR USAGE OF CODE CHARACTER "P"                   /
130 REM/ I,J = LOOP INDICES                                            /
140 REM////////////////////////////////////////////////////////////////
200     DIM M(72),C(40),D(40),E(9)
205 REM  READ THE CODE AND DECODE LISTS (TABLE 8.2)
210     MAT READ C,D
212 REM  READ CODE REPLACEMENTS
213     MAT READ E
215     PRINT "THE MESSAGE IS:"
217     LET P = 0
220 REM* BEGIN LOOP 220
230         READ M$
240 REM* ***EXIT FROM LOOP IF END OF MESSAGE
250         IF M$ = "30" THEN 999
260         CHANGE M$ TO M
270 REM  SET DECODE VALUE FOR CODE I TO 5 IF MESSAGE STARTS WITH B
280         IF M(1) = E(1)                                    THEN 300
290                                                           GO TO 320
300 REM*         THEN
310                 LET D(9) = E(2)
320 REM*     END IF 280
330 REM  THIS LOOP CONVERTS EACH INDIVIDUAL CHARACTER
340         FOR I = 1 TO M(0)
350 REM  CHECK FOR CODE LETTER C
360         IF M(I) = E(3) AND I < M(0)                       THEN 380
370                                                           GO TO 440
380 REM*         THEN (CHECK IF NEXT LETTER IS D)
385                 LET M(I) = E(4)
390                 IF M(I+1) = E(5)                          THEN 410
400                                                           GO TO 645
410 REM*             THEN
420                     LET M(I) = E(6)
430 REM*         END IF 390
435                                                           GO TO 645
440 REM*         ELSE (M(I) <> "C" -- CHECK IF = "P")
450                 IF M(I) = E(7)                            THEN 470
460                                                           GO TO 550
470 REM*             THEN (M(I) = "P" -- REPLACE BY "L")
475                     LET M(I) = E(8)
480                     LET P = P + 1
490                     IF P < 2                              THEN 510
500                                                           GO TO 530
510 REM*                 THEN (DECODE CHAR. FOR "P" IS "O")
520                         LET M(I) = E(9)
530 REM*             END IF 490
540                                                           GO TO 645
550 REM*             ELSE (M(I) <> "P")
```

```
560 REM    NO SPECIAL CASES -- SEARCH FOR C ARRAY TO FIND CORRESPONDING
561 REM    DECODE CHARACTER IN D.
570                         FOR J = 1 TO 40
580                           IF M(I) = C(J)                    THEN 600
590                                                             GO TO 635
600 REM*                         THEN
610                                 LET M(I) = D(J)
620 REM*                      **********EXIT FROM LOOP
630                               GO TO 650
635 REM*                        END IF 580
640                           NEXT J
642                         END IF 450
645                       END IF 360
650              NEXT I
655 REM  CONVERT DECODED NUMERICS BACK TO STRING
660              CHANGE M TO M$
670              PRINT M$
680                                                             GO TO 220
690 REM* END LOOP 220
695 REM    ARRAY C (TABLE 8.2)
700 DATA 65,66,67,68,69,70,71,72,73,74,75,76,77,78,79,80,81,82,83,84
701 DATA 85,86,87,88,89,90,48,49,50,51,52,53,54,55,56,57,32,36,62,60
715 REM  ARRAY D (TABLE 8.2)
720 DATA 72,78,84,32,88,50,46,82,77,85,73,80,90,89,87,76,81,83,49
721 DATA 48,66,70,75,69,79,68,74,67,86,54,52,57,84,71,69,77,65,51,55,56
745 REM  ARRAY E -- EQUIVALENTS OF B,5,C,T,D,E,P,L,O.
750 DATA 66,53,67,84,68,69,80,76,79
795 REM    MESSAGE STARTS HERE
800 DATA "I886D9CDKBDCACD7 HZ8BGCBPYBDCY9YHHYOG"
810 DATA "1Y98D PYB8GDMG"
998 DATA "30"
999 END
```

Output:

```
THE MESSAGE IS:
MEET ME IN THE GARDEN. NOON TOMORROW.
COME ALONE.  Z.
```

As shown here, Example 8.6 assumes that the user has already provided the data before running the program. The program might have been written differently; it could accept the entire message as a string array from a MAT INPUT statement. It should have a check to be sure that all the code characters exist in the array C; that is, what will happen if the program never gets an equal compare in the loop given in lines 570–640?

Observe the important use of M(0) to delimit the loop, starting in line 340.

The data in lines 700–701 represent the values to be assigned to the array C, that is, the numeric equivalents of the code characters in Table 8.2. The data in lines 720–721 correspondingly are assigned to the array D and are the numeric equivalents of the decode characters in Table 8.2. The coded message is given in lines 800–810.

8.2.3   **Comparing Strings**   One detail not yet adequately discussed is how strings compare with one another. We have already compared strings, indicating that they can be compared like numbers. One question that may arise, however, is, How do strings such as "SMITH", "SMITHE"," SMITH", and "SMITH " compare?

To find out, let's write a program to sort a list of names into alphabetical order. We shall use the simple exchange-sort algorithm discussed in Chapter 6 (Example 6.3). Since the procedure has already been discussed, the program, modified to sort strings, is shown in Example 8.7.

EXAMPLE 8.7

Program:

```
10 REM/////////////////////////////////////////////////////////////
15 REM/ PROGRAM NAME: NAMSRT                                        /
20 REM/ THIS PROGRAM SORTS A LIST OF NAMES IN ALPHABETICAL          /
30 REM/ ORDER.  THE NUMBER OF NAMES, FOLLOWED BY THE NAMES          /
40 REM/ ENCLOSED IN QUOTES MUST BE SUPPLIED ON DATA STATEMENTS      /
50 REM/ STARTING AT LINE 500.                                       /
60 REM/ PROGRAMMER:  S. TOWNDING              12/12/78               /
70 REM/                 VARIABLES                                    /
80 REM/ S$ = THE ARRAY OF NAMES      N = NUMBER OF NAMES            /
90 REM/ W  = SWITCH TO DETERMINE IF SORT IS COMPLETE                /
100 REM/ T$ = TEMPORARY STRING FOR INTERCHANGE                       /
110 REM/////////////////////////////////////////////////////////////
150     DIM S$ (50)
160 REM  READ IN THE NAMES
170      READ N
180      MAT READ S$(N)
190 REM  SORT THE NAMES
200 REM* BEGIN LOOP 200
210         LET W=0
220         FOR I = 1 TO N-1
230            IF S$(I) > S$(I+1)                          THEN 250
240                                                        GO TO 300
250 REM*            THEN (EXCHANGE)
260                   LET T$ = S$(I)
270                   LET S$(I) = S$(I+1)
280                   LET S$(I+1) = T$
290                   LET W=1
300             END IF 230
310           NEXT I
320 REM* ***EXIT FROM LOOP IF SORT COMPLETE
330          IF W <> 0 THEN 200
340 REM* END LOOP 200
350      PRINT "NAMES"
360      PRINT "-----"
370      PRINT
380      FOR I = 1 TO N
390        PRINT S$(I)
400      NEXT I
500 DATA 8
510 DATA "SMITHE J.","SMITHE E.","SMITH A.","SMITH A. "
520 DATA "AARDVARKER P.","SMITH B."," SMITH A.","SMITHE J.D."
999 END
```

```
Output:
NAMES

 SMITH A.
AARDVARKER P.
SMITH A.          (no trailing blank)
SMITH A.          (trailing blank)
SMITH B.
SMITHE  E.
SMITHE J.
SMITHE J.D.
```

Note that in Example 8.7, the name with the leading blank is printed first. This is because the blank precedes the other characters in the ASCII character set (Table 8.1). Also, shorter strings are printed first, and thus "SMITH A." appears before "SMITH A. " and "SMITHE J." before "SMITHE J.D." Different versions of BASIC will yield different results, and you can use the above example to test your BASIC system.

8.2.4 **Additional String Functions** Many versions of BASIC include numerous other functions to facilitate the manipulation of strings. Several additional functions are presented in this section. We suggest strongly that you compare these with the functions allowed (if any) in your version of BASIC. The formats of the instructions, and even the function names themselves, differ from system to system. A given system is likely also to have several string functions besides those given here.

First we consider the **INDEX** function. Some of the forms used are

$$n \text{ LET } v = \text{IDX (string 1, string 2)}$$

or
$$n \text{ LET } v = \text{INDEX (string 1, string 2)}$$

or
$$n \text{ LET } v = \text{POS (string 1, string 2, N)}$$

or
$$n \text{ LET } v = \text{SER (string 1, string 2)}$$

where v is a numeric variable, and string 1 and string 2 are string variable names or constants. In the third form, N is a numeric variable or constant. The first form is probably the most common.

The INDEX statement is used to determine whether or not string 1 contains string 2, and if so, where string 1 is situated within string 2. Thus, v is set equal to the position in string 1 of the *first* character of the substring that exactly matches string 2 (counting from left to right). If no match is found, v is set to zero. In the third case, the search for the string 2 begins in the Nth position of string 1.

For example, in

```
100 LET M$ = "MANY EARTHQUAKES ARE LOST BENEATH THE SEA."
110 LET N   = IDX (M$, "EARTH")
```

N is given the value 6.

This function is not particularly useful by itself. To be effective, it must be used together with some other functions.

Another fairly common function is the **LENGTH** function, which determines the length of a string. This is useful in handling strings of varying length, in the same way that the zeroth element of an array is used with the CHANGE statement.

The general form of this instruction is

$$n \text{ LET } v = \text{LEN (string)}$$

where v is a numeric variable; v is set equal to the number of characters in the string segment. For example, after execution of

$$5\emptyset \text{ LET K\$} = \text{``A} + \text{B} * \text{C} + \text{D}/(X^{\wedge}2 + Y^{\wedge}2 + Z^{\wedge}2)\text{''}$$
$$6\emptyset \text{ LET K } = \text{LEN (K\$)}$$

K is equal to 21. This value can be used anywhere an arithmetic expression is valid. For example,

$$2\emptyset\emptyset \text{ IF LEN (P\$)} > = 3\emptyset \qquad \text{THEN } 3\emptyset\emptyset$$

and

$$35\emptyset \text{ PRINT LEN (A\$)}$$

are valid statements.

Another useful function is **CONCATENATION,** which refers to constructing strings by combining other strings. We have already seen how to do this in a PRINT statement, using the semicolon to invoke concatenation for output strings. What is needed is to be able to do the operation in a more general setting. Again, the format varies from system to system, but a common technique is to use the operator "+" to perform concatenation; for example,

$$1\emptyset \text{ LET A\$} = \text{B\$} + \text{C\$}$$

would concatenate strings B\$ and C\$ with B\$ as the left part and C\$ as the right and store the result in A\$. Thus,

$$1\emptyset \text{ LET X\$} = \text{``ATOMIC ENERGY IS ''}$$
$$2\emptyset \text{ LET Y\$} = \text{``A BOON TO MANKIND''}$$
$$3\emptyset \text{ LET Z\$} = \text{``A CURSE''}$$
$$4\emptyset \text{ LET A\$} = \text{X\$} + \text{Y\$}$$
$$5\emptyset \text{ LET B\$} = \text{X\$} + \text{Z\$}$$

results in

$$\text{A\$} = \text{``ATOMIC ENERGY IS A BOON TO MANKIND''}$$
$$\text{B\$} = \text{``ATOMIC ENERGY IS A CURSE''}$$

Note that a blank space was included as the last character in X\$ to provide proper spacing.

With the above functions we can locate substrings and put strings together, but we also need functions that enable us to **copy** substrings from strings. The variant of the extract function used in this book is given by

$$n \text{ LET string 1} = \text{CPY\$ (string 2, N1,N2)}$$

This statement copies from string 2 a substring of N2 characters, starting with the character position (from the left) given by N1, and stores that substring in string 1.

For example,

10 LET S$ = "GOD REST YE MERRY GENTLEMEN"
20 LET P$ = "CPY$(S$, 19, 6)

would set P$ = "GENTLE".

Other variations of this function may copy everything to the left or right of a given character, or they may copy a substring and concatenate it with another string as well. One version of BASIC uses

n LET string 1 = SEG$ (string 2,N1,N2)

where string 1 becomes the string consisting of the characters in positions N1 through N2 in string 2.

The above collection of functions represents a complete set for manipulating strings. They allow us to

1. Locate substrings
2. Copy substrings
3. Concatenate strings

Remember that the length and starting position values can be specified by variables that allow these functions to be used effectively in loops and the like. For example,

50 LET S$ = CPY$(P$,K,L – 1)

is a valid statement. Additional string functions simply combine some of these features; otherwise equivalent programs can sometimes be written with fewer statements. All these operations can be accomplished with the CHANGE statement. But using it is more cumbersome than concatenation and requires more statements to do the same job.

Let us now consider another application of string manipulation. A common feature of many computer systems is a **text editor,** which is an assemblage of programs to enable users to modify collections of data by easy-to-use commands. A text editor written in BASIC must use string functions.

One typical feature of an editor is the provision for replacing one string (a word, for instance) by another. The following example will illustrate how this can be done. We assume that we have some English text from a book in the form of strings coded in DATA statements (ordinarily this information would be stored in a *file*—see the next section of this chapter). In this example it is convenient to use the so-called **null string,** which is a string with no characters at all (not to be confused with a string consisting of a blank character); consequently, it has length zero. Such a string is useful, for example, as the initial value in a series of concatenations. We can define a string P$ to be the null string by

10 LET P$ = ""

that is, using two successive quotes without an intervening space.

The short program following illustrates simple editing. We shall follow the outline,

FIGURE 8.4 Researchers in the humanities sometimes use computers to analyze texts.

which simply extracts the appropriate substrings from the original and puts them together.

I.   Input the string to be changed: O$

II. Compute the length L1 of O$

III. Input the string to replace O$; N$

IV. For each line of data, D$(I):

    A. Initialize P$ to the null string.

    B. Begin loop:

        Use index function to locate O$ in D$(I)—

        If found (index value K $\neq$ 0)

          then

          1. Concatenate string P$ with the substring of D$(I) consisting of characters 1 to K − 1.

          2. Concatenate P$ with N$

          3. Compute the length L2 of D$(I)

          4. Using CPY function, redefine D$(I) as the characters in positions K + L1 to L2 of D$(I).

          else

          5. Exit from loop.

    C. Concatenate P$ with D$(I).

    D. Print P$

The example seems artificial, since we simply print out the edited result. In a true application, the result could be saved (say in a file) for use later or for further editing.

To clarify what is being done, we apply this outline to the string

$$D\$ = \text{"ROSES ARE RED, VIOLETS ARE BLUE."}$$

where we intend to replace "RED" by "WHITE". Initially,

$$P\$ = \text{""} \text{ (null string)}$$

and

$$L1 = 3 \text{ (the length of "RED")}$$

The index value K is set to 11 (location of RED).

$$P\$ = P\$ + \text{"ROSES ARE "} = \text{"ROSES ARE "} \text{ (step B.1)}$$
$$P\$ = P\$ + \text{"WHITE"} = \text{"ROSES ARE WHITE"} \text{ (step B.2)}$$
$$L\$ = 32 \text{ (length of D\$—step B.3)}$$
$$D\$ = \text{", VIOLETS ARE BLUE."}$$

Repeating step IV.B, K = 0 this time; therefore

$$P\$ = P\$ + D\$ = \text{"ROSES ARE WHITE, VIOLETS ARE BLUE"}$$

and the result P$ is printed.

The program is given in Example 8.8.

EXAMPLE 8.8 ==

Program:

```
 10 REM//////////////////////////////////////////////////////////////////
 15 REM/ PROGRAM NAME: EDIT                                                /
 20 REM/ THIS PROGRAM PERFORMS AN EDITING FUNCTION ON A COLLECTION         /
 30 REM/ OF STRING DATA ENABLING THE USER TO REPLACE ONE SUBSTRING         /
 40 REM/ BY ANOTHER (AS LONG AS THE STRINGS REMAIN WITHIN THE LENGTH       /
 50 REM/ LIMITS).                                                          /
 60 REM/                      VARIABLES                                    /
 70 REM/ D$ = THE ARRAY OF ORIGINAL DATA                                   /
 80 REM/ O$ = THE SUBSTRING TO BE REPLACED                                 /
 90 REM/ N$ = THE SUBSTRING TO REPLACE O$                                  /
100 REM/ P$ = THE OUTPUT STRING      K = THE LOCATION INDEX                /
110 REM/ L1,L2 = THE LENGTHS OF O$ AND D$(I), RESPECTIVELY                 /
120 REM/ T$ = TEMPORARY STRING                                            /
130 REM//////////////////////////////////////////////////////////////////
200     DIM D$(90)
205     READ M
210     MAT READ D$(M)
230     PRINT "WHAT IS THE STRING TO BE CHANGED";
240     INPUT O$
250     LET L1 = LEN(O$)
260     PRINT "WHAT IS THE REPLACEMENT STRING";
270     INPUT N$
280     FOR I = 1 TO M
285        LET P$ = ""
290 REM*    BEGIN LOOP 290
295 REM  FIND STARTING POSITION OF SUBSTRING O$
300           LET K = IDX(D$(I),O$)
400 REM*     ***EXIT FROM LOOP IF SUBSTRING NOT FOUND
410            IF K = 0  THEN 490
415            LET R$ = D$(I)
418 REM  COPY LEFT PART OF STRING UP TO O$
420            LET T$ = CPY$(R$,1,K-1)
430            LET P$ = P$+T$
440            LET P$ = P$+N$
450            LET L2 = LEN(R$)
455 REM  NOTE THAT D$ IS NOW EVERYTHING TO THE RIGHT OF O$; ORIGINAL
457 REM  D$ IS DESTROYED.
460            LET D$(I) = CPY$(R$,K+L1,L2-K-L1+1)
470                                                           GO TO 290
480 REM*    END LOOP 290
490        LET P$ = P$+D$(I)
500        PRINT P$
510     NEXT I
550 REM  NUMBER OF INPUT LINES
599 DATA  10
600 DATA "      ********          "
601 DATA "KEEPING TIME, TIME, TIME,"
602 DATA "  AS HE KNELLS, KNELLS, KNELLS,"
603 DATA "IN A HAPPY RUNIC RHYME,"
604 DATA "       TO THE ROLLING OF THE BELLS --"
605 DATA "   OF THE BELLS, BELLS, BELLS: --"
606 DATA "       TO THE TOLLING OF THE BELLS --"
607 DATA "OF THE BELLS, BELLS, BELLS, BELLS,"
```

```
6Ø8 DATA "         BELLS, BELLS, BELLS --"
6Ø9 DATA "TO THE MOANING AND THE GROANING OF THE BELLS."†
999 END
```

Output:

```
WHAT IS THE STRING TO BE CHANGED?  "BELLS"
WHAT IS THE REPLACEMENT STRING?    "SEA SHELLS"
    ********
KEEPING TIME, TIME, TIME,
  AS HE KNELLS, KNELLS, KNELLS,
IN A HAPPY RUNIC RHYME.
       TO THE ROLLING OF THE SEA SHELLS --
   OF THE SEA SHELLS, SEA SHELLS, SEA SHELLS: --
       TO THE TOLLING OF THE SEA SHELLS --
OF THE SEA SHELLS, SEA SHELLS, SEA SHELLS, SEA SHELLS,
       SEA SHELLS, SEA SHELLS, SEA SHELLS --
TO THE MOANING AND THE GROANING OF THE SEA SHELLS.
```

8.3 Files

Example 8.8 would be much more useful if the data could somehow be stored apart from the program. As it is now, the data can be saved with the program in their original form but not in their revised form. Generally, collections of data in this form can be updated only by the tedious process of retyping the revised lines of data.

Furthermore, to use the program with a *different* set of data means replacing the original data with the new; the original data are lost and must be retyped if the program is to work them again. The impractical alternative is to have a copy of the program for each set of data and to save the data by saving the program.

Finally, data used in this form are limited on some systems to relatively small collections, usually because of the limits on the number of lines in a program, in addition to the above problems. Practical problems often require data collections that run into thousands, or even tens of thousands of lines.

All programs considered so far have had the data supplied either in DATA statements or through INPUT statements during execution of the program. These limitations and their drawbacks as described can be eliminated by using *files*.

Definition: A *file* is an organized collection of information.

This is a very general definition, since a file's contents can vary greatly. A file can contain a program or a set of programs (a *program* file), or it can contain a set of data (a *data* file). Here we shall concern ourselves with data files. Implicit in our using the term *file* is the assumption that the data are stored apart from a program; and like programs when they are saved, data files are stored in auxiliary memory (see Chapter 1).

---

†From "The Bells," by Edgar Allen Poe, as it appears in *The Complete Poems and Stories of Edgar Allen Poe, with Selections from His Writings,* 2 vols., ed. Arthur Hobson Quinn (New York: Alfred A. Knopf, 1946), p. 90.

Generally, a file is organized into *records,* which are themselves collections of *related* items of data (called *fields*). In a payroll file, for example, each record contains items of information about a given employee; the name, the social security number, the home address, the salary or hourly rate, and the like. The collection of all such employee records for a given company or department makes up the file. A payroll file is shown schematically in the accompanying diagram.

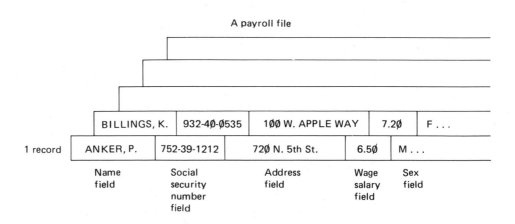

A payroll file

Because data files are stored outside a program, they require special instructions for processing. Like the string processing statements, the file processing instructions vary significantly from system to system. Thus, we can only present some representative sets here.

8.3.1   Sequential Files Although there are other possibilities, data files are usually organized either sequentially or randomly. (We shall discuss random organization in the next section.)

In a *sequential* organization, data are retrieved from the file in the order they have been written, proceeding sequentially from the first record. Consequently, the records are often—particularly in business applications—entered into a sequential file sorted on one (or more) of the fields. For example, the employee records in the payroll file given above might be sorted in alphabetical order by name, by social security number, by age, and so on. The records are written in the order most suitable for a given program, but since the data can be used by more than one program, the file must often be sorted into different sequences. Also, files can be erased, modified, or merged with other files.

Some systems require that a line number precede each line of data (that is, each record) in the file. If this is done, the data will be arranged in order of increasing line numbers. The fields themselves can be separated by commas or blank spaces, depending on the system; in most systems, string data should be enclosed in quotes.

The data in the above payroll file can appear in the form

    1Ø "ANKER, P.", "752-39-112", "72Ø N. 5TH ST.", 6.5Ø, "M", . . .
    2Ø "BILLINGS, K.", "932-4Ø-Ø535", "1ØØ W. APPLE WAY", 7.2Ø, "F", . . .

How can we create sequential files in BASIC? Like a BASIC program, a data file must be given a name, and the file is created in the process of naming it. Files can be created and built up entirely independent of any program by the same process used to create the program itself. Alternatively, they can be created by instructions within a BASIC program. The instruction used in this book to create files, or to make existing files available for processing, is the **FILES** statement. It has the form

n FILES   list of filenames

The filenames in the list are separated by commas. A number is used in place of the filename to refer to the file and is determined by the name's position in the list; the first name is assigned the number 1, the second 2, and so on. For example,

5Ø FILES   PAYROLL, TEMP, MASTER

assigns the numbers 1, 2, and 3 to the files PAYROLL, TEMP, and MASTER. In this format, all files in the list are assumed to be input files, unless a statement of the form

n   SCRATCH # m

appears later in the program. In this case the mth file in the list can be used as an output file.

One variation is of the form

n   #k = filename

where k is the number to be assigned to the filename. The filename must be in quotes. For example,

5Ø # 21 = "PAYROLL"

would assign the number 21 to the file named PAYROLL.

A third variation of this statement has the form

$$n \text{ OPEN filename, } \left\{ \begin{array}{c} \text{INPUT} \\ \text{or} \\ \text{OUTPUT} \end{array} \right\}, \quad m$$

where m is any arithmetic expression that has the value of an integer between 1 and 9. This number is then used in place of the filename to refer to the file. As long as a file is OPEN (or available for processing), no other file can be assigned that number. This system is limited to nine files that can be open at the same time; other systems have different limits or no limits at all. The word INPUT is required for an input file, OUTPUT for an output file. Also, there must be one OPEN statement for each file created in the program. For example,

1ØØ OPEN PAYROLL, INPUT, 3

assigns the number 3 to the INPUT file PAYROLL. Whichever variation is used, the files are said to be OPEN.

Actually, opening a file either creates a new file (for output) or makes available (for input) a file that was saved previously. The system searches its *catalog* to see whether a file with that name already exists; if none is found, a new one is established. In this way, data files can be saved and reused just like programs. Sometimes additional control statements outside of BASIC are required for the system to save and retrieve files properly. On some systems a string variable can be used for the filename, thereby allowing the user to select the filename during execution.

Reading data from sequential files is much like reading data in DATA statements.

Corresponding to the FILES format to open files, typical statements to read files are

n INPUT # m, list of variables

or   n READ # m, list of variables

where m is the number assigned to the file by the FILES statement.[†] This instruction works just like the standard INPUT statement except that the values are read from file m. For example,

12Ø INPUT # 3, N$,S$,A$,W,T$,T,W1,Y

could be used to read records from the payroll file described above.

The format of this instruction corresponding to the OPEN statement is

n INPUT FROM m: list of variables

where m is the number assigned to the appropriate file by the OPEN (or FILE) statement.

If more data are requested than what are on a given line in the file, data will be read from successive lines until all the variables in the list are assigned.

Finally, on systems that require a line number for each line of data in the file, a variable must be included in the input list to account for the line number, even if it is not used in the program.

In addition, most BASIC systems provide an automatic *end-of-file* to determine when the end of a file has been reached. In this case there is no need for a counter or trailer to detect the end of data. The following statement is used with the FILES format:

n IF END # m THEN p

where n and p are line numbers and m is the number of the file. When the statement is executed, control transfers to line number p after an end-of-file condition is encountered on the given file.

The statement

n ON END FILE m GO TO p

is used with the OPEN statement.

Just as with DATA statements, it is sometimes desirable to *reread* the data from the beginning of the file. On many systems this can be done with a statement like

n CLOSE filename

followed by another OPEN statement for the given file. The file cannot be opened again

---

[†]Most systems actually allow m to be zero, in which case input (or output) will be from (or to) the terminal instead of a file.

without first being closed. Reading can then take place from the beginning of the file again. Also, it is usually desirable to close each file when the program is finished with it.

An alternative form of the CLOSE statement is

n CLOSE # m

or on some systems simply

n # m

where m is the number associated with a given file (by the OPEN or FILES statement). Also, some systems have an instruction of the form

n RESTORE # m

which is analogous to the RESTORE instruction for DATA statements.

Finally a user can, besides reading data from a file, *write* information on another file, rather than on the printer, or terminal, using a statement of the form

n PRINT # m,   list of expressions.

Again, m represents a file number, and the rules for the list are the same as for the ordinary PRINT statement; for example,

100 PRINT # 5, V$;A + B;50/29; P1

is a valid statement of this form. One must remember that the file must be opened before it can be used for input or output.

Other forms of this statement include

n PRINT ON m: list of expressions

and

n WRITE # m,   list of expressions

Many systems sometimes require that the first PRINT or WRITE to a given file should be preceded by a SCRATCH statement (see above) which *erases* the data (if any) in the specified file so that the new output will begin in the first line of the file. Other systems allow the appending of data already in the file.

Example 8.9 is a simple example that illustrates the above features.

EXAMPLE 8.9

Program:

```
10 REM//////////////////////////////////////////////////////////////////////
20 REM/ PROGRAM NAME:  MERGE                                                 /
30 REM/ THIS PROGRAM READS NAMES FROM TWO FILES,                             /
40 REM/ FILE A AND FILE B, AND MERGES THEM ALTERNATELY INTO                  /
50 REM/ THE OUTPUT FILE FILE C.  IT ASSUMES THE LENGTHS                      /
60 REM/ OF BOTH FILES ARE THE SAME.  NOTE THAT VARIABLE NAMES                /
70 REM/ CAN BE USED FOR THE FILE NAMES.                                      /
75 REM//////////////////////////////////////////////////////////////////////
80      PRINT "ENTER THE NAMES OF THE TWO FILES TO MERGE"
90      INPUT P$,Q$
95 REM   OPEN THE FILES
100     FILES P$,Q$,FILEC
110     SCRATCH #3
130 REM* BEGIN LOOP 130
140        INPUT  #1, N$
150 REM* ***EXIT FROM LOOP IF END OF FILE
160        IF END #1 THEN 210
170        INPUT  #2, M$
175 REM  WRITE RESULTS ON FILEC.
180        PRINT  #3, N$
190        PRINT  #3, M$
200                                              GO TO 130
210 REM*  END LOOP 130
220     END
```

The contents of FILEA, FILEB, and FILEC after the run are (assuming that the user had entered "FILEA", "FILEB" in response to line 90)

FILEA	FILEB	FILEC
ALWORTHY, A.	BORST, B.	ALWORTHY, A.
CRUNK, C.	DIMWITTY, D.	BORST, B.
ELFY, E.	FRUMP, F.	CRUNK, C.
		DIMWITTY, D.
		ELFY, E.
		FRUMP, F.

Note that the contents of FILEA and FILEB are unchanged by the program.

We mention, without going into details, that many BASIC systems also provide formatted input-output (that is, PRINT USING or PRINT IN IMAGE, INPUT USING) for files. In addition, MAT READ and MAT PRINT statements exist for files on some systems.

Let us now consider an application for a sequential file. Rocket Robot Corporation (RRC) manufactures robots. They also supply parts from their warehouse to their dealers throughout the country. Because of the increased demand, the warehouse has expanded tremendously, and RRC is having problems keeping track of its inventory. Consequently, the managers have decided to computerize the inventory procedures.

Using a computer terminal in the warehouse, the shipping clerk is to enter records of (1) incoming parts from the manufacturing plant and (2) outgoing parts to the dealers. These records are to provide information to a computer PARTS master file, which will be read, updated, and written out to a new file. If it has been requested, the program should also print a listing of overstocked parts and parts that must be ordered. Each part record in the file is to contain numbers that represent the minimum and maximum quantity that should be on hand. Each record, then, will have the following form:

PART NAME	PART NO.	NO. IN STOCK	BIN NO.	MAXIMUM	MINIMUM
(1–15 characters)	4 digits	1–5 digits	2 digits	2–5 digits	1–3 digits

for example,

"HEAD", 0973, 1012, 21, 2000, 100.

FIGURE 8.5 Inventory management is a common computer application. (Courtesy of International Business Machines Corporation)

A record to update the parts file has the form:

Part no.   No. parts in shipment   Shipping code (1 if incoming, 2 if outgoing)

Rusty Gates, RRC's swinging programmer-analyst, has been given the task. After a thorough discussion of the requirements of the program and potential problems, Rusty produces the following initial outline:

I.   Compare (on part no.) update records to master records.

II. Update the "in-stock" numbers in the matching master records.

III. If a listing is requested, print the records of overstocked and understocked parts.

This outline requires considerable refinement before a program can be written. After further study, Rusty notes that a set of nested loops is needed, the outer loop for the update records and the inner loop to read and process the master records.

Since the master file is sorted by part number, for the matching to work properly the update file must also be sorted by part number. Most of the records in the master file will not be updated—they will simply be read and then written to the output file. This is because there are normally many more master records than update records. When there is a match on the part number, the number in stock can be updated according to whether the part is coming in or going out. If a report is requested, the on-hand amount can be checked against the minimum-maximum limits.

These considerations enable Rusty to produce the following expanded outline:

I.   Loop on update file (given on DATA statements).
   A. Read an update record—leave loop if trailer.
   B. Loop on master file.
     1. Read master record.
     2. If part numbers match
       then
       a. Update the "in stock" amount.
       b. If a report is desired,
         then
         i. Print record with appropriate amounts.
     3. Write updated master record.
     4. Exit from loop if there was a match.

II. Read in and write out the rest of the master file.

After carefully testing this revision on some sample data, Rusty refines the outline again:

I.   Open the PARTS master file and the NEWPRT file to hold the updated master records.

II. Is a listing desired for over- and understocked parts? (Answer: A$)

III. If A$ = "YES"
   then
   A. Print report heading.

IV. Loop until the end of the update file is encountered:

  A. Read an update record, with part number P1.

  B. Loop on master file:

    1. Read a master record, with part number P2.

    2. If P1 = P2,

      then (matching records)

      a. If shipping code S = 1 (incoming),

        then (incoming shipment)

        i. Add no. of parts in shipment, N1, to no. of parts in stock, N2.

        else (outgoing shipment)

        ii. Subtract N1 from N2.

      b. If A\$ = "YES"

        then (report wanted)

        i. Set M\$ = "OK"

        ii. If N2 > M1 (maximum)

          then

          a. Set M\$ = "OVERSTOCKED"

          b. Set A = N2 - M1

        iii. If N2 < M2 (minimum)

          then

          a. Set M\$ = "UNDERSTOCKED"

          b. Set A = N2 - M2

        iv. If M\$ <> "OK"

          then

          a. Print part name, part no., bin no., N2, A, M\$.

    3. Write the master record onto the NEWPRT file.

    4. Exit from inner loop B if P1 = P2 (match).

    End of Inner Loop B

  End of Outer Loop

V. Read rest of master file PARTS, and write it to NEWPRTS.

For simplicity Rusty assumed that the update file is always sorted by part number in ascending order. But in a real application you should always check for records out of sequence. Rusty made other careless assumptions as well. He assumed that the update records are never in error, and that the part number always corresponds to the number of a record in the master file. He also assumed that there are always enough parts in stock to fill an order. See problem 15 in the exercises.

This outline is detailed enough to produce the program in Example 8.10. The outline and the program are long and you should study both carefully.

EXAMPLE 8.10

Program:

```
  10 REM/////////////////////////////////////////////////////////////////////
  15 REM/ PROGRAM NAME: INVENTORY                                             /
  20 REM/ THIS PROGRAM MONITORS THE INVENTORY FOR ROCKET ROBOT               /
  30 REM/ CORPORATION.  IT UPDATES THE MASTER FILE AND OPTIONALLY            /
  40 REM/ PRINTS A REPORT OF UNDER/OVERSTOCKED ITEMS.  THE UPDATE            /
  50 REM/ ITEMS MUST BE ENTERED AS DATA BETWEEN LINES 1100 AND 8900 BEFORE   /
  60 REM/ RUNNING THE PROGRAM.  THE RECORD FORMAT IS:                        /
  70 REM/    PART #, # OF PARTS IN SHIPMENT, SHIPPING CODE                    /
  80 REM/ THE SHIPPING CODE = 1 IF INCOMING, 2 IF OUTGOING                    /
  90 REM/ A TRAILER IS ALREADY PROVIDED FOR THE UPDATE FILE.                  /
 100 REM/ PROGRAMMER: RUSTY S. GATES              3/10/78                     /
 110 REM/                   VARIABLES                                         /
 120 REM/ P$ = PART NAME        P2 = PART NO. (MASTER)                        /
 130 REM/ P1 = PART NO.(UPDATE)   N2 = PARTS ON HAND                          /
 140 REM/ N1 = NO. OF PARTS IN SHIPMENT   B = BIN NO.                         /
 150 REM/ M1 = MAXIMUM STOCK      M2 = MINIMUM STOCK                          /
 160 REM/ S = SHIPPING CODE   M$ = MESSAGE TO BE PRINTED ON REPORT            /
 180 REM/ A$ : DETERMINES IF REPORT IS TO BE GENERATED                       /
 200 REM/////////////////////////////////////////////////////////////////////
 250      FILES   PARTS, NEWPRT
 260      SCRATCH #2
 370      PRINT "IS A REPORT DESIRED OF OVER/UNDERSTOCKED PARTS (YES OR NO)";
 380      INPUT A$
 390      IF A$ = "YES"                                        THEN 410
 400                                                           GO TO 440
 410 REM*      THEN
 420               PRINT TAB(24);"STOCK REPORT"
 430               PRINT TAB(5);"PART";TAB(16);"NO.";TAB(23);"BIN";
 431               PRINT TAB(30);"ON HAND";TAB(42);"OVER/UNDER STOCK"
 440 REM* END IF 390
 450 REM* BEGIN LOOP 450 (UPDATE FILE)
 460        READ P1,N1,S
 470 REM* ***EXIT FROM LOOP IF END OF UPDATE FILE
 480        IF P1 < 0 THEN 920
 490 REM*    BEGIN LOOP 490 (MASTER FILE)
 500            INPUT   #1,    P$,P2,N2,B,M1,M2
 515 REM      CHECK FOR MATCHING PART NUMBERS
 520            IF P1 = P2                                      THEN 540
 530                                                            GO TO 850
 540 REM*        THEN (UPDATE MASTER RECORD)
 550               IF S = 1                                     THEN 580
 560                                                            GO TO 610
 580 REM*            THEN (INCOMING SHIPMENT)
 590                   LET N2 = N2 + N1
 600                                                            GO TO 630
 610 REM*            ELSE (OUTGOING SHIPMENT)
 620                   LET N2 = N2 - N1
 630 REM*          END IF 550
 640              IF A$ = "YES"                                 THEN 660
 650                                                            GO TO 845
 660 REM*            THEN (PREPARE REPORT)
 670                   LET M$ = "OK"
 680                   IF N2 > M1                                THEN 700
 690                                                            GO TO 730
 700 REM*                THEN (OVERSTOCKED)
 710                        LET M$ = "OVERSTOCKED"
```

```
720                                     LET A = N2 - M1
730 REM*                        END IF 680
740                             IF N2 < M2                            THEN 760
750                                                                   GO TO 790
760 REM*                    THEN (UNDERSTOCKED)
770                             LET M$ = "UNDERSTOCKED"
780                             LET A = N2 - M2
790 REM*                        END IF 740
800                             IF M$ <> "OK"                         THEN 820
810                                                                   GO TO 840
820                         THEN (PRINT RECORD)
830                             PRINT P$;TAB(15);P1;TAB(23);B;
831                             PRINT TAB(31);N2;TAB(42);A;TAB(50);M$
840 REM*                    END IF 800
845 REM*                END IF 640
850 REM*            END IF 520
860                 PRINT #2,P$,P2,N2,B,M1,M2
870 REM*       ***EXIT FROM LOOP 490 IF THERE WAS A MATCH
880             IF P1 = P2 THEN 900
890                                                                   GO TO 490
900 REM*      END LOOP 490
910                                                                   GO TO 450
920 REM* END LOOP 450
930 REM* BEGIN LOOP 930 -- WRITE OUT REMAINDER OF MASTER FILE
940        INPUT #1,P$,P2,N2,B,M1,M2
950 REM* ***EXIT FROM LOOP IF END OF FILE
960        IF END #1  THEN 990
970        PRINT #2, P$,P2,N2,B,M1,M2
980                                                                   GO TO 930
990 REM* END LOOP 970
1100 DATA 0057,50,1
1101 DATA 0210,100,2
1102 DATA 0395,200,2
1103 DATA 0923,10,2
1104 DATA 1790,50,1
1105 DATA 2321,100,1
1106 DATA 3927,1000,1
1107 DATA 4205,500,2
1108 DATA 6101,200,1
1109 DATA 8530,500,1
9000 DATA -1,0,0
9999 END
```

Output:

```
IS A REPORT DESIRED OF OVER/UNDERSTOCKED PARTS?    YES
                          STOCK REPORT
          PART       NO.    BIN   ON HAND    OVER/UNDER STOCK
SPINNEROO            210    10     700       -50    UNDERSTOCKED
CLAW                 923    31     47        -53    UNDERSTOCKED
TRINKUS              1790   27     139       114    OVERSTOCKED
BATTERY              2321   77     450       50     OVERSTOCKED
RIGHT ARM            3927   83     2400      900    OVERSTOCKED
MIDDLE ARM           4205   84     2         -198   UNDERSTOCKED
```

Example 8.10 is almost completely self-descriptive, especially if you follow the detailed outline and description preceding the program. But the file processing deserves comment. Note that another file besides PARTS (namely NEWPRT) must be used to contain the updated master records. It is not possible to write the updated record back into the PARTS file. To retrieve this file next time, the file NEWPRT would have to be used in place of PARTS. This means that (1) the file names would have to be changed each time in the program, or (2) the name of the file NEWPRT would have to be renamed PARTS, outside of BASIC, or (3) NEWPRT would have to be *copied* into PARTS. This necessary step is one of the disadvantages of working with sequential files in BASIC. Keep this in mind when you read the next section.

Only the printed output (that is, the report) is shown in Example 8.10. The master input and output files are not shown because they are not part of the program. The files PARTS (input) and NEWPRT (output) contain the records shown in Table 8.3.

TABLE 8.3 ══

PARTS	NEWPARTS
"LEFT LEG", 55, 350, 20, 600, 300	"LEFT LEG", 55, 350, 20, 600, 300
"RIGHT LEG", 57, 510, 21, 600, 300	"RIGHT LEG", 57, 560, 21, 600, 300
"WIDGET", 200, 580, 50, 800, 500	"WIDGET", 200, 580, 50, 800, 500
"SPINNEROO", 210, 800, 10, 1000, 750	"SPINNEROO", 210, 700, 10, 1000, 750
"EYEBALL", 395, 351, 15, 400, 100	"EYEBALL", 395, 151, 15, 400, 100
"CLAW", 923, 57, 31, 100, 25	"CLAW", 923, 47, 31, 100, 25
"HEAD", 973, 202, 25, 300, 200	"HEAD", 973, 202, 25, 300, 200
"LASER", 1501, 285, 12, 500, 200	"LASER", 1501, 285, 12, 500, 200
"TRINKUS", 1790, 89, 27, 100, 25	"TRINKUS", 1790, 139, 27, 25, 100
"BATTERY", 2321, 350, 77, 400, 200	"BATTERY", 2321, 450, 77, 400, 200
"HIPS", 2570, 87, 45, 100, 25	"HIPS", 2570, 87, 45, 100, 25
"LEFT ARM", 2621, 310, 82, 500, 200	"LEFT ARM", 2621, 310, 82, 500, 200
"RIGHT ARM", 3927, 1400, 83, 1500, 750	"RIGHT ARM", 3927, 2400, 83, 1500, 750
"MIDDLE ARM", 4205, 502, 84, 600, 200	"MIDDLE ARM", 4205, 2, 84, 600, 200
"TRUNK", 5505, 71, 67, 100, 50	"TRUNK", 5505, 71, 67, 100, 50
"FLIMMERJIM", 6101, 973, 95, 1500, 750	"FLIMMERJIM", 6101, 1173, 95, 1500, 750
"KLAKERJAC", 8530, 1525, 97, 2500, 1000	"KLAKERJAC", 8530, 2025, 97, 2500, 1000
"FOOTWHEEL", 9100, 725, 56, 1000, 500	"FOOTWHEEL", 9100, 725, 56, 1000, 500

The changes are due to the update records in the data lines. Obviously, the files here are very small; in a real application they would be much larger.

The files are shown here with commas between the values. Many systems will print the data in the same manner as an ordinary PRINT statement. In this case, semicolons should separate the variables in the PRINT list. Also, a QUOTE statement is necessary for enclosing string data in quotes for reading at a later time (for example, QUOTE #2).

8.3.2   Random Files   Sequential files, as the name implies, are designed for processing records in the sequence in which they were written. The main advantage of sequential processing is its simplicity—there is very little overhead in the bookkeeping aspects of the programs, and consequently it can be very efficient for some applications.

In the previous example, one of the disadvantages of treating the master file as a sequential file is that all the records in the file must be read and written to the output file, even if only a small percentage of them will be changed. For this reason, in practice update records are **batched** before they are processed against a sequential master file. That is, the records are collected and processed periodically in a group instead of being processed immediately when the individual records are generated. This periodic processing—or batching—was done in the previous example. Depending on the situation, batches might be processed once each month, once each week, or even once each day. Because the records are batched, some files are out of date and this can present serious problems.

Another disadvantage of sequential files is that an output file other than the original master file must be available if the records are being updated. Also, the batched records must be sorted in the same order as the master files for ease of processing.

Random files do not have these disadvantages.[†] They are called random because the records are not arranged in any particular order. In a random file, one can directly access a given record; it is not necessary first to read all the records that precede it. Consequently, searching for *particular* records is usually made faster on a random file. Also, one can read a record, update it, and write it back to the same location in the same file; a separate output file is not needed. Records do not need to be batched either. They can be processed immediately; the result is a more up-to-date file.

The price paid is in the complexity of processing. Much more bookkeeping is required to handle records in random files. In BASIC, some of the bookkeeping tasks are handled by the BASIC processor; the user does not have to write the routines. But you must remember that with random files much processing is going on "behind the scenes"—more so than with sequential processing. Consequently if every record is processed, the processing time per record is much higher than with sequential files. Thus, random files are usually used only when relatively few records are to be processed.

Most BASIC systems handle random files, but the detailed instructions vary greatly from system to system. You should consult the manual of your particular system for the details.

First, files can be established for random (direct) input or output operations or both by the FILES statement or its equivalent.

Some systems using the FILES statement use the characters % and $ as suffixes on the file names, to designate random files: % for numeric files and $ for string files. For example,

100 FILES STUDNT$, ACCPAY%

defines STUDNT and ACCPAY to be random string and numeric files, respectively.

Another version has the form

$$n \text{ OPEN filename, RANDOM} \left\{ \begin{array}{c} \text{INPUT} \\ \text{or} \\ \text{OUTPUT} \\ \text{or} \\ \text{IO} \end{array} \right\}, m$$

[†]Perhaps a better term, which is also widely used, is *direct access files.*

where IO means that the file can be read or written without reopening, and m is the number used to refer to the file in the program. For example,

5Ø OPEN MASTER, RANDOM INPUT, 3

assigns the number 3 to the RANDOM INPUT file MASTER.

Suppose now a user wants to write a record to a random file so that the record can be retrieved directly from the file without reading any others. For this to happen, each record must have a **key,** or **pointer,** which is a number that represents the relative location of the record in the file. For example, if a record has a key equal to 150, we should expect to find the record as the 150th record from the beginning of the file.

The key is usually computed from one of the fields in the record, for example, from the part number or the employee numbers or even the name, that is unique to that record. Choosing a key for a given file is usually the subject of much study, which we cannot consider here. The important point is that BASIC uses the key to locate a given record directly for reading or to determine a position in the file for writing. The key usually must appear as the first field in the record. Finally, special read-print instructions must be used for random files.

Systems that use the FILES statement have relatively simple random read and write statements. The read has the form

n READ: m, list

and the write has the form[†]

n WRITE: m, list

where m is the file number and list is the list of items to be read or written. Note that the colon (:) is used in place of a pound sign (#) to distinguish random from sequential I/O.

Since the latter forms have no facility for setting the pointer or key, a statement of the form[‡]

n SET: m, v

is used for this purpose. The value m is the file number and v is the value to which the key will be set. With this statement, we can access data in any order we desire; v can be determined sequentially or by a formula.

In this formulation, each time a READ or a WRITE is executed, the key is advanced by one. Thus, to read, update, and write back the same record, you must reset the key back one.

Finally, two functions, LOC and LOF, are useful in dealing with random files:

LOC(m) and LOF(m)

are set equal to the current key value for file m and the number of records in file m, respectively.

These functions are all illustrated by Example 8.11.

[†]The form is n PRINT: m, list on some systems.
[‡]The form is n RESET: n, v on some systems.

Another system, quite different from the one just considered, uses a random read statement of the form

$$n \; RRD \; (m,n,k,A)$$

where m is the number assigned to the random file, k is the number of characters to read, starting at character position n to be stored in the one-dimensional array A. Note that the characters are stored as numeric equivalents; the array A is numeric. For example,

$$5\emptyset \; RRD \; (1,2\emptyset1,1\emptyset\emptyset,M)$$

would read a 100-character record from file 1 starting at character position 201 into the array M.

Similarly,

$$n \; RWR(m,n,k,A)$$

is the form of the random WRITE statement.

EXAMPLE 8.11 ══

Program:

```
1Ø  REM////////////////////////////////////////////////////////
2Ø  REM/ PROGRAM NAME:  CITIES                                  /
3Ø  REM/ THIS PROGRAM READS A RANDOM FILE, CITIES, IN           /
4Ø  REM/ SEQUENTIAL ORDER.  EACH RECORD                         /
5Ø  REM/ CONSISTS OF A CITY OR TOWN IN WISCONSIN.  THE          /
6Ø  REM/ PROGRAM APPENDS THE STRING ",WIS." TO EACH             /
7Ø  REM/ CITY AND WRITES THE RECORD BACK IN THE SAME            /
8Ø  REM/ LOCATION IN THE FILE.                                  /
9Ø  REM////////////////////////////////////////////////////////
1ØØ     FILES CITIES$
11Ø     FOR I = 1 TO LOF(1)
12Ø        READ: 1,S$
13Ø        LET S$ = S$+",WIS."
14Ø        SET :1,LOC(1)-1
15Ø        WRITE: 1,S$
16Ø     NEXT I
17Ø     CLOSE:1
18Ø     END
```

In Example 8.11, the random string file is opened in line 1ØØ. In line 11Ø, the function LOF(1) determines the limiting value in the loop—the number of records in the file. In line 14Ø, the SET instruction resets the key back one from the current location, since it had been automatically increased by one in the previous statement. Thus the new string is written back into the same location in line 15Ø.

Let us now reconsider the example of Section 8.3.1. Rocket Robot Corporation discovered that the inventory program did not work very well since the update records were batched and run only once each week. Consequently the file was never up to date. The company fired Rusty and hired Wilma Wunupem, who decided to run the inventory file as a random file.

She decided to use the part number as the key, without any modifications. Again, this is an oversimplification of reality. In practice, the determination and use of the key would be much more complex. For one thing, there are large gaps between successive part numbers, which means there will be large gaps—and consequently much wasted space—in the file. (Can you find any other problems with this key?)

The master record will then have the form

| Part no. (key) | Part name | No. in stock | Bin no. | Maximum | Minimum |

Thus, considering that there may be one or more update records, and that they now do not have to be sorted, Wilma produces the following outline after studying the approach used for the sequential file:

I. Loop on update file (on DATA statements)
    A. Read an update record—exit from loop if trailer.
    B. Use the key from update record to read corresponding record from master file.
    C. Update the "on hand" amount.
    D. If a report is desired,
       then
       1. Print record with appropriate amounts.
    E. Using the key, write updated master record back into same file.

Note carefully the differences between this approach and the record outline for the sequential file. There is no inner loop here because only *matching* master records are read; there is no need to read the others. Consequently there is also no test for matching part numbers; with the key, the matching record is selected automatically. With the details of a particular system, it would be easy to perhaps refine this outline a step further and then produce a working program. See problem 16 in the exercises.

Exercises

1. Using the MAT functions, solve the following systems of equations and note the results:

    a. $X_1 - 5X_2 + X_3 = 2$ b. $X_1 + 2X_2 + X_3 = 3$
        $X_1 + X_2 + X_3 = 0$ $3X_1 + 5X_2 + 2X_3 = 1$
       $2X_1 + 4X_2 + X_3 = 1$ $2X_1 + 3X_2 + X_3 = 5$

2. Given matrices

$$A = \begin{bmatrix} 1 & 2 & -1 \\ 2 & -1 & 1 \\ 1 & 2 & 2 \end{bmatrix} \text{ and } B = \begin{bmatrix} 1 & 2 & 0 & 5 \\ -3 & 9 & 2 & 6 \\ 14 & -1 & 0 & 3 \end{bmatrix}$$

compute A^{-1}, the determinant of A, A * B, $(A * B)^T$, and $B^T * A^T$. Note particularly the last two results.

3. Write a program to compute the matrix equation

$$Y = B^{-1} * (I + A + A^2 + A^3 + A^4 + A^5) * B$$

where

$$A = \begin{bmatrix} 1 & 0.5 & -0.2 \\ 0.5 & 3 & 0.6 \\ 0 & 0.7 & 2 \end{bmatrix} \text{ and } B = \begin{bmatrix} 30 & 0 & 0 \\ 0 & 16 & 0 \\ 0 & 0 & -3 \end{bmatrix}$$

4. Using Example 8.4 or the first problem of the exercises as a guide, write a program that will solve a set of up to 25 simultaneous linear equations, where the number N of equations equals the number of unknowns. The value N should be an input value. Also, there should be a check to be sure a solution exists.

5. ABC Manufacturing Company produces three products: widgits, gidgits, and fidgits. Three different machines process each of the three products. The management of ABC would like to determine the number of each product that should be produced during each eight-hour day so that none of the machines is idle at any time. The following table gives the number of minutes each product is processed by each of the machines, M1, M2, and M3.

	WIDGIT	GIDGIT	FIDGIT
M1	4	8	8
M2	6	6	4
M3	3	15	2

Use the program written for the fourth problem of the exercises to solve this problem. *Hint:* Let N1, N2, and N3 be the total number of widgits, gidgits, and fidgits, respectively. Then 4 · N1 is the total number of minutes that machine M1 is occupied with widgits. One equation is formed by equating the total time for all three products to occupy M1 to 480, the total number of minutes in an eight-hour day.

6. The following problem could be solved in several ways, but use the MAT statements to compute solutions for each question.

Wingit Airlines has five flights daily to and from Farcry, Alaska. The accompanying table lists the number of passengers for a typical day's flight.

FLIGHT NO.	FIRST CLASS	SECOND CLASS	LOW CLASS
127	5	23	14
326	8	31	22
405	0	5	83
727	17	21	15
909	25	14	2

The prices for first-, second-, and low-class tickets are $245, $199, and $110. Wingit Airlines would like a program to compute

a. The total dollars in ticket sales for each flight (*Hint:* Form a 5 X 3 matrix A with the tabular values as elements. Multiply A on the *right* by the appropriate column vector of prices.)

b. The total number of ticket sales in each class (*Hint:* Multiply A on the left by an appropriate CON matrix.)

c. The total number of ticket sales for each flight

d. The total dollars in ticket sales for all flights together

7. In an application of matrices to economics, we consider the following model—called a Leontief model—of a simplified economy with *n* basic commodities.[†] The production of each commodity uses at least some of the other commodities. The amount of each commodity used in the production of one unit of the other commodities can be represented as an *n* X *m* matrix T, called the *technological matrix* of the economy.

Suppose, for example, an economy has just three commodities: fuel, grain, and transportation. Producing 1 unit of fuel requires 1/2 unit of grain and 1/4 unit of transportation; producing 1 unit of grain requires 1/4 unit of fuel and 1/3 unit of transportation; producing 1 unit of transportation requires 1/4 unit of grain and 1/4 unit of fuel. For this example,

$$
T = \begin{bmatrix} 0 & 1/2 & 1/4 \\ 1/4 & 0 & 1/3 \\ 1/4 & 1/4 & 0 \end{bmatrix} \begin{matrix} \text{(fuel)} \\ \text{(grain)} \\ \text{(trans.)} \end{matrix}
$$

with column headers (fuel) (grain) (trans.)

We can use T to determine *gross production* G of each commodity for a given *net production* N. The elements G and N can be represented as row vectors. The relation is given by

$$ N = G - GT $$

where GT represents consumption. Then, by properties of matrices,

$$ N = G(I - T) \quad \text{or} \quad G = N(I - T)^{-1} $$

where I is the identity matrix.

Write a program to determine G, given N and T.
Let

$$ N = [258 \quad 516 \quad 129] $$

which represents the net production of 258 units of fuel, 516 units of grain, and 129 units of transportation.

8. Rewrite Example 8.6 to include the option of reading a message in English and writing out the message in code. The user should be given the option of an INPUT parameter.

[†]From *Mathematics: With Applications in the Management, Natural, and Social Sciences* by Margaret L. Lial and Charles D. Miller. Copyright © 1974 by Scott, Foresman and Company, Chicago. Reprinted by permission.

9. Write a program to translate Morse code strings into English and vice versa. Assume that the "characters" are separated by a single space.

A	· —	H	· · · ·	O	— — —	V	· · · —
B	— · · ·	I	· ·	P	· — — ·	W	· — —
C	— · — ·	J	· — — —	Q	— — · —	X	— · · —
D	— · ·	K	— · —	R	· — ·	Y	— · — —
E	·	L	· — · ·	S	· · ·	Z	— — · ·
F	· · — ·	M	— —	T	—		
G	— — ·	N	— ·	U	· · —		

10. Write a program that will print out a concordance. First, code several paragraphs from some text, say the Declaration of Independence, as strings of DATA. The program should count the number of times each word appears and print out a list containing (1) the word, (2) the number of times it appears, and (3) a copy of the line or lines in which the word appears. Extra credit: Print the list in alphabetical order.

11. Write a program to read a paragraph in the form of string data and print all the words backwards; for example, "GOOD MORNING" should print "DOOG GNINROM".

12. Write a program to simulate the game "Life" (developed by John Conway; see *Scientific American*, October 1970, p. 120). The game represents an interesting development of the changes that occur in a colony of organisms.

The game is played as follows. Start with a 30 × 30 matrix on which the "organisms" are placed. Each configuration in the matrix represents a "generation." The organisms give birth to others, survive, and die according to the following rules:

Survival Organisms with exactly two or three neighbors survive to the next generation. A neighbor means an organism on an adjacent—including the diagonal—element (eight possible). Survival means that the organism remains in the matrix for the next generation.

Death Organisms with no neighbors or only one die from isolation. Organisms with four or more neighbors die from overcrowding. They are deleted from the matrix so that they do not appear in the next generation.

Birth Each empty position with exactly three organisms as neighbors is a birth—an organism is entered there on the next generation.

For example:

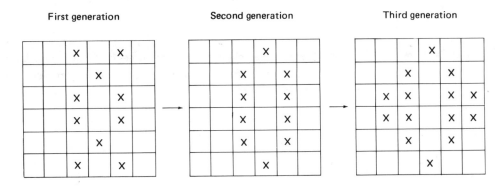

First generation   Second generation   Third generation

Read in the row and column positions of a set of organisms. Print out the matrix using 1's for the organisms. Compute a new generation and print the results. Repeat, for say, ten generations or until the matrix is empty. *Hint:* Use two matrices, each the next generation of the other.

13. Write a program that will add 2 integers, each having up to 50 digits. Treat the numbers as strings.

14. Try an experiment in code breaking. Write several lengthy paragraphs from a book as string data for a program that will count the number of A's, B's, blank spaces, and so on, and compute the percentage of use of each character. The program should print a table of these results. Then take a different paragraph as string data for a second program that encodes this paragraph into a cryptogram. (You can use Example 8.6, or you can devise your own code.) Now write a third program that assigns characters to those in the cryptogram based solely on the relative percentages obtained in the first program. For example, if E has the highest percentage of use in the first program, E should replace the character in the cryptogram with the highest percentage. Print out the result. How close is this result to the original sentence? This problem could be used as a team project for two or three students.

15. Modify Example 8.10 to check that the update file is sorted in ascending order and that there is a part number in the master file corresponding to each update record. The modified program should also handle the situation for which not enough parts are in stock to fill an order (print an error message but continue to process the rest of the records); that is, the processing should not result in a negative stock.

16. Write a program based on the outline of the program to update a random master inventory file (Section 8.3.2).

17. Modify Example 8.8 to read text from a sequential file and write the edited text to another file.

18. First, create two files: (1) a master customer file with the customer name, number, address, and code (= 1, 2, or 3); and (2) an invoice file with customer number, description of item sold, price per unit item, and total number of units sold. Both files should be sorted on customer number. Write a program to read the files, match the records on customer number, and print out an appropriate invoice using all the above information. The customers with code 1 get no discount, those with code 2 get 5 percent discount, and those with code 3 get 10 percent discount.

19. Write an information retrieval program. Create a file of 20 to 25 book titles from the library, preferably from two or three fields of study. Each record should contain call number, book title, author or authors, and subject keyword list with four to six subjects covered in the book. For example:

NUMBER	TITLE	AUTHOR(S)	KEY WORDS
QA 729.1	COMPUTERS AND SOCIETY	J. D. JONES	COMPUTERS, SOCIETY, TECHNOLOGY, FUTURE
AQ 327.5	COMPUTER SCIENCE	K. P. TATER	COMPUTERS, PRO-GRAMMING, LAN-GUAGES, PROBLEM SOLVING
T 129.3	LEARNING THEORY	P. A. PIPP	LEARNING, PSYCHO-LOGY, COMPUTERS, EX-PERIMENTS
R 923.5	THE BIONIC PERSON	T. R. SMITH	SCIENCE FICTION, COM-PUTERS, FUTURE, BIONICS, VIOLENCE

The program should ask the user to input up to three key words. The program should select records from the file that have any of the key words in the title or in its list of key words. If so, the program should print the call number, title, and author or authors. Furthermore, the user should have the option of obtaining only those records that contain *all* the key words in the input list.

20. Create a sequential file of records, each of which contains the name of a student and a set of test scores for that student. For your example, have three scores per student. The file should be in alphabetical order according to student names. The program should read a set of records of which each contains a student name and the student's score for the latest test. Input the number of the test. The program should match the score file with the records for the latest test and write out a new file that contains the latest score. It should also print a report giving the average score for each student, the class average for the latest test, and also the cumulative averages.

9. Functions and Subroutines

BASIC has features, in addition to those earlier described, that can help to reduce the programming effort and also improve the chances that the program is correct.

FIGURE 9.1   The end is at hand.

9.1   User-Defined Functions

Subroutines enable a programmer to break up a program into relatively small sections; this practice promotes a better understanding of how the program works and makes it easier to correct errors. Coding a program by subroutines is akin to modular program design, in which problem solutions are constructed for parts of a program independently of the other parts.

Functions simplify programming by eliminating repetition. We have already encountered BASIC's built-in functions (Chapter 6). These functions are provided by BASIC in an easy-to-use format, since they are needed frequently. Imagine the work required to code all the instructions (approximately 10 lines of code) for the square root function every time you want to use it!

Sometimes a programmer, particularly one who works on mathematical applications, uses functions not included among the built-in functions. BASIC provides features for handling these so-called *user-defined functions.*

9.1.1 Single-Line Functions

Here we consider functions that can be defined by a single statement. The **DEF** statement enables the user to define such functions for use in a program. The general form of the statement is

$$n \text{ DEF FN}g(d_1, d_2, \ldots, d_k) = e$$

where n is a line number, g is a letter of the alphabet, and $d_1, d_2, \ldots, d_k$ are the arguments of the function, called *dummy arguments* for reasons given below.[†] These arguments must be *nonsubscripted* variable names. The symbol e can be any valid arithmetic expression representing the function.

Examples include

```
100 DEF FNA(X) = (1 + (X – 3)^2 + (X – 3)^4)/X^.5
110 DEF FNP (A,B) = SQR (A^2 + B^2)
150 DEF FNK(Y) = 1/FNA(Y)
200 DEF FNT(N) = N/(1 + A * 3)
```

Note that other functions, including user-defined functions, may appear in the expression, as in the second and third cases; other variables besides the dummy arguments may also be in the expression, as in the fourth example.

The DEF statement simply defines the function for BASIC; it doesn't compute anything during the execution of the program. Its advantage is that the function names FNA, FNP, and the like can be used in place of the expressions that define them, wherever they are needed in the program, thereby shortening the coding necessary for solving a problem. Thus, to compute the value of

$$\frac{(1 + (X – 3)^2 + (X – 3)^4)}{\sqrt{X}}$$

for X = 4 in line 100 and for X = 9 in line 500 of a program, we could write

```
90 LET X = 4
100 LET L = (1 + (X – 3)^2 + (X – 3)^4)/SQR(X)
      • • •
```

[†]Some versions of BASIC permit only one dummy argument. Also, some versions permit a function definition with no arguments at all, in which case the parentheses are omitted.

$$490 \text{ LET } X = 9$$
$$500 \text{ LET } M = (1 + (X - 3)^{\wedge}2 + (X - 3)^{\wedge}4)/\text{SQR}(X)$$
. . .

or by the definition of FNA above, we could write instead

$$10 \text{ DEF FNA}(X) = (1 + (X - 3)^{\wedge}2 + (X - 3)^{\wedge}4)/\text{SQR}(X)$$
. . .

$$100 \text{ LET } L = \text{FNA}(4)$$
. . .

$$500 \text{ LET } M = \text{FNA}(9)$$

The savings are in the reduction of the number of times the expression must be given. Clearly, if the function value is computed in only one line of the program, there is nothing to be gained.

Note from the above sequence that BASIC computes the function value wherever the function name appears in an expression. The function name can be used anywhere an ordinary variable name can be used, except when a variable is assigned a value (in INPUT, READ, or the left-hand side of an assignment statement, for example); this use is sometimes referred to as a function call. The values of the arguments in the function call, which can be any valid arithmetic expressions, are substituted into the function expression in place of the dummy arguments. After the resulting expression is evaluated, the value replaces the function name in the call. See Figure 9.2.

The arguments in the DEF statement are referred to as dummy arguments because no values are ever assigned to them—they are simply placeholders for values appearing in the function call. On the other hand, variables that appear in the definition, except for the arguments (for instance, A in the fourth example on page 272, line 200), must be defined before a function call takes place.

The DEF statements can be placed anywhere in the program; here we shall follow the customary practice of placing them at the beginning.

Let us now consider an application for the DEF statement.

Newton Leibnitz is a college freshman taking a course in beginning calculus. His professor has assigned a large number of analytic geometry problems, which include determining roots of functions; that is, given a function $f(x)$, he must find x such that $f(x) = 0$. Since Newton knows BASIC he decides to write a program to compute the roots.

Generally, the roots of a function can only be approximated with a computer. There are many proven ways to compute approximations of roots; Newton decides to use the

dummy argument
↓

function definition } ⟶ $150 \text{ DEF FNA}(X) = \text{SQR}(X)/(1 + X * X)$
. . .

$600 \text{ PRINT FNA } \underline{(A + 1)}/5$ ⟵ function call
argument substituted for X during execution

FIGURE 9.2 The function call

FIGURE 9.3 Mathematicians were among the first to use computers. (Courtesy of Tektronix, Inc.)

bisection method, which is one of the simplest and also one of the most reliable procedures for this purpose.

To keep the problem simple, Newton will consider only functions that have one and only one root in an interval A < X < B. In general then, the function will be positive at one endpoint and negative at the other, and the product $f(A) * f(B)$ will be negative. Such a function is shown in Figure 9.4.

The method can be outlined as follows:

I. Repeat the following until the root is located as accurately as desired (or to within the accuracy limits of the computer).

    A. Compute the midpoint of the interval: M = (A + B)/2.

    B. Compute P = $f(A) * f(M)$.

        1. If P = 0, the root is M.

        2. If P < 0

            then

            a. f must cross the axis between A and M—the root is in the left half-interval (Figure 9.5). Reset B = M and repeat.

            else (P > 0)

            b. f does not cross the axis between A and M—the root is in the right half-interval (Figure 9.6). Reset A = M and repeat.

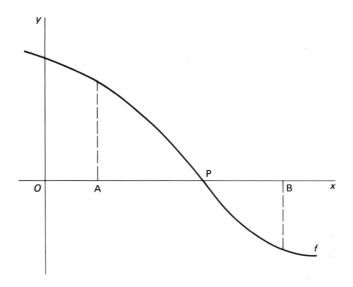

FIGURE 9.4   Graph of a function with a root at X = P

Thus, the interval that is searched is successively *bisected* until the interval becomes small enough. If the last computed M is assumed to be the root, the error in the approximation will be no larger than one-half the size of the final interval.

Newton will use the algorithm as specified above, but he must first provide more details before he codes the program.

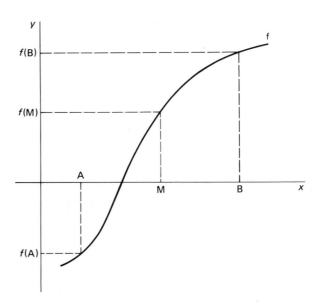

FIGURE 9.5   Graph of a function with a root between A and M

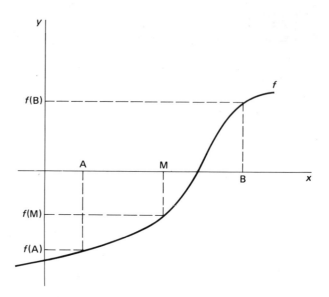

FIGURE 9.6   Graph of a function with a root between M and B

Like the graphing program of Chapter 7, this program should inform the user how to define the function. Further, it should request the interval limits A and B in which the search is to be made. It should also check to be sure $f(A) \cdot f(B) < 0$.

Furthermore, Newton considers the phrase in the above procedures, "Repeat . . . until . . . accurately as desired" to be ambiguous. He decides to use the value $1/2 \cdot (B - A)$ as the measure of accuracy, where $(B - A)$ is reduced by a factor of $1/2$ at each stage of the procedure. He will leave the loop when $1/2 \cdot (B - A) \leqslant E$, another input value.

With these points in mind, Newton produces the following outline:

I.   Print "Have you defined the function (yes or no)?"
II.   If answer is not "yes,"
    then
    A. Print "Enter your function as 2ØØ DEF FNA(X) = (function in terms of variable X) and then run the program again."
    B. Stop.
III. Print "Enter the left and right endpoints of the interval, separated by commas."
IV.   Input A, B.
V.   If FNA(A) * FNA(B) $\geqslant$ Ø
    then
    A. Print "Error—F(A), F(B), should have opposite signs."
    B. Stop.
VI.   Print "Enter accuracy desired".

VII.   Input E.

VIII. If E $<$ 1.E-6
> *then*
>   A. Set E = 1.E-6

IX.   Begin loop.
> A. Set M = (A + B)/2.
> B. Set P = FNA(A) $*$ FNA(M).
> C. If P = 0
> > *then*
> > > 1. Print "Root is exact:", M
> > > 2. Stop.
> D. If P $<$ 0
> > *then* (root in left half)
> > 1. Set B = M.
> > *else* (P $>$ 0—root in right half)
> > 2. Set A = M.
> E. Exit from loop if (B - A) $\leqslant$ E.

X.   Set M = (A + B)/2.

XI.   Print "Approximate root is"; M; "and value of F there is"; FNA(M). "The error is less than"; E/2.

XII. Stop.

Newton writes the program shown in Example 9.1 directly from this outline.

EXAMPLE 9.1 ==

Program:

```
10 REM//////////////////////////////////////////////////////////////////////
15 REM/ PROGRAM NAME:  ROOT                                                  /
20 REM/ THIS PROGRAM COMPUTES A ROOT OF A FUNCTION F OF A SINGLE             /
30 REM/ VARIABLE IN AN INTERVAL (A,B) USING THE BISECTION ALGORITHM.         /
40 REM/ F MUST HAVE OPPOSITE SIGNS AT A AND B.   THE USER MUST DEFINE        /
50 REM/ THE FUNCTION AT LINE 200 BEFORE RUNNING THE PROGRAM: THE DUMMY       /
60 REM/ FUNCTION F(X) = X ^ 2 WILL THEN BE REPLACED BY THE USER'S            /
70 REM/ FUNCTION.                                                            /
80 REM/ PROGRAMMER:  NEWTON LEIBNITZ          3/15/78                        /
90 REM/                        VARIABLES                                     /
100 REM/ A = LEFT ENDPOINT                  B = RIGHT ENDPOINT               /
110 REM/ M = MIDPOINT               E = ERROR BOUND (MUST BE > = 1.E-6)      /
120 REM/ P = PRODUCT OF TWO FUNCTION VALUES      FNA = FUNCTION              /
130 REM//////////////////////////////////////////////////////////////////////
200      DEF FNA(X) = X ^ 2
210      PRINT "HAVE YOU DEFINED YOUR FUNCTION";
220      INPUT A$
230      IF A$ <> "YES"                                       THEN 250
240                                                           GO TO 280
250 REM*     THEN
260              PRINT "ENTER YOUR FUNCTION AS 200 DEF FNA(X) = ..."
261              PRINT "(THE FUNCTION IN TERMS OF VARIABLE X) AND RUN"
262              PRINT "THE PROGRAM AGAIN."
270              STOP
280 REM* END IF 230
290      PRINT "ENTER THE LEFT AND RIGHT ENDPOINTS OF THE INTERVAL,"
291      PRINT "SEPARATED BY COMMAS."
300      INPUT A,B
310      IF FNA(A)*FNA(B) > = 0                                THEN 330
320                                                           GO TO 350
330 REM*     THEN
340              PRINT "ERROR -- FUNCTION NOT OF OPPOSITE SIGNS"
341              PRINT "AT ENDPOINTS."
342              STOP
350 REM* END IF 310
360      PRINT "ENTER ACCURACY DESIRED"
370      INPUT E
380      IF E < 1.E-6                                          THEN 400
390                                                           GO TO 420
400 REM*     THEN
410              LET E = 1.E-6
420 REM* END IF 380
430 REM* BEGIN LOOP 430
440      LET M = (A + B)/2
450      LET P = FNA(A)*FNA(M)
460      IF P = 0                                              THEN 480
470                                                           GO TO 510
480 REM*         THEN
490              PRINT "ROOT IS EXACT:";M
500              STOP
510 REM*     END IF 460
520      IF P < 0                                              THEN 540
530                                                           GO TO 570
540 REM*        THEN (ROOT IN LEFT HALF)
550              LET B = M
560                                                           GO TO 590
570 REM*        ELSE (ROOT IN RIGHT HALF)
580              LET A = M
590 REM*     END IF 520
```

```
600 REM* ***EXIT FROM LOOP IF ERROR < = BOUND E.
610      IF (B-A) < = E THEN 630
620                                                    GO TO 430
630 REM* END LOOP 430
640      LET M = (A + B)/2
650      PRINT
651      PRINT "APPROXIMATE ROOT IS ";M;"AND THE VALUE OF F THERE IS";FNA(M)
652      PRINT
653      PRINT "THE ERROR IS LESS THAN ";E/2
660      END
```

Output:

```
HAVE YOU DEFINED YOUR FUNCTION?  NO
ENTER YOUR FUNCTION AS 200 DEF FNA(X) = ...
(THE FUNCTION IN TERMS OF VARIABLE X) AND RUN
THE PROGRAM AGAIN.

200 DEF FNA(X) = X ^ 2-.9*X-8.5
RUN

HAVE YOU DEFINED YOUR FUNCTION?  YES
ENTER THE LEFT AND RIGHT ENDPOINTS OF THE INTERVAL,
SEPARATED BY COMMAS.
?  0,  5
ENTER ACCURACY DESIRED
?  1E-04
APPROXIMATE ROOT IS  3.4000015 AND THE VALUE OF F THERE IS 9.05991E-06

THE ERROR IS LESS THAN 5E-05
```

Note that the function name (the function call) appears five times in this program (twice in lines 310 and 450, and once in line 651). Without the DEF statement, the user would have to type in the function in place of each of these calls.

One feature of Example 9.1 that wasn't discussed but was included in the outline and the program is limiting E to a value $\geq 10^{-6}$ (lines 380–420). This prevents the user from requesting accuracy greater than the machine can handle, which might cause the program to go into an infinite loop.

A possible source of trouble that was unchecked is that a user may input the interval endpoints in the wrong order, that is, the largest first. What will the program do in this case? In a real application, the program should be written to exchange the values if they are entered incorrectly.

Newton would not have provided all the documentation and error checks if he were going to use the program only a few times. He felt, however, that he might use it again sometime next year or might lend it to a friend. These features would then be very helpful—the friend could use the program without studying the program statements.

9.1.2 Multiline Functions Many functions cannot be coded in a single line. An example is the built-in function SQR. Another example is the function g defined in Section 6.1:

$$g(x) = \begin{cases} x \text{ if } x < 0 \\ x^3 - x + 1 \text{ if } x \geq 0 \end{cases}$$

Fortunately, most versions of BASIC have features to handle such functions so that they can be used—or called—as easily as single-line functions.

The first statement in a multiline function also uses the keyword DEF, but in a different format

$$n \text{ DEF FN}g (d_1, d_2, \ldots, d_k)$$

where n is a line number, g is a letter of the alphabet, and $d_1, \ldots, d_k$ are the dummy arguments, which follow the same rules as those for single-line functions.[†] Note that no equals sign or expression follows the argument list.

Following the DEF statement are the lines that define the function; these statements are called the *body* of the function. At the end of the function definition must be a statement of the form

$$m \text{ FNEND.}$$

In the body of the function, the function name must be assigned a value in at least one line. This is done with a statement of the form

$$k \text{ LET FN}g = e$$

where k is a line number, g is the same letter that was used in the DEF statement, and e is any valid arithmetic expression representing the function. There may be more than one of these statements in the body—the last one executed before BASIC encounters the FNEND determines the value of the function for a given call.

The body of the function is like an independent program, contained within the program that uses it. The difference is that none of these statements is executed until the function is called; then the values of the arguments in the call replace the dummy arguments in the definition, and the function value is computed.

Multiline functions should be placed either at the beginning or at the end of the program. If they are placed at the end, a STOP statement should be placed immediately before the DEF statement; otherwise in some versions BASIC tries to execute the statements in the function body at the end of the program. Finally, transferring into or out of the body of a function (say with a GO TO) is illegal—the function must terminate by execution of the FNEND statement. Example 9.2 illustrates *illegal* transfers.

EXAMPLE 9.2

Program (segments only):

```
    100 LET Y = FNP(A)          200 GO TO 650
   110 PRINT Y                   . . .
    . . .                       500 STOP
   600 STOP                     510 DEF FNK(A)
   610 DEF FNP(X)                . . .
    . . .                       650 LET T = T + S
   750 LET FNP = 1 + X ^ 2       . . .
   760 GO TO 110                700 LET FNK = T ^ A
    . . .                        . . .
   900 FNEND                    800 FNEND
```

[†]Some versions of BASIC permit only one argument. Some versions allow functions to have no arguments.

Consider also Example 9.3.

EXAMPLE 9.3

Program:

```
10       DEF FNG(X)
15       LET Y = 2
20           IF X < 0                                    THEN 40
30                                                       GO TO 70
40 REM*          THEN
50                   LET FNG = X
60                                                       GO TO 85
70 REM*          ELSE
80                   LET FNG = X^3 - X + 1
85 REM* END IF 20
90       FNEND
93       LET Y = 1
95       PRINT "Y BEFORE:";Y
97       PRINT
100      FOR I = -3 TO 3 STEP .5
110          PRINT I,FNG(I)
120      NEXT I
123      PRINT
125      PRINT "Y AFTER:";Y
130      PRINT
140      PRINT "DUMMY ARGUMENT X:";X
150      END
```

Output:

```
Y BEFORE: 1
-3                    -3
-2.5                  -2.5
-2                    -2
-1.5                  -1.5
-1                    -1
-.5                   -.5
0                     1
.5                    .625
1                     1
1.5                   2.875
2                     7
2.5                   14.125
3                     25
Y AFTER:  2
DUMMY ARGUMENT X:  0
```

Example 9.3 tabulates the function g defined at the beginning of this section. The function definition is in lines 10-90. Note that there are two lines (50 and 80) that assign the value to the function; the line used depends in this case on the value of X.

For legibility, it is a good idea to indent the body of the function definition, as in this example.

Note that the variable X, used as a dummy argument in the function definition, is still zero even though the function has been called using other values; again this illustrates the point that dummy arguments are simply placeholders for the actual values. The dummy variable X in the function definition and the variable X outside the function definition are different, just as the array A and the variable A are different.

But consider Y, which is not a dummy argument for the function and is defined in the body of the function. This variable Y has the value 1 before the function is called (line 95) and 2 afterward (line 125). How can this be?

The variable Y is said to be a **global** variable in the sense that it refers to the same location both inside and outside the function. This is because Y is not a dummy argument. Therefore you must be careful that any global variable used outside and inside a function body is not redefined in the body, or it may have unexpected and possibly catastrophic effects on the results. A variable like X that is not global is said to be **local.**

Like the single-line functions, the multiline functions can reduce the programming effort—the body of the function needs to be coded only once, no matter how many calls are required. The effect here is more dramatic, since the multiline functions may require a large number of statements.

Furthermore, since multiline functions are self-contained, they readily lend themselves to modular program design and testing (but be wary of global variables). It is easier to test a function for correctness by a simple calling program before you include it in the program for which it is intended. The function can then be used in different places and you don't have to concern yourself with it while writing other parts of the program. Furthermore, the function can be changed easily.

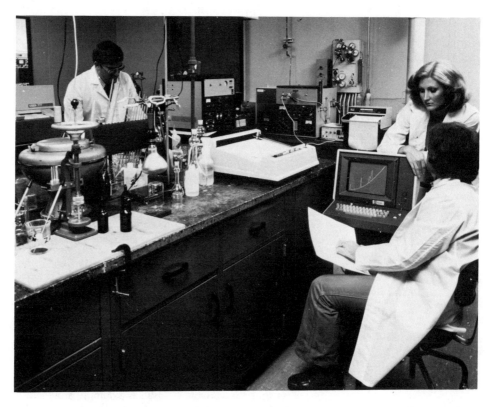

FIGURE 9.7 Computers are used extensively for biology applications. (Courtesy of Tektronix, Inc.)

For an application, we consider the problems of Alma Applecore, a biology student. She has to solve a number of problems like the following: If a pair of gnus have 16 offspring, what is the probability that at least 6 are males? The science genetics gives the solution to such problems by the formula

$$(m + f)^n$$

where n is the number of offspring; m represents the probability that the offspring will be male and f the probability that it will be female. When this expression is expanded (multiplied out), it has the form

$$m^n + C(n, 1)m^{n-1} f + C(n, 2)m^{n-2} f^2 + \cdots + C(n, n-1)m f^{n-1} + f^n$$

where $C(n, k)$ are coefficients (called the *binomial coefficients*) whose values depend on n and k; in other words, $C(n, k)$ is a *function* of n and k. If the probability that each offspring is male is 0.5 (a 50 percent chance), then

$$\frac{C(n, n-k)}{\text{sum of } all \text{ the } C(n, k)}$$

is the probability that of n offspring exactly k are males. Then the quantity

$$P = \frac{1 + C(n, 1) + C(n, 2) + \cdots + C(n, n-k)}{\text{sum of all the } C(n, k)}$$

is the probability that at least k offspring are males. This is the quantity Alma needs for the above problem.

Furthermore the function $C(n, k)$ can be defined as

$$C(n, k) = \frac{n!}{k! \, (n-k)!}$$

where $n!$ (n factorial) = $1 \cdot 2 \cdot 3 \cdot \cdots \cdot (n-1) \cdot n$. For example,

$$C(5, 2) = \frac{5!}{2! \; 3!} = \frac{1 \cdot 2 \cdot 3 \cdot 4 \cdot 5}{(1 \cdot 2) \, (1 \cdot 2 \cdot 3)} = \frac{120}{12} = 10$$

Since Alma makes many errors computing these quantities by hand, she decides to write a BASIC program to do the computation. She also decides to make the program handle slightly more general problems by requesting the user to input the starting and ending values of k in the numerator of P above ($0 \leqslant k \leqslant n$). In this way Alma can get results for such equations involving

"at least 1 female"   (k runs from 1 to n)

or   "between l_1 and l_2 males"   (k runs from $n - l_2$ to $n - l_1$)

or   "exactly 1 male"   (k runs from $n - 1$ to $n - 1$).

By the above formulas, she derives the following outline:

I.   Ask, "What is the number of offspring?" (N).

II.   Ask, "What are the lower and upper limits for the offspring in question?" (L1 and L2)

III. Initialize sums S1 = 0 and S2 = 2.

IV. For K = L1 to L2 (compute numerator)
    A. If K = 0
        then (first term)
        1. Set S1 = S1 + 1
        else
        2. If K = N
            then (last term)
            a. Set S1 = S1 + 1
            else (all other terms)
            b. Set S1 = S1 + C(N,K)

V.   For K = 1 to N – 1 (compute denominator)
    A. Set S2 = S2 + C(N,K)

VI. Set P = S1/S2

VII. Print "The probability of the requested offspring outcome is:"; P

Note that S2 is initialized to 2; the first coefficient and the last equal 1. This outline assumes that N $\geq$ 2.

The outline is not yet complete. Parts IV.A.2.b and V.A refer to C(N,K), which conveniently represents a function call. Before Alma codes the program, she needs first to write the function definition for C(N,K). It is tempting to define it as follows:

VIII. Define Function C(N,K):
    A. Set P1, P2, P3 = 1
    B. For I = 1 to K
        1. Set P1 = P1 * I
    C. For I = 1 to N – K
        1. Set P2 = P2 * I
    D. For I = 1 to N
        1. Set P3 = P3 * I
    E. Set C = P3/(P1 * P2)

This will do the job, assuming that the function is always called with $\emptyset < K < N$, but with a little study Alma realizes that she can easily improve its efficiency. She notes that C(N,K) can be written as

$$C(N,K) = \frac{N!}{K!\,(N-K)!} = \frac{(K+1)\cdot(K+2)\cdot\cdots\cdot(N-1)\cdot N}{(N-K)!}$$

Using this form, she rewrites the definition of C:

VIII. Define Function C(N,K):
- A. Set P1, P2 = 1
- B. For I = K + 1 to N
    - 1. Set P1 = P1 * I
- C. For I = 1 to N – K
    - 1. Set P2 = P2 * I
- D. Set C = P1/P2

This is much more efficient. There are only $(N - K - 1) + N - K = 2N - 2K - 1$ multiplications here versus $N + (N - K) + K = 2N$ in the first attempt. Also, BASIC must increase the loop index by increments and test for the exit from the loop $(N - K - 1) + (N - K - 1) = 2N - 2K - 2$ times here versus $(K - 1) + (N - K - 1) + (N - 1) = 2N - 3$ times in the first case.

You should be aware that even with these improvements the above solution of the problem is far from the best one. For one thing, the values can easily become too large for the computer to store, with resulting *overflow* and invalid quantity. Many more efficient and accurate schemes exist; this one is used simply to show how to use the function definition.

The resulting program is in Example 9.4.

EXAMPLE 9.4 ═══

Program:

```
10 REM//////////////////////////////////////////////////////////////////
15 REM/ PROGRAM NAME:  OFFSPRING                                        /
20 REM/ USING BINOMIAL COEFFICIENTS THIS PROGRAM COMPUTES THE           /
30 REM/ PROBABILITY OF A RANGE OF THE NUMBER OF MALE OR FEMALE          /
40 REM/ OFFSPRING GIVEN THE TOTAL NUMBER OF OFFSPRING.                  /
50 REM/ PROGRAMMER:  A. APPLECORE                    12/6/77            /
60 REM/                        VARIABLES                               /
70 REM/ N = NUMBER OF OFFSPRING (N > = 2)  K = COUNTER FOR COEFFICIENTS /
80 REM/ L1,L2 = LOWER AND UPPER LIMITS FOR COEFFICIENTS                 /
90 REM/ S1 = SUM FOR NUMERATOR OF PROBABILITY                          /
100 REM/ S2 = SUM FOR DENOMINATOR OF PROBABILITY                       /
110 REM/ P = PROBABILITY OF OUTCOME        C = BINOMIAL COEFF. FUNCTION /
120 REM/ P1,P2 = PRODUCTS ACCUMULATED IN COMPUTATION OF C              /
130 REM/ N1,K1 = DUMMY ARGUMENTS CORRESPONDING TO N AND K              /
140 REM//////////////////////////////////////////////////////////////////
150      DEF FNC(N1,K1)
160          LET P1 = 1
170          LET P2 = 1
175 REM  COMPUTE NUMERATOR
180          FOR I = K1+1 TO N1
190              LET P1 = P1*I
200          NEXT I
205 REM  COMPUTE DENOMINATOR
210          FOR I = 1 TO N1-K1
220              LET P2 = P2*I
230          NEXT I
240          LET FNC = P1/P2
250      FNEND
260      PRINT "WHAT IS THE NUMBER OF OFFSPRING";
270      INPUT N
280      PRINT "WHAT ARE THE LOWER AND UPPER LIMITS FOR THE OFFSPRING"
281      PRINT "IN QUESTION";
290      INPUT L1,L2
300      LET S1 = 0
310      LET S2 = 2
320      FOR K = L1 TO L2
330          IF K = 0                                    THEN 350
340                                                       GO TO 380
350 REM*         THEN (FIRST TERM)
360                 LET S1 = S1 + 1
370                                                       GO TO 470
380 REM*         ELSE
390              IF K = N                                THEN 410
400                                                       GO TO 440
410 REM*             THEN (LAST TERM)
420                     LET S1 = S1 + 1
430                                                       GO TO 460
440 REM*             ELSE (ALL OTHER TERMS)
450                     LET S1 = S1 + FNC(N,K)
460 REM*         END IF 390
470 REM*     END IF 320
480      NEXT K
485 REM  SUM UP ALL TERMS IN DENOMINATOR
490      FOR K = 1 TO N-1
500          LET S2 = S2 + FNC(N,K)
510      NEXT K
520      LET P = S1/S2
530      PRINT "THE PROBABILITY OF THE REQUESTED OFFSPRING IS:";P
540 END
```

```
Output 1:

WHAT IS THE NUMBER OF OFFSPRING?    16
WHAT ARE THE LOWER AND UPPER LIMITS FOR THE OFFSPRING
IN QUESTION?    1,5
THE PROBABILITY OF THE REQUESTED OFFSPRING IS:  .1050415

Output 2:

WHAT IS THE NUMBER OF OFFSPRING?    8
WHAT ARE THE LOWER AND UPPER LIMITS FOR THE OFFSPRING
IN QUESTION?    3,7
THE PROBABILITY OF THE REQUESTED OFFSPRING IS:  .8515625

Output 3:

WHAT IS THE NUMBER OF OFFSPRING?    36
WHAT ARE THE LOWER AND UPPER LIMITS FOR THE OFFSPRING
IN QUESTION?    8,8
 FLOATING OVERFLOW IN 200.
 FLOATING OVERFLOW IN 200.
         *
         *
         *
```

The main point to observe in Example 9.4 is the use of the function definition (lines 150–250). These N1 and K1 are dummy arguments. The alternatives would be to replace the function calls (lines 450 and 500) with code equivalent to the eight lines of the function definition.

Note that the output in the third case indicates an overflow error. In this case, the value of P1 became too large because of the large choice for N. A different way of programming this algorithm could prevent the overflow in this example.

9.2   Subroutines

Subroutines are similar to functions in several respects. They can be referred to from other places in the program. They promote modular design of programs, enabling the programmer to divide long programs into workable pieces. They also eliminate repetition; a sequence of statements required more than once in a program needs to be coded only once as a subroutine.

Why use a subroutine instead of a function? Sometimes a segment of code is constructed more conveniently as a subroutine. Unlike functions, subroutines do not have names or arguments. Therefore the variables used in the body of a subroutine are *global*—they have values that have meaning outside the subroutine. Furthermore, the subroutine concept is much more important in other programming languages like FORTRAN, where subroutines are much more powerful. Often subroutines will execute faster than functions. In many cases, especially in BASIC, the choice is simply a matter of preference.

Since subroutines do not have names in BASIC, they can begin with any valid statement. We recommend that a REM statement be used to initiate the beginning of the subroutine and its purpose. However, the last statement in the subroutine must be a **RETURN** statement, which transfers control back to the statement immediately following the latest reference, or call, to the subroutine. The statement has the form

$$n \text{ RETURN}$$

where n is a line number.

Note that the action of the RETURN statement depends on where the subroutine was called from, unlike a GO TO, which always returns control to the same line number. Thus, *only a* RETURN *statement is allowed to terminate a subroutine;* one cannot "exit" from a subroutine with a GO TO or an IF-THEN or an ON-GO-TO statement. There may be more than one RETURN statement in a subroutine, however.

A simple subroutine is given by Example 9.5.

EXAMPLE 9.5

Program (segment only):

```
500 REM  SUBROUTINE TO COMPUTE AREA OF TRIANGLE:
510      IF W = 1                             THEN 540
520                                           GO TO 570
530 REM*      THEN (RIGHT TRIANGLE)
540              LET A = .5*S(1)*S(2)
550              RETURN
560 REM*      ELSE (NOT RIGHT TRIANGLE)
570              LET P1 = (S(1) + S(2) + S(3))/2
580              LET T1 = P1
590              FOR I1 = 1 TO 3
600                 LET T1 = T1*(P1-A(I1))
610              NEXT I1
620              LET A = SQR(T1)
630              RETURN
640 REM* END IF 510
```

This subroutine (it is not a complete program) computes the area of a triangle using

$$A = 1/2\, S(1) \cdot S(2) \qquad \text{(if it is a right triangle)}$$

and

$$A = \sqrt{P \cdot (P - S(1)) \cdot (P - S(2)) \cdot (P - S(3))}$$

otherwise, where S(1), S(2), S(3) are the lengths of the sides and P = (S(1) + S(2) + S(3))/2. It is more efficient to use the first formula if the triangle is a right triangle. Note that two RETURN statements are used (lines 550 and 630).

For the subroutine to be used properly, the variables S(1), S(2), S(3), and W should be assigned values before the subroutine is called. The other variables P1, T1, and I1 are global and used strictly for the intermediate computation. These variables should not be used in the rest of the program since their value will be changed each time the subroutine is called. The variables S(1), S(2), S(3), W, and A (area), however, act like arguments in the sense that they contain the values of interest on return from the subroutine.

Referring to a subroutine in BASIC is much simpler than calling functions. A subroutine is called by means of the **GOSUB** statement. To the user, it behaves in part like a GO TO statement—to control transfers to the given line number. The distinction is that the GOSUB statement also sets up the linkage necessary for control to RETURN from the subroutine to the statement immediately following the GOSUB. The general form of the statement is

n GOSUB m

where m is the line number of the first statement in the subroutine.

Thus, a program may have more than one call (GOSUB) to a given subroutine; control will always return to the statement following the latest GOSUB to call the routine. Furthermore, since a GOSUB may appear in the body of a subroutine, one subroutine may call another. The call cannot be circular, however; having subroutine A call subroutine B, which calls subroutine A again, is illegal. Thus, a program of the form in Example 9.6 is illegal.

EXAMPLE 9.6 ===

Program (segment only):

```
                    1ØØ GOSUB 5ØØ
                         . . .
                  ┌─►5ØØ REM SUBROUTINE 1
                  │  51Ø LET A = X + Y
                  │  52Ø GOSUB 8ØØ ──────┐
        call      │       . . .          │
     subroutine 1 │                      │
                  │  65Ø PRINT X         │
                  │  66Ø RETURN          │ call subroutine 2
                  │  8ØØ SUBROUTINE 2◄───┘
                  │  81Ø LET X = A + B
                  └─ 82Ø GOSUB 5ØØ
                         . . .
                    9ØØ RETURN
```

Like multiline functions, subroutines should be kept apart, in a sense, from the rest of the program. Generally, all the subroutines are placed at the end of the program. One must be careful, then, to place a STOP statement immediately before the first subroutine; otherwise BASIC will execute the statements in the body of the first subroutine. When BASIC encounters a RETURN statement in this case, it will terminate execution with an error message similar to

RETURN WITHOUT GOSUB IN n

where n is the line number of the RETURN statement.

Example 9.7 illustrates how subroutines can be used to reduce the coding effort.

EXAMPLE 9.7 ══

Program:

```
 10 REM//////////////////////////////////////////////////////////////////
 15 REM/ PROGRAM NAME: SUMS                                                /
 20 REM/ THIS PROGRAM COMPUTES THE SUMS OF (1) ALL THE ELEMENTS OF AN      /
 30 REM/ ARRAY, (2) THE ODD NUMBERED ELEMENTS, AND (3) EACH FOUR           /
 40 REM/ ADJACENT ELEMENTS, EACH SUM COMPUTED USING A SINGLE SUBROUTINE. /
 50 REM/ DATA MUST BE PROVIDED STARTING AT LINE 500.  THE FIRST NUMBER     /
 60 REM/ IS THE NUMBER OF VALUES.                                          /
 70 REM/                               VARIABLES                           /
 80 REM/ A = ARRAY OF NUMBERS           N = NUMBER OF VALUES IN A          /
 90 REM/ U = UPPER LIMIT IN SUM         L = STARTING ELEMENT IN SUM        /
100 REM/ D = STEP SIZE IN SUM           T = SUM                           /
110 REM//////////////////////////////////////////////////////////////////
150       DIM A(50)
160       READ N
170       FOR I = 1 TO N
180          READ A(I)
190       NEXT I
195 REM   SPECIFY UPPER AND LOWER LIMITS IN SUM.
200       LET U = N
210       LET L = 1
220       LET D = 1
230       GOSUB 360
240       PRINT "TOTAL, ALL NUMBERS, IS:";T
241       PRINT
245 REM   SUM ODD NUMBERED ELEMENTS
250       LET D = 2
260       GOSUB 360
270       PRINT "TOTAL, ODD NUMBERED VALUES, IS: ";T
271       PRINT
280       LET D = 1
285 REM   SUMS OF 4 SUCCESSIVE ELEMENTS
290       FOR I = 1 TO N STEP 4
300          LET L = I
310          LET U = I+3
320          GOSUB 360
330          PRINT "TOTAL, FOUR SUCCESSIVE VALUES, IS:";T
340       NEXT I
350       STOP
360 REM   SUBROUTINE TO COMPUTE SUMS
370       LET T = 0
380       FOR I1 = L TO U STEP D
390          LET T = T + A(I1)
400       NEXT I1
410       RETURN
500 DATA 14,5,-13,15,-7,20,-21,15,-4,25,-18,125,-40,55,-8
510 END
```

Output:

```
TOTAL, ALL NUMBERS, IS:  149

TOTAL, ODD NUMBERED VALUES, IS:  260

TOTAL, FOUR SUCCESSIVE VALUES, IS:  0
TOTAL, FOUR SUCCESSIVE VALUES, IS:  10
TOTAL, FOUR SUCCESSIVE VALUES, IS:  92
TOTAL, FOUR SUCCESSIVE VALUES, IS:  47
```

Example 9.7 effectively uses a subroutine (lines 360–410) to add numbers. The numbers must be in the array A, and limits must be provided for the starting, ending, and step values (L, U, and D) for the loop index. The total is returned as the variable T. By varying L, U, and D one can sum a wide variety of subsets of elements of A.

There are three GOSUB statements that transfer control to the subroutine (lines 230, 260, and 320). Although the subroutine consists of only five lines, this sequence would have to be included in place of the GOSUB statements if a subroutine were not to be used.

Observe that there is only one variable I1 that is used neither for input to the subroutine nor output from it. Again I1 should not be used in the rest of the program if possible. It is a good idea to code each such variable name with a digit unique to a given subroutine if possible; for subroutine 1, for instance, code these variables as I1, S1, P1, and so on.

Finally, observe that the same job could have been done as efficiently using a multiline function in place of the subroutine.

Before we go on to the next topic, we should mention that some versions of BASIC include an **ON-GOSUB** statement that is analogous to the ON-GO TO statement. The general form of the statement is

$$n \text{ ON } e \text{ GOSUB } n_1, n_2, n_3, \ldots$$

where e is an expression that evaluates to a positive integer and $n_1, n_2, n_3, \ldots$ are line numbers of subroutines.[†] If the value of e is k, control is transferred to the subroutine at line n_k. The ON-GOSUB statement represents a more economical and more easily readable alternative to a sequence of nested selection structures (IF-THEN-ELSE) when there are a number of subroutines. For example, the sequence of steps

1. If $0 \leqslant N < 10$ then GOSUB to 500
2. If $10 \leqslant N < 20$ then GOSUB to 1000
3. If $20 \leqslant N < 30$ then GOSUB to 2000
4. If $30 \leqslant N < 40$ then GOSUB to 2500

in a program outline could be coded in the single line

$$50 \text{ ON INT}(N/10) + 1 \text{ GOSUB } 500, 1000, 2000, 2500$$

9.3 Further Considerations of Program Design: Efficiency

For most of the programs we have written, a modular approach to the design problem is not critical. But as programs get longer, they become increasingly difficult to handle as a complete unit. Then modular design, the use of functions and subroutines, becomes important, since it is much easier to deal with smaller, less complex segments.

As we pointed out in Chapter 5, writing the outline for the individual modules—completing the most elementary segments and then stepping to higher levels by combining these elements—is in a sense the opposite of top-down program design. Both

[†]Other forms of the statement are

$$n \text{ GOSUB } (n_1, n_2, n_3, \ldots) e$$

or

$$n \text{ GOSUB } n_1, n_2, n_3, \ldots e$$

approaches have proponents. For large programs, we recommend a combination of the two, in the sense that the modules, as functions and subroutines, should be coded and tested individually after the final outline is completed.

How large should the modules be? If the modules are too large, understanding and debugging them will be more difficult. If they are too small, their very number can be confusing. There are no set rules for such modules, but some rules of thumb can be followed.[†]

1. Modules should not extend beyond one page (say 30 lines).
2. They should contain no more than two IF statements.
3. They should contain no more than five variables.

These rules are to promote clarity. Obviously exceptions must be made, since each module should also be a complete unit.

Finally, each module should be written as generally as possible without sacrificing clarity. This means that variable names should be used as parameters in place of constants. For example, if the loop beginning with

$$100 \text{ FOR I} = 1 \text{ TO } 10$$

is used to print out the rows of an array, it is better to write

$$100 \text{ FOR I} = 1 \text{ TO N}$$

where the value of N is provided to the subroutine or function. In this way the code can be used, unaltered, in other programs. Save work!

Furthermore, your analysis of a program should not stop with eliminating bugs, unless it is a one-shot program. You should peruse the code to see whether you can improve the program in some way. Remember, of course, that efficiency should have been considered in the design stage. But it is often possible to improve efficiency—saving space or time—without sacrificing clarity and without major changes in the outline. Quite often, improving the run time of a program means increasing the memory space used, and vice versa. If you do make a change, you have to decide which one is more important. If the speed improvements do not seriously affect the memory space requirements (for example, to the point at which the program will not run without major modifications), you should make the changes. And after making such changes, you may want to test the programs or modules again to be sure they do the same things as before.

Reducing the memory requirements of a program is difficult without a lengthy rewriting job or without more advanced features that are generally not available in BASIC. Therefore we shall concentrate on efficiency of execution. Many things can be done to improve the run time; here are a few of the simplest ones.

First, **remove unnecessary computations from loops.** Loops result in repetition, and consequently any statement whose value or condition does not depend on the parameters that are changing with each repetition should not be there. This matter was considered in Example 6.7. Consider the following segment:

[†]From C. B. Kreitzberg and Ben Shneiderman, FORTRAN *Programming—A Spiral Approach* (New York: Harcourt Brace Jovanovich, 1975), p. 336.

```
100 FOR I = 1 TO 100
110       LET S(I) = 0
120       FOR J = 1 TO 100
130            LET S(I) = S(I) + A * B * R(I) - T(J)
140       NEXT J
150 NEXT I
```

The product A * B, although constant throughout both loops, is evaluated 10,000 times.[†] Similarly, S(I) and R(I) do not depend on the inner loops and need not be there. An improved segment is

```
100 LET C = A * B
110 FOR I = 1 TO 100
120       LET V = 0
130       FOR J = 1 TO 100
140            LET V = V - T(J)
150       NEXT J
160       LET S(I) = 100 * C * R(I) - V
170 NEXT I
```

Careful examination will show that this segment accomplishes precisely what the first one does, with less work. The product A * B is computed only once, and the product C * R(I) only 100 times (versus 10,000 in the first case). Also, the variable V is used in place of S(I) in the inner loop. This is possible since I does not change in the loop, and BASIC needs less time to find the location of a nonsubscripted variable than a subscripted variable. (See below.) Even with the above improvements, a further saving can easily be made. Can you find it?

Second, **remove common subexpressions.** Another inefficient way of coding is illustrated by the following segment:

```
100 LET R1 = (-B + SQR(B^2 - 4 * A * C))/(2 * A)
110 LET R2 = (-B - SQR(B^2 - 4 * A * C))/(2 * A)
```

It is wasteful to do all this computation a second time, since none of the variables has changed value. A better way is to remove the common subexpressions:

```
100 LET D = 2 * A
105 LET V = SQR(B^2 - 4 * A * C)
110 LET R1 = (-B + V)/D
120 LET R2 = (-B - V)/D
```

This results in five less arithmetic operations (multiplied by the number of times these statements are executed in a loop). The only drawback is a slight loss of clarity.

Third, **nest FOR loops with increasing range of the FOR index if possible.** Sometimes

---

[†]An efficient BASIC compiler might remove such a product from the loop during the translation, but don't trust that your compiler will do it.

the order in which loops are nested does not affect results. If we assume, for example, that three-dimensional arrays are legal, the loops

```
200 LET S = Ø
210 FOR I = 1 TO 20
220      FOR J = 1 TO 5
230          FOR K = 1 TO 1Ø
240              LET S = S + A(I,J,K)
250          NEXT K
260      NEXT J
270 NEXT I
```

can be written, say, with K = 1 TO 1Ø as the outer index with no effect on the sum S. But remember that in each loop, BASIC must increase by increments and test the index for exit from the loop. In the

"I" loop: increment and test occur 20 times
"J" loop: increment and test occur 100 times
"K" loop: increment and test occur 1000 times

Simply rearrange the loops so that nesting occurs with increasing range of the FOR index:

```
200  LET S = Ø
210  FOR J = 1 TO 5
220      FOR K = 1 TO 1Ø
230          FOR I = 1 TO 2Ø
240              LET S = S + A(I,J,K)
250          NEXT I
260      NEXT K
270  NEXT J
```

This results in substantial savings. In the

"J" loop: increment and test occur 5 times
"K" loop: increment and test occur 50 times
"I" loop: increment and test occur 1000 times

Fourth, "unroll" a loop if decreasing the execution time is critical. Sometimes increased speed can be realized by unrolling, or reducing the number of loop increments and tests. For example, changing

```
FOR I = 1 TO 1ØØØ
    LET A(I) = Ø
NEXT I
```

to

```
FOR I = 1 TO 1ØØØ  STEP 2
    LET A(I) = Ø
    LET A(I + 1) = Ø
NEXT I
```

reduces the frequency of the loop incrementing and testing code by the factor 2. Extra computation is introduced, however, because of the subscripted variable A(I + 1). Generally, the loop increment and test code are more complex, resulting in a savings. Also, more storage space is used for the extra line or lines of code. This can be carried further by increasing the step value and the corresponding number of statements. In the limit (which is impractical) in this case, there would be 1000 assignment statements and no loop at all.

Five, **use simple variables in place of one-dimensional arrays and one-dimensional arrays in place of arrays of higher dimensions if clarity is not sacrificed.** As we mentioned above, some computation is needed for locating elements in arrays. The name of the array determines the starting point for the elements, and the subscript is used to locate the item relative to the starting point. Without going into details, we remark that the amount of computation required increases with the number of dimensions. Thus, never use an array or especially an array of higher dimensions unless there is a good organizational reason for doing so. The segment

```
300 LET S = 0
310 FOR I = 1 TO 25
320     FOR J = 1 TO 50
330         LET S = S + A(I,J)
340     NEXT J
350 NEXT I
```

will require more execution time than

```
300 LET S = 0
310 FOR I = 1 TO 1250
320     LET S = S + B(I)
330 NEXT I
```

even though the same number of elements is involved.

There are many other steps you can take to make a program more efficient. You must be careful, however, not to lose the clarity you strove so hard for earlier.

9.4   The CHAIN Statement

Most versions of BASIC include the **CHAIN** statement, which provides, in a sense, a more general method of linking program segments than either multiline functions or subroutines do.

The CHAIN statement terminates execution of the current program and transfers control to a specified program that has been saved. The general form of the statement is

n CHAIN P, m

where P is the name of a saved program and m is a line number in P where execution is to begin. If m is not given, execution starts at the first line of P. For example,

200 CHAIN PLOT, 50

would terminate execution of the current program and begin executing the program PLOT, starting at line 50.

On some systems, the CHAIN statement has the option of passing the values of single arithmetic variables (no arrays) to the chained program. The system we use here uses the modified form (the colon)

n CHAIN: P, m

to accomplish this. On some systems, character strings or files can be passed also. If data cannot be passed to the chained program, then the CHAIN statement is severely limited.

Besides providing the advantages of modularity, the CHAIN statement yields another advantage. Some systems have a limit on the number of lines per program. Chaining several programs together will enable you to get around this restriction.

Furthermore, a chained program can also contain CHAIN statements. This means that you can chain from program A to program B, execute program B, and then chain back to the line number in A immediately following the first chain. In this way the programs act like a GOSUB-RETURN combination, but in a more general way—they don't have to be stored physically together within the same program, in contrast with a program having a subroutine. Also, each program is then calling the other. In a sense, these programs can be called **coroutines** for that reason; there is no subordinate relation. For this scheme to work properly, both programs must first be saved.

It is difficult to give any applications of meaning here, but a simple example, 9.8, shows how the CHAIN statement works.

EXAMPLE 9.8

```
Program (1):

100 REM PROGRAM 1 - SAVED UNDER THE NAME FIRST
110 READ A,B,C
120 PRINT "EXIT FROM FIRST"
130 CHAIN:  SECOND, 20
140 PRINT "ENTER FIRST"
150 PRINT "S = ";S, "T = ";T
160 DATA 6,30,64
170 END

Program (2):

10 REM PROGRAM 2 - SAVED UNDER THE NAME SECOND.
20 PRINT "ENTER SECOND"
30 LET S = A + B + C
40 LET T = SQR(S)
50 PRINT "EXIT FROM SECOND"
60 CHAIN:  FIRST, 140
70 END

Output:  (RUN FIRST)

EXIT FROM FIRST
ENTER SECOND
EXIT FROM SECOND
ENTER FIRST
S = 100     T = 10
```

In Example 9.8, the program FIRST reads values A, B, and C and saves the values for the program SECOND, which uses them to compute S and T. The values of S and T are then passed to FIRST by the CHAIN statement in line 6∅.

9.5   Functions and Recursion

We have seen that it is possible and useful for a function to call another function. You may have already asked the related question, "Can a function call itself too?" The answer is that some BASIC systems do allow a function to call itself. Such a function is said to be **recursive,** and the process itself is known as **recursion.**

At first glance you may wonder how this could possibly work. It may seem that executing such a procedure would result in an infinite loop. To understand how it works, we consider a *recursive definition* of a function. Certain functions lend themselves nicely to being defined in terms of themselves. The classic example of such a function is the *factorial function F.* We can write

$$\text{For } n \text{ a positive integer, } F(n) = n! = 1 \cdot 2 \cdot 3 \cdot \cdots \cdot n$$

which is a nonrecursive definition, since F does not appear on the right-hand side. Alternatively, we can write

$$\text{For } n \text{ a positive integer, } F(n) = \begin{cases} n \cdot F(n-1) & \text{if } n \neq 0 \\ 1 & \text{if } n = 0 \end{cases}$$

which is recursive; F is defined in terms of itself. The key to the significance of the definition is that for any positive integer n, the repetitions generated by the definition eventually terminate (when $F(0)$ is called); a value for F is eventually determined.

Suppose we apply the function F to the argument $n = 5$, using the latter definition. We have

$$F(5) = 5 \cdot F(4)$$

since $5 \neq 0$. Now to get the value of $F(4)$, we have to return to the definition

$$F(4) = 4 \cdot F(3)$$

which requires a value of $F(3)$. Thus, from successive applications of the definition, we have

$$F(3) = 3 \cdot F(2)$$
$$F(2) = 2 \cdot F(1)$$
$$F(1) = 1 \cdot F(0)$$

and finally we get out of the cycle, since

$$F(0) = 1$$

which does not require applying the definition again.

Now the values of F can be completed in the reverse order:

$$F(1) = 1 \cdot 1 = 1$$
$$F(2) = 2 \cdot F(1) = 2 \cdot 1 = 2$$
$$F(3) = 3 \cdot F(2) = 3 \cdot 2 = 6$$
$$F(4) = 4 \cdot F(3) = 3 \cdot 6 = 24$$
$$F(5) = 5 \cdot F(4) = 5 \cdot 24 = 120$$

giving us the final result. A recursive function in BASIC operates in the same way. Clearly, this example does very little to illustrate the value of recursion; obviously the computation could be done more efficiently using iteration in a loop (with the first definition). It is unfortunate that most simple examples of recursion can usually be solved more easily by other approaches. Recursion finds useful application in such areas as compiler writing and in *data structures*, a topic concerned with representing large collections of data in computer memory.

Defining a valid recursive function in BASIC is analogous to the above definition. You must be sure to have a statement that defines the function nonrecursively for at least one value that will terminate the sequence of function calls.

Example 9.9 illustrates the use of recursion in BASIC to compute the above function.

EXAMPLE 9.9

Program:

```
10 REM/ THIS PROGRAM COMPUTES N! FOR N A NONNEGATIVE INTEGER
15 REM/ USING A RECURSIVE FUNCTION.
20      DEF FNF(N1)
30          IF N1 < = 1                              THEN 50
40                                                   GO TO 80
50 REM*      THEN
60              LET FNF = 1
70                                                   GO TO 100
80 REM*      ELSE
90              LET FNF = N1 * FNF(N1 - 1)
100 REM*     END IF 30
110      FNEND
200      PRINT "WHAT VALUE OF N DO YOU WANT";
210      INPUT N
220      LET V = FNF(N)
230      PRINT "FOR N = ";N;" N! = ";V
240 END
```

Output:

```
WHAT VALUE OF N DO YOU WANT?    7
FOR N = 7    N! = 5040
```

In Example 9.9, the function FNF will continue calling itself (line 90) until the argument is less than or equal to 1. Then it will return function values in the opposite order (like the computation using the definition) until the final value is computed.

Here the sequence of function calls is FNF(7), FNF(6), FNF(5), . . . , FNF(2), FNF(1), after which the products are computed successively using these values as factors in the reverse order. Line 6Ø ensures that the procedure will terminate.

Note that the function has a built-in protection against an infinite loop. What will happen if you input N as –5? The program could be improved to print a warning for invalid values of N.

9.6   A Final Application: Computer Art

An interesting application for subroutines is computer art. This application also illustrates to what extent computer uses are being explored today. The examples presented here are

FIGURE 9.8 Computers have been used by artists to generate sometimes startling results. This example is entitled, *Claustrophobia,* **by Aldo Giorgini, drawn by the help of the program FIELDS by Giorgini-Chen.**

primitive, but they convey some of the possibilities available to an artist using only a line printer.

To do this work, we can think of a two-dimensional array as our "canvas" on which to produce our picture. Once the picture is completed, it is a simple matter to print out the array to display the result. Since the canvas is numeric, we should first convert the array row by row to a string array for printing; we can replace zeros by blanks, for example.

Our pictures will consist of collages of rectangles. It should be evident after this discussion how other shapes could be included.

Suppose now that we want to "paint" a rectangle into our array. What information must we provide? Some thought will show that we need only

1. The height H and width W in terms of the number of array locations (assuming that the rectangle will have sides parallel to the page)
2. The location in the array of the upper left-hand corner of the rectangle (given as row R1, column C1, of the array)
3. The number used to fill in the rectangle (this number will be converted by the CHANGE statement to a special character)

We shall write a subroutine that uses this information to construct a rectangle. Furthermore, we shall need a subroutine to "erase" the array—to initialize the array elements to "32", which is converted to a blank space by the CHANGE statement.

We can now outline a solution for each job.

(Subroutine to erase the array)

I. For I1 = 1 to R (no. of rows)
    A. For I1 = 1 to C (no. of columns)
        1. Set A(I1,J1) = B(1) (B(1) represents the numeric equivalent of a blank)

(Subroutine to construct the rectangle)

Given the upper left-hand corner of the rectangle in A as row no. = R1, col. no. = C1:

I. For I1 = R1 to R1 + H − 1 (height)
    A. For J1 = C1 to C1 + W − 1 (width)
        1. Set A(I1,J1) = F (the fill-in character)

The latter subroutine is to be called once for each rectangle generated. By manipulating the variables R1, C1, W, and H appropriately, we can generate interesting patterns of overlapping rectangles.

We have outlines of routines to erase the array A and to construct the rectangles; we also need a routine that will determine the variables H, W, R1, C1, and F. This routine then determines the overall pattern—the shape of the rectangles, their relative position, and the fill character for each one. The above routine determined the fundamental shape of the basic object to be used (rectangles versus, say, circles).

For the first example, we intend to produce a sequence of overlapping squares, similar to Figure 9.9. This pattern is easily produced in a loop. Input variables for this subroutine include an array (V) of fill characters, the number of rectangles to generate (N), and the array limits R and C.

There are many different ways to build such a pattern. We choose to add a fixed

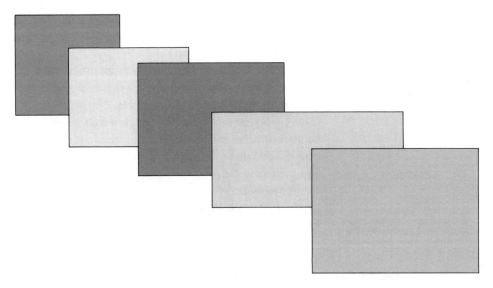

FIGURE 9.9   Overlapping rectangles

amount to the height H and width W of each successive square (different dimensions must be used because the scale across the page is about two-thirds that down the page). We choose to increase the starting point of each successive square by an amount dependent on the loop index.

The resulting outline is

I.   Initialize H, W, R1, and C1 to zero.

II. For I = 1 to N (number of rectangles)

    A. Choose fill character F = V(I)

    B. Add 4 to H, 6 to W, and (I + 1) to each of R1 and C1.

    C. EXIT from loop if R1 > R or C1 > C (outside limits of array).

    D. Choose upper limit for the row element as H1 = min(R, R1 + H – 1)

    E. Choose upper limit for column element as W1 = min(C, C1 + W – 1)

    F. Call subroutine to generate the rectangle.

Steps II.D and II.E ensure that the rectangles do not overflow beyond the boundaries of the array A. Since H1 and W1 are computed here, they may be used in place of R1 + H – 1 and C1 + W – 1 as the upper limits in the loops to generate the rectangles (see the previous outline). Note that this subroutine calls the second subroutine.

For consistency it is reasonable to write the code to print A as a subroutine also:

I.   For I = 1 to R

    A. For J = 1 to C

        1. Set P(J) = A(I,J)

    B. Set P(∅) = C

    C. CHANGE P to P$

    D. Print P$

Note that we print the array one row at a time; the values in each row are changed to character form for printing. This is necessary, since most versions of BASIC do not accept two-dimensional string arrays.

The complete program, then, will consist of calls to the above subroutines. Making minor changes in the overall pattern means changing some of the statements in the third subroutine (for example, adding I to H, 2 * I to W in step II.B). Important changes can be made simply by replacing this subroutine by an entirely different one (see the second example below) or by replacing the rectangle generator with, for example, a triangle generator, or doing both. More routines could be added to produce patterns with rectangles and circles and the like. The possibilities are endless, and it is easy to experiment with different parameters.

The first example is given in Example 9.10, with the complete program (to save space, leading comments are not given).

EXAMPLE 9.10

Program:

```
  10 DIM A(50,50),V(50),P(50)
  15 REM READ LIST OF FILL CHARACTERS
  20     READ V$
  25 REM CONVERT TO NUMERIC EQUIVALENT
  30     CHANGE V$ TO V
  35 REM DEFINE BLANK SPACE FILL CHARACTER
  40     LET B$ = " "
  45     LET B(0) = 1
  50     CHANGE B$ TO B
  51 REM NO. OF RECTANGLES TO GENERATE; ARRAY LIMITS
  52     READ N,R,C
  55 REM CALL SUBROUTINE TO BLANK OUR ARRAY A.
  60     GOSUB 1000
  65 REM CALL SUBROUTINE TO GENERATE THE OVERALL PATTERN.
  70     GOSUB 3000
  75 REM CALL SUBROUTINE TO PRINT THE ARRAY A.
  80     GOSUB 4000
  90     STOP
1000 REM SUBROUTINE TO BLANK OUT A.
1010     FOR I1 = 1 TO R
1020        FOR J1 = 1 TO C
1030           LET A(I1,J1) = B(1)
1040        NEXT J1
1050     NEXT I1
1060     RETURN
2000 REM SUBROUTINE TO GENERATE A RECTANGLE
2010     FOR I1 = R1 TO H1
2020        FOR J1 = C1 TO W1
2030           LET A(I1,J1) = F
2040        NEXT J1
2050     NEXT I1
2060     RETURN
```

```
3000 REM SUBROUTINE TO SELECT PARAMETERS
3050    LET W = 0
3080    LET H = 0
3090    LET R1 = 0
3100    LET C1 = 0
3110    FOR I = 1 TO N
3114 REM CHOOSE FILL CHARACTER
3115       LET F = V(I)
3119 REM SET HEIGHT,WIDTH,LOCATION PARAMETERS
3120       LET H = H + 4
3130       LET W = W + 6
3140       LET R1 = R1 + I + 1
3150       LET C1 = C1 + I + 1
3160 REM* ***EXIT FROM LOOP IF STARTING POINT > ARRAY SIZE
3170       IF R1 > R THEN 3370
3180       IF C1 > C THEN 3370
3185 REM CHOOSE UPPER LIMIT FOR ROW
3190       IF R < = R1+H-1                              THEN 3210
3200                                                    GO TO 3240
3210 REM*        THEN
3220               LET H1 = R
3230                                                    GO TO 3260
3240 REM*        ELSE
3250               LET H1 = R1+H-1
3260 REM*  END IF 3190
3265 REM CHOOSE UPPER LIMIT FOR COLUMN
3270       IF C < = C1+W-1                              THEN 3290
3280                                                    GO TO 3320
3290 REM*        THEN
3300               LET W1 = C
3310                                                    GO TO 3340
3320 REM*        ELSE
3330                LET W1 = C1 + W - 1
3340 REM*  END IF 3270
3345 REM CALL SUBROUTINE TO GENERATE A RECTANGLE.
3350       GOSUB 2000
3360    NEXT I
3370    RETURN
4000 REM SUBROUTINE TO PRINT ARRAY
4366 REM CHANGE THE NUMERIC EQUIVALENT TO CHARACTERS FOR PRINTING
4367 REM ROW BY ROW.
4370    FOR I = 1 TO R
4380       FOR J = 1 TO C
4390          LET P(J) = A(I,J)
4400       NEXT J
4405       LET P(0) = C
4410       CHANGE P TO P$
4430       PRINT P$
4460    NEXT I
4470    RETURN
5000 DATA "ABCDEFGHIJKLMNOPQRSTUVWXYZ)-+ = &$*(%:?!"
5005 REM NO. OF RECTANGLES; ARRAY LIMITS
5010 DATA 10,50,50
9999 END
```

```
Output:

AAAAAA
AAAAAA
AAAAAA
AAABBBBBBBBBBB
    BBBBBBBBBBB
    BBBBBBBBBBB
    BBBBBBBBBBB
    BBBBCCCCCCCCCCCCCCCCCCC
    BBBBCCCCCCCCCCCCCCCCCCC
    BBBBCCCCCCCCCCCCCCCCCCC
    BBBBCCCCCCCCCCCCCCCCCCC
        CCCCCCCCCCCCCCCCCC
        CCCCCDDDDDDDDDDDDDDDDDDDDDDDDDD
        CCCCCDDDDDDDDDDDDDDDDDDDDDDDDDD
        CCCCCDDDDDDDDDDDDDDDDDDDDDDDDDD
        CCCCCDDDDDDDDDDDDDDDDDDDDDDDDDD
        CCCCCDDDDDDDDDDDDDDDDDDDDDDDDDD
        CCCCCDDDDDDDDDDDDDDDDDDDDDDDDDD
        CCCCCDDDDDDEEEEEEEEEEEEEEEEEEEEEEEEEEEEEEEE
              DDDDDDEEEEEEEEEEEEEEEEEEEEEEEEEEEEEEEE
              DDDDDDEEEEEEEEEEEEEEEEEEEEEEEEEEEEEEEE
              DDDDDDEEEEEEEEEEEEEEEEEEEEEEEEEEEEEEEE
              DDDDDDEEEEEEEEEEEEEEEEEEEEEEEEEEEEEEEE
              DDDDDDEEEEEEEEEEEEEEEEEEEEEEEEEEEEEEEE
              DDDDDDEEEEEEEEEEEEEEEEEEEEEEEEEEEEEEEE
              DDDDDDEEEEEEEEEEEEEEEEEEEEEEEEEEEEEEEE
              DDDDDDEEEEEEEEEEEEEEEEEEEEEEEEEEEEEEEE
              DDDDDDEEEEEEEEFFFFFFFFFFFFFFFFFFFFFFFFF
                    EEEEEEEFFFFFFFFFFFFFFFFFFFFFFFFF
                    EEEEEEEFFFFFFFFFFFFFFFFFFFFFFFFF
                    EEEEEEEFFFFFFFFFFFFFFFFFFFFFFFFF
                    EEEEEEEFFFFFFFFFFFFFFFFFFFFFFFFF
                    EEEEEEEFFFFFFFFFFFFFFFFFFFFFFFFF
                    EEEEEEEFFFFFFFFFGGGGGGGGGGGGGGGGG
                    EEEEEEEFFFFFFFFFGGGGGGGGGGGGGGGGG
                    EEEEEEEFFFFFFFFFGGGGGGGGGGGGGGGGG
                    EEEEEEEFFFFFFFFFGGGGGGGGGGGGGGGGG
                    EEEEEEEFFFFFFFFFGGGGGGGGGGGGGGGGG
                          FFFFFFFFGGGGGGGGGGGGGGGGG
                          FFFFFFFFGGGGGGGGGGGGGGGGG
                          FFFFFFFFGGGGGGGGGGGGGGGGG
                          FFFFFFFFGGGGGGGGGGGGGGGGG
                          FFFFFFFFFGGGGGGGGGGGHHHHHHH
                          FFFFFFFFFGGGGGGGGGGGHHHHHHH
                          FFFFFFFFFGGGGGGGGGGGHHHHHHH
                          FFFFFFFFFGGGGGGGGGGGHHHHHHH
                          FFFFFFFFFGGGGGGGGGGGHHHHHHH
                          FFFFFFFFFGGGGGGGGGGGHHHHHHH
                          FFFFFFFFFGGGGGGGGGGGHHHHHHH
```

Interesting patterns can result if we use a random number generator to define the fill characters, and dimensions and locations of the rectangles. We only need to replace the subroutine at line 3000 in the above program; everything else can remain exactly the same.

Once again, we shall let N be the number of rectangles. We must also limit H and W to, say,

$$1 \leqslant H, W \leqslant 20$$

and the starting position must also be bounded:

$$1 \leqslant R1 \leqslant R, \quad 1 \leqslant C1 \leqslant C$$

Recall that

$$INT(RND * K + 1)$$

generates a random integer in the range 1 to K. Using this fact, we obtain the following outline for our new subroutine:

I. For I = 1 to N
    A. Choose fill character: F = V(INT(RND * 50 + 1))
    B. Set H = INT(RND * 20 + 1)
    C. Set W = INT(RND * 20 + 1)
    D. Set R1 = INT(RND * R + 1)
    E. Set C1 = INT(RND * C + 1)
    F. Choose upper limit for the row element as H1 = min(R, R1 + H − 1)
    G. Choose upper limit for column element as W1 = min(C, C1 + W − 1)
    H. Call subroutine to generate rectangle.

Note that steps F, G, and H are precisely the same as in the subroutine being replaced. This suggests that these three steps would be appropriate as another separate subroutine. (See problem 9 in the exercises.)

Example 9.11 shows only this subroutine and the resulting output. The rest of the program is precisely the same as in Example 9.10.

EXAMPLE 9.11 ══

Program (segment):

```
3000 REM SUBROUTINE TO GENERATE RANDOM PATTERN OF RECTANGLES
3005    RANDOMIZE
3008 REM RANDOMLY SELECT SHAPE AND POSITION.
3010    FOR I = 1 TO N
3020       LET F = V(INT(RND*40 + 1))
3030       LET H = INT(RND*20 + 1)
3040       LET W = INT(RND*20 + 1)
3050       LET R1 = INT(RND*R + 1)
3060       LET C1 = INT(RND*C + 1)
3070       IF R < = R1+H-1                                 THEN 3090
3080                                                       GO TO 3120
3090 REM*       THEN
3100               LET H1 = R
3110                                                       GO TO 3140
3114 REM CHOOSE FILL CHARACTER
3115               LET F = V(I)
3119 REM       SET HEIGHT, WIDTH, LOCATION PARAMETERS
3120 REM*       ELSE
3130               LET H1 = R1+H-1
3140 REM*  END IF 3070
3150       IF C < =C1+W-1                                  THEN 3170
3160                                                       GO TO 3200
3170 REM*       THEN
3180               LET W1 = C
3190                                                       GO TO 3220
3200 REM*       ELSE
3210               LET W1 = C1 + W - 1
3220 REM* END IF 3150
3230 REM CALL SUBROUTINE TO GENERATE A RECTANGLE
3240       GOSUB 2000
3250    NEXT I
3260    RETURN
```

Output:

```
                          <<
                          <<
            TTTTTTTTTTT<     JJJJJJJJJJJJJ
            TTTTTTTTTT<      JJJJJJJJJJJJJ
            TTTTTTTTTT<      JJJJJJJJJJJJJ
            TTTTTTTTTT<      JJJJJJJJJJJJJ
            TTTTTTTTTT<      JJJJJJJJJJJJJJFFFF
          EETTTTTTTTTTTE     JJJJJJJJJJJJJFFFF
          EETTTTTTTTTTTE     JJJJJJJJJJJJJ0000
          EETTTTTTTTTTTE     JJJJJJJJJJJJ0000
          EETT0000%%%%%%%JJJJJJJJJJJJJ0000
        %%EEE0000%%%%%%%JJJJJJJJJJJJJ0000
        %%EEE0000%%%%%%%JJJJJJJJJJJJJ0000
        %%EEE0000%%%%%%%JJJJJJJJJJJJJ0000
        %%EEE0000%%%%%%%JJJJJJJJJJJJJ0000
        %%EEE0000%%%%%%%JJJJJJJJJJJJJ0000
        %%EEE0000000000000000??????000000
        %%     0000000000000000??????00000:::::
        %%     0000000000000000??????00000:::::
        %%        !!!!        ??????00000::::::::::
        %%        !!!!        ??????00000::::::::::
        %%        !!!!        ??????00000::::::::::
    AAAAAA%%AAAAA  !!!!        ???????    ::::::::::
    AAAAAAAAAAAAA  !!!!        ???????    ::::::::::
    AQQQQQAAAAAAAA  !!!!       ???????    ::::::::::
    AQQQQQAABBBBBBBBBBBBBBBB&&&&&&&&&&&&    ::::::::::
    AQQQQQAABBBBBBBBBBBBBBBB&&&&&&&&&&&&    ::::::::::
     QQQQQ   BBBBBBBBBBBBBBBB&&&&&&&&&&&&
     QQQQQ   BBBBBBBBBBBBBBBB&&&&&&&&&&&&
     QQQQQ   BBBBBBBBBBBBBBBB&&&&&&&&&&&&
             BBBBBBBBBBBBBBBB&&&&&&&&&&&&ZZZZZZZZZZZZZ
         BBBBBBBBBBBBBBBB))))    ZZZZZZZZZZZZZ
         BBBBBBBBBBBBBBBB))))    ZZZZZZZZZZZZZ
         BBBBBBBBBBBBBBBB))))    ZZZZZZZZZZZZZ
         BBBBBBBBBBBBBBBB))))    ZZZZZZZZZZZZZ
       GGGGGBBBBBBBBBBBBBBBB))))    ZZZEEEEEZZZZZZZ
       GGGGGBBBBBBBBBBBBBBBMMMMMMMMMM    ZZZEEEEEZZZZZZZ
       GGGGGBBBBBBBBBBBBBBBMMMMMMMMMM    ZZZEEEEEZZZZZZZ
       GGGGGBBBBBBBBBBBBBBBBB))))    ZZZEEEEEZZZZZZZ
       GGGGGBBBBBBBBBBBBBBBBB        EEEEE      X
       GGGGGGGGGGGGGG              EEEEESSSSSSS
       GGGGGGGGGGGGGG              EEEEESSSSSSS
       GGGGFFFFFFFFGG              EEEEESSSSSSS
       GGGGFFFFFFFFGGPPPPPPPPPPPPPPPPPP    EEEEESSSSSSS
       GGGGFFFFFFFFGGPPPPPPPPPPPPPPPPPP    EEEEEGGGSSSS
```

Because of the RANDOMIZE statement, the program generates a different pattern each time it runs. Experimenting with different limits, fill characters, and so forth will produce varying results.

Care to try circles? See the tenth problem of the exercises.

9.7 Concluding Remarks

With this section you have come to the end of the book; but we hope you have not completed your programming experiences. If you continue to write programs, to use programs for further study and interest, or even entertainment, then this book will have met its purpose. Programming can be a powerful and useful skill. But like any other skill, it must be practiced regularly. With practice, your ability can only improve; without it, the skill will ebb away until you forget most of what you learned.

With time, programming should become increasingly important. The availability of computers is growing at a phenomenal rate—the computer industry, some predict, will be the country's largest industry by 1985. It is also predicted that at that time, hand-held computers (not calculators) will be available for much less than $100! Computer technology is advancing so rapidly that possibly by the time this book appears in print, such predictions may well be outdated.

Whatever the details, all indicators point to a tremendous proliferation and resulting influence of computers in our lives. Already they affect us more than most of us are aware. Expanding computing networks and the availability of inexpensive minicomputers will provide a wealth of computing power for a variety of needs and interests. Consequently, one's need, and perhaps obligation, to understand and use these machines cannot be understated. You are now well on the way to fulfilling that need.

Exercises

1. What is wrong with each of the following program segments?

a.
```
100 GOSUB 500
    . . .
210 GO TO 550
    . . .
500 REM SUBROUTINE A
510 LET S = 0
    . . .
550 PRINT S
    . . .
610 RETURN
```

b.
```
50 GOSUB 200
   . . .
200 SUBROUTINE B
    . . .
350 IF S > 5 THEN 150
    . . .
500 RETURN
```

c.
```
100 DEF FNC(X)
110 IF X < 0     THEN 140
120              GO TO 170
130 REM*  THEN
140        LET C = ABS(X) + 1
150        RETURN
160 REM*  ELSE
170        LET C = X * X + 1
180        RETURN
190 FNEND
```

d.
```
10 READ S
20 GOSUB 40
30 PRINT T
40 REM* SUBROUTINE D
50 LET T = SQR(S)/S
60 RETURN
70 END
```

2. Write a BASIC function for each of the following:
   a. Evaluate the function

   $$y = \frac{(x^{1/2} - 1)}{(x^{1/2} + 1)}$$

   b. Evaluate the function

   $$x = \begin{cases} \dfrac{-b + \sqrt{b^2 - 4ac}}{2a} & \text{if } t = 1 \\ \\ \dfrac{-b - \sqrt{b^2 - 4ac}}{2a} & \text{if } t \neq 1 \end{cases}$$

   c. Evaluate the *step function* $S(x) = n$ for $n \leq x < n + 1$ where $n = 0, 1, 2, \ldots$.
   d. Concatenate the three strings A\$, B\$, and C\$ in alphabetical order.
   e. Compute the sum of the even-numbered elements of the array A for $x > 0$ and the odd-numbered elements for $x \leq 0$.
   f. Evaluate the function

   $$g(x, y, t) = \begin{cases} x^2 - y^2 & \text{if } t < 0 \\ x^2 + y^2 & \text{if } 0 \leq t < 5 \\ (x - y)^2 & \text{if } t \geq 5 \end{cases}$$

3. a. Use the function in problem 2.a to compute

   $$\frac{(a - b)^{3/2} - 1}{(a - b)^{3/2} + 1}$$

   that is, exhibit the appropriate function call.

   b. Use the function in 2. f above to compute

   $$\begin{array}{ll} (a - x)(1 + x) & \text{if } a^2 < 7 \\ (x^2 + 1) & \text{if } 7 \leq a^2 < 12 \\ (1 - 2x + x^2) & \text{if } a^2 \geq 12 \end{array}$$

   c. Use the function in 2.e to compute the smallest of (1) the absolute value of the sum of all the elements in the array A (dimensioned at 50), (2) the absolute value of the sum of the even-numbered elements, and (3) the absolute value of the sum of the odd-numbered elements.

4. Rewrite the program of Example 9.4 so that it can compute larger coefficients C(N,K) without overflow. *Hint:* Overflow happens unnecessarily in many cases because the large numerator and denominator of C(N,K) are computed separately. Why not compute C(N,K) as

   $$C(N,K) = \left(\frac{K + 1}{1}\right) \cdot \left(\frac{K + 2}{2}\right) \cdot \left(\frac{K + 3}{3}\right) \cdot \ldots$$

5. Another way to compute the C(N,K) (see problem 4) is to use the formula

   $$C(N,K) = C(N-1,K-1) + C(N-1,K)$$

Use this formula to improve Example 9.4. Note that the C(N,K) correspond to the entries in the Pascal triangle (see problem 17 of the exercises in Chapter 7).

6. Rewrite Example 9.7 so that it uses a multiline function instead of a subroutine.

7. In Section 9.3, it was mentioned that the improved segment under the topic "removing unnecessary computations from loops" could be improved further. Do it.

8. Assuming that three-dimensional arrays are valid, make the following program segment as efficient as you can:

```
FOR I = 1 TO N
      LET A(I) = I^2 + I
      FOR J = 1 TO N1
            LET V(J) = 2 * Y – X
            FOR K = 1 TO N2
                  LET P(K)  = (X – 2 * Y + I)/T(I,J,K) – R(K)
                  LET M(K) = (X – 2 * Y) * T(I,J,K) + A(I)
                  LET S(J)  = R(K) + T(I,J,K) + X^3 – A(I)
            NEXT K
      NEXT J
NEXT I
```

9. Rewrite Example 9.10 to include more subroutines.

10. Write a subroutine similar to Example 9.11 to generate a random pattern of circles instead of rectangles. Parameters for the subroutine should include the centers for the circles and the radius, in terms of the array coordinates.

In the following problems try to use functions or subroutines or both. Think modularly!

11. Redo the calendar problem (number 15 in exercises of Chapter 7) using subroutines.

12. Redo the bowling problem (number 14 in exercises of Chapter 7) using functions.

13. Rocket Robot Corporation manufactures between 1,000 and 5,000 robots a month. The cost of materials for each robot is $850, and the labor required costs between $1,100 and $1,400. Other costs, including overhead, amount to $23,000 a month. Write a program to produce a report listing the number of robots produced, the material, labor, and other costs, total costs, and average costs for each month of the year. The program should also give totals for the year in each category. Simulate the number of robots produced and the labor costs for each month using the RND function. The formula for average costs is

$$\text{average cost} = \frac{\text{material cost} + \text{labor cost} + \text{other cost}}{\text{number of robots produced}}$$

14. Rewrite number 12 of the exercises in Chapter 7 using a function.

15. Write a program to determine the maximum value of a function. The program should be written to enable the user to define the function, the interval in which the maximum is to be found, and the error tolerance (that is, the error should be less than this value). For simplicity you can assume that the function has only one "peak" in the interval. You should be able to use a procedure like the bisection method (Example 9.1).

16. When a function is given only at a set of tabulated values (for example, in a table), the function can be easily approximated at other points besides the tabulated values by *linear interpolation.* If the function $f(x)$ is given at the points $x_1, x_2, \ldots, x_n$, if $x_k < x < x_{k+1}$, then $f(x)$ can be approximated by the formula

$$f(x) = \frac{1}{x_{k+1} - x_k} \cdot (f(x_{k+1}) \cdot (x - x_k) - f(x_k) \cdot (x - x_{k+1}))$$

Write a program to read N pairs of numbers, $x_1, f(x_1), x_2, f(x_2), x_3, f(x_3), \ldots, x_N, f(x_N)$, and a value x at which an interpolated value is desired. Print x and the interpolated value.

17. Write a program to accept a checkerboard configuration (describe the unoccupied positions, and red's and black's men and kings, using some numbering scheme) and to compute the total number of possible moves by which black can jump at least one of red's pieces (multiple jumps should be counted only once).

18. For calculus students: Many important applications of mathematics require knowing the area between the curve given by the graph of a function and the x-axis. Computing this area is known as *integration.* One way to approximate this area (usually not the best way) is by Monte Carlo integration, which uses the area under the curve given by the function $f(x)$ between a and b (see Figure 9.10). In this process a random number r_1 is

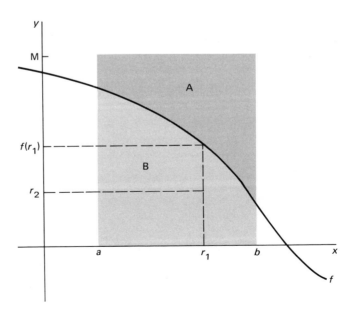

FIGURE 9.10   Example of Monte Carlo integration

computed such that $a \leqslant r_1 \leqslant b$. A second random number r_2 is computed where $0 \leqslant r_2 \leqslant M$, where M is larger than f in $[a, b]$. Then r_2 is compared with $f(r_1)$. If $r_2 > f(r_1)$, then it lies in region A above the curve (see Figure 9.5). Otherwise it lies under the curve (region B). This process is repeated many times; two counts are kept, one for the total number of times the process is repeated and the other for the number of times r_2 falls in region B. The area is taken as the ratio of the second to the first count, times the area of the rectangle containing the curve $(M \cdot (b - a))$. Write a program to do this. The user should input f, a, b, and M. Try it for 500, then 1,000, repetitions and compare with the exact answer.

19. Write a program that uses the RND function to simulate a game of craps. The RND function should be used twice to give an integer result between 1 and 6 each, representing a toss of two dice. If the total is a 2 or 12, the shooter (user) loses. If the result is 7 or 11, the user wins. If the result is anything else, the user continues to throw until the person either repeats the number on the first toss (a win) or throws 7 or 11 (a loss). The program should allow the user to repeat the process and to bet (up to $100) each time. The program should print the outcomes for both dice on each toss. When the user decides to stop, the program should print the total winnings or losses.

20. Write a computer-assisted instruction (CAI) tutorial program on a subject of your choice. The program should ask 5 to 10 fill-in-the-blank or multiple-choice questions. The user should get a second chance at each question and if both answers are wrong, the program should display the correct answer. The program should also keep score.

21. Using the formula in problem 5 of these exercises, write a program that uses a recursive function to compute the binomial coefficients.

22. The classic Fibonacci sequence,

$$1, 1, 2, 3, 5, 8, 13, 21, 34, \ldots$$

can be computed by the formula

$$F_n = F_{n-1} + F_{n-2}$$

where F_n is the nth term of the sequence. Write a program that uses a recursive function to do this.

Appendix A. Summary of BASIC Statements, Functions, and Commands

In this summary,

e	=	an expression (numeric or string, whichever is applicable)
n, m	=	line numbers
R	=	relation ($<, >, =, =, =, <>$)
L	=	logical operator (AND, OR, NOT)
S$	=	string constant
C	=	numeric variable
V	=	numeric variable
V$	=	string variable
U	=	nonsubscripted numeric variable
g	=	letter of the alphabet
A, B, C =		matrix or vector
D	=	vector (one-dimensional array)
list	=	list of variable names, with or without subscripts, separated by commas
s-list	=	list of subscripted variables only
d-list	=	list of numeric or string constants
$\begin{Bmatrix} X \\ Y \end{Bmatrix}$	=	indicates choice of required portion (here the choice is between X and Y)
. . .	=	indicates pattern can be repeated
[ ]	=	indicates equivalent forms for other systems

A.1   Statements

In this section a brief description of the action of the statement is given only for statements not used frequently in this book. The items on the right exemplify the category of statement commands. This list is not complete; furthermore, the commands may not be valid on all systems.

Comments
n REM S$ 1Ø REM THIS IS A SAMPLE COMMENT

Allocate Memory Space
n DIM s-list   2Ø DIM A(5Ø), B(5,7), C$(3Ø)

313

Assignment Statements

$$n \text{ LET} \begin{Bmatrix} V \\ V\$ \end{Bmatrix} = e$$

5Ø LET P1 = X + Y + Z

$$\begin{cases} n_1 \text{ READ list} \\ n_2 \text{ DATA d-list} \\ n_3 \text{ RESTORE (reset pointer to start of} \\ \qquad\qquad\qquad \text{data list)} \end{cases}$$

$$\begin{cases} 25 \text{ READ C\$, A(I), P} \\ 5\text{ØØ DATA "SMITH, J.", 25, –3.75} \\ 8\text{Ø RESTORE} \end{cases}$$

n INPUT list

1ØØ INPUT N\$, K1, R(2)

Print Statements

n PRINT $e_1, e_2, \ldots$

10 PRINT A\$, B(1)/2, INT(X)

n PRINT $e_1; e_2; \ldots$

2Ø PRINT "SUM="; S; "AND T="; T

n PRINT TAB $(e_1); e_2;$ TAB$(e_3); e_4; \ldots$

3Ø PRINT TAB(1Ø); X; TAB(C/2); Y

Control Statements

n END

999 END

n GO TO m

5Ø GO TO 31Ø

n STOP

15Ø STOP

$$n \text{ IF} \begin{Bmatrix} e_1 \text{ R } e_2 \\ (e_1 \text{ R } e_2)\text{L}(e_3 \text{ R } e_4) \\ (e_1 \text{ R } e_2)\text{L}_1(e_3 \text{ R } e_4)\text{L}_2 \ldots \end{Bmatrix} \begin{matrix} \text{THEN m} \\ \text{[GO TO]} \end{matrix}$$

$$\begin{cases} 10 \text{ IF X + Y1 THEN 9}\text{ØØ} \\ 7\text{Ø IF A\$ = "JOE" THEN 5}\text{Ø} \\ 8\text{Ø IF A} < 9 \text{ AND B\$ = "NO" THEN 25} \end{cases}$$

n ON e GO TO $n_1, n_2, \ldots$

5Ø ON N/2 + 1 GO TO 5Ø, 75, 75, 1Ø

[n GO TO $(n_1, n_2 \ldots) e$]

[n GO TO $n_1, n_2, \ldots e$]

[n ON e THEN $n_1, n_2, \ldots$]

$$\begin{cases} n_1 \text{ ON e GOSUB m} \\ \qquad \cdots \\ n_2 \text{ RETURN} \end{cases}$$

$$\begin{cases} 5\text{Ø ON INT(X) + 1 GOSUB 5}\text{ØØ} \\ \qquad \cdots \\ 1\text{Ø9Ø RETURN} \end{cases}$$

Loops

$$\begin{cases} n \text{ FOR U} = e_1 \text{ to } e_2 \\ \quad \bullet \\ \quad \bullet \\ \quad \bullet \\ m \text{ NEXT U} \end{cases}$$

$$\begin{cases} 10 \text{ FOR I} = \text{L TO (U + 1)}^\wedge 2 \\ \quad \bullet \\ \quad \bullet \\ \quad \bullet \\ 9\text{Ø NEXT I} \end{cases}$$

$$\begin{cases} n \text{ FOR U} = e_1 \text{ TO } e_2 \text{ STEP } e_3 \\ \quad \bullet \\ \quad \bullet \\ \quad \bullet \\ m \text{ NEXT U} \end{cases}$$

$$\begin{cases} 10 \text{ FOR K} = 1 \text{ TO N STEP SQR(X)} \\ \quad \bullet \\ \quad \bullet \\ \quad \bullet \\ 5\text{Ø NEXT K} \end{cases}$$

Matrix Statements

n MAT READ A,B,C, . . .

10 MAT READ X, Y

$$[\text{A}(c_1, c_2), \text{B}(c_3), \ldots]$$

n MAT PRINT A,B,C   50 MAT PRINT A;B
                [A;B;C; . . .]
n MAT INPUT A   ⎧ 10 MAT INPUT R
        (with NUM)   ⎪   •
        (NUM = no. of elements)   ⎨   •
                                                     ⎪   •
                                                     ⎩ 20 FOR I = 1 TO NUM

n MAT A = B + C   100 MAT P = X + Y
n MAT A = B – C   50 MAT B = Q – B
n MAT A = (e) * B   (scalar mult.)   60 MAT Y = (K/2) * A
n MAT A = B * C   (matrix mult.)   90 MAT V = A * X
n MAT A = INV(B)   (inverse of matrix)   ⎧ 10 MAT Y = INV(X)
        (with DET)   (Determinant of   ⎪   •
                          inverted matrix)   ⎨   •
                                                     ⎪   •
                                                     ⎩ 50 PRINT DET

n MAT A = TRN(B)   (transpose of   50 MAT Y = TRN(X)
                          matrix)
n MAT A = ZER   (zero matrix)   100 MAT K = ZER
        [ZER (c_1,c_2)]
n MAT A = CON   (matrix of ones)   40 MAT Y = CON
        [CON (c_1,c_2)]
n MAT A = IDN   (identity matrix)   80 MAT R = IDN
        [IDN (c_1,c_2)]

String Processing Statements
n CHANGE V$ TO D   50 CHANGE R$(1) TO A
n CHANGE D TO V$ 80 CHANGE X TO P$

$$n\ LET\ V = IDX\left(\begin{Bmatrix}S\$_1\\V\$_1\end{Bmatrix}, \begin{Bmatrix}S\$_2\\V\$_2\end{Bmatrix}\right)$$ 20 LET N = IDX (A$, "ALP")

$$\left[INDEX\left(\begin{Bmatrix}S\$_1\\V\$_1\end{Bmatrix}, \begin{Bmatrix}S\$_2\\V\$_2\end{Bmatrix}\right)\right]$$

$$\left[POS\quad\left(\begin{Bmatrix}S\$_1\\V\$_1\end{Bmatrix}, \begin{Bmatrix}S\$_2\\V\$_2\end{Bmatrix}, C\right)\right]$$

$$\left[SER\quad\left(\begin{Bmatrix}S\$_1\\V\$_1\end{Bmatrix}, \begin{Bmatrix}S\$_2\\V\$_2\end{Bmatrix}\right)\right]$$

$$n\ LET\ V = LEN\left(\begin{Bmatrix}S\$\\V\$\end{Bmatrix}\right)$$ 100 LET L = LEN (P$)

$$n\ LET\ V\$_1 = \begin{Bmatrix}S\$_1\\V\$_2\end{Bmatrix} + \begin{Bmatrix}S\$_2\\V\$_3\end{Bmatrix}\ (concatenation)$$ 20 LET S$ = A$ + "END"

$$n\ LET\ V\$_1 = CPY\$\left(\begin{Bmatrix}S\$_1\\V\$_2\end{Bmatrix}, \begin{Bmatrix}V_1\\c_1\end{Bmatrix}, \begin{Bmatrix}V_2\\c_2\end{Bmatrix}\right)$$ (copy substring)
                                                     10 LET P$ = CPY$(A$,N,5)

File Processing Statements

n_1 FILES list of filenames	5Ø FILES PAYRLL,BETAR,GENLG
n_2 SCRATCH # c	6Ø SCRATCH # 2
$(1 \leqslant c \leqslant 9)$	

$$\left[n \text{ OPEN filename,} \left\{ \begin{array}{c} \text{INPUT} \\ \text{OUTPUT} \end{array} \right\} , c \right]$$

$(1 \leqslant c \leqslant 9)$

n INPUT #c, list	1ØØ INPUT #3, N$,A,X
[n READ #c, list]	
[n INPUT FROM c: list]	
n IF END #c THEN m	2ØØ IF END #8 THEN 999
[n ON ENDFILE c GO TO m]	
n CLOSE #c	5ØØ CLOSE #4
[n CLOSE filename] (terminate processing of given file)	
[n RESTORE #c]	
n PRINT #c, list	1ØØ PRINT #1, A,B,X(1),P$
[n WRITE #c, list]	
[n PRINT ON c: list]	

A.2   Functions

Built-In Functions	*Examples*
INT(e)	2Ø LET Y = INT(X/2) + 1
ABS(e)	5 LET K = ABS(Y − 5)
SQR(e)	25 LET Z = SQR(INT(X + 1))
RND	5Ø IF RND < .5 THEN 2ØØ
[RND(e)]	
SGN(e)	3Ø LET P = SGN(T) ∗ X
CLK	8Ø PRINT CLK
SIN(e)	3Ø LET P = SIN(P/2)
COS(e)	1ØØ LET C1 = COS(X) ∗ 2
TAN(e)	5Ø FOR I = 1 TO TAN(P)
ATN(e)	1Ø PRINT ATN (X − 22.7)
COT(e)	2Ø IF COT(X) < .1 THEN 5
EXP(e)	1ØØ LET Y = EXP(−X)/2
LOG(e)	4Ø PRINT LOG (T^2) − LOG(T)
LGT(e)	3Ø LET A = LGT(X)/LGT(2.71)
MAX(e_1, e_2)	5Ø LET M = MAX(A,B)/A
MIN(e_1, e_2)	8Ø PRINT MIN (MAX(X,Y),V)

User-Defined Functions

n DEF FN g $(V_1, V_2, \ldots)$ = e

$\left\{ \begin{array}{l} n_1 \text{ DEF FN g } (V_1, V_2, \ldots) \\ \quad \bullet \\ \quad \bullet \\ \quad \bullet \\ n_2 \text{ LET FN g = e} \\ \quad \bullet \\ \quad \bullet \\ \quad \bullet \\ n_3 \text{ FNEND} \end{array} \right.$

Examples

$\left\{ \begin{array}{l} 1\emptyset \text{ DEF FNY (A,B) = A } * \text{ B/2} \\ \quad \bullet \\ \quad \bullet \\ \quad \bullet \\ 1\emptyset\emptyset \text{ LET T = FNY (6, X + Y)} \end{array} \right.$

$\left\{ \begin{array}{l} 1\emptyset\emptyset \text{ LET P = FNA(X,.1, Y/2)} \\ \quad \bullet \\ \quad \bullet \\ \quad \bullet \\ 5\emptyset\emptyset \text{ DEF FNA (A,B,C)} \\ \quad \bullet \\ \quad \bullet \\ \quad \bullet \\ 55\emptyset \text{ LET FNA = N } * \text{ (B } * \text{ A/3 + C)} \\ \quad \bullet \\ \quad \bullet \\ \quad \bullet \\ 59\emptyset \text{ FNEND} \end{array} \right.$

A.3 System Commands

COMMAND	DESCRIPTION
BYE [OFF]	Terminates access to BASIC.
CATALOG	Produces a list of programs (and sometimes files) that are saved under the active account number.
DELETE [EDIT DELETE]	Format varies from system to system. Deletes a specified number of lines from the program.
LENGTH [STATUS]	Gives the size of the current program.
LIST	Produces a printout of the entire current program. Some systems provide for options to print a given segment of the program.
NEW [NAME]	Permits a new program to be entered.
OLD	Retrieves a previously saved program and makes it available for processing.
RENAME [NAME]	Changes the name of the current program to that given in this command.
REPLACE [RESAVE or SAVE]	Replaces a previously saved version of the current program with the current version.

RESEQUENCE [EDIT RESEQUENCE or RENUMBER]	Resequences the line numbers beginning with a given line and with the given uniform increment.
RUN	Executes the current program.
SAVE	Stores a copy of the current program in the user's file or library.
SCRATCH	Erases the working copy of the current program.
STOP	Terminates execution of the program. STOP without a line number (used, for example, on INPUT) is a system command. With a line number it is a BASIC language statement.
TAPE	Tells the computer to read statements from the paper tape reader or its equivalent.
UNSAVE	Erases the saved version of the current program.

Appendix B. Error Messages

Error messages vary widely from system to system. Some statements considered to be in error on one system might be legal on another. Thus the list of error messages given here is incomplete, containing only the most common errors. Furthermore, many of the messages are paraphrased versions of the actual error messages.

Some of the messages are given during the compilation and others during the execution. Many of the messages identify the line number (although this is not shown in the list below) at which the error occurred as well as the type of error. If an error message appears immediately after you transmit a statement during the construction of a program, it is likely that the given statement has been automatically deleted from the program. Finally, during execution some of the errors do not stop the program but only warn the user of some irregularity. The most serious errors terminate execution.

Unfortunately, because of the complexities of the programming language, the BASIC processor may sometimes have difficulty pinpointing the cause of the error. Thus a given error message may not refer to the actual problem. For that reason, an error message should be considered only a crude clue about where to start looking. You may still have much detective work before you find the actual error.

Suppose, for example, a user intends to input the line

$$50 \text{ LET } X = C * (A + B)$$

but transmits

$$50 \text{ LET } X = C(A + B)$$

by mistake.

When the program runs it is likely that a message similar to the following will occur:

SUBSCRIPT OUT OF RANGE IN 50

This is at first a confusing message, since perhaps the programmer was not using any arrays in this part of the program (and if $A + B \leqslant 10$, the situation is much worse, since BASIC will assume that C is an array—automatically dimensioned at 10—and will assign the value zero to X; no error message is produced).

Sometimes the actual error may exist because of the presence or absence of a statement in another part of the program. For example, the program

```
10 READ X
20 GOSUB 40
30 PRINT X,Y
40 REM   SUBROUTINE TO COMPUTE Y = X^2 - 1
50 LET Y = X^2 - 1
60 RETURN
70 DATA 6, 9
80 END
```

produces the error message

RETURN WITHOUT GOSUB IN 6Ø

At first glance this seems incorrect because there is clearly a GOSUB 4Ø in line 2Ø. The problem is that there is no STOP statement immediately before line 4Ø, and after printing (line 3Ø) the program enters the subroutine and eventually encounters the RETURN again. In a lengthy program, such errors can be difficult to find.

We first present errors detected during compilation.

B.1   Compilation Errors

ERROR MESSAGE	MEANING
CUT PROGRAM OR DIMS	The total space needed by the program and arrays is too large. Trim useless instructions from the program. Reduce array sizes if possible; if an array requires less than 10 locations be sure to dimension it to save space.
DIMENSION TOO LARGE	Self-explanatory. The limit of the size of an array varies from system to system.
FILE NOT $\left\{ \begin{array}{l} \text{OPEN} \\ \text{DEFINED} \end{array} \right\}$	The file reference statement is missing (format depends on the system).
FORS NESTED TOO DEEPLY	The limit on nested loops has been exceeded. Try to rewrite this part of the program with fewer nested loops.
FOR WITHOUT NEXT	A NEXT statement is missing. Possibly the control variable is not the same as the FOR index.
ILLEGAL CONSTANT	A number exceeds the bounds for numbers on this computer, or it has an incorrect form. Check for commas, extra decimal points, or other typing errors.
ILLEGAL FORMULA	This message covers a variety of errors: missing parentheses, missing operators, illegal variable names, and the like. Check the statement carefully.
ILLEGAL INSTRUCTION	The instruction is not legal in BASIC. Check for misspellings and typographical errors.
ILLEGAL LINE NUMBER	The number has an incorrect form; it contains a letter, for example, or has more than five digits.

ILLEGAL MAT	Several errors are possible. Check the dimensions in a matrix multiplication, format of scalar multiplication, and the like.
ILLEGAL PROGRAM NAME	Something is wrong with the program name in a CHAIN statement. Check to be sure that program is saved and that it has less than 7 characters in the name.
ILLEGAL RELATION	There is an error in the relational expression in an IF-THEN statement. Check the relational symbol.
ILLEGAL STRING OPERATION	Self-explanatory. Look for illegal operation (say multiplying strings or other arithmetic operations on string variables).
ILLEGAL VARIABLE	An illegal variable name was used (for example, AB or V16$).
INCORRECT NO. OF ARGUMENTS	The number of arguments in a function call doesn't match the number of dummy arguments in a function definition.
INCORRECT NO. OF SUBSCRIPTS	The number of subscripts in an array reference doesn't match the number in the DIM statement.
NEXT WITHOUT FOR	A FOR statement is missing. It is likely that the wrong variable is given. Also check for incorrect nesting of FOR loops.
NO DATA	No DATA statements were provided.
PLEASE? (WHAT? HUH?)	BASIC encountered an unrecognizable instruction. Usually this means a line number was omitted or there was a misspelling.
REDIMENSIONED ARRAY	An array has been dimensioned previously.
STRING TOO LONG	Self-explanatory. The limit varies from system to system.
UNDEFINED FUNCTION	A function reference (for instance, FNF(X)) has been used in a statement, but there is no DEF statement for it. Check both the present statement and the corresponding DEF statement for typographical errors.
UNDEFINED IMAGE	A PRINT IN IMAGE (USING) statement has an incorrect reference to an image string.
UNDEFINED LINE NUMBER	The line number in the GO TO, IF-THEN, or similar statement does not exist.

B.2 Execution Errors

ERROR MESSAGE	MEANING
ABSOLUTE VALUE RAISED TO A POWER	A computation $A^{\wedge}B$ was attempted, where $A < 0$ and B is a noninteger (say, 3.6). BASIC substitutes $(ABS(A))^{\wedge}B$ and continues execution.
DIVISION BY ZERO	The denominator was zero. BASIC replaces the result with the largest value that can be represented in the computer and continues execution.
INPUT DATA INCORRECT	Data entered in an INPUT statement is in error. The data may not contain operations; for example, 1Ø * 2 is incorrect data. Retype the line.
INSUFFICIENT DATA	The number of data items is less than the number of variables in the INPUT statement. When the rest is transmitted, the program continues execution.
LOG ERROR	The argument for the LOG function is zero or negative.
OVERFLOW, UNDERFLOW	A numeric result exceeded the permissible bounds (it was too large or too small). There is a logic error somewhere. Execution continues with the "largest" number (if overflow) or zero (if underflow) as the result.
RETURN WITHOUT GOSUB	A RETURN was encountered without first executing a GOSUB. Execution is terminated. Check whether a GO TO was used instead of a GOSUB. Also, recall the example at the start of this appendix.
SQUARE ROOT OF A NEGATIVE NUMBER	Self-explanatory. Program continues execution using the square root of the absolute value of the argument.
SUBSCRIPT ERROR	A subscript is outside the range provided by the DIM statement. Execution terminates. This usually indicates a logic error.
TOO MUCH INPUT	The number of data items is greater than the number of variables in the INPUT statement. The excess is ignored and execution continues.
ZERO TO A NEGATIVE POWER	Self-explanatory. Action is the same as DIVISION BY ZERO.

Appendix C. A DEC BASIC-PLUS-2 Program

Digital Equipment Corporation has a version of BASIC called BASIC-PLUS-2, which includes the control structures that we constructed in Chapter 5 using REM and GO TO statements. Clearly, such built-in facilities for construction will make programming easier.

The accompanying example is like Example 5.1 but written in BASIC-PLUS-2. Note the differences.

```
1Ø REM THIS PROGRAM DETERMINES WHETHER A NUMBER
2Ø REM N IS POSITIVE, NEGATIVE, OR ZERO. IF POSITIVE,
3Ø REM N, N^2, AND N^3 ARE PRINTED. IF NEGATIVE,
4Ø REM -N, N^2, AND (-N)^3 ARE PRINTED.
5Ø REM
6Ø PRINT "TYPE A NUMBER."
7Ø INPUT N
8Ø IF N > Ø                                              &
        THEN PRINT "N IS POSITIVE."                      &
   \        PRINT N, N^2, N^3                            &
        ELSE IF N = Ø                                    &
            THEN PRINT "N = Ø"                           &
            ELSE PRINT "N IS NEGATIVE."                  &
   \            PRINT -N, N^2, (-N)^3
9Ø END
```

This example is much cleaner than PROGRAM(2) in Example 5.1 because the REM and GO TO statements are not necessary to effect the program. The ampersand (&) signifies to the compiler that the line is to be continued. Also, the backslash (\) is used to separate multiple statements. The lines 8Ø plus all the lines between 8Ø and 9Ø are thus treated as a single statement. No END IF is required.

Ideally the backslashes and ampersands will also not be needed. In time, such powerful control structures will be available in many versions of BASIC.

Index

ABS function, 156, 201
Accumulating, 63–65
Address, 6, 32
Algorithm, 3, 4, 13, 16, 80–81, 88, 107
AND operation, *see* Operations, logical
Arguments, *see* Functions, arguments of
Arithmetic expressions, 34–35, 38, 40–41, 58,
 220, 272, 293
 parentheses in, 34–35
Arrays, 132–152, 213–214, 216, 219, 232,
 234–235, 295. *See also* Matrices; MAT
 functions
 advantages of, 135
 changing dimensions in, 228
 defined, 132
 rules for subscripts in, 133, 149–150, 214,
 228
 strings, 134–135, 136n, 142, 149n, 203
 two-dimensional, 147–152, 154, 167
ASCII code, 233, 239, 243

Backspace key, 27
BASIC, 5, 7, 13, 31
 basic, 31–52, 57–89
 interactive, 15, 51–52
 program structure, 13–14
BASIC-PLUS-2, 98n, 101, 323
Batch processing, 19–20, 261
Binary number system, 7, 75
Binomial coefficients, 210, 283
Birthday paradox, 164–166
Bisection method, 274
Bit, 6–7
Blank spaces, 14
Byte, 6

CAI, *see* Computer-assisted instruction
Card reader, 8
CASE structure, 176, 179–183
 general form of, 178–179
Central processing unit, 11–12, 16
CHAIN statement, 295–296
CHANGE statement, 232–241, 245
Collating sequence, 241–243
Comparisons, *see* Operations, relational
Compilation errors, 320–321
Compiler, 5–6, 13, 49, 293n

Computer
 analog, 2
 digital, 2
 functional unit of, 6–10
Computer art, 299–307
Computer-assisted instruction, 163
Constants, 32–33
 numeric, 33, 40–42
 string, 33, 39–42, 49
Control paths, 97
Control statements, 57–58
Control structures, 96–98. *See also* Structured
 programming
 elementary, 96
 eliminating multiple exits from, 117–119
 exits from, 97, 103–104, 117–118
 undesirable types, 97, 102, 119–120
Corrections, 25–28
Coroutines, 296
Counting, 45, 64, 70–71, 101
CPU, *see* Central processing unit
Cryptography application, 236–241, 268

Data, 3, 58, 62, 66, 70–71, 214, 239
DATA statement, 46–48, 51
Data structures, 298
Debugging, 87–89, 95, 319–322
DEC BASIC-PLUS-2, *see* BASIC-PLUS-2
DEF statement, 272, 280
Deletions, 28
Depreciation, 91
Determinant, 226n
DIM statement, 135–136, 141, 149–150
 for MAT functions, 214
 determining dimensions using NUM, 217
Direct access files, *see* Files, random

Editing data, 69. *See also* PRINT IN IMAGE
 statement
 use of string functions, 188–190
Editing programs, 25–28
 correcting, 25–27
 deleting, 28–29
 inserting, 28
Editing symbols, table of, 188–190
Efficiency, 284–285, 291–295. *See also* Loops,
 improving efficiency of

END statement, 37, 47
Equations, systems of linear, 230–232
Error checking, 87–89, 319–322
    for logic, 87
    for syntax, 87
Error condition, 16, 19
Error messages, 6, 319–322
ESC (ALTMODE) key, 28
Exchange, 139
EXCHANGE function, 139n
Execution errors, 322
Exponential notation, 33, 130–131, 167

Fields, 250
File operations, 251–264
    close statement, 252
    FILES (OPEN) statement, 251, 261–262
    IF END (ON END), 252
    INPUT (FROM), 252
    LOC statement, 262
    LOF statement, 262–263
    MAT functions for files, 254
    PRINT (ON), 253, 260, 262n
    PRINT USING for files, 254
    QUOTE statement, 260
    READ, 252
    RESTORE statement, 253
    RRW statement, 263
    RWR statement, 263
    SCRATCH statement, 251, 253
    SET statement, 262–263
    WRITE, 253, 262
Files
    closing of, 252
    defined, 249
    end of file indicator, 252
    input, 251
    key, 262, 264
    opening of, 251
    random, 260–264
    sequential, 250–260
Flowchart, see Algorithm
FNEND, 280
FOR-NEXT statement, 72–78, 101, 115
    improper use of, 76
    increment in, 72
    index in, 72
    rules, 72
    step option, 72–73
    test value in, 72
Function(s), 153–154, 316–317. See also MAT
        functions; String functions
    arguments of, 272–273, 280–282
    body of, 280
    built-in, 155–169
    calling of, 273, 280
    defined, 153
    factorial, 297

FNEND statement, 280
    greatest integer, 154–155
    illegal use of, 280
    mathematical, 153
    multiline, 279–287
    plotting of, 193–198
    recursive, 297–298
    roots of, 273–279
    single line, 272–279
    user defined, 271–287

GO SUB statement, 291, 298
GO TO statement, 60–61, 64
    misuse of, 61, 98, 120
    to implement control structures, 98–100, 104,
        106, 179

Histogram, 206

IF-THEN statement, 58–59, 66, 79–80
    in control structure, 96
IF-THEN (IF-THEN-ELSE) structure, 98–101,
        120, 183, 204
Increment, 72
Index, see Subscripts
INPUT statement, 15, 43, 51–52, 64n, 67,
        194
Input unit, 8–9
Insertions, 28
Instructions, 3
    arithmetic assignment, 12
    data handling, 12–13
    data structure, 13
    input/output, 13
    sequence control, 13
Integration, 311
Interactive programming, 51, 80
Interest calculation, 91
Interpolation, 311
Interpreter, 6, 49
INT function, 114, 123, 126, 140, 154–155,
        156, 157–161
    use in CASE structure, 176–177, 181
    use in rounding, 160–161
Inventory application, 254–260, 263–264
Iterative statements, 45, 65, 298

Jumps, 17. See also GO TO statement; IF-
        THEN statement
    conditional, 58
    unconditional, 60

Leontief economic model, 266
LET statement, 43–46, 51
    errors in, 46
Life (game), 267–268
Line numbers, 13, 38

Loop, 17, 37, 61, 62-71, 96-97, 213, 228,
    231. *See also* FOR-NEXT statement
constructing, 63-65, 68-69, 74
as a control structure, 96-97, 101-102
defined, 63
exits from, 69-70, 103-104, 117-118
improper use, 61, 78
improving efficiency of, 159, 292-294
indefinite, 102-104
index, 72
infinite, 61, 64n
necessary properties of, 66
nested, 77-78, 293-294
parameters, 72

Machine language, 5
MAT functions, 214-229
changing dimensions in, 228
DET function, 226n
MAT addition, 219
MAT assignment, 219
MAT CON (constant), 224, 228
MAT IDN (identity), 224-225, 229
MAT INPUT, 214, 216-217, 219, 227, 241
MAT INV (inverse), 225-226
MAT multiplication, 220-222
MAT PRINT, 214-216, 224
MAT READ, 214-215, 227-229, 239
MAT subtraction, 219
MAT TRN (transpose), 225
MAT ZER (zero), 224, 228
NUM function, 217
scalar multiplication, 220
strings, 227-228
Matrices, 171, 213-215, 219-220, 230
addition of, 219
identity, 224
inverse, 225
multiplication of, 220-221
square, 224-225
subtraction of, 219
Mean, 93
Median, 137-138, 140-141
Memory unit, 6-7, 12
Merging, 173, 250, 254
Modularity, 109, 110, 137, 140, 142, 147, 194,
    202, 271-272, 282, 291
size of modules, 292
Morse code, 267

Nesting, 77-78, 293-294
NOT operation, *see* operations, logical

ON-GOSUB statement, 291
ON-GO TO statement, 176, 178
Operations
arithmetic, 34-35, 41

logical, 204-205
relational, 58
OR operations, *see* Operations, logical
Outline, 4, 230, 238, 245, 247, 256, 274, 284.
    See also Algorithm
Output unit, 9-11
Overflow, 285, 287

Parentheses, 34
PRINT IN IMAGE statement, 187-191, 201
different forms of, 187
examples of, 190-191, 199-203
rules for editing (table), 188-190
PRINT statement
basic form, 37-43
columns feature, 40, 42
legal items in, 43
need for quotation marks, 39
punctuation at end of list, 185-186
semicolon, use of, 183-186, 215
skipping lines, 40, 42
TAB function, 185-186, 195
use with INPUT, 52
PRINT USING statement, *see* PRINT IN
    IMAGE statement
Problem solving, 2
Program, 2, 4-5, 7, 11, 13. *See also* Statements,
    program
defined, 4
Programming language, 5
high level, 5
machine, 5
Pseudorandom numbers, 163

Random number, *see* RND function
RANDOMIZE statement, 163-164
Read statement, 43, 46-49, 51
Records, 250
Recursion, 297
Refinement, *see* Structured programming, top-
    down design
Relations, *see* Operations, relational
REM (remarks) statement, 35-36
as comment, 35-36, 85-87, 113
to describe control structures, 36, 99-100,
    102-105
to initiate subroutine, 287
jumps to, 178n
RESTORE statement, 191-193, 193n
RETURN key, 20
RETURN statement, 287-288
RND function, 156, 162-165, 173, 209, 211
to produce a range of random
    numbers, 164
random number generator, 173
Round-off error, 38, 75, 115n, 130, 132, 161,
    199

Scattergram, 206
Scientific notation, 130
Semicolon, 183-184
SGN function, 156, 180-181
Simulation, 1, 211
Sorting, 59, 138-139, 173-174, 242, 250, 257
SQR function, 156, 161, 180-181
Standard deviation, 93, 171
Statements, program, 12-13, 313-316
Stopping a program, 49, 64n, 71
STOP statement, 58, 71, 99n, 280
Storage, *see* Memory unit
String(s), 33, **44.** *See also* Constants, string
  comparing, 59, 241-242
  concatenation of (on printing), 183-184
  in INPUT statement, 51-52
  in LET statement, 44
  in MAT functions, 227-228
  null, 43, 133, 245
  printing, 38-39
  in PRINT IN IMAGE statement, 187-190
  in PRINT statement, 38-40, 42-43, 183-184, 201
  processing, 232
  in READ statement, 48-49
  table of numeric equivalents of string characters, 233
  use in editing, 245-249
String functions, 232-249. *See also* CHANGE statement
  concatenation operator, 244
  COPY (SEG) function, 244-246
  INDEX (IDX, POS, SER) function, 243
  LEN function, 244
Structured programming, 95-120
  control structures, 96, 104-105
  defined, 95
  flow of control in, 96-97, 105
  indenting, nested structures, 104
  stepwise refinement, 80-85, 107, 180-181, 194-195, 201, 238, 256
  top-down design, 83, 99, 107-114, 291-295
Subprogram, 108

Subroutines, 271, 287-291, 301-302, 305
  illegal use of, 289
Subscripts, 133. *See Also* Arrays, rules for subscripts in
Switch, 117-118, 139, 144
Syntax errors, 87
System commands, 22, 317-318
  LIST, 23-24
  NEW, 20-22
  OLD, 21-25
  REPLACE, 23
  RUN, 24-25
  SAVE, 22
  UNSAVE, 23

TAB function, *see* PRINT statement
TAB key, 190
Tables, *see* Arrays, two-dimensional
Terminals, 9-10
  CRT, 9-10, 13
  display, 9
  logging off, 21
  logging on, 20-21
  special keys, 20, 27, 28, 190
  teletype, 8-9
  use in time sharing, 19-20
Text editor, *see* String functions
Time sharing, 20
Top-down design, 83, 99, 107-114, 291-295. *See also* Structured programming
  flow of control, 96-97, 105
Trailer, 16, 70-71, 138, 146
Truncation, 130, 160-161, 176n

Variables, 21, 32-33, 50, 71, 273
  assigning values to, 43-52
  global, 282, 287-288
  local, 282
  numeric, 33, 43-44, 46-49, 51-52
  string, 33, 43, 46-49, 51, 84-95
Vector, 214, 217, 219-220, 222, 230

Word, 7n